Crossing the Color Line

NEW AFRICAN HISTORIES

SERIES EDITORS: JEAN ALLMAN,
ALLEN ISAACMAN, AND DEREK R. PETERSON

*Books in this series are published with support from the
Ohio University National Resource Center for African Studies.*

David William Cohen and E. S. Atieno Odhiambo, *The Risks of Knowledge: Investigations into the Death of the Hon. Minister John Robert Ouko in Kenya, 1990*
Belinda Bozzoli, *Theatres of Struggle and the End of Apartheid*
Gary Kynoch, *We Are Fighting the World: A History of the Marashea Gangs in South Africa, 1947–1999*
Stephanie Newell, *The Forger's Tale: The Search for Odeziaku*
Jacob A. Tropp, *Natures of Colonial Change: Environmental Relations in the Making of the Transkei*
Jan Bender Shetler, *Imagining Serengeti: A History of Landscape Memory in Tanzania from Earliest Times to the Present*
Cheikh Anta Babou, *Fighting the Greater Jihad: Amadu Bamba and the Founding of the Muridiyya in Senegal, 1853–1913*
Marc Epprecht, *Heterosexual Africa? The History of an Idea from the Age of Exploration to the Age of AIDS*
Marissa J. Moorman, *Intonations: A Social History of Music and Nation in Luanda, Angola, from 1945 to Recent Times*
Karen E. Flint, *Healing Traditions: African Medicine, Cultural Exchange, and Competition in South Africa, 1820–1948*
Derek R. Peterson and Giacomo Macola, editors, *Recasting the Past: History Writing and Political Work in Modern Africa*
Moses E. Ochonu, *Colonial Meltdown: Northern Nigeria in the Great Depression*
Emily S. Burrill, Richard L. Roberts, and Elizabeth Thornberry, editors, *Domestic Violence and the Law in Colonial and Postcolonial Africa*
Daniel R. Magaziner, *The Law and the Prophets: Black Consciousness in South Africa, 1968–1977*
Emily Lynn Osborn, *Our New Husbands Are Here: Households, Gender, and Politics in a West African State from the Slave Trade to Colonial Rule*
Robert Trent Vinson, *The Americans Are Coming! Dreams of African American Liberation in Segregationist South Africa*
James R. Brennan, *Taifa: Making Nation and Race in Urban Tanzania*
Benjamin N. Lawrance and Richard L. Roberts, editors, *Trafficking in Slavery's Wake: Law and the Experience of Women and Children*
David M. Gordon, *Invisible Agents: Spirits in a Central African History*
Allen F. Isaacman and Barbara S. Isaacman, *Dams, Displacement, and the Delusion of Development: Cahora Bassa and Its Legacies in Mozambique, 1965–2007*
Stephanie Newell, *The Power to Name: A History of Anonymity in Colonial West Africa*
Gibril R. Cole, *The Krio of West Africa: Islam, Culture, Creolization, and Colonialism in the Nineteenth Century*
Matthew M. Heaton, *Black Skin, White Coats: Nigerian Psychiatrists, Decolonization, and the Globalization of Psychiatry*
Meredith Terretta, *Nation of Outlaws, State of Violence: Nationalism, Grassfields Tradition, and State Building in Cameroon*
Paolo Israel, *In Step with the Times: Mapiko Masquerades of Mozambique*
Michelle R. Moyd, *Violent Intermediaries: African Soldiers, Conquest, and Everyday Colonialism in German East Africa*
Abosede A. George, *Making Modern Girls: A History of Girlhood, Labor, and Social Development in Colonial Lagos*
Alicia C. Decker, *In Idi Amin's Shadow: Women, Gender, and Militarism in Uganda*
Rachel Jean-Baptiste, *Conjugal Rights: Marriage, Sexuality, and Urban Life in Colonial Libreville, Gabon*
Shobana Shankar, *Who Shall Enter Paradise? Christian Origins in Muslim Northern Nigeria, ca. 1890–1975*
Emily S. Burrill, *States of Marriage: Gender, Justice, and Rights in Colonial Mali*
Todd Cleveland, *Diamonds in the Rough: Corporate Paternalism and African Professionalism on the Mines of Colonial Angola, 1917–1975*
Carina E. Ray, *Crossing the Color Line: Race, Sex, and the Contested Politics of Colonialism in Ghana*

PRAISE FOR *CROSSING THE COLOR LINE*:

"A fascinating exploration of sex across the color line in colonial Ghana. This book is a brilliant addition to the literature on sex, gender and empire."

—Kwame Anthony Appiah, professor of philosophy and law, New York University

"*Crossing the Color Line* uses a wide-angle lens to think broadly and adeptly about the fate of sexual liaisons against the backdrop of imperial change in the twentieth century. Ray pays scrupulous attention to the embeddedness of sexual relations in local contexts through textured personal stories and fine-grained analyses of how race, gender, and class intertwined to produce both African agency and British unease. In the process, this book makes a persuasive case for the indispensability of interracial histories to any account of imperial power and anticolonial resistance."

—Antoinette Burton, author of *The Trouble with Empire*

"With *Crossing the Color Line*, Carina Ray has produced a leading work on the intricate interracial relationships in colonial Ghana. Her study builds on so-far fragmented studies for the eighteenth and early nineteenth century, giving us a comprehensive understanding of the development of interracial relations during the height of colonialism in Ghana in the twentieth century and beyond. Theoretically and methodologically, the book is of seminal importance for the study of the subject in general."

—Michel R. Doortmont, University of Groningen & African Studies Centre Leiden

"This is a smart, well-researched, and nuanced account of the politics of sexuality and race that animated the establishment and contestation of colonial rule in Ghana. Drawing from transnational scholarship on gender and colonialism, the book explains how anxieties about racial mixing remain fraught into the present."

—Durba Ghosh, author of *Sex and the Family in Colonial India: The Making of Empire*

"Carina Ray has produced an ambitious monograph about interracial relationships in the colonial period, transnational in its scope and based on vivid biographical examples and fascinating case studies. . . . The originality of this book lies in its focus on the positive and intimate aspects of interracial sexual relationships during a time when, as Ray carefully documents, a fear of miscegenation took hold of the popular imperialist imagination."

—Stephanie Newell, author of
The Power to Name: A History of Anonymity in Colonial West Africa

"The account that Ray provides in *Crossing the Color Line* is a fine combination of both astonishing insights and disarming lucidity. That she opens up an entire new domain of historical analysis there is no doubt. This book will quickly be recognized as an agenda-setting work and will illuminate debates on race relations not just in Ghana and West Africa, but wherever such relations occurred in the British Empire."

—Ato Quayson, author of *Oxford Street, Accra: City Life and the Itineraries of Transnationalism*

Crossing the Color Line

Race, Sex, and the Contested Politics of Colonialism in Ghana

Carina E. Ray

OHIO UNIVERSITY PRESS ～ ATHENS, OHIO

Ohio University Press, Athens, Ohio 45701
ohioswallow.com
© 2015 by Ohio University Press
All rights reserved

Earlier versions of chapters 6 and 7 appeared, respectively,
in *Gender and History* 21, no. 3 (2009); and *American Historical Review* 119,
no. 1 (2014). I am grateful to both journals for granting permission to reprint.

Cover image: "Unidentified Group Portrait, Ghana," photographer unknown,
ca. 1915. (Basel Mission Gold Coast Photographs, Image no. EEPA 1997–0011–004,
Eliot Elisofon Photographic Archives, National Museum of African Art,
Smithsonian Institution.)

To obtain permission to quote, reprint,
or otherwise reproduce or distribute material from
Ohio University Press publications, please contact our rights
and permissions department at (740) 593-1154 or (740) 593-4536 (fax).

Printed in the United States of America
Ohio University Press books are printed on acid-free paper.♾™

20 19 18 17 16 15   5 4 3 2 1

Library of Congress Cataloging-in-Publication Data

Ray, Carina E.
  Crossing the color line : race, sex, and the contested politics of
colonialism in Ghana / Carina E. Ray.
    pages cm. — (New African histories)
  Includes bibliographical references and index.
  ISBN 978-0-8214-2179-6 (hc : alk. paper) — ISBN 978-0-8214-2180-2
(pb : alk. paper) — ISBN 978-0-8214-4539-6 (pdf)
  1. Miscegenation—Ghana—History—20th century.
  2. Miscegenation—Great Britain—History—20th century.
  3. Great Britain—Race relations—20th century. 4. Ghana—Colonial
influence—20th century. 5. Ghana—Social conditions—20th century.
I. Title. II. Series: New African histories series.
  DT510.4R39 2015
  306.709667—dc23
                                                              2015018325

*For Dean and Tajudean
From Loss to Life*

Contents

List of Illustrations ... ix

Preface ... xi

Acknowledgments ... xiii

Introduction   The Stakes of Studying Sex across the Color Line in Colonial Ghana ... 1

PART ONE   THE GOLD COAST

Chapter 1   From Indispensable to "Undesirable"
African Women, European Men, and the Transformation of Afro-European Power Relations in the Gold Coast ... 29

Chapter 2   "Undesirable Relations"
"Native" Women, European Government Officers, and Administrative Racial Classification ... 56

Chapter 3   "A New Whim of a Most Unpopular Governor"
Embedded Officers and the Local Politics of Concubinage Cases ... 79

Chapter 4   The Crewe Circular
The Life and Death of a Policy on Interracial Concubinage ... 102

Chapter 5   "A Manifestation of Madness"
The Gold Coast's Interracial Marriage "Epidemic" ... 133

PART TWO   METROPOLE AND COLONY

Chapter 6   "The White Wife Problem"
*Intermarriage and the Politics of Repatriation
to Interwar West Africa*   159

Chapter 7   "White Peril"/Black Power
*Interracial Sex and the Beginning
of the End of Empire*   190

Chapter 8   WASU, White Women, and African Independence   212

Conclusion   Sexuality's Staying Power   226

Notes   241

Bibliography   299

Index   323

Illustrations

FIGURES

1.1.	The Zimmerman-Mulgrave family	44
1.2.	Hermann Ludwig Rottmann and Regina Rottmann-Hesse	45
5.1.	Hans and Mercy "Kwadua" Roth	153
6.1.	Janice Noble (née Davies) with her mother, Jenny, and cousin Jean	186
7.1.	Illuminated building, Sekondi	202
7.2.	Bata store, Sekondi	203
7.3.	William Timothy Evans with daughters Mary Emma and Elizabeth	210
8.1.	WASU social gathering	218
8.2.	Frederick and Erna "Miki" Kankam-Boadu and friends	219
8.3.	Joe and Peggy Appiah on their wedding day	221

MAPS

1.1. Map of the Gold Coast and adjacent territories, 1896 — 40

1.2. Map of the Gold Coast,
indicating places of significance in the text — 41

6.1. Map of the United Kingdom,
indicating riot-stricken port cities, ca. 1919 — 166

Preface

Little is known about the photograph that appears on the cover of this book, except that it was taken around 1915 in the Gold Coast. It is one of only a handful of pictures in the Basel Mission's prodigious visual archive that features multiracial families in the colony. Even less is known about the people pictured in the photograph. The men's style of dress, including their pith helmets and characteristic white uniforms, suggests that they may have been French officers. If true, this image offers compelling visual evidence to support the findings of a 1910 French survey that reported that French men stationed in neighboring Ivory Coast regularly crossed into the Gold Coast to find temporary "native wives." Such a phenomenon would surely have contributed to the growing discontent, documented in *Crossing the Color Line*, among Gold Coasters about white men's sexual predations and the frequency with which they abandoned their multiracial children.

Yet the image does not convey the kind of reckless abandon and moral depravity that many Africans and Europeans came to associate with interracial relationships during the colonial period. Two of the couples appear with their children seated on their mothers' laps, indicating that these unions were at least several years old. The hands of the third woman rest on a piece of white cloth curiously placed on top of what appears to be her protruding belly, suggesting that she may have been pregnant. The children's crisp white dresses and the silk handkerchief that adorns the head of the woman who is pictured without a child are imported—perhaps tokens of affection brought back by the men when they returned from home-leave or purchased in one of the colony's European-owned shops. The obvious care and intent with which the group presented itself for the camera suggest that even if such family formations were temporary, they could also be cherished and worthy of memorializing.

I chose this cover image precisely because it stubbornly resists categorical readings, and in doing so it succinctly captures the nuanced complexities and contradictions that characterize the history this book sets out to tell. Amid the racism and exploitative and unequal power relations that surrounded and informed these relationships, affective ties could also grow.

Acknowledgments

So much of my life has been the product of communal enterprise. This book is no exception, and I am deeply grateful to the family, friends, colleagues, and various institutions that made this work possible.

I wish to begin by thanking the two people who most directly influenced my intellectual trajectory, Sandra E. Greene and David H. Anthony III. As an undergraduate at the University of California, Santa Cruz, it was in David's African history courses that I had my first opportunity to channel my childhood obsession with Africa into academic study. I can still vividly recall how at the end of each lecture the densely intricate yet expansive narrative he had woven seemed to spill over the edges of the chalkboard. A masterful teacher, my sense of what it means to truly engage students in the process of learning is rooted in his classroom. It was David who introduced me to Sandra's work and encouraged me to pursue my graduate studies in African history with her at Cornell University; for this I will always be in his debt. Gratitude can be daunting to put into words because the process of translation has a way of making finite what is most certainly not; nevertheless, I want to thank Sandra for being an extraordinary graduate adviser, teacher, mentor, and now colleague in the field. With intense rigor and uncommon generosity, she trained me to think and write like a historian, to trust and value my analytical instincts, and through her own example to teach and mentor with great expectations.

I would also like to thank Viranjini Munasinghe and Mary Roldan for their deep engagement with this work during its earliest inception. I have benefited greatly from the guidance of Carolyn Brown, Judith Byfield, Toyin Falola, and Paul Zeleza, who set high bars for leadership in the field through the rigor of their work and their commitment to mentoring junior scholars. Jean Allman, Antoinette Burton, Stephanie Newell, and Ato Quayson have all made this a much better book—I salute their brilliance and generosity. A very special group of people nurtured this book with their intellects and friendship—for this I am immensely grateful to Abosede George, Toja

Okoh, and Ben Talton. For their inspiring work and friendship I also want to thank Rachel Jean-Baptiste, Michelle Moyd, Naaborko Sackeyfio-Lenoch, and Meredith Terretta. Among the many other scholars and friends who have contributed to my intellectual growth and to the work at hand, I am grateful to Dede Amanor-Wilks, David Amanor, Kofi Baku, Corey Capers, Fred Cooper, Solsiree Del Moral, Francis Dodoo, Florence Dolphyne, Michel Doortmont, Mary Gayne, James Gibbs, Michael Gomez, Hilary Jones, Jeanette Jouili, Kwaku Korang, Dennis Laumann, Christopher J. Lee, Xerxes Malki, Gregory Mann, Idrissou Mora-Kpai, Tejumola Olanyani, John Parker, Marika Sherwood, Rebecca Shumway, Salamishah Tillet, and Ousmane Traore. I also owe a special debt of gratitude to Angela Davis and Ann Lane, both of whom had a profound and lasting impact on my thinking and supported my efforts as an undergraduate to study abroad in Ghana, an experience that seeded this book.

A portion of this book was written during a postdoctoral fellowship at the Center for African American Studies at Princeton University. I am deeply grateful to Wendy Belcher, Daphne Brooks, Eddie Glaude Jr., Tera Hunter, Chika Okeke-Agulu, Imani Perry, Noliwe Rooks, Stacey Sinclair, and Valerie Smith for welcoming me into their community and providing such a rigorous and stimulating environment to think and write in. My stay at Princeton was also made possible by a generous residential faculty fellowship at Butler College, where Sanjeev Kulkarni, along with Mindy Andino, Sue Giranda, Matthew Lazen, Betty Stein, and David Stirk were kind and supportive above all expectations.

When this book comes out I will be starting a new chapter of my career with an especially dynamic group of colleagues at Brandeis University's Department of African and Afro-American Studies. I would be remiss, however, if I did not take this opportunity to acknowledge my profound gratitude to the wonderful colleagues I was blessed to have during my time at Fordham University, where I honed my craft as a teacher and a historian in the History Department. An ardent advocate for faculty in her role as department chair, Kirsten Swinth's efforts created both the time and the funding needed to complete this book. I am especially lucky to count her as a friend as well. Doron Ben-Atar, Elaine Crane, Nancy Curtin, Richard Gyug, David Hamlin, Bob Himmelberg, Maryanne Kowaleski, Mike Latham, Hector Lindo-Fuentes, Wolfgang Mueller, David Myers, Silvana Patriarca, Nicholas Paul, Beth Penry, Thierry Rigogne, Bernice Rosenthal, Christopher Schmidt-Nowara, Asif Siddiqi, Daniel Soyer, Susan Wabuda, and Rosemary Wakeman welcomed me into the department, showed me

kindness, and many generously read portions of this book. For their brilliance, collegiality, and friendship I also wish to thank Salvador Acosta, Christopher Dietrich, Yuko Miki, Durba Mitra, and Ebru Turan.

Numerous institutions generously supported the costly research undertaken for this book, including the Institute of International Education's Fulbright Program; Cornell University's Department of History, Graduate School, Mario Einaudi Center for International Studies, and Feminist, Gender and Sexuality Studies; Pennsylvania State University's Department of History and Religious Studies; One Race Films; and Princeton University's Center for African American Studies. I would especially like to acknowledge the tremendous support I received from Fordham University in the form of several research grants and leaves, as well as a generous publication subvention. In this regard the dean of faculty, John Harrington, deserves special recognition for championing this book at every step of the way. In a moment when funding for research in the humanities is rapidly diminishing, I am truly grateful to these institutions for enabling me to travel widely, read deeply in the archives, and write in peace.

I am also indebted to the many people who shared their homes with me—for both short and much longer periods of time—while researching and writing this book: Anne Adams, (My)Rosina and (My Dearest)Araba Hackman, (Beloved)Nii Obodai, and Sara Piccoli in Accra; Sabine Bieli and Stefan Weigert in Hull; Hans and Mercy "Kwadua" Roth in Switzerland; Christopher and Alice Schemers in London; Samantha Vincent in Los Angeles; Irving and Delora Vincent and Marisa Fuentes in New York City; and Ellen Robinson (née Annan) in Long Island.

One of the most pleasurable parts of the research process was working closely with staff members at the Public Records and Archives Administration Department (PRAAD) in Ghana and The National Archives (TNA) in Kew, Britain. In particular I wish to thank Felix Ampong, Dorothy Armah, Cletus Azangweo, Judith Botchway, Bright Botwe, Amoasi Joe-Mensah, Augustine Mensah, J. J. T. Mensah, and Killian Onai, who facilitated my work in PRAAD's various regional branches with great acumen and generosity. Julie Ash and David Claiden provided cherished moments of levity during long days in TNA's reading room. My gratitude also goes to Eric Acree, Sharon Powers, and Saah Quigee at Cornell's Africana Library and to the very helpful staff at the Colindale Newspaper Library and the Fordham University Library. For their assistance in securing publication rights for a number of the images that appear in this book, I would like to thank Tim Davis (Corbis Images); Paul Johnson (TNA Image Library); Anke Schürer-Ries (Basel

Mission Archives); and Amy Staples (Smithsonian Institution). A special thanks to Kwame Appiah for his help in tracking down the copyright holder of the photograph of his parents on their wedding day and to Erin Haney for sharing her extensive knowledge of Ghana's colonial photographic archives with me and drawing my attention to the book's cover image. Brian Balsley produced two of the maps that appear in this book, and Lisa DeBoer indexed it with great skill.

Family histories form a vital part of this study, and I could not have gathered them without the willingness of the many people who shared their oral histories and other sources with me: Robert and George Annan; Tom and Cathleen Ellis (née Hawe); Erna "Miki" Kankam-Boadu; the late Felicia Agnes Knight and her daughter and granddaughter Barbara and Nicole Amartefio; Janice Noble; Ellen Robinson; Hans and Mercy "Kwadua" Roth; and Reggie Yates. I am also grateful to the members of the International Spouses Association of Ghana who took the time to speak with me about their experiences and allowed me to sit in on several of their meetings.

My own personal and familial networks had both a direct and an indirect bearing on this book's existence. In 1973 I was born into an experimental community called Synanon that, among other things, committed itself to creating a racially inclusive society in part by promoting interracial marriage. Growing up in a multiracial community, where intermarriages and multiracial identities were normalized, heightened my awareness of how deeply segregated American society was upon leaving Synanon in 1981 and left me deeply preoccupied with the question of race even as a young child. For creating that community and exemplifying the commitment to interracial unity through their own marriage, I wish to thank Chuck Dederich and Betty Coleman. Without Synanon, the questions that frame my intellectual agenda would likely be very different. My parents met and married in Synanon, and so I must thank them, too, for having the courage to live differently. I want to honor my father, Dean Ray, who died before I could make him proud, but who bequeathed me his big rig driver's steel backbone and inner quiet, both of which have kept me in good stead. I am blessed to have two mothers, Carmen Rosado and Kathy Coons, who are the yin and yang of motherhood. Together they raised me with tender strength, and they continue to be unflagging sources of love and support. When I was twelve Pete Rozsa sat me down with a tape deck and had me transcribe Bob Marley's music, an experience that sparked a revolution in my mind. I remain grateful to him and to his daughter, Frannie, who has been my lifelong friend, for their love. I also wish to express my gratitude to Tami Acuna, Anna Brown,

Gerri and Terri Coons, Peter Hyman, Noah Kaiser, Bibi Ortiz, Anita Rosan, Rick Runcie, Stephanie Shanks, and the late Ed Arkin and Bill Crawford, among many other Synanon family members.

Friends and family near and far have offered support, laughter, and love throughout the lengthy process of writing this book. In addition to those already mentioned in Ghana, I wish to thank Kati Dagadu, Felicia Frimpong, Penelope Mawuenyega, Haruna Mumuni, Asad Nazir, Michael Kwesi Quist, Pamela and Mark Sackeyfio, Jillian Tay, and Sebastian van Leeuwen. In California I cannot thank enough my beautiful auntie Sajji Cloud and her late husband, Hamilton, as well as Paul Davis, Katie Desai, the Littlejohn-Craft-Scott families, Amy Nevins, Joe Odiase, Joan and Ron Rhodes, and Marcellus and Kane Walker. Words cannot rise to the task of thanking Samantha Vincent for her extraordinary friendship, generosity, and support, including the sustained interest she took in this project, and for sharing with me her remarkable family, who have also rendered tremendous support in service of this book. In Ithaca, I have had the benefit of being surrounded by friends who served as patient sounding boards, readers, and enthusiasts for this project: among them are Iftikhar and Elizabeth Dadi, Ramez Elias, David Ethridge, Bill Gaskins, Oneka LaBennett, Fouad Makki, Barry Maxwell, Shawn McDaniel, Natalie Melas, Renee Milligan, Noliwe Rooks, Lisa Wichman, Shelley Wong, and Dagmawi Woubshet. While in Ithaca, I have also had the continued benefit of Viranjini Munasinghe's brilliance, friendship, and boundless support. I have also had the pleasure of Jennifer Savran Kelly's and Alexis Boyce's company during long days of writing at the Toboggan Lodge. Rick Canfield and Cindy Hazan—both angels disguised as humans—offered friendship and support in ways that simply cannot be quantified. My love and appreciation also go to Ibrahim El-Salahi for giving me the unexpected gift of having a father again. Salah and Carmen Hassan rallied to the cause of seeing this book completed; for their love and encouragement I remain grateful.

This book has been made possible, in part, by invisible support networks that too often go unacknowledged. I owe a special debt of gratitude to Tami Acuna, Victoria Bloch, Sajji Cloud, Kelvin Davis, and Daniel Menta, who in my absence have looked after my mother, Carmen, with such generosity and care. I also want to wholeheartedly thank Lisa Barber, Matt Boardman, Erin Hindes, Jennifer Jones, Erika Riccardi, Leighann Slater, and Gloria Tati for providing my son, Tajudean, with superb care and instruction. My father used to call me "the apple of his eye," an expression that made no sense to me until I had Taj. In everything I do he is foremost in my mind.

Even when writing time meant that I had to sacrifice time with him, his love remained boundless and gave me the best reason of all to finish this book.

Last, but certainly not least, I want to thank the stellar team at Ohio University Press for the tremendous job they have done with this book. Deborah Wiseman copyedited it with an impeccable eye for detail and Nancy Basmajian, Beth Pratt, John Pratt, and Samara Rafert gracefully ushered it—and me—through the publication process. I am especially grateful to Jean Allman, Allen Isaacman, Derek Peterson, and to the extraordinary Gillian Berchowitz for their enthusiasm and commitment to this project. It truly has been an honor and a pleasure to work with them. Their dedication to the field, to producing innovative scholarship, and to mentoring authors should inspire us all to write more new African histories!

Introduction
The Stakes of Studying Sex across the Color Line in Colonial Ghana

As Kwame Nkrumah's cabinet ministers walked through the gates of Flagstaff House on an early January morning in 1961, a disarmingly demure-looking Ghanaian woman lambasted them for threatening to tear her family apart. The woman in question, Felicia Agnes Knight, was the wife of a former British district commissioner, Brendan Knight, who had been in government service since 1940. The government of Ghana had retained Brendan's services for several years after independence in 1957, but at the close of 1960 he was notified that his employment would soon be terminated as part of the ongoing Africanization of the civil service.[1] It was this news that propelled Felicia out of the confines of her comfortable upper-middle-class home in an affluent section of the nation's capital, Accra, to the gates of Flagstaff House, where she launched a one-woman protest to save her husband's job and to ensure the viability of her family's life in Ghana.[2] It was not long before President Nkrumah got wind of what was happening and invited Felicia to his office to explain what the commotion was about. The Knights had been married since 1945 and were raising their children as Ghanaians, explained Felicia, who ultimately convinced Nkrumah that although Brendan was British, he had long ago committed himself to their life in Ghana. Shortly after his meeting with Felicia, Nkrumah granted her husband a special dispensation allowing him to remain in the civil service because, as government documents noted, he "is

1

married to a Ghanaian and has five children with her, all of whom have been brought up as Ghanaians."³

As this brief vignette suggests, decolonization was a fraught moment for families like the Knights, whose affiliations, affinities, and affections did not neatly conform to the reconfigured political landscape of African independence and the retreat of the British Empire. The episode at Flagstaff House also dramatically illustrates how the lives of a relatively small number of people who crossed the colonial color line continued to attract the state's attention, often at the highest levels, even after the Gold Coast gained its independence. Indeed, this was not the first time that the Knights' union was the subject of official attention. Fifteen years earlier, Brendan's plans to marry Felicia had so bewildered the then governor of the Gold Coast, Sir Alan Burns, that he wrote to the Colonial Office in Whitehall (London) to see "what can be done to stop this sort of thing." He even suggested reviving an old circular from 1909, "warning men against living with African women, and adding . . . that the discovery that a man has been living in sin is not going to be over-looked just because he has made an honest woman of her."[4] In the end no official action was taken against Knight, or the three other government officers who had wed Gold Coast women in the preceding months, because the Colonial Office feared it would be accused of racism. Besides, argued a Whitehall adviser, these marriages were "a form of madness" that no circular could cure.[5] Instead, it was reckoned that it would be only a matter of time before the officers' marriages to African women diminished their authority and consequently impaired their performance as government servants such that they could be removed on grounds of "inefficiency."[6]

Administrators' panicked response to these late colonial marriages underscores the persistence and gravity of colonial anxieties about interracial sexual relationships and their assumed adverse consequences for administrative efficiency and repute. But their dire predictions of career suicide never came to pass, suggesting that administrators were wrong to assume that after marriage to an African woman, an officer was no longer "in a position to command respect and confidence."[7] Knight and the other officers in question not only remained in government service throughout the colonial period, they all enjoyed success and promotion, albeit not without some obstacles. Three of their number, moreover, continued to live and work in Ghana well after independence. Still, the four interracial marriages were unprecedented during the formal colonial period, confirming in turn what government officials admitted was the "much more frequent case of an officer living with an African woman without marriage."[8] In accepting this to be true, the Colonial Office implicitly acknowledged the failure of its efforts in the early decades of the twentieth century to stamp out concubinage in an attempt to bring the sexual politics of European government officers in line with the increasingly stratified racial politics of colonial rule.[9]

Colonial administrators were not alone in attempting to regulate sex across the color line. Some Gold Coasters drew on the realm of customary law in an attempt to control European men's access to local women by exacting payment for customary marriage rights and seeking compensation when Europeans fell afoul of the laws regulating marriage and adultery, while others repurposed the colonial state's ban on concubinage to shore up their own interests. While sexual relationships between European men and African women remained commonplace, such unions were rarely publicly legitimized during the first half of the twentieth century—as the shock caused by the four marriages suggests—and thus conferred little in the way of respectability on the women involved. This, in turn, provoked early Gold Coast nationalists to condemn these relationships for corrupting the virtue of the "future mothers of the country," as one Gold Coast writer put it.[10]

ACCOUNTING FOR CHANGE IN THE GOLD COAST'S INTERRACIAL SEXUAL ECONOMIES

Africans and Europeans, including the British, had not always viewed intimate relations between African women and European men as a threat to moral, social, and political order. In fact, they had once been regarded as instrumental to the consolidation of Afro-European economic and political relations. Interracial marriages contracted in accordance with African customary law and, less frequently, those recognized as lawful by the religious and administrative bodies associated with the various European powers present on the coast, were regular features of its trading enclaves during the long period of cross-cultural contact and exchange that preceded the territorial expansion and formalization of British colonial rule from the mid-nineteenth century onward. Evidence of these marriages comes from an array of sources, including travel narratives, wills left by European men, administrative records, official and personal correspondence, genealogical records, and even visual sources. Beginning with Margaret Priestley's pioneering work on the Brew family, historians have used these sources to fashion compelling accounts of prominent Afro-European trading families, making them an iconic feature of the coast's precolonial history.[11] Many scholars credit these relationships with successfully integrating European men into local West African societies and enabling African and multiracial women to carve out entrepreneurial niches for themselves in the transatlantic slave trade by capitalizing on their links to both African and European sources of power and profit.[12] They have also come to symbolize the cosmopolitan and culturally hybrid character of the precolonial Atlantic trading ports and towns interspersed along the West African coast during a period when power was largely in the hands of free Africans, not Europeans.

When set against the precolonial period's centuries-long tradition of intermarriage, the changes in policies, practices, and perceptions that shaped colonial-era interracial sexual relationships appear particularly striking. Gold Coasters lamented this transformation in the pages of the colony's indigenous press. In 1915 Atu, a regular columnist for the *Gold Coast Leader*, reminisced about bygone "Dutch times" when "conditions were wholly different, marriage relations between black and white being honest . . . and fathers of mulattoes made honest efforts to train up their children."[13] The historical moment and attendant socioeconomic and political imperatives that informed Dutch policies and practices in the seventeenth, eighteenth, and early nineteenth centuries were indeed "wholly different" from those of the British in the early twentieth century. The power relations of bygone "Dutch times" contrast markedly with those of the British in 1915 when Atu was writing. Despite their long tenure on the coast, the almost exclusively male Dutch presence remained very small and was highly dependent on support—curried partly through customary law marriages with African women—from local populations. This was hardly the case for the much larger, self-imposed British presence in the opening decades of the twentieth century. The institutionalization of alien political rule, as Ato Quayson astutely observes, was characterized by "a fundamental . . . conversion of what had been the relations of dependency and accommodation that had defined the commercial interactions between Europeans and local groups since the fifteenth century to one of domination without accountability by the end of the nineteenth."[14] Part and parcel of this pronounced but incomplete transformation was the shift away from intermarriage. This, however, had less to do with a distinctively British viewpoint—after all they too had once embraced it, if less systematically than the Dutch—and more to do with the racial politics and grossly uneven power relations of formal colonialism in early twentieth-century Africa and Asia. The Dutch, it should be remembered, similarly renounced intermarriage as Dutch East India Company rule gave way to colonial rule in Indonesia and eventually condemned concubinage, albeit selectively and ineffectively.[15]

Atu's remarks are nonetheless noteworthy because they remind us that Gold Coasters during their own time remembered precolonial interracial sexual relationships in ways that emphasized their honor and respectability, not unlike many historians in more recent times. Historical narratives about the ubiquitous nature of publicly recognized intermarriages between entrepreneurial African women and European men during the precolonial period are important in their own right, but they frequently gloss over the range of other kinds of sexual encounters, including concubinage, prostitution, and rape, that formed less visible—and hence less easily documentable—strata of the interracial sexual economies of the Gold Coast's precolonial trading hubs.[16] Although the rape of enslaved women during the Middle Passage is fairly well documented and remembered, much less has been written about the pre-embarkation period when female captives were confined in the coast's slave forts and castles. It has nonetheless been memorialized in the harrowing narratives that many of the castles' tour guides tell visitors in places like Elmina and Cape Coast.[17] Only recently have scholars begun to grapple with the rape and sexual exploitation of the female slaves who worked for the castles' European residents.[18]

Even where marriages were concerned, we must bear in mind that these unions were a constitutive part of the Gold Coast littoral's trade-based economies, which became almost exclusively focused on the slave trade during the seventeenth and eighteenth centuries. While these commercially minded interracial unions predated and outlived the slave trade, they were nonetheless an integral part of the development of a highly functioning and elaborate slave-trading system that enriched some at the expense of many. European traders and the companies they represented obviously profited the most, but many of the women involved in these relationships also benefitted from being able to exploit the labor of those they enslaved or to profit from their sale. Like their counterparts in Senegal, Guinea-Bissau, and Madagascar—the *signares*, *nharas*, and *zany malattas*—these women were "individuals, who, through chance or by design, were not victims but beneficiaries of the [slave] trade."[19] Thus, the model of female agency that they have often been made to represent is worthy of critical appraisal rather than applause.

It would, however, be a gross oversimplification to assume that African women either enjoyed the status of wife and reaped the respect and financial benefits associated with their lucrative marital ties to European men, or else suffered rape in the bowels of the coast's slave dungeons, or were bought and sold to meet the sexual and domestic needs of European men temporarily living on the coast. The binary opposition between consent and coercion obscures the complex, overlapping, and changing nature of the range of sexual relationships between African women and European men during the precolonial period, as well as the changing dynamics of power between Africans and Europeans within which these relationships were situtuated.[20]

The consent/coercion binary is even less helpful for the formal colonial period, when the sexual terror associated with the slave trade ended as the slave castles were transformed into administrative centers of British colonial power, or fell into disrepair, and publicly recognized intermarriages—no longer of use to a British regime that asserted rather than negotiated its power and presence—were almost unheard of. Indeed, during the opening decades of the twentieth century, Africans and Europeans alike commented on the paucity of marriages between African women and European men.[21] The disavowal of intermarriage reflected and reinforced the changing political climate and increasing, but hardly complete, social distance that separated Europeans and Africans by the early 1900s.

As colonialism's racial prescripts ruled out the possibility of publicly legitimized marriages between European men and African women, they also clearly demarcated customary practices as the exclusive preserve of Africans. This marked a break with the precolonial past, when European men had readily availed themselves of customary marriage rights to African women as part of a wider complex of indigenous sociocultural practices for integrating strangers into local societies and fostering trade. Accommodation and assimilation, whether through marriage or through other kinds of practices, including polygyny and concubinage, ran counter to the entire premise of Britain's "civilizing mission." While colonial ideologues argued that through education and religious conversion, Africans could move from the domain of "barbarism" into "civilization," it was absolutely out of the question for European men to "go native." Colonial officers were expected to become conversant with the traditions and customs of the people they presided over, but they were not supposed to participate in those practices, as many European men before them once had.

Crucially, the demise of publicly legitimized interracial marriages occurred at a time when ideas and expectations about marriage among Africans were rapidly changing in the Gold Coast as the result of the spread of Christianity and Western education and the creation of a dual legal system based on English and indigenous customary law, the latter of which remained malleable and responsive to social change despite its increasing codification. Of particular importance here, the 1884 Marriage Ordinance gave Gold Coasters an alternative to customary marriage. There was no more hotly debated topic in the African-owned Gold Coast press during the decades after its introduction than the 1884 ordinance. With its Christian underpinnings, the ordinance became synonymous with "European marriage," otherwise defined as a monogamous companionate union. Although many elites, especially the small but growing number of educated Christian women, as well as newly educated and recently converted aspirant elites, praised the merits of ordinance marriage, a group of vocal male elites—who were typically Christian themselves—defended the institution of customary marriage and rejected ordinance marriage as an intrusive colonial imposition that fomented moral decay and social chaos by endowing women with too many rights. But even this group of men doubted the legitimacy of customary marriages when contracted across the color line. Thus, regardless of what marriage form Gold Coast elites favored, there was a consensus among this group of literate, relatively prosperous, and politically active Africans that interracial customary marriages were a thin veil for profiting from the sale of the colony's young women to "demoralised whitemen," as one Gold Coast writer put it.[22] In this way elite ideas about interracial customary marriages echoed colonial ideologies that cast the institution of customary marriage among Africans as "slavery in disguise."[23]

The families who brokered interracial customary marriages, some of the women involved in them, and many of the Gold Coasters who observed these unions, however, simply described them as marriages. In turn, the term "native wife" could connote radically different things. For some it marked an African woman as the legitimate wife of a European man by customary law, even if the descriptor "native" implicitly stripped away some of the term's veneer. For others "native wife" was synonymous with concubine or worse yet, prostitute. Given the range and complexity of interracial sexual practices and arrangements, as well as the vastly different ways they were viewed and assigned meaning, the only way to fully understand them is to eschew neat binaries in favor of grappling with the gray area that most of these relationships fell into.

In the early decades of formal colonial rule, British authorities focused their prescriptive powers on one such gray area—concubinage between government officers and local women—because it was a vestige of the past that remained a stubbornly integral part of European men's lives in the African colonies in ways that officials believed diminished their officers' credibility and undermined good governance. These efforts hardly did away with interracial concubinage or customary marriages—practices that were blurred in the minds of many colonial bureaucrats and in the view of growing numbers of Gold Coasters—but they could no longer be publicly recognized without serious consequences for a European man's professional prospects and position in colonial society. As a result, such unions were typically clandestine, which in turn made them a wellspring of derision and shame, and for those willing to expose them, a source of leverage. Thus, the precolonial-colonial divide marked an important shift in perception and practice: unions with European men rarely held out the possibility of conferring elevated status, respectability, and prestige on African women, even as some women sought to empower themselves through these relationships.

As the twentieth century opened, Gold Coasters were publicly confronted with the question of whether they would "continue indifferent when you see your sister, your daughters sold for *prostitutes*—while you aspire to rise and shout Excelsior!" This would not be the last time that the "traffic in 'Native wives'" for European men would be posed as an obstacle to racial uplift.[24] Less than two decades later, white men's sexual exploitation of the colony's young women became the subject of intense public criticism in the African-owned Gold Coast press. Growing indigenous opposition was tied to how these relationships had changed over time, rendering them a source of racial denigration and moral degeneration. And yet, two decades later—in 1944 and 1945—four European officers, Brendan Knight among them, would take the seemingly unfathomable step of publicly wedding Gold Coast women in civil and church ceremonies. In Knight's case as well as others, their civil unions were preceded by customary marriages that were clearly meaningful and binding to the parties involved. Thus these were years of vast change in terms of official policy, public opinion, and everyday practice. Africans and Europeans alike recalibrated their thinking and approach to these relationships in conversation with the shifting terrain of race relations and political power in the colony. But these changes should not obscure the degree to which interracial sexual relations remained an enduring feature of colonial society.

Crossing the Color Line explores how and why interracial unions in the Gold Coast became a source of colonial anxiety and anticolonial agitation during the first half of the twentieth century. Far from being death knells, regulation of and resistance to these relationships signify their staying power, while also serving as indicators of the changing social and political climate within which these relations had to be negotiated. Studies in a similar vein by Ann Stoler, Durba Ghosh, Emanuelle Saada, and Owen White, as well as important edited collections by Julia Clancy-Smith and Frances Gouda, and Frederick Cooper and Ann Stoler, utilize the rubric of empire to challenge and complicate conventional understandings of how colonial empires work by showing how the management of sexuality and allied concerns were at the heart of imperial statecraft.[25] *Crossing the Color Line* shares these intentions, but it has other ambitions too. It seeks to more firmly situate the history it tells within the growing bodies of historical scholarship on race, gender, sexuality, and nationalism in Africa, in order to rethink that history from a more African-centered perspective.

SEEING THE COLOR LINE IN COLONIAL GHANA

In titling this book *Crossing the Color Line*, I was mindful that for many readers, especially those in North America, it would call to mind W. E. B. Du Bois's prescient warning that "the problem of the Twentieth Century is the problem of the color-line," as well as familiar images of those early pioneers of desegregation—the Freedom Riders, Rosa Parks, and Mildred and Richard Loving, among many others—who crossed the color line at their own peril. My intention was to draw on the familiar in the context of a very different locale, that of colonial Ghana, in order to remind readers that the problem of the color line was—and still is—global, even as it played out in locally specific ways. This expansive view of the color line's reach is precisely what Du Bois intended to convey to his readers when he defined the problem as "the relation of the darker to the lighter races of men in Asia and Africa, in America and the islands of the sea."[26] The starkness of the color line in places like southern Africa's settler colonies has rendered visible the racial crossings of people like Ruth and Seretse Khama in Botswana, and South African Communist Party members Ruth First and Joe Slovo, who, though white, were lifelong comrades of the African National Congress, in ways that resonate with US struggles. But ever the visionary, Du Bois understood that even in a place like West Africa, where whites formed a tiny minority, race relations and racism were critical issues nonetheless.

Yet, historians of Africa have only recently begun to grapple with race as a significant analytic category outside the context of settler colonialism. Hitherto, where questions of identity, social formations, and group interactions were concerned, the study of ethnicity and religion preoccupied Africanists. This has enriched our understanding of intra- and intergroup relations across the continent, and their relationship to cultural, political, economic, and social change. It has also left much to be said about the ways in which local histories of race have shaped the historical landscape of a continent that has for centuries been at the heart of the West's racializing discourses. Recent work by Chouki El Hamel on Morocco, Jonathon Glassman on Zanzibar, and Bruce Hall on the West African Sahel, as well as work by Eve Troutt Powell and others on Sudan and Egypt, has met this challenge by broadening our understanding of race in Africa beyond the white/black binary, and offering eloquent and insightful analyses of how Africans constructed and deployed their own ideas about race in ways that upend the stubbornly persistent myth that racial discourses in Africa were the sole provenance of European colonizers.[27] In the process, these pioneering studies demonstrate that white settler colonialism was not the only African context in which race mattered.

While studies of race in Africa are beginning to shift their focus away from the settler colonies, some of the most compelling work probing the intersectional nature of sexuality and race in Africa returns our attention to them. Numerous scholars have skillfully explored how the racial politics of settler colonial rule and the sexual economies and ideologies that developed around African women and men mutually informed one another.[28] This is particularly evident in the robust literature on the region's so-called "black peril" scares—the periodic outbreak of panic in settler colonial communities over the sexual threat that black men allegedly posed to white women—which scholars widely agree had little or no correlation to actual sexual crimes.[29] As a result, we know much about the specter of "black peril" in southern Africa, but very little about intimacies between black men and white women there or elsewhere on the continent. The scholarly preoccupation with "black peril," moreover, has overshadowed and perversely normalized white men's pervasive sexual abuse of African women and in the process undermined its historical significance.

Crossing the Color Line adds another layer of complexity to the scholarship on race and sexuality in Africa by exploring interracial sexual relationships during the opening decades of the twentieth century in the Gold Coast, when a new emphasis was placed on the creation of racial boundaries as a means of consolidating colonial rule. This led to the introduction of segregated European residential areas and social clubs, the exclusion of Africans from higher posts in the administrative service and the West African Medical Service, race-based discrimination in salary and benefits that disadvantaged the colonial service's African officers, and efforts to bring interracial fraternizing to an end. Rather than being self-evident or inevitable, this turn says more about the inchoate nature of the colonial color line at this particular moment and the kind of racial work that was required to further develop and institutionalize it. Sexuality became an important site for delineating these boundaries, but it also emerged as a key site for contesting colonialism and exposing the intensifying racism at work even in administered colonies like the Gold Coast, which lacked large white settler populations. The colonial politics of race and sexuality had profound consequences for Africans and Europeans alike that set the parameters for the kinds of relationships that could develop across the color line, but these boundaries were continuously transgressed, contested and revised over time. Accordingly this book presents the color line as a site of provocation and dissent, foregrounding the ways that it was crossed rather than simply the ways that it divided.

BRINGING COLONY AND METROPOLE INTO A SINGLE ANALYTIC FIELD

Despite almost two decades of scholarship that has powerfully argued for bringing colony and metropole into a single analytic field, most studies of colonial-era interracial sexual relationships remain geographically bounded within either metropole or colony. By extending its analysis to the British ports, where scores of West African seamen who worked for the shipping lines that plied the Atlantic formed relationships with white women, *Crossing the Color Line* vividly illustrates how "the United Kingdom could be as much of 'a contact zone' as the colonies themselves."[30] Intimate relations between black men and white women emerge here as a constitutive part of the history of interracial sex and empire in ways that have been obscured by the far more robust bodies of literature on relations between colonizing men and colonized women and on "black peril" scares. Although hardly racial utopias, Britain's polyglot ports offered black men and white women intimate access to one another in ways that would have been unthinkable in the colonies. This was not lost on black men, who were also well aware that white men had nearly unfettered sexual access to black women in the colonies. Rather than signaling that the racialized sexual economies of metropole and colony were hermetically sealed off from one another, this awareness demonstrates just how entangled they were.

These connections were particularly evident during and after the 1919 race riots when black men were blamed not only for taking jobs away from white port dwellers, but also for taking *their* women. White women who partnered with black men were, in turn, widely disparaged in the press as lascivious race traitors. As the ports became tinderboxes of racial tension, black men were targeted for repatriation back to West Africa. Colonial authorities, however, acted quickly to ensure that they were not sent back with their white wives, whose presence, it was feared, would grossly undermine European prestige in the colonies. By bringing metropole and colony into a single analytic frame, *Crossing the Color Line* shows how "powerful sexual taboos [that] policed white female sexuality" were not the only mechanisms that kept white women and black men from openly coupling in the West African colonies.[31] State power was also used, a move that says more about the vulnerability of colonial rule than it does about its omnipotence.

The 1919 race riots and the state's draconian response to them triggered a powerful critique, on the part of Gold Coasters, of the sexual politics of empire and its potential consequences for nation building. *Crossing the Color Line*'s focus on these kinds of indigenous responses to interracial sexuality offers new vantage points from which to consider questions that have long been important to scholars of gender in colonial Africa, namely, the innovations, transformations, and challenges to gender relations occasioned by the colonial encounter and their political consequences. Established historical arguments about the "gender chaos" that gripped the Gold Coast during the late 1920s and 1930s, for instance, are given even greater historical depth by analyzing an earlier moment when the "wayward" behavior of some of the colony's young women with white men generated fears about national decline among the early vanguard of anticolonial nationalists at the close of World War I.[32] Here, we see a clear example of how contestations over race, gender, and sexuality were deeply implicated in the rise of African nationalism decades before the heyday of political nationalism in the aftermath of World War II.

Anticolonial discourses about white men's sexual exploitation of African women, in turn, offer new insights into the diverse ways that male power holders engaged with the colonial state to assert their authority. Familiar narratives about traditional political authorities who collaborated with the colonial government to reassert their patriarchal control over "disobedient" women get a new twist by focusing on the ways that politically marginalized Gold Coasters discursively constructed the sexual libertinage of the colony's young women as proof of the demoralizing influences of European men, and by extension colonial rule, in order to bolster their own patriarchal claims to power.[33] But like other scholars who have explored similar questions, the goal here is to probe the experiences of African women in ways that attend to their subordination to both indigenous and colonial systems of patriarchal power without obscuring the extent to which they could also be agents of their own sexuality.[34] Indeed, the stories presented here show that Gold Coast women's varied sexual engagements with European men were part of a broader spectrum of self-determination strategies that women employed in their efforts to wield more control over their lives. It would be a fallacy, however, to suggest that these relationships were solely or only ever instrumental. As Jennifer Cole and Lynn Thomas rightly assert, affective ties could coexist alongside or even be forged through exchanges of material resources for sex.[35] Rachel Jean-Baptiste takes this argument a step further by insisting that historians of sexuality in Africa need to do more in the way of analyzing how sexuality is expressed through emotions, "such as desire, pleasure, yearning, and pain," so that we are better able to see how "African historical actors thought of and embodied their sexuality."[36] *Crossing the Color Line* heeds this call by offering a multivalent reading of these relationships that takes their emotive aspects seriously.

The vast literature on empire and sexuality has made clear that colonial paranoia about interracial sexual relationships was the soft underbelly of Europe's new imperial expansion, although such concerns, as Durba Ghosh has persuasively shown, were already evident in older corners of the empire.[37] As Europe's limited governance in service of trade throughout much of Africa and Asia transformed over the course of the second half of the nineteenth century into formal colonization characterized by large-scale land acquisition and the expansion of governance structures, often achieved through military conquest, the dynamics of race relations palpably changed. Yet, the material conditions of dependence underpinning everyday interactions and intimacies between Africans and Europeans in British West Africa remained relatively unchanged. If in the workplace Native officers and clerks were the "hidden lynchpins of colonial rule," in European officers' bungalows and residential areas, African men, in their roles as cooks, stewards and servants, gardeners and watchmen, were the lynchpins of colonial life.[38] So, too, were African women who continued to meet the sexual and domestic needs of European men, even as colonial governments came to view—in different measures and in different ways—such relationships as a hindrance rather than a help to the new colonial dispensation. As a result, administrators and policy makers focused their attention on eradicating interracial concubinage. It is instructive that marriage and prostitution were generally not the targets of these efforts. The racial etiquette of colonialism across Africa was already so deeply entrenched by the turn of the century that interracial marriages sanctioned by civil or church authorities did not require prohibition—they were simply unheard of.[39] At the same time, the vast majority of European men were not permitted to bring their wives to the colonies, and so administrators tacitly, and sometimes explicitly, tolerated prostitution to ward off the even greater perceived threat of homosexuality.[40]

Like heterosexual sex across the colonial color line, the first studies of homosexuality in the context of the colonies largely privileged the perspectives and experiences of the colonizer.[41] This is beginning to change as scholars have increasingly turned their attention toward more African-centered explorations of homosexuality. Apart from documenting the indigeneity of same-sex practices in Africa, helping to counter the myth that homosexuality is a Western import, some of these studies underscore the contemporary origins of the recent headline-grabbing homophobia in a number of African countries by analyzing how African communities responded, historically, to same-sex relationships and the individuals who practiced them, while also illuminating the contingent nature of these practices and the conceptual limitations of Western-derived categories for understanding them in Africa.[42] Among these studies, Stephanie Newell's *The Forger's Tale: The Search for Odeziaku* and Neville Hoad's *African Intimacies: Race, Homosexuality, and Globalization* point us in directions that must be pursued if there is to be a convergence between the new literature on (homo)sexualities in Africa and the older literature on empire and sexuality. Although the focus of *Crossing the Color Line* is on heterosexual sex across the color line—a result of the limits of my sources rather than an accurate reflection of the range of cross-racial sexualities in colonial Ghana—no book of this kind would be complete without acknowledging that interracial sexuality was managed in the colonies in ways that had much to do with colonial assumptions about the dangers posed by homosexuality to the "civilizing mission's" moral credibility—a question I return to in the conclusion.

While colonial approaches to the management of sexuality were relational, they were hardly fixed or uniform. Rather, their form, severity, duration, and targets varied across different colonial contexts and shifted in response to the dangers those contexts presented. The timing of some of the better-known efforts to end concubinage, for instance, occurred in the wake of the forceful application of alien political rule over much of Africa and Asia. Far from confirming the legitimacy of imperial power, conquest at this scale entailed serious risks to European supremacy and thus constituted precisely the kind of moment in which concubinage was ripe for coming "under more direct attack."[43] To minimize these risks, colonial regimes attempted to legitimize, institutionalize, and professionalize their administrations partly through sexual regulation. French Cambodia's Governor-General Doumer attempted to whip his ragtag colonial service into shape at the turn of the twentieth century by taking "immediate steps to police the private lives of French administrators," which included instructing them "to avoid relationships with native concubines."[44] Similar injunctions against concubinage were soon made elsewhere in Indochina. While interracial concubinage was never officially prohibited in French West Africa, by the early 1920s colonial administrators were no longer openly encouraging the practice, although it remained common.[45] This change in attitude was spurred in part by colonial anxieties about the racial status and citizenship rights of the métis offspring of these often-temporary unions and fears that they would cohere into a group of "dangerous *déclassés*" instead of "indispensable auxiliaries."[46]

As Emanuelle Saada observes, in the context of France's second colonial empire, "the phenomenon of *métissage* acquired a new face: it became the '*métis* question,'" or the "métis problem," as it was frequently called.[47] The early twentieth century also witnessed significant changes in official attitudes and policies toward interracial sexual relationships throughout much of British Africa and in many of Britain's Asian and Pacific colonies.[48] Among the African colonies it was the Gold Coast government that led the effort to eradicate what its governor, Sir John Rodger, called "very undesirable relations being maintained by European government officers with Native Women" in a 1907 anticoncubinage circular.[49] Notably, Rodger's anxieties about concubinage were not tied to the progeny of these relationships. Thus, if strikingly similar colonial discourses, authored by the French, British, and Dutch alike, tied the dangers of *métissage* to the "métis problem" in vastly different colonial contexts, the case of the Gold Coast suggests a different trajectory altogether: colonial discourses could condemn interracial relationships, especially concubinage, as problematic without ever constructing "mixed-bloods" as a problem, let alone a problem in need of fixing through state intervention.[50] Indeed, amid the overabundance of colonial correspondence about interracial sexual relations in the Gold Coast, there is relative silence about their progeny. Where the British were concerned, it was domestic authorities and civil welfare groups in Britain who raised the alarm about the offspring of West African men and British women in port towns and cities like Liverpool and Cardiff. The alleged ill fate of such children—as outlined in the infamous "Fletcher Report" of 1930—was used to disparage their parents and to urge authorities to adopt stricter immigration and labor restrictions against West African seamen.[51]

When anxiety over multiracial children was expressed in the colony, it was by Gold Coasters—not Gold Coast administrators—who worried that white men abandoned their offspring "to the precarious protection of needy native families."[52] These concerns, however, were not used to make demands on the colonial state's coffers, but rather to highlight the immoral behavior and paternal failings of white men as part of a wider challenge to the moral legitimacy of British colonial rule. Indeed, I have found only a few cases in which individual Gold Coasters petitioned the colonial government for aid in caring for multiracial children abandoned by their European fathers.[53] Concerns about the burden of care placed on local families underscore the germane point that such families generally assumed responsibility for these children. Even in cases where multiracial children were placed in care facilities, this did not typically signal an end to the maternal familial relationship, but rather an attempt to secure a better future for the child in question.

The tendency of local families to absorb these children and the enduring connections to African societies that absorption fostered, combined with the colonial state's noninterventionist approach and the nature of British nationality law—factors that are explored in greater detail in chapter 1—help to explain why multiracial people in the Gold Coast were not ultimately categorized separately from other Africans; why they did not seek out that distinction for themselves; and why they did not form sociopolitical organizations or mutual aid societies, as they did in numerous other colonial settings, including elsewhere in British Africa.[54] When they confronted the colonial state for increased rights, they did so as part of the larger vanguard of educated elites and anticolonial nationalists in the Gold Coast who hailed from diverse ethnic backgrounds. Thus the narrative that unfolds in *Crossing the Color Line* is not about multiracial people—for such a category of being had little salience in colonial Ghana for Africans and Europeans alike—rather this book is about the deep and enduring, but nonetheless shifting investments that Africans and Europeans made in interracial sexual relationships.

CURBING CONCUBINAGE IN THE GOLD COAST

While curbing concubinage in the Gold Coast was not a prophylactic solution to the thorny problems of racial classification and citizenship status or (presumed) disaffection and alienation that multiracial people raised in other colonial settings, it was certainly in keeping with the postconquest defensive posture assumed by other colonial governments in which imperial security was linked to sexual and racial order. In this regard the timing of Rodger's anticoncubinage decree, released just five years after the Asante Kingdom had finally been militarily defeated and incorporated into the colony in 1902, is telling. Far from signaling the triumph of British rule, we might better understand the end of the "pacification" campaign as marking the onset of even greater uncertainty as the British government was now faced with the challenge of administering the colony. Indeed, a culture of paranoia and doubt was evident throughout the colonial period in the government's efforts to protect itself against a range of perceived threats that was hardly limited to interracial concubinage. Officials actively sought to prevent African American repatriates from settling in the Gold Coast and barred the white wives of working-class Africans from doing the same because it feared their presence would be subversive.[55] For similar reasons, they restricted the entry of Dusé Mohamed, Marcus Garvey, W. E. B. Du Bois, and other "race agitators" to the Gold Coast and sought to ban their "anti-British propaganda" from being disseminated there.[56] Even the showing of a film titled *The White*

Man's Grave in the colony set off a flurry of colonial correspondence over the "harmful" effect that films like this could have on "the half-educated and ... illiterate communities of the African race," a description that says more about the racist assumptions of colonial administrators than it does about the intelligence of Gold Coast filmgoers. Such concerns resulted in tighter import regulations on films and greater censorship powers.[57]

Interracial concubinage was particularly troublesome, however, because unlike the aforementioned examples, it was a threat that came from within. In asserting that these were relationships that European government officers "maintained with" local women, Governor Rodger recognized the purposefulness and intent with which his officers made these arrangements. They were neither accidental nor occasional occurrences; indeed, it was "with much regret" that Rodger said he came to know of their "prevalence in this Colony and its Dependences." Thus despite the phrase's lack of precision, "undesirable relations" referred in the main to concubinage. In Rodger's view, officers diminished their own authority by participating in these relationships and in the process compromised the government, a situation he declared was intolerable.[58] Rodger's circular was followed two years later by the better-known and more widely disseminated Crewe Circular of 1909, which similarly sought to bring European colonial officers' sex lives in line with the new racial politics of British colonial rule. The Colonial Office condemned interracial concubinage because, in the words of the secretary of state for the colonies, Lord Crewe, it was "not possible for any member of the administration to countenance such practices without lowering himself in the eyes of the natives, and diminishing his authority to an extent which will seriously impair his capacity for useful work in the Service."[59]

Although concubinage took many forms involving widely varying degrees of cohabitation, sexual and emotional intimacy, and domestic labor, colonial authorities assumed it was more likely to draw officers into compromising webs of social relations and obligation with local families precisely because it was an ongoing relationship, unlike prostitution or "occasional illicit acts," as one Whitehall adviser put it.[60] Concubinage was thus held responsible for enmeshing officers into local families and communities that apparently they would have otherwise remained aloof from. This reasoning put the cart before the horse. Expanding our view of cross-racial intimacy beyond sex allows us to see how deeply embedded European officers were in the African communities they lived and worked among and how ensconced Africans were in the colonial households and workplaces they inhabited.[61] The highly dependent relations officers formed with their cooks, stewards, headmen, clerks, and other "native" subordinates were the most common conduits through which relations of concubinage came into being. That concubinage was so commonplace—and administrators agreed that it was—reflected the quotidian familiarity that already existed between Europeans and Africans in the colony, while also helping to further it. It also reflected the fact that at this fairly early juncture in Ghana's colonial history, the color line needed to be drawn rather than defended.

Despite their shared intentions, in a number of striking ways the 1907 and 1909 circulars arguably did more to blur the line between colonized and colonizer than they did to clarify it. First, by disciplining the sexual habits of European officers, the circulars raised uncomfortable questions about whose sexuality was actually in need of "civilizing." Second, by making concubinage a punishable offense the circulars put a premium on keeping these matters quiet, which in turn pushed some European men, "anxious to avoid publicity," into native law courts where they could discretely settle their "so-called 'woman palaver[s],'" as a German colonial official curiously noted in his 1912 legal survey of the Gold Coast.[62] Incentivizing colonial officers to have their sexual misdeeds adjudicated by "native" authorities is hardly what Governor Rodger or Lord Crewe could have imagined when they issued their respective circulars. Compounding all of this was the fact that the circulars transformed concubinage charges into powerful tools of coercion and sabotage used by both Africans and Europeans to achieve a range of different goals, chief among them extorting money, redressing workplace grievances, and ruining rival officers' careers. In the process they further undermined British authority and credibility, the very things they were charged with securing. The Crewe Circular's unanticipated adverse consequences prompted the Colonial Office's decision, in 1924, to let it "fade into oblivion," and on these same grounds its distribution was officially discontinued in 1934, although concubinage remained a punishable offense for the duration of the colonial period.[63] While the circulars did not succeed in stopping interracial sexual relationships, they did push them into the recesses of colonial society where they were less visible—or so many Europeans thought. Ironically, then, British efforts to end concubinage helped to create the unseemly and illicit picture of interracial sexual relations that early Gold Coast nationalists increasingly began to draw in the pages of the colony's lively indigenous press.

Not least by showing how these relationships hastened the end of empire, *Crossing the Color Line* contributes to the substantive and still-growing body of research that explores the myriad and changing ways that interracial sexual relations sustained and complicated Europe's new imperialism.[64] These studies have unequivocally demonstrated that interracial sexual relations were the subject of intense discussion, debate, informal and formal policy making, surveillance, and regulation underscoring their central importance to the colonial state. Yet, this prolific body of scholarship has often been less successful in illuminating what these relations meant for the colonized. *Crossing the Color Line* charts British colonial concerns, but it pushes beyond them to show how the "domain of interracial sexual relations"—conceived here as the sphere of knowledge, influence, and activity that constituted, informed, and transformed these relationships—was shaped to a far greater extent by the social practices and interests of the colonized, in this case Gold Coasters, than much of the scholarship has hitherto acknowledged.[65] Together Africans and Europeans coproduced sexuality as a "volatile symbol in debates about the character of national identity," and thus the goal here is not to counterbalance European perspectives with African ones, but rather to show how the interaction between African and European approaches and practices influenced the historical trajectory of these relationships.[66]

METHODOLOGY, SOURCES, AND ORGANIZATION

This book in a narrow sense is about interracial sexual relationships between African women and European men in the Gold Coast, African men and European women in the colonial metropolis, and the various ways in which these geographies of interracial sex collided and influenced one another. My aim in documenting these relationships, however, is not simply to elucidate patterns of continuity and change in the relationships themselves. I use them as an entry point for discussing colonial race relations more broadly and to explore the connective tissue between the racial and sexual politics of colonial rule and its contestation. I am able to do this because the archival link between sexuality and race is profound and persistent: references to sex consistently exposed the contested racial politics of colonialism in the Gold Coast and Britain. Official inquiries into European officers' alleged sexual misconduct with African women, for instance, disclosed vivid details about the tensions between European and African government officers, while also illustrating the often petty but nonetheless vicious intraracial rivalries between European officers.[67] These grievances were strategically expressed through concubinage charges because government prohibition gave them teeth.

In drawing on the records generated by official inquiries into these charges, I have been mindful of the very particular kind of sources they are. Historical actors, whether African or European, who levied sexual misconduct charges against government officers were often motivated by reasons that had little to do with sex itself. Nor were they necessarily concerned by the breach of racial boundaries that such relations represented, even when they exposed such relations in order to assert power over and within the colony's administrative racial hierarchy. Accusers often hoped that the charges would be an effective way of gaining the upper hand over officers with whom they had grievances—they were a means to an end. For their part, the accused were deeply invested in either refuting or minimizing the charges against them because their careers hung in the balance. Depending on the severity of the charges, government officers risked demotion, financial penalties, early termination of their contracts, or dismissal if found guilty. Official censure was compounded by the social disgrace, financial loss, and diminished prospects for future employment that could accompany these kinds of charges.

The expansive corpus of colonial correspondence generated by imperial efforts to manage, prohibit, or otherwise control sex across the color line dramatizes a point that Anjali Arondekar has made about the historical visibility, rather than the oft-assumed invisibility, of sexuality in the colonial archive. What is particularly compelling about Arondekar's argument is her insistence that we seek out "how sexuality is made visible in the colonial archive" in order to "paradoxically disclose the very limits of that visibility."[68] In the case of the Gold Coast, interracial sexuality was made visible in ways that clarified the colonial state's investments and inconsistencies in regulating sex across the color line among its own officers, who were subject to its anticoncubinage circulars. The significantly larger population of privately employed Europeans was not beholden to these directives, and as a result their relations with local women rarely made their way into the colonial archive. The increasingly virulent culture of racism and racial segregation that underpinned these circulars, however, stigmatized interracial relationships in ways that were surely palpable to all Europeans in the colony. Despite the risks, European men in government service and in private employment continued to pursue these relationships, making them a wider phenomenon than this book's emphasis on concubinage between European officers and African women reveals.

Sexuality was also made archivally visible in the ways that accused officers sought to defend themselves by compromising others, both African and European. In a number of cases accused men made similar allegations against their fellow officers in order to diffuse the charges against them, while others painted themselves as the victims of unscrupulous African men and women who blackmailed or thrust involuntary liaisons on them. Drawing on Arondekar's insights, it quickly becomes evident that while the colonial archive provides ample evidence of officers' exculpatory strategies, which frequently drew on the lexicon of colonial racism that painted African women as sexually promiscuous and crafty, and African men as immoral and oppressive, these sources rarely opened up spaces for Africans, especially women, to reverse the gaze.

The voices of African men occasionally entered the evidentiary record as they sought to show how European government officers' sexual relationships with local women interfered with their official duties, biased their actions, or constituted a form of administrative and/or racial abuse. Although sexual relations with African women were supposedly at the heart of these inquiries, they were almost never directly questioned about their relationships with European men. Rather, African and European men spoke for or about them. Only in a few instances, when these women were involved in legal proceedings (as opposed to administrative inquiries), do their voices enter court records. When their voices do emerge, the nature of what they say is circumscribed by the venue of the court and the kinds of questions posed to them. Nonetheless, archival fragments reveal how some women used their relationships with European men to assert their independence and contest their subordination to African and European men. But opportunities for Africans to weigh in on these cases were quickly curtailed because the government became skittish about soliciting evidence from them about European officers' sexual relationships with local women—a fact that worked in the favor of a number of officers charged with sexual misconduct.

Given the scarcity of women's voices and perspectives, it is unwise to suggest that the few female voices we do hear spoke on behalf of anyone but themselves. To frame them as representative of women's experiences, rather than what they are—the experiences of individual women—would be nothing short of asking them to perform the function of the "native female informant," just as European men had once demanded of their "sleeping dictionaries."[69] I do, however, attempt to speak to their individual experiences and motives, when and where I can, by reading between the lines of what was said by and about them and by contextualizing their actions within wider patterns of gender relations and social change in the colony. If we have to work hard to recover the voices and experiences of African women, we must not let the overabundance of male voices minimize our analytical scrutiny of what they had to say. The stakes were high for the men involved in these cases—Europeans faced serious professional repercussions, but so too did Africans who made sexual misconduct charges against Europeans—and thus it is often easier to discern motive than truth in the colonial archive.

Other sources proved more capable of yielding a range of African insights and perspectives less mediated by colonial power and its archival logic. The numerous African-owned Gold Coast newspapers published during the first half of the twentieth century make it possible to access African perspectives—albeit predominately those of African men—outside the colonial archive. While these press sources illuminate the growing discontent in the colony with interracial sexual relations, they also have much to say about the changing and challenging terrain of gender relations between African men and women. Letters, petitions, and oral histories were another rich but limited source for African perspectives. Interviews with two Ghanaian women, Mercy "Kwadua" Roth and the late Felicia Agnes Knight, both of whom married European men in the late colonial period, as well as interviews with the children and grandchildren of a number of the interracially married couples whose histories I take up in several chapters of the book, provided much-needed insight into the experiences of the ordinary and at times extraordinary women and men who, in part, made this history. Because of the sensitive, highly personal, and at times contested nature of the information revealed during these interviews and in the archives, I had to make difficult decisions about what information was appropriate to disclose. While some details might have made for a more gripping read, I refrained from revealing information that made living family members uncomfortable.

Taken together, the sources this book draws upon form a qualitatively and quantitatively rich, if uneven, corpus of evidence. Concubinage cases may have numbered in the tens rather than the hundreds, but the vast correspondence generated by individual cases speaks volumes about the anxieties these relationships generated. Likewise, the number of interracial families that fought to be repatriated to the Gold Coast during the interwar years was small, but their efforts nonetheless left sizable and rich archives. Indeed, one such family generated upward of five hundred pages of correspondence over the span of a decade. As a result of the nature of these sources, the chapters that make up *Crossing the Color Line* move across different registers, shifting from the micro-politics of individual concubinage cases to transatlantic networks of family, empire, and anticolonial resistance.

The first part of this book is organized around a number of key twentieth-century developments that had important implications for the ways in which interracial sexuality was managed in colonial Ghana. Chapter 1 offers a brief overview of shifting practices and perceptions of interracial relationships from precolonial times to the onset of formal British colonial rule. The 1907 and 1909 anticoncubinage circulars, and the spate of cases they spawned, are the subjects of chapters 2, 3, and 4.

My reconstruction and analyses of these cases are grounded in wide-ranging documentation found in official correspondence between the Gold Coast government and the Colonial Office. These files often contain sizable enclosures of supporting materials, including official inquiry reports, internal correspondence between different local government branches, exculpatory statements and other official letters written by accused men, eyewitness accounts, and court proceedings. These sources more easily yield official perspectives, but such perspectives were shaped by the actions of Gold Coasters who initiated sexual misconduct cases or who influenced how such cases unfolded. By attending to the motivations and actions of Gold Coasters and raising questions about how their varied involvements in these relationships could act as levers in their interactions with European officers, these chapters provide a more balanced set of perspectives than my sources, if read only along the archival grain, tend to reveal.[70] Apart from reading along and against the archival grain, I employ a third methodology that I call "reading along the seam," by which I mean carefully and critically examining those places where archival accounts with disparate intentions agree on certain fundamentals. Locating instances when adversarial accounts meet up proved to be a particularly indispensable method for reconstructing the actions of those rendered voiceless in the archive and speculating about their intentions.

The African actors involved in these cases represent a cross section of society—fathers and uncles, literate government officers and clerks, chiefs, headmen, female load carriers, migrant women, mothers and daughters—and thus provide insights into how differently positioned Gold Coasters could at times challenge European officers in the often surprising ways that ultimately led, in part, to the Colonial Office's decision to stop distributing its 1909 circular in 1934. Part 1 concludes with a fifth chapter that looks at a brief moment of reignited debate in 1945 among colonial administrators about whether Lord Crewe's antinconcubinage circular should be revived in the wake of the four interracial marriages mentioned in the opening pages of this introduction. Set against the backdrop of World War II and the rampant interracial prostitution occasioned by the deployment of thousands of European and white American military personnel to the Gold Coast, which administrators were slow to address, the panic over the four interracial marriages underscores that the most dangerous form of heterosexual interracial sexuality was publicly legitimized intermarriage.[71] In order to provide a sense of the long-term trajectory of the four interracial couples whose marriages were at the center of this firestorm, chapter 5 includes brief biographical sketches of each family, as well as a biography of Hans and

Mercy "Kwadua" Roth, who, after a long courtship and a customary marriage, were married in a civil ceremony on the eve of independence. The Roth's history sheds light on intimate relations between privately employed European men and African women in the Gold Coast.

Part 2 begins by moving across the Atlantic to the British ports at the end of World War I to reveal how the raced and gendered systems of sexual access in the Gold Coast and Britain collided in ways that vivify, in the words of Antoinette Burton, "how imperial power was staged at home and how it was contested by colonial 'natives' at the heart of the empire itself."[72] After being subjected to unprecedented forms of racial violence during the riots that swept the British seaports in 1919, black men were targeted for repatriation to the colonies. While some men were willing to return home, they insisted that their white wives go with them. Chapter 6 unearths the sustained but failed attempts of these interracial couples to settle in West Africa and provides vivid insights into the vexed position of white women in the colonies and in the colonial imagination. Thwarted by colonial policies designed to preserve white prestige by keeping the white wives of working-class Africans out of the colonies, these men could be repatriated only if they agreed to leave their wives and multiracial children behind. In this instance colonial concerns shaped metropolitan policy making with often-tragic consequences for interracial couples in Europe. Drawing on interviews, petitions, and official colonial correspondence, the human toll of these policies is dramatically illustrated through the story of the Annans, an Afro-German family that fought for over a decade to settle in the Gold Coast.

Chapter 7 returns to the Gold Coast to explore how the 1919 race riots in Britain triggered public condemnation in the colony's African-owned press of the perceived double standard that allowed white men to have their way with African women in the colonies, while black men were beaten for marrying or cohabiting with white women in Britain. It was not long before Gold Coast commentators took European men to task for sexually exploiting the colony's young women. While unseemly relationships between white men and African women became a focal point of anticolonial agitation, chapter 8 argues that the relationships many leading figures of African independence formed with white women during their sojourns in Britain were central to the struggle against colonialism, even as they complicated it. These deeply intertwined Black Atlantic histories illuminate the profound, yet little-known connection between interracial sexual relations and anticolonial nationalism among West Africans—a fitting historical note on which to end a book about interracial sexual relationships during the colonial period in Ghana.

In charting the continuities and changes that shaped interracial sexual relationships in the Gold Coast, *Crossing the Color Line* demonstrates that these relationships were subject to increasing colonial control and the raced and gendered conventions of their time. But they also emerged as a key space in which these conventions were both accommodated and challenged—in small and big ways—by Gold Coasters who saw in them all of the contradictions, inconsistencies, inequalities, and, at times, opportunities that characterized colonialism. Thus the tale that unfolds across these pages joins together an analysis of the carnal politics of imperial rule in the Gold Coast and Britain with an analysis of how Africans interpreted these relationships and attempted to assert control over them. Race and sex often intersected in combustible ways precisely because racial and sexual boundaries were charged with regulating colonial life even as they were continually crossed. In the process of illuminating the convergence of these competing realities, I hope to tell a layered story about the complex nature of everyday race relations in the Gold Coast, which neither mirrored the extreme form of racial segregation that existed in the settler colonies nor was free of the culture of racial privilege and hierarchy that underpinned it. But like the settler colonies, sexuality was a dense transfer point for relations of (racial) power in the Gold Coast, to borrow from Foucault, and thus became an active locus of contestation.

PART ONE

The Gold Coast

1 ⇝ From Indispensable to "Undesirable"

African Women, European Men, and the Transformation of Afro-European Power Relations in the Gold Coast

"ALL THE EUROPEANS HAVE NATIVE WIVES." So observed US naval officer Horatio Bridge, who published an account of his visit to the Gold Coast in 1845.[1] The label "native wives" surely glossed a range of different kinds of relationships—from concubinage to a small number of church-sanctioned marriages and more prevalent "country marriages," which, as the name implies, often lasted for the duration of a European man's stay on the coast and were contracted in accordance with local customary law.[2] While Bridge's turn of phrase elided less seemly sexual exchanges altogether, his observation indicates just how visible and ubiquitous interracial relationships between African women and European men were during the mid-nineteenth century. What Bridge witnessed was a continuation of practices that European explorers from centuries past documented in published accounts of their voyages to what the Portuguese first called El Mina, or "the mine," because of the abundant gold that adorned the bodies of the coast's indigenous inhabitants. Published in 1602, one of the earliest European accounts of the Gold Kingdom of Guinea, written by Flemish trader and explorer Pieter de Marees, described how the thriving population of Portuguese men "take as their wives many sturdy black women or Mulatto [women], half-white and half-black (that is, yellowish), whom the Portuguese like very much."[3] Interracial unions, from their early beginnings on the coast, were thus regarded as de rigueur.

But there is an even deeper, African history to the marriage practices that traders and explorers like de Marees and Bridge documented. European men were being incorporated into preexisting sociocultural frameworks—what George Brooks calls "landlord-stranger reciprocities"—developed by Africans throughout the West African region to integrate strangers into local societies.[4] One of the reciprocities that this system entailed was the granting of marriage rights to local women as a means of wedding stranger men to their host communities and securing their loyalty.[5] From an African perspective, then, these relationships were of strategic importance to the way in which they negotiated on behalf of their own best interests in the context of the increasingly competitive, politically unstable, and often treacherous conditions that characterized transatlantic trade, especially as the trade in slaves came to dominate the commercial life of the Gold Coast littoral.[6]

For the same reasons, Europeans also found these relationships to be advantageous, but there were more practical motives as well. Medical care, access to food, language instruction, companionship, and sex were all gained through these alliances. But, as Britain put an end to the transatlantic slave trade and wrested control of the coast from its European competitors—a process that was largely complete by the mid-nineteenth century, with the exception of Dutch-controlled Elmina, which was annexed in 1872—it also began to change the tenor of its relationship with local societies. Thomas McCaskie succinctly describes this transformation as "a century-long shift from a Britain that *asked* to one that *demanded* and at last *commanded*."[7] As company rule gave way to colonial rule, official attitudes toward relationships between African women and European officers shifted in ways that dramatically heralded a new colonial order of racial insularity—albeit one that was never fully achieved. Nowhere was this shift more evident than in the release of Governor Rodger's 1907 "undesirable relations" circular. In banning interracial concubinage to help shore up the colonial state's interests, Rodger nonetheless shared a common imperative with his predecessors—whether Portuguese, Dutch, Danish, or, like himself, British—to regulate sexual relations between European men and local women in ways that would advance, in theory if not always in practice, the agendas of their respective regimes.

This chapter explores how Africans and Europeans in the Gold Coast sought to control interracial sexual relationships, with a view to showing continuity, variation, and change in these regulatory strategies across the precolonial and early formal colonial periods. If, as I argue, these relationships broadly went from being indispensable during the precolonial period to being "undesirable" in the view of many Europeans and Africans during the colonial period, we must bear in mind that this shift in opinion was not universal, nor did it bring about the effective end of sex across the colonial color line.

LANDLORDS AND STRANGERS: INTEGRATING EUROPEANS INTO WEST AFRICAN SOCIETIES

An expansive and thriving intracontinental African trade had been in existence long before the Portuguese set foot on the shores of the Gold Coast during the late fifteenth century. During this period, strangers, as purveyors of trade, linked the expansive West African region into an economic unit.[8] Because they had something of value to offer that could not be obtained locally, host societies, or "landlords," welcomed them and often encouraged valued strangers to take up permanent residence. Their presence was regulated through "landlord-stranger reciprocities" to ensure that it remained beneficial. While the origins of these reciprocities cannot be readily identified, their tenets are visible in the social practices of western African societies:

> Historically, travelers were provided food, lodging, and security of possessions. Hospitality and appropriate behavior toward visitors derived from the obligations of kinship affiliations, real and fictive. . . . Concomitantly, the behavior of strangers was conditioned by all of the foregoing; by the dread of spending a night in the bush bereft of the protection of a community; by dependence on hosts for food, shelter, access to commercial networks, land, and other resources.[9]

This system of reciprocities also saw "rulers, village leaders, and lineage heads promote marriage between female relatives or dependent women to favored strangers as a means of binding these men to family and community."[10] Marriages between male strangers and enslaved women were particularly common among many host societies who wished to profit from alliances with strangers, but were wary that they might abscond with a valued female relative. Although the Ga appear to have refrained from this practice in favor of betrothing freeborn women, it was observed elsewhere in the Gold Coast and in other parts of West Africa. In the Anlo region of what was then known as the Upper Slave Coast (southeastern Ghana), "free women were rarely if ever betrothed to stranger men [both African and European], even financially prosperous ones." Instead, "Anlo elders reserved unions with such men for the enslaved women in their families . . . because of the perceived risks involved."[11] While the prevalence of arranged marriages meant that both free and enslaved women often had little control over their marital prospects, the fact that enslaved women were more frequently betrothed to strangers not only suggests that families were well aware that these unions did not always produce positive outcomes, it also underscores the greater risks enslaved women faced as they sought to negotiate their position in society.[12] Despite the circumstances surrounding their betrothal to stranger men, women often sought the advantages to be gained from these relationships. Even enslaved women were sometimes able to accumulate substantial wealth, particularly through trade, precisely because they had valuable connections to the worlds of their free families and their stranger husbands.[13] For their part, male strangers had much to gain from their alliances with women from their host societies, who often served as linguistic and cultural interpreters and partners in commercial exchanges, in addition to providing male strangers with sex, companionship, and a range of domestic services.

Starting in the late fifteenth century, when West Africa's trade networks were increasingly reoriented toward the Atlantic, landlord-stranger reciprocities were extended to Europeans. The first three and a half centuries of Afro-European contact were characterized primarily by the commercial relationships that various European powers, including the Portuguese, Dutch, Danes, and British, established with the various ethnic groups inhabiting the Gold Coast littoral. Like African strangers, Europeans were expected to comply with the dictates of these reciprocal arrangements. To help ensure compliance, West African landlords strategically restricted the amount of land Europeans were given such that they had only enough to meet their need for shelter and trade. As a result, Europeans were rendered dependent on host societies for their daily subsistence needs, giving Africans considerable leverage in times of conflict. Apart from the obvious trade benefits and the ability to contain Europeans in specified zones, these agreements allowed landlords to "regulate the introduction of change and technology and maintain for themselves those by-products beneficial for continuance of local power."[14] Gold Coasters adapted these practices to meet the demands of Atlantic trade and the new situations and stresses it created. For instance, Ty Reese has shown how the Fante integrated Britain's Company of Merchants Trading to Africa into the structures of local society through a tenant-patron relationship. Reese observes that "by making the company react to the structures . . . the local peoples kept the company in a subservient position," which not only gave the Fante control over the company, but also "allowed for the continued growth of the Gold Coast Atlantic trade during the second half of the eighteenth century" because both parties accepted a common framework for minimizing disputes that otherwise would have disrupted trade.[15]

Coastal ethnic groups, such as the Fante and the Ga, drew on their own pre-European traditions of using marriage alliances to foster stranger integration and strengthen their political and economic positions when they extended the privilege of marriage and/or cohabitation with free and enslaved women to Europeans. This was particularly important to the establishment of the almost entirely male European presence in the Gold Coast as elsewhere in West Africa.[16] To simply suggest that in lieu of European women, European men turned to African women to meet their sexual and domestic needs, however, neglects the range of services and skills these women uniquely possessed and were able to provide Europeans with. In addition to locally sourced food supplies, language and cultural instruction, and companionship, African women were the primary conduit through which European men accessed indigenous medical knowledge and care during their frequent illnesses in the centuries before advances in tropical medicine transformed the "fever coast" into a relatively livable environment for Europeans. But relationships with local women were not merely a matter of basic survival, they also allowed European men to cement profitable commercial and political alliances with local families whose social, political, and trade networks were opened only to trusted strangers whose loyalty could be assured.

Africans arranged these relationships according to their own purposes and in accordance with their own rules and regulations, which they expected Europeans to follow. As Rebecca Shumway notes, "Failure to follow the African law and custom in this regard resulted in expensive disputes" when Europeans gained sexual access to women without prior negotiation, approval, and payment.[17] Among the Fante, customary law was used to encourage marriage over concubinage by enforcing the custom of forfeiture, or *sarwie*, which mandated that "whatever is given or entrusted by a man or woman, to the person with whom he or she is living in concubinage, cannot be reclaimed on any consideration whatsoever." According to the Fante lawyer and legal scholar John M. Sarbah, *sarwie* "placed a great check or restraint on the wealthy, and those traders, European and native, who were in the habit of keeping a host of women under their protection as concubines."[18]

Although it has been widely argued that African women found room to act with agency within the context of their relationships with European men, their entry into these relationships was often not of their own making. The standard interpretation of the role of women in landlord-stranger relationships tends to obscure the contours of patriarchal power and exchange that controlled these women's destinies. Although not without its own conceptual limits, a more analytically fruitful framework for understanding the position of women in these reciprocities is Gayle Rubin's theorization of the "traffic in women," which contends that "if it is women who are being transacted, then it is the men who give and take them who are linked." According to Rubin, "Women are in no position to realize the benefits of their own circulation," because "it is the partners, not the presents, upon whom reciprocal exchange confers its . . . power of social linkage."[19] If Rubin leaves no room for countenancing the possibility that some women did benefit from their exchange, her emphatic stance makes powerfully clear that these gains were often made against great odds. Perhaps more telling, however, is that the women who acquired wealth and power through their relationships with European men typically did so because they were willing to treat others, just as they had once been treated, as tradable commodities.

FROM STRANGERS TO LANDLORDS: EUROPEAN APPROACHES TO INTERRACIAL SEXUAL RELATIONSHIPS

While European men frequently secured their own physical and emotional well-being, as well as their personal fortunes and those of the companies, crowns, and governments they represented, through their relationships with local women, there was considerable variation in the management of these relationships among the European powers that vied for control of the coast. In the context of the tightly controlled institutionalized trade that came to characterize the Portuguese presence in Elmina during the late fifteenth and sixteenth centuries, the Portuguese Crown disapproved of marital unions between local women and its traders and officers.[20] The officially authorized Portuguese contingent was confined to their coastal fort, São Jorge da Mina, built in 1481 to protect King João II's royal monopoly on trade.[21] As with the construction of the fort, all regulations were geared toward the promotion and protection of trade.[22] Thus, the administration's disapproval of intermarriage likely stemmed from concerns that access to local women's networks would increase opportunities for illicit private trade. Instead, the administration supplied officers with female slaves who tended to their domestic needs.[23] Their sexual demands were met through a system of prostitution, in which women who were surely enslaved were housed in the fort expressly for this purpose, even as the fort's vicar objected to the practice.[24] Despite these provisions, some of the men who resided in the fort also maintained relationships with townswomen.²⁵ The contacts made through these alliances may even partially account for the rampant illicit trade that was occurring between the fort's residents and local townspeople. Beyond the confines of the castle, as Pieter de Marees observed in the early seventeenth century, intermarriage between Portuguese interlopers and local women, known as *calisare*, was commonplace. Surely these relationships further undermined the Crown's monopoly on trade and help to explain its opposition to intermarriage. Although seemingly ignored even by those men who were directly under its authority, the Portuguese Crown's disapproval of marital unions in favor of a system of slave-based domestic and sexual labor must be understood as an explicit attempt to manage interracial sexual relations in a manner intended to advance the Portuguese Crown's agenda in Elmina.

When the Dutch wrested control of Elmina from the Portuguese in 1637, it signaled the end of Portuguese dominance on the coast and ushered in an era of intense competition among Europeans for control over the coast's lucrative trading settlements. Officers of the Dutch West India Company (WIC) participated in relationships ranging from marriages recognized by Dutch and Akan law to cohabitation that may have lacked formal recognition but often lasted for the duration of a man's stay on the coast.²⁶ Given that the majority of the company's officers lacked the financial resources needed to marry, concubinage was the most affordable and hence commonly practiced alternative, which helped to ameliorate officers' poor living conditions and paltry food supplies.²⁷ Suggestive of the extent to which local practices were adopted, some Dutch men, presumably those of greater means, "may have practiced polygyny, following Akan custom."²⁸ The WIC was favorably disposed to intermarriage and cohabitation with local women because these unions created stability among officers and produced male offspring who could be incorporated into the company's organizational structure. By the close of the eighteenth century, the Dutch employed between 100 and 150 multiracial men who assisted in a variety of administrative, commercial, and military tasks.²⁹ Responding to another group of Afro-Dutch children who lived wholly immersed in their mothers' societies, the Dutch administration established an Orphan Fund "to give assistance to poverty-stricken mulatto children."³⁰ But even children acknowledged by their Dutch fathers, trained in the castle's school, and employed by the company retained strong ties with their African families and often served as intermediaries.

Elmina remained a stronghold of the Dutch until 1844, but their sphere of influence from Accra eastward began to contract by 1780 due to increased competition from the British, which led them to attack a number of Dutch forts. This in turn enabled the Danes to expand their influence farther east beyond Fort Christiansborg in Osu (Accra), which had served as their headquarters since the late seventeenth century.[31] By the latter part of the eighteenth century, they had succeeded in building Fort Kongensten in Ada and Fort Prinzensten in Keta, giving them a dominant position in the lucrative slave trade eastward from Accra.[32] An initial attempt at improving the morality of the Danish garrison by prohibiting sexual relations with local "heathen women," as Governor Frants Boye put in 1711, failed.[33] A different approach was soon taken when the Danish administration received a special dispensation from Copenhagen's prominent reformist Bishop Christen Worm encouraging formal unions with local women in order to stave off homesickness among Danish officers and to cater to their domestic needs, while also reducing the level of sexual promiscuity among them.[34] The African wives of Danish officers were entitled to a monthly allowance and a biannual provision of cloth.[35] These incentives helped to gradually break down the prohibition against sexual intercourse with uncircumcised men among Ga women in Accra, who made up the primary pool of partners for the Danes stationed in and around Fort Christiansborg. Prior to the easing of this prohibition, unions between Ga women and Danish men were less common—a powerful reminder that indigenous sociocultural norms determined the course of these relationships, even as European practices and policies transformed them.[36]

Administrative approval of these unions also depended on a prospective husband's willingness to pay a portion of his salary to the "Mulatto treasury," established to care for Afro-Danish children who were "not otherwise supported."[37] By ensuring these children were educated and materially and spiritually cared for, the Danes hoped to maintain them in a way that distinguished them from other Africans.[38] To achieve this and to promote the spiritual welfare of the fort's officers, the Danish government invited Basel missionaries to minister and teach in Christiansborg, which led to the mission's establishment in the Gold Coast in 1828.[39] On a more practical level, the Danes, like the Dutch, sought the reciprocal benefits of training their offspring, as indicated by their employment of multiracial boys, starting at a very young age, as fort soldiers.[40] As was the case with the Dutch, this policy helped to meet the ongoing demand for skilled manpower in the face of high mortality rates among Europeans. Multiracial girls were also groomed for marriage to Danish officers.[41] While the administration appears to have closely monitored the upkeep of Afro-Danish children and the local women that Danish employees were involved with, the permanency of such unions was evidently not regulated, leading one contemporary observer to hyperbolically note, "The new husband can send his wife packing the next day if he feels like it."[42] When these relationships endured, however, the women who participated in them were often able to claim "particularly powerful position[s] in the racialized social hierarchy of the Atlantic slave trade," which, as Pernille Ipsen points out, they used to protect themselves and their families from enslavement, while selling others into slavery.[43] But, as the slave trade peaked at the end of the eighteenth century, the balance of power steadily shifted in favor of Europeans in ways that had important ramifications for interracial marriage practices. Ga-Danish marriages looked less like Ga marriages and more like Danish marriages precisely because "marrying and living with a Danish man was a way to signal belonging to the right side of the slave trade."[44] Thus we must acknowledge that although these intermarriage practices were initially rooted in indigenous sociocultural frameworks for integrating strangers, the longer Europeans remained on the coast and the more power they wielded, the less like strangers and the more like landlords they became. This arc especially characterized the British experience on the coast.

Like the Portuguese, Dutch, and Danes, relationships between British men and local women were an integral feature of African-British socioeconomic and political networks, which helped stabilize the British presence on the coast. Between the late seventeenth century and the mid- to late nineteenth century British traders and administrators who did not form unions with local women were, in fact, the exception.[45] While these relationships were occasionally fleeting, most were stable and many persisted for the duration of a man's stay on the coast. This was certainly true for the subject of Margaret Priestley's research, Richard Brew, an Irish slave trader and progenitor of the Brew family. Brew married Effua Ansah, the daughter of John Currantee, the principal *caboceer* (headman) of Anomabu, an important trading enclave during the mid-eighteenth century. Through his marriage to Ansah, Brew gained and cemented a direct line of access to local power holders.[46] While Richard Brew is perhaps the best-studied example, he was by no means alone in using "kinship connections" gained through marriage to Fante women to bolster his commercial enterprises.[47] These alliances were clearly no small advantage in the fiercely competitive slave trade.

Although a small number of church weddings did occur, British men typically married according to local custom. Several late eighteenth-century wills left by British men made provisions for multiple wives, indicating that some of these unions were polygamous.[48] These wills, which often reference the good service provided by the deceased man's "wench," not only suggest that some British men sought the advantages to be gained through multiple alliances with African women, but also indicate the degree to which they adopted local practices like polygamy. Concubinage was also prevalent, suggesting that British men took advantage of the full range of domestic and sexual arrangements available to them, selecting the one that best suited their personal, social, and commercial needs. The extent to which these relationships permeated the upper reaches of the British administration during the first half of the nineteenth century is indicated by the fact that during periods of company rule (1800–1822; 1828–1843), only two out of the ten British governors at Cape Coast appear not to have been intimately involved with African women.[49] These relationships were common knowledge, and the women involved in them were often regarded as wielding considerable influence over their partners, who, as governors, were the highest-ranking British officials on the coast. But even at this early stage, there were signs of administrative unease over these relationships and the competing loyalties they were thought to produce. After the 1803 siege on Cape Coast Castle, Governor Jacob Mould (1798–1799; 1802–1805) was unfavorably reported on for having been more concerned about his African wife than the safety of the castle's British inhabitants.[50] Mould's successor, Governor George Torrane (1805–1807), was accused several years later of allotting the castle chamber normally reserved for the vice president of the Committee of Merchants to his female companion.

The complications created by these relationships extended beyond in-house castle politics. The Asante believed the increase in British hostility toward them after 1817 resulted from the influence of Governor John Hope Smith's (1817–1822) Fante wife, Fannie Smith.[51] The Fante had long been at odds with the Asante, and the suggestion here is that Fannie Smith's identity as a Fante led her to encourage her husband to pursue a more confrontational policy toward the Asante. As Mary McCarthy points out, "The frequency with which these unions were successfully negotiated by Fante families and the long period of time over which the practice continued" not only stemmed from "the potential commercial advantage accruing to a trading family with personal connections to a European," but also from the Fante's efforts "to solidify their [political] position . . . through marriage alliances."[52] Although the African women who (were) partnered with European men are generally described as cultural and commercial intermediaries, the example of Fannie Smith suggests that they could also act as political advocates.

The benefits to be gained through alliances with local women—ranging from health care, companionship, and domestic work to the supervision of business interests and the provisioning of commercial contacts and political alliances—were critical to the success of the commercial interests that characterized the British presence on the coast prior to the second half of the nineteenth century. In this regard it does seem noteworthy that the last governor openly rumored to have had such a liaison, Sir George Maclean (1830–1843), was also the last to govern on behalf of the Committee of Merchants.[53] In 1844 the British Crown permanently retook control of the nascent colony from the Committee of Merchants. Horatio Bridge's observation a year later that "all Europeans have native wives" suggests the obvious: Crown rule did not immediately do away with this common social practice. Nonetheless, the transfer of power to the Crown marked the beginning of the slow march toward formal colonization and the myriad social changes that accompanied it.

FROM COMPANY RULE TO COLONIAL RULE

As the foregoing suggests, historians have rightly emphasized the centrality of relationships between African women and European men to the growth of trade along the Gold Coast stretching as far back as the late fifteenth-century arrival of the Portuguese.[54] Comparatively little, however, has been written about what became of such relationships during the period of formal British colonial rule, except to note that they were increasingly frowned upon.[55] It is a curious omission given the investment historians have made in showing how well established and commonplace this particular social practice was in the four centuries leading up to the late nineteenth-century consolidation of British rule in the Gold Coast.

Although no single date marks the beginning of the formal colonial period, the transition from company to colonial rule occurred in fits and starts during the first half of the nineteenth century as the British aggressively moved to eliminate their European competitors from the coast, asserted their authority with Asante, and shifted their official representation from the Committee of Merchants to the Crown on a number of occasions. When the Crown finally dissolved the committee in 1843, this marked the end of company rule. Britain's aggrandized role beyond commerce was signified a year later by the Bond of 1844, which regularized and helped to expand the British administration's limited judicial powers. During the last quarter of the century, Britain's commitment to full-scale colonization was made evident not only by the purchase of the Dutch Gold Coast (Elmina) and the proclamation of the coastal zone and its hinterland as a Crown colony in 1874, but also by its determination to finally defeat and annex Asante, which was accomplished at the end of a costly series of Anglo-Asante wars (1824–1901).

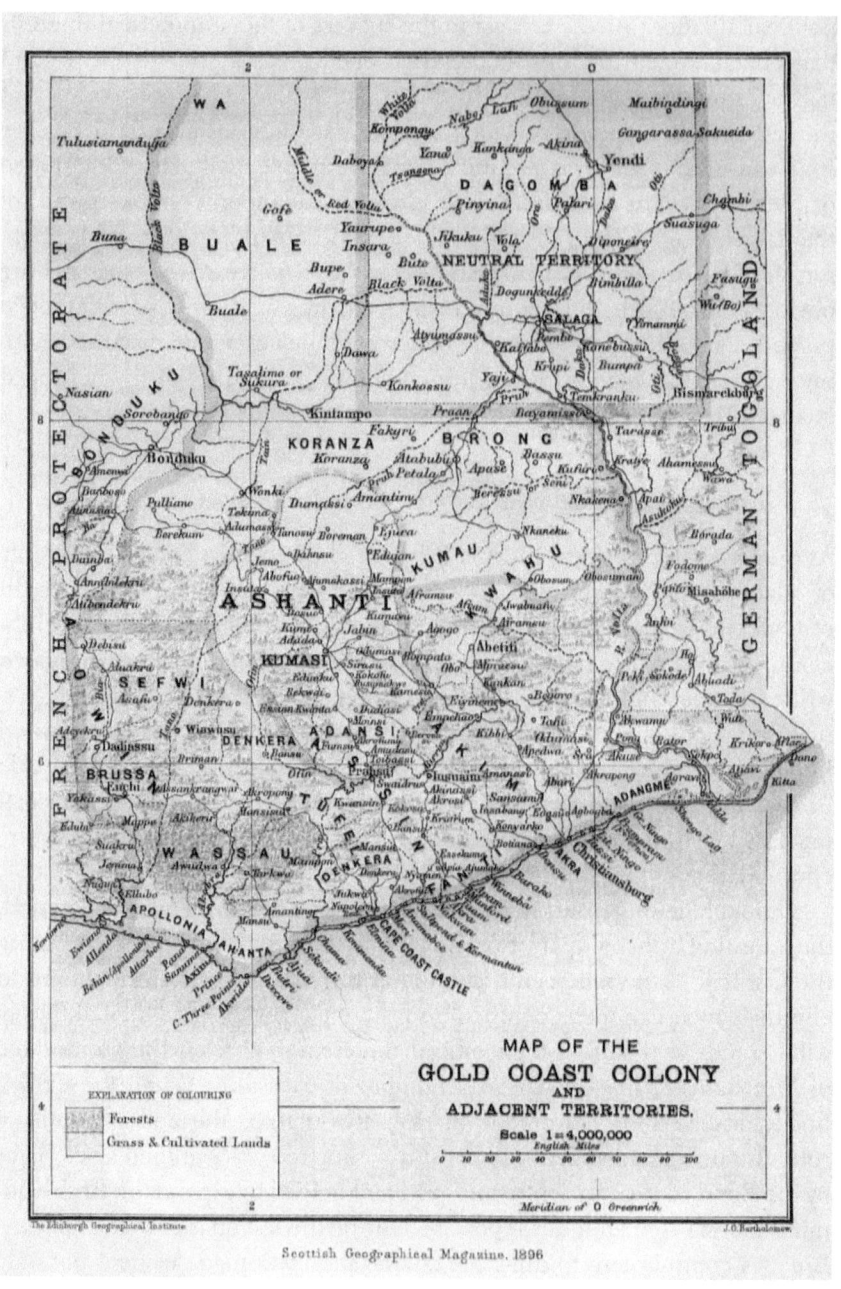

MAP 1.1. "Gold Coast Map, 1896," by John George Bartholomew. (*Scottish Geographical Magazine* 17, Royal Scottish Geographical Society, 1896.)

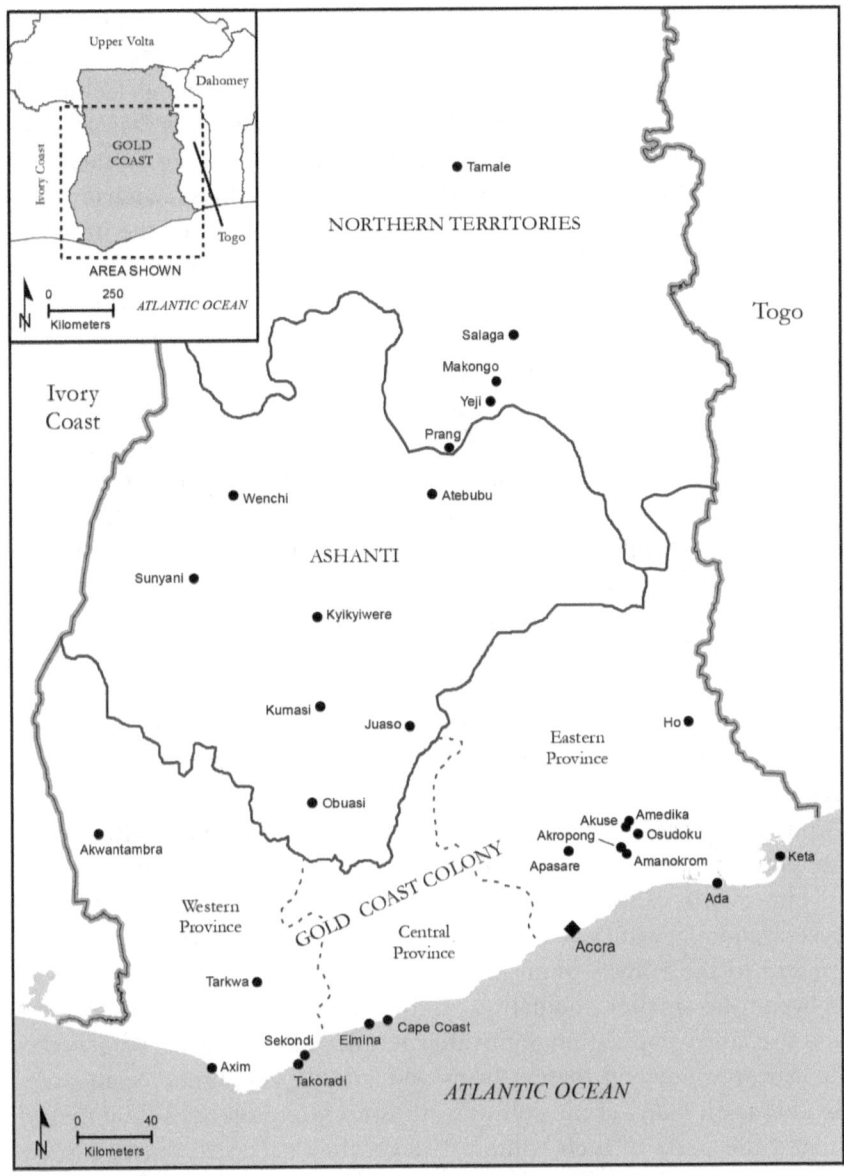

MAP 1.2. Map of the Gold Coast, indicating places of significance in the text. (Map by Brian Edward Balsley, GISP.)

As the twentieth century opened, the British had consolidated their control over the coastal zone, Asante, and the Northern Territories. Together they were colloquially known as the Gold Coast colony, although technically the Northern Territories were governed as a protectorate rather than a Crown colony. In the half century leading up to this, several key developments occurred that help to contextualize the increasingly racialized character of colonial rule. The rise of scientific racism not only legitimized the invention of racial hierarchies, it also condemned race mixture and pathologized its progeny. The idea that multiracial people were "the moral marker of contamination, failure, [and] regression" gained wide currency, especially in colonial circles.[56] Although administrators in the Gold Coast did not link their campaign to end interracial concubinage to its reproductive consequences, the pervasiveness of these kinds of pseudoscientific discourses found expression in the ways that multiracial Africans were excluded from top government posts they had once enjoyed special access to. In this regard, the brief acting governorship between 1850 and 1851 of James Bannerman, the son of a Scottish father and a Fante mother, is instructive. Bannerman would be the last of his kind to hold high office in the colony's government. The supplanting of multiracial Africans in government office by Europeans, however, could not have happened without contemporaneous advances in tropical medicine, particularly the discovery of quinine as a treatment for malaria, which greatly reduced European mortality rates and allowed greater numbers of European men to be employed in West Africa—hitherto known as the "white man's grave."[57] Developments in steamship technology also allowed for more frequent and efficient travel between metropole and colony.

The growth of the colony's civil service, infrastructure, and resource-based economy witnessed a dramatic rise in the number of European men present in the colony. With this came an increasingly clear distinction between the smaller population of government officers and employees, and the larger population of privately employed Europeans, who worked for European-owned trading firms and mining and timber companies, as well as on many of the colony's infrastructure projects. While they all shared the perks of their white privilege, they occupied different social and professional worlds in the colony even as those worlds often had significant overlap.

The increase in the European population is illustrated by the census returns of 1891, 1901, and 1911. The 1891 census recorded a total of 493 Europeans in the colony, 65 of whom were "Official" Europeans, while 428 were "Commercial" Europeans.[58] Of this number, 206 resided in the sixteen principal towns of the Gold Coast.[59] A decade later that figure had risen to 646, with an additional 53–70 "officials and others" who were "travelling in the Colony at the time of the Census," bringing the estimated total to around 700.⁶⁰ Of that number, only 283 were identified as "European members of the Civil Service." Development projects influenced the population growth of specific towns. For instance, the 1891 census did not record any "Whites" in Sekondi, but in 1901—three years after construction commenced on the railway connecting mining and timber production sites in the hinterland to the coastal town's natural harbor—the census showed a total of 67 "Europeans" living in Sekondi. The growth of the mining sector also influenced European settlement: in 1891 Tarkwa was not included as a "principal town" on the census, but in 1901 it not only appeared as one, it was also home to 176 Europeans (including 19 Americans), the single-largest concentration in the colony at that time. Accra, the administrative capital, had the second-largest European population, estimated at 138, for both district and town.⁶¹

The 1911 census recorded a total of 1,389 Europeans in the colony proper, 12 percent of whom were women. Of this number 1,184, were British, including 48 women.⁶² Tarkwa continued to be home to the largest concentration of Europeans, numbering 557 men and 3 women. Accra came in second with a population of 242 Europeans, including 32 women.⁶³ Of the 1,389 Europeans in the colony, 258 of them, all British, were employed in administrative services, while approximately 200 more were to be found in non-administrative government posts, including just over 100 men who were employed in the railway sector.⁶⁴ The majority of Europeans in the colony were still privately employed: 332 worked in the mining sector, while 253 were employed in the commercial sector. Mission work ranked third, with a total of 90 European missionaries, including 11 women, in the colony.⁶⁵ This had implications for the demographic makeup of mining towns like Tarkwa which were home to a much greater percentage of privately employed Europeans. Separate figures were given for Asante, which had a total European population of 223, of which 193 were British, but these numbers were not broken down further by occupation or gender.⁶⁶

Thus, during the early twentieth century, the European presence in the colony was primarily British and predominantly made up of men who were privately employed rather than members of the colonial service. For the purpose of this study, one of the most significant aspects of this division was that only the smaller number of government employed Europeans—almost all men—fell under the purview of the colonial government's

FIGURE 1.1. Married in 1851, Catherine Zimmerman (née Mulgrave) and Johannes Zimmermann, who are pictured here with their five children and Zimmerman's cousin, were members of the Basel Mission. By the end of the nineteenth century, publicly recognized church-sanctioned intermarriages of this kind were almost unheard of. ("The Zimmerman-Mulgrave Family," unknown studio, 1872–1873, Ref. No. QS-30.002.0237.02, Basel Mission Archives/Basel Mission Holdings.)

regulations concerning sexual relations with local women.[67] The level of sexual regulation varied among the majority of privately employed Europeans. Missionary societies, not surprisingly, expected their members, both black and white, to adhere to strict moral codes of conduct. Basel missionaries were discouraged from marrying African women, but in a few cases exceptions were made. During the mid- to late nineteenth century it appears that "the trading section of the Basel Mission applied standards which were less rigid than the mission proper" in allowing some missionary traders to marry well-connected local women whose familial connections, it was hoped, would bolster the mission's trading prospects.[68] Multigenerational marriage patterns in the Zimmerman-Mulgrave and Rottmann-Hesse families, pictured in figures 1 and 2, exemplify this trend, but such marriages were unheard of even among Basel missionary traders by the early twentieth century.

FIGURE 1.2. Basel Mission members Hermann Ludwig Rottmann and Regina Hesse wed in 1857. The Basel Mission approved their marriage because it hoped that Regina's local family connections would enhance the mission's trading efforts. ("Rottmann, Hermann Ludwig and Rottmann-Hesse, Regina," Ehlers Gebrüder, Altona, Germany, 1857/1898, Ref. No. QS-30.003.0276.02. Basel Mission Archives/Basel Mission Holdings.)

Of the various European commercial firms that were active during the twentieth century in the Gold Coast, the Union Trading Company (UTC), which had its origins in the Basel Mission, strictly enforced its prohibition against "indecent or illicit intercourse with members of the opposite sex." Instead of preventing these liaisons, this injunction forced UTC employees to act with absolute caution so as not to be detected.[69] Other trading firms, like the Swiss African Trading Company Limited (SAT), had similar prohibitions, although they were less rigorously enforced.[70] Mining managers were said to have discouraged relations with "native women" but the prevalence of venereal diseases among European miners and the extent to which their sexual promiscuity was commented upon suggests that managerial disapproval did little to improve standards.[71] In short, while there was a tightening of interracial sexual regulation across the colony's variously employed European populations, especially in the government sector, it remained uneven.

SEXUAL MORALITY, RACE, AND COLONIAL GOVERNANCE

Although administrative concerns about the sexual morality of European government officers came to focus in a particularly dramatic way on interracial concubinage, it was by no means the first or only form of moral misconduct to garner official attention in the Gold Coast. Drunkenness and chronic indebtedness frequently led to disciplinary action against officers because both were viewed as moral failings that brought the administration into disrepute. Where sexual conduct was concerned, disapprobation of interracial concubinage between European government officers and African women proceeded rather than preceded other forms of censurable sexuality. While the question of race loomed large in all of these cases, they were also informed by Victorian sexual mores, the state's aggrandized role in regulating morality, and the particular way in which these factors converged in the context of colonial rule, the legitimacy of which was closely tied to moral respectability as a marker of fitness to rule.

A particularly illustrative case involved Elizabeth Brew, who hailed from the prominent Afro-European Brew trading family. Her father, Samuel Collins Brew, was a merchant; her mother, Amba Opanwa, was a member of the stool family of Abura Dunkwa.[72] Educated during the 1850s in Britain alongside her better-known brother James Hutton Brew (Prince Brew of Dunquah), Elizabeth returned to the Gold Coast and eventually found employment as a teacher in Accra's government school.[73] She was dismissed from her teaching post in 1884 "when it was officially discovered that she had been co-habiting with a European trader ... since 1864."[74] Given the autonomy that European traders now had, the government did not have the authority to censure Brew's partner, Lyall. Although it is impossible to say whether he would have been similarly punished if the tables were turned, the lack of any cases in which European officers were reprimanded for cohabiting with local women during the late 1800s suggests not – it was simply not yet an offense.

Brew's dismissal might well have been a harbinger of the change in official attitudes that would come in later decades, but in 1884 it was arguably less a pronouncement against interracial concubinage and more a censure of her participation in a domestic arrangement that called into question her moral credibility.[75] Victorian-era sexual mores placed a premium on female chastity and regarded premarital sex as deeply immoral, thus as a woman Elizabeth was judged more harshly for the lack of moral discretion she showed by cohabiting with Lyall outside of marriage. Brew's dismissal from the service, moreover, constituted a particularly severe punishment and is suggestive of the gravity with which her misconduct was regarded given that she was expected to serve as a role model for her female pupils. Finally, the colonial government's intervention into Brew's personal affairs must also be understood as a product of what historian Lesley Hall describes as the Victorian era's "growing secularization of the regulation of moral conduct," which had previously been the "purlieu of the church and ecclesiastical courts."[76] Thus, far more was at play here than the interracial character of their relationship.

For British administrators looking to defend their increasing exclusion of educated Africans from government posts, Brew's relationship with Lyall would have also been convenient fodder for justifying why Africans were ill suited to leadership positions. So too was another case involving Charles Barnes, a high-ranking Native officer, who was accused in 1897 of contracting a "native marriage" with the daughter of another Native officer, Mr. Hyde, while already married under the Marriage Ordinance of 1884 to someone else, thereby contravening its clause against polygamy.[77] Summing up the whole affair as an "illustration of the low standards of native morality" on the coast, governor Sir William Maxwell proposed that Barnes be prosecuted under the Criminal Code if found guilty and contemplated dismissing Mr. Hyde from the government service for allowing his daughter to live with Barnes.[78] The Brew and Barnes cases give a good indication of not only the increasing reach of the colonial state's arm into the private affairs of its officers' lives, but also the way in which sexual morality had already emerged as a particularly powerful racialized marker of a credible governing profile in the decades preceding Governor Rodger's 1907 "undesirable relations" circular.

The case of Accra's European postmaster, H. Selfe Leonard, who was dismissed from government service in 1904 after an internal investigation found him guilty of gross indecency and indecent assault against two "Krooboys" who worked as domestic servants, illustrates the point that the administration was frequently more concerned with containment rather than prosecution.[79] Fearful of the scandal that would erupt if the charges were made public, the local government forwent a criminal prosecution against Leonard in favor of dismissing him from the service and sending him back to England. But, the case was only brought to official attention when Leonard's European bungalow mate, Mr. Guppy, realized that he was not sleeping with African women, but rather with "boys." Guppy even acknowledged having seen a "native figure" in Leonard's bed, but did not report it because he assumed it was a woman.[80] This serves as one indication of the acceptability of heterosexual interracial sexual relationships during the early 1900s. By virtue of being the exception that proves the rule, the singular presence of this case in the colony's archival record stands as a reminder of all the other sexual encounters across the color line, both heterosexual and homosexual, that did not make their way into the archive or were intentionally kept out of it.

Sexual misconduct was also defined by acts that adversely affected the financial interests of the colonial state and endangered its labor supply. The government maintained a policy of financially penalizing officers who contracted venereal diseases through their own misconduct by withholding sick pay. This policy was established by Governor William Maxwell in 1896 for Native officers and then extended to Europeans on an ad hoc basis until 1910, when it became official policy for both Native and European officers.[81] Like the policy on venereal diseases, officers who became ill through their own insobriety were also financially penalized.[82] Thus, while the 1907 circular marked a watershed moment in official British policy toward sexual relations between European officers and African women, the foregoing cases demonstrate that it was an extension of a preexisting decades-old tendency, on the part of the administration, to punish acts it perceived as sexually immoral, indiscreet, and unprofessional.

This proclivity was directly linked to the new era of formal colonial rule, characterized as it was by an almost obsessive concern with the racial respectability of European officers and the repute of the colonial service, as well as the need for increased social and spatial distance between Africans and Europeans. Racial respectability was not defined solely in terms of sexual morality; work ethics, fiscal discipline, sobriety, and general good health were all measures by which the administration evaluated its officers' integrity. Sexual misconduct was, however, particularly threatening because the fundamental categories of colonial rule—"colonized" and "colonizer"—were so persistently constructed and legitimized through the idea of sexual difference; hence the need for the kind of sexual vigilance enshrined in Governor Rodger's circular.[83] Constructions of sexual difference were, of course, primary modes through which racial difference and hierarchy were also produced and legitimized. By engaging in interracial concubinage, European officers undermined all of this by participating in a social institution that was deemed the backward preserve of Africans. In the process they shortened the social and spatial distance between Africans and Europeans that the colonial government sought to enforce in multiple facets of colonial life through the creation of European residential areas, segregated hospitals and social clubs, and race-based appointments and salary scales.

When set against the Gold Coast government's investments in creating racial boundaries, it appears particularly striking that in seeking to end interracial concubinage it was *not* motivated by its reproductive consequences, nor was it guided by the eugenic discourses then becoming influential in Britain and elsewhere in its empire and the wider colonial world. After all, as numerous scholars have pointed out, across disparate colonial settings multiracial people came to embody, in the most literal sense, the "dangers of *métissage*" in ways that set off protracted debates and policy struggles to define the "criteria by which Europeanness could be identified, citizenship accorded, and nationality assigned."[84] Different colonial regimes arrived at different answers to the "métis question," but one common response was to take an increasingly hard line against concubinage in the hopes that this would, at the very least, reduce the size of the "problem" population.

While there is certainly evidence of deliberation over how multiracial Gold Coasters were to be racially classified, these debates were hardly contentious or protracted. Nor did they ever inform policy discussions about interracial concubinage. Instead, they occurred briefly during the last two decades of the nineteenth century in relation only to the census and the construction of the Native Jurisdiction Ordinance, which governed the application and exercise of customary law in the context of the colony's dual legal system. Per the 1883 Native Jurisdiction Ordinance, the term "native" was defined to include "mulattos, and all persons resident in the country other than those commonly known as Europeans."[85] In subsequent draft ordinances in 1894, 1895, and 1896, British administrators proposed to exclude "mulattos" from this category. But when the ordinance was finally amended in 1910, there was no mention of "mulattos" at all. Rather, the term "native" was redefined as "any person who is under native customary law or under any Ordinance a member of a native community of the Colony, Ashanti, or the Northern Territories," a definition that could still incorporate multiracial people depending on the context.[86]

The consolidation of colonial thinking about the appropriateness of categorizing multiracial people as "natives" was also evident in the evolution of census categories. The 1891 Gold Coast census, the first of its kind in the colony, was also the only census in which "Mulattos" appeared as a separately enumerated category. For the sixteen principal towns along the coast, the total size of the "Mulatto" population was counted at 1,200 in comparison to 69,436 "Blacks" and 206 "Whites."[87] As of 1901, census takers found that "it was not . . . practicable to ascertain the numbers of the various tribes, nor to sub-divide the population into Mulattos, Quadroons, etc."[88] Instead, they were counted as part of the African population, with

Europeans continuing to be counted separately, although over the course of the following decades the terminology shifted from "White Races" to "Non-African Races," presumably to account for the growing presence of Syrians in the colony.[89] Thus, by the opening decade of the twentieth century, colonial administrators agreed that the "mulatto" population was part and parcel of the African population.

This resonated with how multiracial Gold Coasters generally positioned themselves during the period of formal British rule. While they had always tended to be closely allied with their African families, in previous centuries many of them had also enjoyed a special relationship with the various European powers, including the very early British colonial state, on the coast. But, as racism emerged as the primary organizing principle of British colonialism across the latter half of the nineteenth century, they responded by joining other educated Africans in pursuit of racial equality. Unlike the case of British Central Africa, which Christopher Lee has skillfully explored, there was no mobilization on the part of multiracial Gold Coasters to gain exemptions or special dispensations from the colonial government on the basis of a separate racial status.[90] For instance, rather than provoking a split along racial lines, the Native Jurisdiction Ordinance, as David Kimble has pointed out, "prompted the first serious discussion among the educated community of the nature of the Chiefs' jurisdiction."[91] Instead of asking the government to be exempted from the realm of customary law and tradition, educated elites, of whom many were multiracial, frequently positioned themselves as custodians of it. Some of their number, moreover, wielded significant power within indigenous power structures, as Augustus Casely-Hayford's genealogical history of Cape Coast stool families suggests.[92] Battles on the part of Native officers for access to higher posts in the colonial service and pay equity with their European counterparts also illustrate this point neatly. Multiracial individuals were employed by the colonial administration as Native officers, and accordingly were saddled by the same institutionalized discrimination, but instead of seeking amelioration through reclassification as European officers or the creation of a third category, they petitioned as Africans, alongside other Africans, for greater parity with Europeans.[93]

Multiracial Gold Coasters were categorized as Africans regardless of their cultural orientation, but the way in which British nationality law was configured largely obviated the kinds of tensions that emerged over the citizenship status of multiracial people in other colonial contexts where cultural competency and race were key determinants of citizenship.[94] The 1914 British Nationality and Status of Aliens Act codified for the first time existing common law and statute stipulating that British subject status "was acquired by birth within the Crown's 'dominions and allegiance.'"[95] This meant "all people in the United Kingdom, throughout the Colonies, and throughout the countries of the Commonwealth were British subjects with only one form of nationality—they were all British subjects."[96] Thus, prior to the 1948 British Nationality Act, there were British subjects, but not citizens. The 1948 act introduced the concept of the citizen, also called "Commonwealth citizen," by creating a new legal status, Citizen of the United Kingdom and the Colonies (CUKC), which remained synonymous with the term "British subject." It also recognized separate national citizenships for Commonwealth countries, through which their citizens maintained their common status as British subjects.[97]

In the case of the Gold Coast, this meant that until independence in 1957 inhabitants of the Gold Coast colony—home to the vast majority of multiracial people—and Asante were deemed British subjects, and after 1948, CUKCs, thereby sharing the same nationality status and entitlements to domicile in Britain as British-born British subjects. By no means egalitarian in practice, this configuration was undermined by other pieces of legislation, most notably the Special Restriction (Coloured Alien Seamen) Order of 1925, which put the onus on Gold Coasters in Britain—who were presumed to be aliens because they were black—to prove their status as British subjects lest they risk deportation, among myriad other forms of discrimination.[98] In the colony, sharing the same nationality status with their European counterparts did not free Africans, including those of multiracial background, from the restrictions and inequalities that were part and parcel of colonial racism, as epitomized by and embedded in the category "native" and the application of indirect rule.[99] Yet, as indicated earlier, multiracial people opted to fight against these inequities as Africans, even as they, like other educated elites, saw themselves as different from—and often superior to—their nonliterate counterparts and the rural masses. Moreover, this configuration did not include "protected persons" from the Northern Territories who were deprived of many of the privileges that came with British subject status. Nonetheless, the broadly inclusive framing of British nationality law meant that battles over citizenship would generally come much later, in the decades after empire's end, when Britain began introducing new legislation to stop the flow of nonwhite immigration from the former colonies, a subject I return to in the book's conclusion.[100]

The small size of the Gold Coast's multiracial population, combined with its integration into African society, further helps to account for why it never materialized as a "problem" for the colonial state. The only hard figure available for the time period under consideration comes from the 1891 census, which, as previously indicated, listed a total population of 1,200 "Mulattos" in the sixteen principal coastal towns. A decade later census takers found it more sensible to count them as part of the African population, a move that reflected the reality of their lives. By the turn of the century, most multiracial Gold Coasters traced their lineage back to a European male ancestor, but were not the immediate offspring of a European father.[101] While marriage patterns reveal that people of multiracial ancestry frequently married one another, they also married other Africans, especially elites.[102] The comparatively small number of first-generation multiracial people that were born during the formal colonial period continued, with few exceptions, to be absorbed into their African mothers' families, as had been the case even when, in earlier centuries, some European fathers played more prominent roles in the lives of their African-born offspring.[103] This meant that they never "constituted a distinct social class," even in places where they had a sizable presence, as J. T. Lever has noted with regard to Elmina.[104] While the matrilineal social organization of Akan groups, such as the Fante, has been posited as an explanation for this, patrilineal organizations, like the *asafo* companies in Elmina and Cape Coast, as well as patrilineal ethnic groups, such as the Ga in Accra, also incorporated multiracial people into their social structures in ways that suggest a willingness to integrate rather than exclude them. But, as John Parker points out, multiracial Gas periodically had their "ethnic credentials" challenged by political rivals, suggesting that their integration into Ga society could be contested, at least when it was politically expedient.[105] Nonetheless, the overall trend was one of absorption into indigenous matrilineages and the wider African society.

Multiracial people regarded themselves and "were regarded by their contemporaries . . . as being Africans," even as many of their number had European-style educations and bore other signs of Westernization in their religious, social, material, and civic lives—as did other educated African elites.[106] The elevated class status of the majority of this population also meant that it did not raise the same kinds of welfare concerns and affronts to European prestige that so vexed colonial regimes elsewhere. Nor did they cohere into a distinct class of alienated dissidents, a prospect that piqued anxieties in other colonial settings, even when there was little evidence to support the idea that multiracial children were abandoned or destined to become enemies of the state.[107] While British administrators in the colony had once disparaged so-called "mulattoes" as "discontented and unprincipled," largely because they were assumed to be the driving force behind the demand for self-government during the latter decades of the nineteenth century, such concerns were fleeting and never materialized into a set of policies aimed at blunting their supposed discontent or currying their allegiance.[108]

Periodic attempts were made by the British to provide education and religious instruction to not only the multiracial offspring of European men, but also to the children of local chiefs at Cape Coast Castle during the late eighteenth and early nineteenth centuries. Thus the Western educated elite was always diverse in its racial makeup, helping to connect rather than divide Africans and their multiracial counterparts, even if the latter were overrepresented in comparison to their actual numbers. These kinds of targeted educational efforts were abandoned later in the nineteenth century as the missionary presence greatly expanded and more mission schools, followed by government-run schools, were opened throughout the colony with the aim of educating a much wider cross section of "native" children. While the spread of Western education in the Gold Coast was intended to create a class of literate Africans who could be employed by the colonial government and private firms, British efforts there hardly resemble those undertaken by the French in West Africa and Indochina, where métis children were removed from their "native" milieus and placed in state-run institutions with the intention of culturally encoding and educating them to become loyal auxiliaries. Nor do they resemble what occurred elsewhere in British Africa, in places like Nyasaland and the Rhodesias, where the so-called "coloured question," no doubt inflected by the racial politics of settler colonialism, was pronounced. Exemplifying the ways in which this group of precariously positioned people came to constitute a "problem" in the minds of British colonial administrators were the numerous commissions of inquiry into the status of "half-castes" and "Coloureds" that were established in these territories and the various and often contradictory policies devised to "fix" the problem.[109] Underscored here is not only the way that colonial anxieties and policies differed between European imperial powers, but also how dramatically they could differ within a single imperial sphere, in this case the British Empire in Africa.

As a result of this combination of factors the status of multiracial Gold Coasters never spurred the kinds of panic over "European prestige" that gave way to attacks on concubinage elsewhere in the colonial world. In the case of the Gold Coast the "problem" of concubinage was neither constituted through its progeny, nor embodied by it. Rather, where questions of cultural competency, racial respectability, and imperial loyalty were raised in relationship to concubinage, it was with regard to the European officers who engaged in it. While European degeneracy came to be linked to concubinage in most colonial settings, such fears were typically provoked by "poor whites." But in the Gold Coast, the lewd behavior of lower-class white immigrant workers seldom garnered the attention of colonial authorities. Perhaps this was because the government's own officers posed the more immediate threat, entrusted as they were with "safeguard[ing] the colonies against the physical weakness, moral decay, and inevitable degeneration that long residence in the colonies encouraged and against the temptations that interracial domestic situations had allowed."[110] These expectations were apparently still far from self-evident to the majority of European officers, whom Governor Rodger ruefully admitted "kept" local women. By enforcing these new standards Rodger's 1907 "undesirable relations" circular heralded a new colonial era of sexual behavior and racial insularity. In this way it was prescriptive rather than defensive.

CONCLUSION

The transition from trade-based company rule to formal colonial rule in the Gold Coast, as elsewhere in Africa, depended to a far greater degree than ever before on creating and maintaining racial boundaries in all spheres of colonial life. Ending the most physically intimate form of cross-racial sociability was an integral component of a wider effort to professionalize the colonial government's administration and to ensure that the behavior of its officers preserved a firm line between colonizer and colonized. Yet, in acknowledging the prevalence of interracial concubinage, Rodger's circular underscored the lag time between the newly articulated racial politics of formal colonial rule and everyday social relations across the color line, which still had much in common with precolonial conventions. The continued dependence that Europeans had on the range of services provided to them by African men and women and the varied intimacies that grew out of dependency and proximity were at odds with the stark line now drawn between Africans and Europeans.

While "ratios of men to women" typically "*followed* from how sexuality was managed . . . rather than the other way around," in the case of the Gold Coast the ban on concubinage was not accompanied by efforts to increase the number of European women in the colony.[111] Just a year before the release of his 1907 circular, Governor Rodger mandated that only "higher officials" stationed in the colony's main coastal towns, as well as in Kumasi and Obuasi, would be allowed to bring their wives to the colony if their jobs did not require frequent travel.[112] The demographic consequence of this was made evident in the 1911 Gold Coast census, which recorded that 47 percent of British men in the colony were married, but only 7 percent of them were accompanied by their wives.¹¹³ A decade later this number had only risen to 17 percent. Given these numbers, the ban on concubinage necessitated a more lenient attitude on the part of administrators toward prostitution and other forms of occasional indiscretion. In practice, however, European officers also continued to engage in concubinage.

Some Gold Coasters continued to see concubinage with European officers as an acceptable arrangement or at least advantageous enough to pursue, but others were slowly beginning to voice their disapproval of the increasingly informal and illicit nature of these liaisons. As early as 1889, the famous Gold Coast pastor and historian Carl Christian Reindorf, who was of Ga and Danish ancestry, condemned the profiteering he associated with customary marriages between "mulatto ladies" and white men, whom he chastised as "mockers" for spoiling their paramours' chances of being respectably married to "their own country men."¹¹⁴ Even Reindorf's contemporary, Oxford-trained Fante barrister Joseph Renner Maxwell, objected to what he called the "illegitimate miscegenation originating from Europeans" in West Africa, despite ardently advocating "race mixing" on the grounds that it would improve the physical characteristics of the "negro race."¹¹⁵ In the pages of the newly established *Gold Coast Leader*, occasional rumblings over interracial sex were also to be found. In 1902, its inaugural year in print, an anonymous writer for the *Leader* bemoaned the "large influx of male whites of loose and indiscriminate morals into the Colony" as "an evil, and danger, almost insurmountable danger that menaces the people of this country."¹¹⁶ He went on to second previously published remarks condemning parents who "sold the priceless pearl of your daughter's chastity to a European or other alien, of whom you know nothing."¹¹⁷ Several years later, a writer from Nigeria left no doubt about his feelings when he quipped, "Black women marrying White men! . . . If it pays you, praise the devil by all means; and . . . if it pays you, damn the gods and do so quickly."¹¹⁸ These disquieted commentaries about interracial sex suggest that Governor Rodger was neither first nor alone in being troubled by "undesirable relations," even though what made them "undesirable" was hardly something that Africans and Europeans agreed upon.

2 ∽ "Undesirable Relations"
"Native Women," European Government Officers, and Administrative Racial Classification

ON 6 NOVEMBER 1906, Quasie Yarn, a self-identified "native doctor," took Marcus Clarke, a European supervisor of customs, to court for backing out of a customary marriage he had entered into several months earlier with Yarn's young daughter, Abba Saraku, in the coastal town of Sekondi. Yarn sued for £13.10/- in damages, an amount that included an unpaid balance of £8.10/- of the original £10 "dowry" and £5 in compensation for his failure to follow through with the marriage after having consummated it. The case was tried in Sekondi's divisional court before District Commissioner W. P. Michelin, who ruled that Clarke had entered into a valid marriage "according to native law" with Abba Saraku. Although not the full amount sued for, Michelin awarded Yarn the upaid portion of the dowry.[1]

Flabbergasted by the ruling, Clarke's efforts to put the whole affair behind him were derailed when details of the lawsuit appeared in a damning memorandum issued the following year by his boss, Inspector A. Smith of the Gold Coast's maritime customs department. The memorandum outlined several charges of "gross official misconduct" against Clarke, the first of which was his "native marriage" to Abba Saraku and the unseemly spectacle that had been created by the ensuing lawsuit.[2] Apart from the settlement Clarke was ordered to pay, Inspector Smith noted that no further action was taken against him because "the scandal had more or less died away." Smith's attention, however, was subsequently drawn to another "ugly fact" regarding Clarke: in early 1907 he had entered into negotiations with one of his Native subordinates, Elias Therson, to contract a marriage with his stepdaughter, Sarah Helden. Although these negotiations did not result in marriage, Smith nonetheless claimed that Helden was so young that had Clarke succeeded, "he would run a grave risk of committing a criminal offence." Smith also made a similar allegation about the age of Abba Saraku. As quickly as he raised the specter of child molestation, Smith brushed it off as a "side issue," instead identifying the "main point" as Clarke's having "grossly misused his position as Supervisor, to attempt to tamper with the step-daughter of a native officer." Smith concluded his memorandum by deeming Clarke's "offence so prejudicial to discipline, and so calculated to bring the Service into disrepute," that were he to let it pass unnoticed, he himself would deserve the severest censure.[3]

The memorandum quickly made its way from the comptroller's office to the desk of the Gold Coast's governor, Sir John Rodger, who surely must have appreciated Smith's diligence in heeding his recent call for vigilance over matters like these. In his circular issued just four months earlier, in March 1907, Rodger condemned "undesirable relations maintained by European Government Officers with Native women" as "demoralizing," and worse yet, in his view, capable of "seriously detract[ing] from the value of an officer's services, not merely by creating jealousy and ill-feeling among the Natives, but also by destroying their confidence in his integrity and impartiality."[4] He instructed the colony's commissioners and heads of departments "to take every means in their power to put an end to this abuse; and, if their Subordinates disregard the warning, to report the matter officially."[5] If an offending officer failed to exculpate himself, Rodger made it clear that he would report the case to the secretary of state for the colonies.[6] All European officers employed in the colony were to be confidentially made aware of the circular's contents. While the circular was consistent with the British colonial administration's tendency since the late nineteenth century to censure acts it perceived as sexually immoral, provided they had or could tarnish the administration's reputation, its specific condemnation of sexual relations between African women and European officers was unprecedented. In forbidding these relationships the circular, by definition, made them disreputable.

Rodger's circular attempted to bring the sexual politics of the colony's European officers in line with the administration's racial politics, but the gap between official prescription and everyday practice was wide. The disciplinary provisions of the circular, however, created a mechanism for trying to narrow the gap. Marcus Clarke was the first officer investigated for violating

Rodger's circular, and the only officer curiously punished for events that had occurred prior to its release. The accusations against Clarke rehearsed the concerns mapped out in the circular: Clarke had arranged these relationships using his official position as leverage at the expense of the colonial government's reputation and by extension its administrative efficiency.

What at first glance appears to be a model case of "undesirable relations" is far more complicated in ways that dramatically illustrate how the messy racial politics of colonialism often found expression in charges of sexual misconduct. Marcus Clarke, European supervisor of customs, was in fact a West Indian of partial African descent. At the root of the case brought against him was a conflict that had developed around West Indian officers of African descent employed in the colonial service. These officers were categorized by the Gold Coast's system of administrative racial classification as European. This unwittingly subversive system sparked a campaign of racism against West Indians of African descent by white European officials who resented having to work on equal terms with them. These officials attempted to legitimize their campaign by claiming they were acting on behalf of Native officers, who, they alleged, were aggrieved that West Indians had access to positions and benefits that they as Africans were denied.

Racism against West Indians arguably motivated the charges made against Clarke, but it was Rodger's circular that gave them traction. The contradiction inherent in drawing stark lines between "colonized" and "colonizer" with instruments like Rodger's "undesirable relations" circular, while simultaneously blurring those lines by employing West Indians of African descent as proxy-colonizers, reveals the kinds of inconsistencies that were part and parcel of colonial rule at a systemic level. While the Clarke case offers compelling reason to believe that anti–West Indian racism found expression in sexual misconduct charges, it also foreshadows how local and imperial efforts to ban interracial concubinage transformed allegations of concubinage into a powerful tool of coercion and sabotage. In Clarke's case the charges against him were narrowly intended to ruin his career, but in a wider sense they might also be read as a means to an end: European officials used them to reorder an administrative racial hierarchy that had been undermined by the categorization of West Indians of African descent as Europeans. To understand the complexities of this case, we must first unpack the contentious history surrounding the employment of West Indians in British West Africa's colonial service.

WEST INDIANS AND ADMINISTRATIVE RACIAL CLASSIFICATION

Marcus Clarke was a West Indian of African and European descent who was categorized as European by the British colonial government's system of official administrative classification.[7] This system placed officers into one of two categories: European or Native. Job postings and attendant salary and benefits were determined by this classification. By virtue of the colony's 1883 Native Jurisdiction Ordinance, "mulattos, and all persons resident in the country other than those commonly known as Europeans" were broadly defined as "natives."[8] The unclear position of West Indians in this rather ambiguous definition was well recognized by the administration: three subsequent draft ordinances, submitted between 1894 and 1896, proposed to clarify that "West Indians of African descent" as well as "mulattos" were not "natives."[9] Although these proposals were never adopted, West Indian officers continued to be administratively classified as Europeans, while African-born "mulatto" officers continued to be administratively classified as Natives.

The incorporation of nonwhite West Indians as European officers into Britain's West African colonial governments offers ample evidence of how "colonial projects were fundamentally predicated on a tension between notions of incorporation and differentiation that were weighted differently at different times."[10] Tensions surrounding West Indian officers played themselves out first in the British colony of Sierra Leone during the mid-nineteenth century and then again in the Gold Coast at the turn of the century. The original impetus for hiring West Indians was to counteract the shortage of European officers employed in Sierra Leone in the wake of an 1839 fever epidemic that killed several officials, further reducing the willingness of Europeans to apply for positions there amidst heightened concerns about their mortality.[11] As of 1840, when the colony's government began hiring West Indians, the majority of recruits were from multiracial backgrounds with a minority who were of "purely African origin."[12] The Colonial Office hoped this recruitment effort would supply the colony with officers who were more resistant than Europeans to tropical illnesses, while also tempering political agitation among West Indians who were stymied at home by the color bar in government service.[13] While administrators viewed West Indians as sharing a common biological heritage with Africans, they saw them as culturally distinct in ways that would ideally influence Africans to embrace Western education and Christian values. Many West Indians concurred; having envisioned themselves as "sons of Africa," they were now returning to do their part in the "civilizing mission."[14]

Given the prominence of these racial considerations in the recruitment of West Indians, many of whom served in the highest reaches of the government during the 1840s and 1850s, it is paradoxical that they were classified by the administration as Europeans.[15] By the end of the 1850s, however, the elevated position of West Indians in the Sierra Leone administration began to provoke discontent among both Europeans and the colony's black settlers and their Creole descendants. While many Europeans resented holding positions subordinate to West Indians, some black settlers and Creoles felt excluded from government posts, which they believed educated members of their community could fill as successfully as West Indians. This brought an end to West Indians in government office in Sierra Leone, although a few were still employed in nonadministrative posts.[16] They were replaced by Europeans, who the colony's governor, Stephen Hill, claimed could render Africans obedient.[17]

In short, a shift had taken place by the late 1850s from a "positive" rhetoric of race used to incorporate West Indians into the Sierra Leonean service to a "negative" one used to exclude them. A consensus was quickly reached between local and metropolitan colonial authorities in 1858, when Secretary of State Lytton concurred with Governor Hill that Africans would more readily accept the authority of Europeans over them.[18] The decision to stop hiring West Indians of African descent was thus legitimized on the grounds that it protected the interests and reflected the desires of the colony's black settlers and Creoles. Avoiding unsavory indictments against the performance of West Indians, largely because most complaints were proven baseless, the Sierra Leonean administration made it a question of whether people of African descent could rule one another, not whether they could rule in general.

The downhill course of the West Indian experiment in Sierra Leone did not deter the Gold Coast government from pursuing its own policy of recruitment from the West Indies. By the early twentieth century, large numbers of West Indians were seconded to the Gold Coast to work as technicians and train guards on the newly opened railways; they also filled junior and executive posts in the colonial service—like Marcus Clarke, many were to be found in the colony's customs and police departments.[19] In contrast to Sierra Leone during the 1840s and early 1850s, West Indians were rarely found in the higher echelons of the Gold Coast's administration during the early twentieth century when their employment was at its peak.

Like educated African elites in the Gold Coast, the exclusion of West Indians from the highest ranks of the colonial administration reflected the increasing influence of scientific racism and advances in tropical medicine that made it possible for greater numbers of European men to serve in the West African colonies with minimized risks to their health.[20] Combined, these shifts made it ideologically imperative and physically possible to exclude West Indians of African descent, as well as Gold Coasters, from high office.[21] Nonetheless West Indians continued to be administratively classified as Europeans and Gold Coasters as Natives. As a result of this system, West Indians were entitled to the same pay and benefits as Europeans, and were subject to the same rules and regulations regarding their interactions with local Africans.[22] Why this classification system persisted despite the profound changes that had occurred in how the relationship between race and the right to rule was conceived and practiced is difficult to ascertain. Perhaps the most convincing reason is that there still remained a great need for skilled officers that surpassed the number of white British officers available. By its own admission, the administration looked to the West Indies to effectively meet this need.[23] It is unlikely that West Indians would have been persuaded to take up posts in West Africa on the terms and conditions given to Native officers; however, this does not adequately explain why the government decided against placing them in a category of their own.

In addition to multiracial and black West Indians, typically referred to respectively as "mulatto" or "colored," and "negroe" or "pure negroe," the Gold Coast service employed a sizable number of "white" West Indians. Given their racial diversity, it appears that by the turn of the century the perceived pros and cons of racial proximity to Africans were less important than the need for trained officers and skilled laborers. For instance, in 1897 the Gold Coast police vigorously recruited superintendents from the British Guiana police force, irrespective of their racial backgrounds. The same was the case in 1901 when Governor Nathan proposed reorganizing the Gold Coast police force using sergeants from the West Indies.[24] Yet, where West Indians of obvious African descent were concerned, ideas about their biological suitability for work in West Africa persisted even as the fallibility of these ideas emerged in the Gold Coast, just as they had in Sierra Leone. Governor Nathan's belief that West Indian recruits "would undoubtedly tend to economy, less[en] sickness and [promote] greater continuity of service" was quickly dispelled by several instances in which the government was forced to expend more resources on their medical care and general upkeep than expected.[25] The persistence of this kind of racial logic, despite having proved false, suggests that it remained useful to administrators who wanted to push through their requests for additional manpower from the West Indies. Others within the administration, however, were less keen on hiring West Indians, and it is from this group that an explicitly negative racial rhetoric emerged about West Indians.

The campaign against West Indian officers occurred in 1904, just a few months after John Rodger replaced outgoing governor Matthew Nathan, who had vigorously supported their recruitment. This attack, spearheaded by Comptroller of Customs George Attrill, who was also Marcus Clarke's top departmental supervisor, employed a racial rhetoric that positioned West Indians of African descent as a problematic interstitial group between Natives and Europeans; as such they disturbed the racial dichotomy that underpinned colonial rule. In their professional lives their detractors viewed them as unable to command the kind of respect needed to effectively direct both Africans and Europeans, although their actual capabilities were never called into question. In their social lives, multiracial West Indians were constructed as "marginal men" who had no place in the social worlds of Africans or Europeans.[26]

"A STRANGER IN THE LAND"

In the course of making a standard request for a replacement officer to fill the position of an outgoing supervisor of customs, Governor Rodger informed the Colonial Office that Comptroller of Customs George Attrill had requested that no more "Native West Indians" be hired as supervisors in the customs department. According to Attrill, "Such officers are not satisfactory, either when dealing with Europeans or with Natives of this Colony."[27] Rodger took Attrill's request a step further, stating: "If, in future, a Native West Indian be appointed in any capacity, to a post in this Colony, I venture to suggest that, in justice to Native West Africans, he should receive only the 'Native' terms" as specified by the rules governing the appointment of African officers.[28] Framed as protecting the interests of African officers, what the governor called for was the administrative reclassification of West Indian officers from European to Native.

Rodger's dispatch created confusion among Whitehall advisers who were perplexed by the term "Native West Indian," which Comptroller Attrill had evidently coined himself. In an attempt to discern to whom the term referred the Colonial Office undertook a survey of the racial makeup of the West Indians employed by the colony's customs department. The survey concluded that of the thirteen West Indians, five were "white," two were "slightly coloured," and two "a good deal coloured." While the racial identity of the remaining four was unknown, it was suggested that "none are black or even nearly so."[29] This prompted the secretary of state's advisers to wonder whether Rodger objected to West Indians of all skin tones or "only to the deeper tinges" and in turn to suggest that perhaps he would be satisfied if future West Indian appointees were "white or nearly so."[30]

Secretary of State Alfred Lyttelton asked Rodger to clarify what was meant by the term "Native West Indian" and requested evidence to support the claim that they were unsatisfactory employees. Lyttelton's remarks are worth repeating at length because they reveal how the discourse on West Indians was shaped in large part by the question of skin color and its perceived relationship to eligibility to hold office and job performance, as well as the challenge posed by the ambiguous nature of the racial identity of West Indians to begin with:

> I am not sure that I understand what is intended by the expression "native West Indians." . . . Most West Indian officers have some admixture of African blood, and, if selection is to be restricted to men of pure European descent, the number of candidates available will be greatly reduced. If on the other hand men who are only slightly coloured are to be regarded as eligible, it is not clear how dissatisfaction has arisen, since nearly all of the present members of the Gold Coast Customs who are of West Indian origin are not more than slightly coloured. It is as you are aware a most difficult thing to define the race of a West Indian officer, and if the men are selected [sight unseen] in this Office from such information as is available it must sometimes happen that a man more deeply coloured than usual is chosen.[31]

Given that most West Indians employed in the colonial service were "not more than slightly coloured," it is not surprising that Lyttelton rejected Rodger's suggestion that they be reclassified as Native officers. He likely foresaw the difficulties involved in reclassifying racially ambiguous West Indians, when some of their number could probably pass as Europeans in London. Instead, he suggested that a new tactic could be employed to further ensure that darker-skinned candidates were kept out by making the governors of the West Indian colonies responsible for selecting candidates for positions in West Africa.[32] This would allow them to physically see the candidates before appointing them. Ultimately, however, Lyttelton found it "impracticable to draw a colour line between West Indians and European Supervisors of Customs or to pay them on different scales of salary," but added the caveat that "there is of course no difficulty in offering lower terms to West Indians than would be offered to Europeans if the former are employed in a class by themselves with distinct duties."[33] In short, instead of classifying them as Native or European, he suggested that they be placed into a third category of their own, with rights and responsibilities assigned accordingly. Such a category, had it been instituted, would have reflected the third space that West Indians were already unofficially inhabiting in the colony's administrative and social spheres.

In asking for the full particulars of why "Native West Indians" were not found to give satisfaction in their jobs, Lyttelton expressed his surprise at Comptroller Attrill's claims and pointed to the consistently favorable reports received by the Colonial Office on their performance, including reports that commended Marcus Clarke's "good work."[34] The local colonial government's official response to Lyttelton's request for clarification on the "West Indian problem" articulated the complicated set of racial dynamics that was, in its view, at work in the Gold Coast. Although administratively categorized as Europeans, West Indians described as "negroes" or "mulattos" were in practice viewed as "coloured" by white European and Native officers, and it was to this group that the term "Native West Indian" referred.[35] According to Attrill, "Native West Indians" were indeed competent in their work; however, he argued that there was "undoubtedly a feeling of jealousy towards them on the part of the natives of the Colony." He attributed this jealousy to the fact that "Native West Indians" had the same leave privileges as Europeans and that they were "placed in a position of authority over Natives and Mulattos of this Colony who are unable to see any superiority in them, and who, if not openly expressing resentment, work less willingly and cordially under their supervision."[36] Given that Native officers had long campaigned for equal access to appointments and equality in salary and benefits, it is hardly surprising that they resented West Indians for receiving better postings and remuneration packages, but there is little evidence to suggest that these grievances were more pronounced against West Indians than against Europeans.[37] Attrill's explanation was clever nonetheless because it placed the blame for the "Native West Indian" problem on Native officers rather than the administration's racist employment practices that disadvantaged Native officers.

Comptroller Attrill then turned to the question of the position of "Native West Indians" vis-à-vis Europeans. In addition to being "frequently treated with less courtesy than is due their position" by European traders, he argued that "Native West Indians" were "worse situated on the Coast than a white man as regards recreation and society and is more a stranger in the land." Citing their exclusion from the pastimes of both Europeans and Africans, he described them as leading "a broody and forlorn existence." Conspicuously, he limited his negative comments to European traders—never suggesting that European government officers mistreated their "Native West Indian" colleagues, although their admitted exclusion from white social circles suggests otherwise. With regard to the lack of popularity "Native West Indians" experienced in their professional lives, Attrill accused them of bringing it on themselves because of their inclination to "watch for treatment from both [their] brother officers and [European] traders which [they] can wrongly construe as a slight or insult." He then insinuated that this inclination resulted from their fraught racial status, which caused them to be "extremely sensitive." Attrill concluded his report by singling out Marcus Clarke and two other "Native West Indians," as "wanting in tact and difficult for the other [white] Supervisors to get on with."[38] Several years after Clarke's case another one of the "difficult" West Indians Attrill had named in his report was falsely accused of concubinage by a European coworker, and subsequently acquitted by the Executive Council.[39]

Upon receipt at the Colonial Office, Attrill's report and Governor Rodger's accompanying dispatch solicited great interest. The claims made by Rodger and Attrill garnered a far less favorable response from the Colonial Office than similar ones made by Sierra Leonean administrators in the late 1850s. In 1858 Edward Lytton, secretary of state for the colonies, summed up the West Indian experiment as "a complete failure as it was likely to prove according to the ordinary principle of prejudice by which society is held together. The Blacks have little respect, [and] jealous dislike for one of their own colour in authority—and we all know how the Whites dislike the idea of being made inferior to a Black."[40] In striking contrast to this, Secretary of State Lyttelton, in 1905, responded to Governor Rodger's request to cease employing West Indians in the following manner:

> West Indians are only employed because they are supposed to be more competent than West Africans, and, if they are so, I consider that the Colonial Government should not allow itself to be influenced by a jealousy which is not well founded. With regard to colour prejudice as such, apart from capacity and efficiency in other respects, I am disposed to think that it is futile and shortsighted statesmanship to make unnecessary concessions to it.[41]

Given that their competency was not in question, Lyttelton concluded, "I do not think that a case has been made out for discrimination against West Indians of mixed blood for employment in West Africa."[42] That Lyttelton's pronouncement was qualified by an emphasis on "mixed blood" West Indians suggests that he may have made some concessions to the idea that West Indians of "full" African origin were more problematic to employ.

In the end neither Rodger's proposal to reclassify West Indians of African descent as Native officers nor Lyttelton's suggestion that they be "employed in a class by themselves with distinct duties" was adopted. While the lack of consensus surrounding the West Indian question reveals its contentious nature, it also suggests that where race was concerned colonial policies did not follow a rigidly linear or uniform path—after all, in 1860 a consensus excluding West Indians of African descent from holding office in Sierra Leone had been arrived at between metropolitan and local authorities, but this was not the case in 1905 with respect to the "Native West Indian" question in the Gold Coast. Disagreements over how to classify West Indians, instead, signaled how practical concerns, such as the need for skilled manpower, could trump the oft-cited need for clear racial hierarchies when administrative efficiency and colonial purse strings were at stake. Ultimately, the lack of consensus on this issue resulted in the continued classification of West Indians as European officers, despite subsequent efforts by Governor Rodger in later years to revive the issue.[43] Led by administrators who had spearheaded the campaign against "Native West Indians," the customs department remained a hotbed of discontent over the West Indian policy in ways that visibly played themselves out in the Marcus Clarke case.

MORE THAN JUST "UNDESIRABLE RELATIONS": THE POLITICS OF MARCUS CLARKE'S RACE

As indicated earlier, at the end of July 1907 the inspector of maritime customs, Mr. A. Smith, reported a "case of gross official misconduct" on the part of Marcus Clarke to the comptroller of customs, George Attrill.[44] The timing of Smith's disclosure, four months after the release of Rodger's "undesirable relations" circular, gave his accusations greater currency given the severity of the government's newly articulated policy toward sexual relationships maintained by European officers with African women. Smith's memorandum detailed not one but two cases in which Clarke was accused of misconduct with "native girls." Within a day the memorandum was on Governor Rodger's desk. He immediately forwarded it, along with other documents from a previous case in which Clarke had been accused of financial irregularities and intoxication, to the secretary of state for the colonies, the Earl of Elgin.

The governor's course of action deviated from the terms of his own circular, which stipulated that the secretary of state for the colonies would be notified *only* if an officer failed to exculpate himself. Skirting around his own protocol, Rodger requested the Earl of Elgin to communicate a copy of Inspector Smith's report to Clarke, who was on leave in England at the time. If Clarke was "unable to furnish a satisfactory reply to the allegations in the report," Rodger made it clear that he would "recommend his dismissal from the Government Service."[45] Rodger's dispatch to the secretary of state gave way to sixteen months of back-and-forth correspondence, totaling more than two hundred pages, between the Colonial Office, the government of the Gold Coast, and Marcus Clarke.

Included in this correspondence was a copy of the transcript from the 1906 court case brought against Clarke by Quasie Yarn, which formed the basis of the first set of charges proffered against him. Before exploring the transcript in greater detail, it is worth pausing for a moment to consider the simple but rather extraordinary fact that this case was tried at all because it raises fascinating questions about how Gold Coasters interacted with the colonial court system as plaintiffs when the defendant was "European." It also begs the question of how Quasie Yarn read Marcus Clarke's racial identity. Did he perceive Clarke to be different from other European officers? If so, does Yarn's perception of Clarke's difference help account for his willingness to take him to court? Asked differently, had Clarke been a "white" European officer would Quasie Yarn have sued him just the same? Likewise, if, as Heike Schmidt has argued for German East Africa, colonial "courts were mostly concerned with maintaining European authority in the eyes of the colonized African population," then the Sekondi divisional court's willingness to hear "native" witnesses testify about the sexual impropriety of a "European" officer makes sense only if the court did not really regard Marcus Clarke as a European.[46] Still, as an officer representing the colonial service, the case against Clarke was bound to reflect badly on the government and thus suggests a more complex relationship between the colonial state and its courts than might first be supposed.

The transcript detailed the circumstances under which Clarke had allegedly contracted a "native marriage" with Abba Saraku in August of 1906. According to the girl's father, Quasie Yarn, a cook named Cudjoe Annan had come to see him about procuring a companion for his employer, Marcus Clarke. Interested in Annan's proposition, Yarn and his wife, Ambah Effie, along with Albert Edward Yates, an interpreter engaged by Annan, all proceeded to Clarke's house in Sekondi with Abba Saraku in tow. Ambah Effie testified that Annan took her daughter upstairs to be viewed by Clarke, and when she, Yarn, and Yates joined them a few minutes later Clarke asked her husband "how much he would take *for* the girl."[47] In his testimony, the interpreter, Yates, recalled this same exchange slightly differently. He told the court that Clarke had said, "I like the girl" and then asked "how much am I to pay *to* the girl."[48] This discrepancy—whether the result of an actual difference in testimony or an error in the court transcript—makes it difficult to know whether Clarke said he would pay money *to* Abba Saraku or pay *for* her. Nonetheless, Yarn's, Yate's, and Ambah Effie's testimony is consistent with regard to the fact that they all agreed that Clarke's expressed interest in Abba Saraku amounted to a marriage proposal.

According to the transcript, Yarn asked Clarke to pay him £10 to cover the cost of "cloth and dowry" for Abba Saraku. The provision of a piece of cloth by a man to his intended bride has long been recognized as a common practice among the Fante of south-western coastal Ghana; so, too, has the payment of a dowry, although it is not technically required to legitimize a customary marriage.[49] Yarn's request was notably different, however, because he asked Clarke for a strictly cash payment. Had Clarke been a "native," Ambah Effie explained, her husband would have expected him "to supply cloth and other things, but for defendant he charged £10."[50] Some of this money was to be used to purchase cloth and handkerchiefs for Abba Saraku on Clarke's behalf.

On the face of it the family's actions suggest that they saw Clarke as an outsider who, being unfamiliar with how to procure the appropriate material goods required to contract the marriage, needed their assistance to fulfill his obligations. The sizeable sum of £10 chosen by the family suggests that their motivations were not, however, strictly altruistic. Rather, they were also looking to achieve the greatest profit possible from the arrangement, something that was not out of step with the colony-wide trend of the "rising costs of obtaining a wife," as Penelope Roberts has noted for Sefwi Wiawso.[51] When Clarke made it known that he did not have the funds immediately available to conduct the transaction in full, an installment plan was agreed upon. He made a small initial payment of £1.10/- and Abba Saraku was left with him that very day.[52] She testified that on that evening, she and Clarke had their first "connection" as she "slept with him in the same bed the whole night."[53] The next day she went back to her father's house, but periodically returned to Clarke's home to provide him with eggs, oranges, and, according to her testimony, sex on the ten occasions she visited him. Abba Saraku further testified that Clarke had given her a small sum in payment of oranges and £2 as a *dash* (gift) for cloth. These moneys, she said, were separate from the dowry he still owed her father. Clarke's cook, Cudjoe Annan, delivered a second installment of £1.10/- to Quasie Yarn; after this no other sum was paid toward the allegedly agreed-upon dowry of £10.

After twice demanding that he make good on the outstanding balance, Yarn claimed that Clarke refused to pay and told him he "could take [his] daughter away."[54] The definitive break in the relationship occurred when Yarn filed a summons against Clarke in October 1906, after which he says Abba Saraku stopped living with Clarke—presumably this meant that she stopped periodically spending the night at his house, since by her own admission she did not stay with him habitually.[55] Her periodic visits to Clarke's home would not have been out of the norm for a married couple given that husbands and wives frequently lived in separate residences after marriage, which is precisely how she and her family represented the relationship. Throughout the course of their testimony, Yarn, Ambah Effie, and Abba Saraku referred to the latter as Clarke's "wife" and to their relationship as a marriage. Clarke's own testimony confirms that the family's intention was to give Abba Saraku to him in exchange for a "dowry." Subsequently, however, Clarke would clarify that he did not view their request for a dowry as indicative of their wanting to contract a legitimate "native marriage," but rather an attempt to profit from a "liaison" dressed up in the language of respectability. The discrepancy between how the two parties presented the nature of the relationship foreshadowed the differing ways Gold Coasters and colonial officers involved in such liaisons represented them: the former often referred to them as "marriages," while the latter consistently made them out to be illegitimate or temporary sexual relationships. That this was the case reflects not only the discursive strategies that colonial officers employed as they tried to minimize their participation in forbidden relations with local women, but also the way in which many Europeans, and growing numbers of Gold Coasters, disparaged customary unions as a lesser form of marriage that was prone to easy dissolution, and where interracial customary marriages were concerned as a thin veil for prostitution.[56]

Clarke, represented by a respected local African barrister, Mr. Peter Renner, testified in front of the district commissioner that he had never agreed to take Abba Saraku as his wife or to pay a dowry for her. Rather, in an attempt to repel their advances, Clarke claimed he told Yarn that his daughter was "too small" and when that did not deter him, he tried to simultaneously placate the family while holding them at bay by promising to pay them £5 at a later date. Clarke further testified that the £1.10/- he gave to Yarn on the day he left Abba Saraku in his possession was for drink money and for help with his trading business, but that Yarn promised to apply it toward the £5. According to Clarke, Yarn insisted that Abba Saraku stay with him that night, but he swore that he "did not have connection with her."[57] While also admitting that she had spent the night at his house on other occasions, he again denied having had sex with her. Their exchanges, by his account, were limited to eggs and oranges for small sums of cash.[58] The essence of his defense was that he had reluctantly given money to the family in an attempt to shake free of them, but he never regarded this money as a dowry payment or his interactions with Abba Saraku as a customary marriage or any other kind of liaison. Clarke's testimony failed to persuade District Commissioner Michelin, who ruled that Clarke and Abba Saraku did indeed have a "valid marriage entered into according to native law" and ordered Clarke to pay £6 to Yarn.[59] This amount was much less than the £13.10 Yarn had sued for, as Michelin deducted the compensation fee, as well as all moneys given to both Yarn and Saraku over the course of their involvement, from this amount. Although shocked by the verdict, Clarke did not contest it. It was not until Inspector Smith brought this old case to official attention, along with a new set of allegations that the full extent of Clarke's defense came out.

"I AM NOT AS BLACK AS IT IS DESIRED TO PAINT ME": MARCUS CLARKE'S SELF-DEFENSE

Inspector Smith's memorandum also alleged that shortly after Clarke had lost the case brought against him by Quasie Yarn—details of which were not previously disclosed to a wider audience—he "grossly misused his position as Supervisor, to attempt to tamper with the step-daughter of a native officer."[60] Thus, in October of 1907, one year after Clarke lost the case, he was now defending himself against old and new charges of sexual immorality. In one of the first of many long letters penned by Clarke to the Colonial Office, he asked for more time to clear himself because, in his words, "it is of the greatest importance to me to rehabilitate myself in His Lordship's opinion and for me to show to His Lordship that *I am not as black as it is desired to paint me.*"[61] Clarke's metaphorical use of this loaded phrase typified how he evoked his racial persecution without ever naming it. Instead, Clarke chronicled in painstaking detail the six years of ill-treatment he had endured under his superior, Inspector A. Smith.

Clarke's career in the colonial service began in British Guiana, where he had also worked as a customs officer before being transferred to the Gold Coast in October 1901, shortly before his thirtieth birthday. According to Clarke, Smith "forcibly expressed his disappointment when I arrived as a Supervisor, that I did not come from the Imperial Customs," and immediately displayed "his chagrin which germinated into malice and hatred."[62] Men from the imperial customs were recruited directly from Britain's domestic customs service and were invariably white. Receiving a nonwhite recruit disappointed Smith; Clarke evoked the same meaning by substituting "white" with "Imperial Customs."

In laying the foundation of his defense against the charges brought against him, Clarke further detailed the nature of Smith's hatred toward him:

> Mr. Smith is to me an enemy implacable, hating me with a virulence which will call forth surprise, and who, during my whole connection with the Gold Coast Customs, set himself out, without any justification, to annoy and to mar and always to injure, and now to further do so to me. I can only attribute this long continued hostility to firstly, a prejudice, and ultimately, and encouraged by himself, dislike, as I proved myself a dependable and capable officer.[63]

This hatred manifested itself in different forms, but particularly egregious to Clarke was Smith's penchant for degrading him in front of "native Staff." Smith often forced Clarke to work in the "native Officer's Office" and was fond of sending him telegrams, which were processed by Native officers, offering Clarke posts that were, in his words, "inferior to my education and respectability" in an attempt to "ridicule me and to humiliate me in their [Native staff's] eyes and in the opinion of my European brother Officers." His humiliation at being dressed down in front of Native officers points to his own investments in being viewed as distinct from and superior to his African colleagues, not unlike the kinds of investments that "white" European officers made in their own racial superiority over West Indians and Africans.

Clarke was at pains to make clear that Smith's treatment of him could not be compared to a fraternal initiation of some sort. He alluded again to his racial persecution at the hands of Smith by describing his torment as worse than "bullying" because of his "surroundings in a strange country," followed by the rather cryptic rejoinder "and the complexion of these actions as my being so differently circumstanced in position, and in other features."[64] According to Clarke, Smith's antics grew more and more "sinister" with the passage of time. Clarke's innuendo-laced lamentations leave no room for doubting that he believed Smith's racially motivated hatred of him was at the heart of the charges brought against him. His inability or unwillingness to name his racial persecution, however, offers some insight into the psychology behind Clarke's own complicated identity politics and the social history of the reverse migrations that increasingly shaped the Black Atlantic world after abolition.[65]

Born in British Guiana, Clarke was part of a group of privileged multiracial West Indians who had access to education at home and in Europe, jobs in the colonial service, and connections beyond the West Indies that allowed him and others like him to move back and forth between different parts of the British Empire, including Britain itself.⁶⁶ Clarke made every effort to present himself as an Anglophile:

> My first standard and highest ideal is that of the English gentleman, and I copy and endeavour to live up to that standard and ideal. British colonially born, my whole life is British and my love and devotion is for and to England, and everything English. I am greatly Anglicized and as greatly Anglophile. My political opinions are distinctly those of your Government and have ever been. . . . I am and endeavour to be very credible in appearance and I dress and comport myself in accordance with the standards of an English gentleman.⁶⁷

Passages such as this and others expressing similar sentiments might be read as revealing the extent to which Clarke's unwillingness to explicitly admit that the attacks against him were racially motivated was a product of a colonized psyche that prevented him from admitting that he was not white.⁶⁸ As such, we might understand Clarke's psyche as emblematic of the type articulated so trenchantly by Frantz Fanon in his seminal study, *Black Skin, White Masks*, in which the desire to be white is produced in people who live in a society "that makes [their] inferiority complex possible, in a society that derives its stability from the perpetuation of this complex, in a society that proclaims the superiority of one race" — in other words, a colonial society.⁶⁹ Yet, the nature of the claims Clarke made about his identity suggests another possibility worth considering.

Clarke consistently positioned himself as British, as an Anglophile, and as an Englishman, but he never claimed to be white. In other words, the stated terms of his affiliations were cultural and national rather than racial. In this sense, he demanded to be seen and treated in the same manner as those who shared the same affiliations. His expectations for equal treatment were grounded not only in his privileged upbringing in the West Indies and his education in Europe, but also in his participation in a colonial system that categorized him as a European. Effectively, Clarke and other West Indians who were employed in West Africa as Europeans were proxies for white British men — they were hired as Europeans, they were paid as Europeans, they were administratively categorized as Europeans, and they lived with Europeans — indeed, Clarke shared a bungalow with the senior supervisor of customs for a year — but clearly they were not always treated as Europeans. Perhaps Clarke's inability to admit he was being racially persecuted stemmed from his own uncertainty about where he really fit into a system that defined him in one way and treated him in another. Admitting to being the target of racial discrimination would require him to acknowledge that he was different in some fundamental way from those he saw himself as being akin to, in his words, his "European brother officers."

While Clarke's status as a European officer was challenged by his "brother officers," he claimed to be regarded as fair game for what he described as the fleecing of European officers by their domestic servants, whom he disparaged as a "very clever and scheming body of men."[70] According to Clarke, African domestic workers were infamous for taking advantage of European officers, particularly those stationed without their wives:

> They [cooks and stewards] know perfectly that the new arrival is only out for a year, and concluding his interest and stay is transitory . . . as a bird of passage he is well plucked before his tour expires. This is incontrovertible and a usual experience . . . especially [for] unmarried officers, who are in a great measure wholly dependent on these servants.[71]

In an account that offers a glimpse into a domain of colonial life where Africans could and did wield greater power than is often assumed, Clarke bemoaned how European officers became "the prey and source of profit" of their local staff, who made their living by "thrusting liaisons on European officers and pronouncing blackmail." This, according to Clarke, was precisely what had happened to him. After finding that he was "perpetually worried and made disagreeable" by having been mixed up in such a proposition, and after his attempts to keep the family at bay had failed, he dismissed his cook, who had orchestrated the whole affair.[72] He claimed that his cook and the Yarn family retaliated by trying to extort money from him. When Clarke refused to give in to their demands, he found himself in court.

Clarke suggested that the sexual blackmail of European officers was part of a larger indigenous phenomenon whereby "natives do purposely seek and plan, and desire these state of affairs [liaisons] from a pecuniary, as well as from their own local point of view."[73] What Clarke described as blackmail might very well have been a variation of preexisting local practices in various parts of the colony whereby men, often of rank, allowed, if not encouraged, their wives to seduce other men in order to profit from the prescribed monetary compensation for adultery.[74] Known as *ayefare sika* among the Asante, similar systems of adultery compensation obtained among the Fante, Ewe, and others. If compensatory transactions were being expanded to include other kinds of sexual infractions, then the incorporation of comparatively well-paid European officers, like Clarke, into the system, would have certainly enhanced opportunities for even greater profit.[75] This, according to Clarke's trial lawyer, Peter Renner, made European officers especially vulnerable to sexual blackmail by "natives."[76] Although Renner's line of defense fell flat in court, blackmail and even the system of adultery compensation would reemerge as factors in officers' exculpatory strategies in some of the cases that followed Clarke's.

In concluding his written defense to the Colonial Office, Clarke turned to the second charge proffered against him by Inspector Smith: that he had abused his official position in an attempt to "tamper" with Sarah Helden, his Native subordinate's stepdaughter. Clarke admitted that he wished to marry Helden, but denied that he had abused his official position in trying to carry out his wishes. He made use of the sworn statements given by Helden's mother, stepfather, and grandmother to show that he dropped the matter once it had been made absolutely clear to him that she was already engaged. Clarke further pointed out that by her own family's admission, Helden was between the ages of fifteen and seventeen and already engaged, facts he asserted proved that Smith had intended to discredit and disgrace him by falsely and maliciously insinuating that Helden was so young that had he carried out his intentions toward her, he would have risked committing a criminal offense.[77] In returning to Smith's hatred of him, Clarke reaffirmed the cornerstone of his defense as Smith's long-standing prejudice against him, which had led to a doggedly willful attempt, on the part of Smith, to destroy him by any means necessary. While we will never really know whether Clarke was completely innocent of the charges against him, the important point, here, is that the levying of charges appears to have been racially motivated. Members of the Colonial Office who reviewed his case shared this belief.

"ORDINARY IMMORALITY" OR A "SPECIES OF SLAVE-DEALING"?

On 11 November 1907, the Colonial Office received the last of four lengthy letters Clarke had authored in his defense. All but one of the advisers handling the case were in agreement that Clarke should be allowed to retire from the service rather than be dismissed, but that at the discretion of the Gold Coast government, his pension might be reduced. In support of this course of action, it was argued that while Clarke's behavior appeared irregular in the first case, whatever scandal, if any, resulting from the lawsuit had subsided and therefore had not brought the colonial service into disrepute.[78] Those who argued for leniency also agreed that Smith's claims in the second case were baseless and therefore found that Clarke was not guilty of any wrongdoing on those charges. Having rejected the "sinister view" of Clarke fabricated by Smith, Colonial Office staff member Alexander Fiddian accepted that "there is more truth in Mr. Clarke's charges of personal malice against Mr. Smith than one would naturally suppose." Immediately following this statement Fiddian declared that a colleague had recently informed him that Clarke was "at least a ~~quadroon~~ mulatto." At last, three months after the investigation of the charges had commenced, an explicit link had been made between Clarke's (perceived) race and his persecution at the hands of Smith. This marked the first and only discussion of Clarke's race, which was mired in confusion, as the crossing out of the term "quadroon" in favor of identifying him as a "mulatto" in the original document suggests.

Still, the muddled disclosure about Clarke's race reads as an intervention designed to bring some kind of sense and racial order to the charges. Fiddian used the information about Clarke's race to explain Smith's actions, but he also used it to make sense of Clarke's behavior and its repercussions. Clarke's alleged laxity of morals in the first case was normalized, in Fiddian's mind, by the revelation about his race, as he doubted the justifiability of "expecting the same standards of morals from [Clarke]" as were expected of white European officers. Here, Clarke's sexuality stood in for his race. Moreover, because disciplinary action was typically calculated in relation to the severity of the public scandal created, Clarke's "colour" worked in his favor, since Fiddian deemed his behavior less scandal-provoking than had he been a "white" European. To this he added, "His colour would also account for the diffuse and partly irrelevant character of his explanations."[79] Thus, by introducing the single fact of Clarke's racial identity, all the pieces of the puzzle fell into place for Fiddian, and presumably for all those who supported the more lenient course of disciplinary action he proposed.

There was, however, one lone figure in the Colonial Office, Reginald Antrobus, who vehemently disagreed with the "soft approach" taken by his colleagues. In calling for Clarke's dismissal from the colonial service, Antrobus drew upon an unfavorable report authored by the Gold Coast's attorney general in which Clarke's actions in the first case were scandalously portrayed. The attorney general believed that Clarke had "entered into an arrangement for concubinage with the parents of [Abba Saraku] . . . for the performance of an immoral act." Because the marriage contract was, in his opinion, "null and void as being *contra bonos mores* [against good morals]," it "should never have been upheld by the Court."[80] Moreover, the attorney general argued that "non-natives" could not, "by merely going through the customary forms used in the native contract of marriage, enter into a legal marriage with a native woman."[81] Thus, while the attorney general rejected the legality of the marriage, he wholeheartedly believed that Clarke had nonetheless sought out an immoral relationship with Abba Saraku. Antrobus categorically accepted the attorney general's statements and used them to support his contention that Clarke's intentions in the second case were no different than in the first: so far as he was proposing marriage to a "native woman," he was doing nothing more than contracting illicit sex.[82] Antrobus went so far as to suggest that his actions were not "ordinary immorality," but were "a species of slave-dealing."[83] Antrobus's accusation drew its intelligibility from the very real fact that despite its abolition in 1874, slavery was still a social fact in the Gold Coast. As the most likely to be enslaved, women necessarily bore the brunt of the incomplete transition from slavery to freedom, whilst even those that were freeborn found their freedom curtailed by patriarchal power, especially where matters of productive and reproductive labor were concerned.

In equating customary marriages between nonnative men and "native" women to a form of "slave-dealing" in which parents sold their daughters for profit to licentious men, Antrobus shared the concerns of other Europeans and Gold Coasters before and after him. As mentioned earlier, in 1889 Carl Reindorf lamented that local women were "sold by their parents to white men," who in turn ruined their prospects for respectable marriages to African men. In a speech delivered in 1902 to the "educated natives of Dixcove and Bushua" on the social problems facing West Africans, Dr. J. Murray, a European medical officer, told his audience that the "'Native wife' question of West Africa . . . amounts to nothing short of [the] sale of your young, tender, pure virgins to dissolute European[s] . . . for their vile temporary uses."[84] And during the first two decades of the twentieth century, even African proponents of customary marriage challenged the legitimacy of such unions when contracted between European men and African women in the pages of the *Gold Coast Leader*.[85] In short, interracial customary marriages aroused the suspicions of Africans and Europeans alike. Nevertheless, Antrobus's colleagues at the Colonial Office rejected his suggestion that Clarke's actions had been tantamount to "slave-dealing." Instead of dismissing Clarke from the service, he was allowed to retire on grounds of ill health at the age of thirty-five with a reduced pension.[86]

CONCLUSION

Marcus Clarke's case reveals how at odds with itself colonial policy making could be. On one hand, the "undesirable relations" circular was meant to draw a firm line between "colonized" and "colonizer," while on the other hand the employment of West Indians of African descent as European officers subverted that very distinction by removing colonial subjects from their colonies of origin and turning them into proxy colonizers vis-a-vis other colonized populations. Underscoring their contingent and shifting nature, colonized and colonizer became in this instance geopolitically bounded categories rather than racially demarcated ones. In less than a decade, however, this unintentionally subversive system of administrative categorization produced a backlash against West Indian officers, whose presence in the Gold Coast unsettled the tidy binaries that structured the racial logics of colonial rule. Governor Rodger's proposal to end the recruitment of "non-white" West Indians, or reclassify them as Natives, was an attempt to redefine the proper racial place of "non-white" West Indians as being either in the West Indies or in the Native sphere of the colony's administration.

The inability of Governor Rodger and Secretary of State Lyttelton to arrive at a consensus regarding this proposal signals how unresolved and contentious views on race within the colonial administration could be, especially between local and metropolitan colonial authorities. The particular concerns of local colonial authorities were often different from, and at times conflicted with those of metropolitan colonial authorities who were more concerned with keeping the entire imperial apparatus running efficiently. Indeed, Lyttelton's refusal to cave into Governor Rodger's demands exemplifies how the racial logic of colonialism could be selectively suspended in the name of expediency, even as it continued to uphold fundamental assertions about African inferiority. But this policy stalemate arguably only made matters worse for West Indians like Marcus Clarke. One possible reading of the charges brought against him, after all, is that they reveal the extent to which disgruntled members of the customs department were willing to go to reorder and fortify the colony's administrative racial hierarchy to protect the supremacy of white Europeans, when they felt that the Colonial Office would not do it for them. In this way the Clarke case reminds us that even fundamental categories of colonial rule—like Native and European—were hardly fixed.

A final word: although written in ways that were clearly meant to exculpate himself from any wrongdoing, Marcus Clarke's letters, when read along the seam joining them to other pieces of evidence, reveal how entangled he was with the Gold Coasters he worked and lived among. In pursuing Sarah Helden, Clarke not only approached her stepfather about the matter but also subsequently spoke to her mother and grandmother—making at least two visits to their family home to discuss his interest in her with them. Clearly no stranger to him, Helden's grandmother said she had known Clarke during his early years of service in the coastal town of Ada. Thus rather than abusing his official position, it seems more likely that Clarke hoped he could leverage his personal connection to the family to get them to agree to his marriage proposal. In the case of Abba Saraku, Clarke came to know her family through his cook, Cudjoe Annan. We know that Clarke received the family inside of his home and on several occasions Quasie Yarn returned to Clarke's residence to pressure him to make good on the dowry. We also know that Abba Saraku spent the night at Clarke's home on multiple occasions. Her overnight presence in his home suggests a familiarity and proximity that connote intimacy, even if, as Clarke claimed, they were never sexually intimate. In Clarke's account of colonial life, relations of dependence fostered an atmosphere of familiarity between officers and their cooks and stewards, many of whom were prepared to cater to the sexual demands of their almost exclusively male employers. The mundane entanglements of colonial life across the color line fostered colonial intimacies that included sex but were hardly limited to it. This would prove true in other cases that followed Clarke's.

3 ~ "A New Whim of a Most Unpopular Governor"
Embedded Officers and the Local Politics of Concubinage Cases

AN EXTRAORDINARY SCENE UNFOLDED on the grounds of the Amedika Customs Station in the colony's Eastern Province on 5 June 1908. As Provincial Commissioner Clarence Napier Curling took his tea on the station's veranda, he was accosted by Narkoyo Otibo, a young woman he knew well, for she had been one of his load carriers for many years. According to Curling, Otibo approached him with "a small bottle in her hand" and soon "commenced crying bitterly and talking very fast."[1] Curling's orderly tried to stop her, but "she shook him off angrily" and began "shaking the bottle" at the commissioner, whom she accused of giving her the bottled medicine to "spoil" her pregnancy. When Otibo threatened to have Curling put in prison, he summoned a nearby Native officer to escort her to the Police Station. But less than an hour later she was back on the veranda of Curling's nearby residential bungalow levying the same accusations against him. The scene soon escalated, with some reports suggesting that Curling struck and threatened to kill her in front of a crowd of people.[2] While Curling later admitted to having made "an involuntary movement," he denied hitting Otibo or threatening her.[3] She was once again removed from the premises and handed over to her father, Moses Ogbe, who was instructed by the acting district commissioner, Dr. Harold Palmer, to return to the customs station the next morning to "settle" the matter.

Accompanied by her father, brothers, and uncles, Narkoyo Otibo explained on the following day that she had been pregnant, although by whom she did not say, and that she believed Curling had given her an abortifacient that caused her to miscarry. When the bottle turned out to contain only cod-liver oil, she recanted by swearing on the Bible that "all that I have said against my master is untrue."[4] Despite her admission, in Acting District Commissioner Palmer's view the episode confirmed his suspicions about a sexual relationship between Commissioner Curling and Narkoyo Otibo. Months later Palmer disclosed his knowledge of this episode in an attempt to discredit Curling, who he believed had negatively implicated him in a series of subsequent intrigues involving members of the Otibo family. Palmer's disclosure gave way to a lengthy investigation into Curling's relationship with Narkoyo, her cousin Owusi, and other members of their family, leaving a paper trail of close to four hundred pages.

Over the course of the investigation and ensuing disciplinary proceedings, the Gold Coast government was confronted with the scale of the concubinage problem that Governor Rodger had hoped to curb with his 1907 "undesirable relations" circular. Like the case of Marcus Clarke, the Curling case and the cluster of cases that followed it reveal the intricate web of social relations that colonial officers were drawn into through their varied associations with Gold Coasters. While the administration assumed that sexual relations between its officers and African women fostered competing loyalties that threatened officers' impartiality and good judgment, this reasoning missed a crucial point: these sexual relationships were often procured through other kinds of preexisting intimate or dependent relationships that European government officers, by necessity, forged with Africans. Thus the administration could hardly hope to curb interracial concubinage without first dismantling the larger grid of cross-racial relations it was embedded in – something it was never fully able to do.

Although Rodger's circular was part of a larger vision to create a more racially segregated society in the colony, it was issued in the years before the creation of European residential segregation areas gained momentum in the wake of a 1910 yellow fever outbreak that killed nine Europeans in Sekondi.[5] As a result, the mixed residential geography of Europeans and Africans continued to foster rather than militate against interracial fraternizing, including concubinage, in the years that followed the 1907 circular. Even when segregation came into force in the major towns and cities with large European populations, it was hardly complete, as indicted by the presence in these zones of African domestic workers and their families, as well as the African mistresses of European men.[6] While the uncoordinated timing of these efforts makes it appear as though the color line was drawn haphazardly, there was some logic to it. Governor Rodger clearly believed that concubinage posed a credible threat worthy of responding to by drawing a color line that he felt would preserve British authority by reducing "ill-feeling among the Natives." He also believed that mixed residential areas posed a threat to the health of Europeans, but it was only after the deadly 1910 yellow fever outbreak that he was persuaded that it constituted a serious enough threat to warrant enforcing a form of racial segregation that he knew would provoke massive discontent among Africans. Thus rather than a uniform broad stroke application, the color line was strategically drawn in ways calculated to best preserve British authority, even if in the end it had had the opposite effect.

The spate of disciplinary cases that followed in the wake of the circular reveal that it provided a ready-made outlet for workplace grievances that frequently had little to do with sex. Rather, Africans and Europeans alike who brought these charges recognized the circular as a convenient yet potent weapon to attack those who were subject to it. The new policy had extraordinary visibility because it was filtered down the chain of command from the governor's office to department heads, who were charged with conveying it to their European subordinates. It must have made quite a stir given that the majority of European government officers were suspected of "keeping" local women. How widely news of the circular and its contents spread among Gold Coasters is difficult to quantify, but it was typed locally in Governor Rodger's record office, leading one government officer to conclude that it "soon became generally known amongst the black population."[7] This was presumably the case, because African clerks were responsible for much of the work performed not only there, but also in the various government offices throughout the colony where the circular was sent for local distribution. One can easily imagine that salacious content of the kind contained in the circular would have been just the type of information to spread quickly by word of mouth among the service's clerks, many of whom had frequent cause to be disgruntled with their European supervisors and thus had plenty of reason to make news of the circular more widely known. As the circular became a pivot for seemingly disparate grievances, it revealed the extent to which the government's workforce, both white and black, was rife with discontent, petty jealousies, fear, and inequality. Personal and professional animus among the colony's officers found expression in charges, whether true or false, of sex with local women because these charges now had political capital. As the cases unfolded they revealed additional layers of conflict and connection not only among officers, but also between officers and the local communities they lived and worked with.

THE CURLING CASE:
SEX, ANIMUS, AND MALADMINISTRATION

Several months after Narkoyo Otibo's heated encounter with Commissioner Curling, he was once again involved in a dispute with the Otibo family. This time, however, he was advocating on behalf of four Otibo men, including the fathers of Narkoyo and her cousin Owusi, who he claimed were wrongfully arrested and cruelly treated by police officers.[8] According to Curling, the men had been "tied up to a beam and left swinging" by the police. Two of the four men were later imprisoned for four weeks without any evidence produced against them.[9] The men in question, Tsutsu Otibo, Amanquah Otibo, Moses Ogbe, and Aporchie, had been arrested on suspicion of aiding the jailbreak of Ogbe's son—and Narkoyo's brother—Theophilus Kwabla Otibo (hereafter T. K. Otibo). T. K. Otibo was serving a prison sentence, handed down to him by acting district commissioner Palmer for forging signatures on a series of letters that had spawned a dispute over a creek between the Otibos and *Mantse* Animli of Osudoku. Curling further claimed that T. K. Otibo had been illegally caned by his prison warder. Outraged, he ordered the policemen and prison warder to be tried on charges of ill-treatment. When the officer investigating Curling's charges, Acting Commissioner of Police (hereafter, ACP) E. V. Collins, issued his report they contained startling accusations, not against the policemen and prison warder, but against Commissioner Curling.

ACP Collins found that the actions of some of the policemen involved were "contrary to law" and warranted punishment, but he claimed that Curling had exaggerated the charges and submitted them without proper inquiry. Furthermore, he accused Curling of being responsible for an unduly harsh jail sentence passed against T. K. Otibo's prison warder. Curling's misguided actions, Collins contended, were the result of "his intimate relations" with the Otibo family, through which he "allowed his sense of justice to be biased."[10] In an appended statement Collins clarified the nature of the "intimate relationship" between the Otibos and Curling. Curling, he alleged, had kept a "native wife," Narkoyo, until June 1908, when he discarded her in favor of her cousin Owusi. Eschewing the possibility that Curling's defense of the four Otibo men was motivated by his decade-long relationship with the family, some of whom served as his headman and load carriers, Collins alleged that the commissioner's sexual relationships with Narkoyo and Owusi were to blame for his failure to impartially judge matters concerning the Otibo family. These factors, in Collins's estimation, added up to "an indictment of serious maladministration on the part of Mr. Curling," which had implications for the "whole question of administration both of Governmental departments and Native affairs in the Eastern Province."[11]

At the close of 1908, Commissioner Curling was called upon to exculpate himself from nine different charges that had been formed against him in relationship to Collins's report.[12] Each of the charges stemmed from the sexual relationships he was alleged to have formed with Narkoyo and Owusi. Central to the severity of the allegations against him were several factors: (1) he was the commissioner of the province to which Narkoyo, Owusi, and their family belonged, and therefore it was suggested that he abused his official position in procuring sexual relationships with the two women and brought disrepute to the position itself; (2) his relationship with Narkoyo, in particular, had resulted in two "violent scenes" that caused public scandals and further tarnished the service's reputation; (3) upon receipt of Governor Rodger's "undesirable relations" circular in 1907, he failed to bring an end to his relationship with Narkoyo and proceeded to commence a new sexual relationship with her cousin Owusi; and (4) his relationships with the Otibo women had led the Otibo family to believe that he would act in their favor vis-à-vis other families in the Eastern Province.[13]

Curling plainly admitted to "intermittent intercourse" with Owusi in 1907 and then again in 1908, stating that he had been experiencing grave marital difficulties with his English wife and "was lonely and very anxious to improve my knowledge of the [Adangbe] language."[14] But he steadfastly denied that he had ever had a sexual relationship with Narkoyo. In his written defense Curling recounted the circumstances under which he came to know his alleged "native wife," Narkoyo:

> I have known the girl Narkoyo since she was a little girl and indeed she carried her first load in my service. On this occasion she was ill-treated and I interposed on her behalf and I suppose earned her gratitude. She was a very intelligent child speaking four languages and she had a habit of running along just behind me and pointing to birds and things and telling me their native names.[15]

In a few short lines, Curling's Pocahontas-like narrative evoked the paternalistic ideologies used to legitimize colonialism. Couched in the language of altruistic paternalism, he constructed himself both literally and figuratively as a protective father figure who had "earned" Narkoyo's loyalty. If not for the fact that Curling tells us that Narkoyo was "a little girl," his description of her is hardly distinguishable from his characterization of Owusi, who had also been his load carrier, as a "sleeping dictionary"—a euphemism for "native" women who simultaneously provided sex and instruction in local languages and folkways to European men.[16] In depicting Narkoyo like this, Curling drew on the centuries-old narrative trope of the "helpful young native woman" to explain her value to him, while his paternalistic tone neutralized its sexual implications.[17] Curling was clearly at pains to emphasize that his interactions with Narkoyo were not sexual, but the fact that he used language instruction to justify his relationships with her and Owusi suggests that he hoped this rationale would resonate with a colonial logic that was on the wane, but perhaps still intelligible.

The long tenure of his relationship with Narkoyo was an outgrowth of the fact that two of her older brothers, Matte and Tettey, were Curling's headmen, who were responsible for choosing his hammockmen and load carriers. The brothers tended to select members of their immediate family, as well as members of the surrounding Osudoku and Kasunya communities. Although it is unclear when Curling's working relationship with Matte and Tettey began, he had been in the colony since early 1899, making his claim that Narkoyo had served as one of his regular carriers throughout her adolescence plausible. Sometime between late 1906 and early 1907, Curling "made an excessively long march" in inclement weather, during which time Narkoyo fell seriously ill with consumption in his service. From then on Curling was, in his own words, "much distressed as it seemed to me that I was responsible."[18] Consequently, he arranged for Narkoyo to be seen by Dr. Fisch of the Basel Mission, who predicted she would not live more than six months and insisted that she stop working immediately and have complete rest and good food. To this end, Curling supplied Narkoyo with thirty shillings a month.

Some months later it came to his attention that she had been "posing in the Town [Akropong] as [his] native wife," while at the same time living as the wife of a Native policeman, Arabara Berrago, in the same town.[19] Curling ordered Narkoyo to leave Akropong at once for Accra, where she could be hospitalized for her continued illness. Under the impression that she had followed his orders, he arranged for money to be distributed to her for her maintenance. Rather than go to the hospital, however, Narkoyo went to the seaside town of Ada where Curling's English wife lived and obtained money from her. After a brief stay with Mrs. Curling—who knew Narkoyo but was apparently unaware that she had been posing as her husband's "native wife"—she traveled to Apasare with Berrago, who Curling reported had "left the Police Force and was openly boasting that he had no need to work further as the white man gave his wife enough to keep him."[20] Angered by Narkoyo's behavior, Curling stopped paying for her upkeep.

Shortly thereafter Curling went on leave to England only to discover that letters soliciting money written in Narkoyo's name had been sent to his mother and aunt there. The letters appear to have resulted in part from the desperation that Narkoyo, too ill to work anymore, felt after losing Curling's financial support. Curling, however, suspected that Narkoyo's brother, T. K. Otibo, was behind both the letter-writing campaign and Narkoyo's antagonistic behavior toward him upon his return to the Gold Coast, including the row at Amedika.[21] It was precisely this probability that Curling later used to defend himself against the accusations of favoritism toward the Otibo family. As put to Colonial Secretary Bryan by Curling, "Why should I wish to favour this young man [T. K. Otibo] who was beaten by the warder, when it was he who had instigated his sister to make a vile charge against me, he who had written letters to my Mother and Aunt in England in her name asking for money on the grounds that she was my native wife?"[22]

Curling was only partially successful in defending himself against the numerous charges he faced. Apart from his alleged sexual relationships with Narkoyo and Owusi, the most serious of these charges was the "violent scene" that had supposedly taken place between Curling and Narkoyo "before a crowd of people to the prejudice of [Curling's] authority as the Commissioner of the Province."[23] The committee of inquiry formed by Governor Rodger to determine the veracity of the charges agreed that a scene had occurred, but they did not believe it was before a crowd, nor did they believe Curling hit and threatened to kill Narkoyo.[24] While the committee dismissed the public scandal charges, it ruled that there was sufficient evidence to find Curling guilty of having had "illicit intercourse" with Narkoyo, a charge that he continued to deny. Central to the committee's conclusion was the testimony of Narkoyo's uncles, Tsutsu and Amanquah Otibo. Tsutsu testified that he had come to know of Curling's relationship with Narkoyo because she had told him "that she was his concubine," a fact that was confirmed in his mind when Curling later told him that "he would no more marry Narkoyo" because she had stirred up problems for him in England.[25] The most damning evidence, however, came from Amanquah Otibo, Owusi's father, who alleged that Curling had given up Narkoyo for his daughter. In a statement given to ACP Collins, he stated in Adangbe through his interpreter:

> Owissy is a daughter of mine.... I know Mr. Curling gave up Narkoyo as his wife. After that he took another wife viz: Owissy who is my daughter. He paid head money. He paid £5. She is still his wife. Mr. Curling told me at Amedica if I wanted my daughter back

> I would have to pay back a sum of money about £7. . . . Mr. Curling paid the head money for Owissy about 4 months ago.²⁶

But Otibo later claimed in his sworn statement to the committee of inquiry that he had been misquoted and that he did not regard the money given to him as head money for Owusi, but rather as payment for load carriers.²⁷ Unbeknownst to Amanquah, however, Curling had already admitted to paying him £5 plus an additional £2 in "expenses" in order to "to keep the matter [of his intercourse with Owusi] absolutely quiet."²⁸ Thus it appears that Amanquah was amending his testimony in the hopes that it would reflect more favorably on Curling. His redaction, however, was only partial. While he asserted that Curling had not taken Owusi as his wife, he said that the commissioner had "come and asked for her i.e. he has engaged her" after he had sent Narkoyo away.²⁹

While it is difficult to determine exactly how Amanquah perceived the relationship, we know he was aware of it, and we also know that he had accepted money from Curling in exchange for his discretion. Moreover, after a long break in their relationship, Curling again took Owusi on a two-month trek, after which he sent her home with "a substantial present," perhaps suggesting to Amanquah that his interest in Owusi continued, despite the "hush" payment.³⁰ Whatever the inconsistencies in his testimony, it confirms that he believed Curling had successive relations with Narkoyo and Owusi. Yet, none of the statements made by the Otibo men suggest that they were aggrieved at Curling's relations with the two young women. Otitso Otibo, the head of the Otibo family, testified that they regarded Curling as "our big man," and this may provide a clue as to why his relations with Narkoyo and Owusi were accepted. Curling was the man who settled "all these disputes between ourselves," and as a powerful man of strategic importance to the Otibos perhaps they were amendable to granting him sexual access to the family's young women, provided he was willing to pay for it.³¹ Such a scenario would not have been altogether implausible given the ways in which compensatory transactions where matters of sexual rights were concerned "came to reflect and articulate power relations" between men elsewhere in the colony.³²

Satisfied that they had proven the existence of the relationships with Narkoyo and Owusi, the committee of inquiry decided not to investigate the remainder of the charges against Curling due to his ill health. But the process of substantiating just these two relationships was long and involved extracting multiple sworn statements from "natives" about their familiarity with the sexual arrangements of their European provincial commissioner. Nothing about this undertaking could have served the administration's purposes, and so while the decision to stop the investigation was allegedly based on Curling's ill health, we must consider the possibility that the administration decided that its probe was doing more harm to its reputation than the actual offenses being investigated. Although truncated, the inquiry revealed just how deeply involved Commissioner Curling was with the Otibo family. Even if he was truthful about not having had a sexual relationship with Narkoyo, his admitted involvement with her was clearly of an emotionally intimate nature—seemingly more intimate than the sexual relationship he had with Owusi. He was also closely tied to other members of the Otibo family whom he went out of his way to defend when he felt they were being mistreated, even after Narkoyo and her brother caused him so much grief, both in the colony and in England. Thus any bias in favor of the Otibo family Curling exhibited was more likely to have stemmed from his decade-long interactions with them rather than the brief sexual relationship he had with Owusi and possibly Narkoyo.

IGNORING THE "WHIM OF A MOST UNPOPULAR GOVERNOR"

Having already admitted to the charge of illicit intercourse with Owusi, in a series of increasingly frantic exculpatory letters Curling sought to minimize the severity of his behavior by contextualizing it in the past and present nature of sexual relations between European officers and African women in the colony. Stationed in the Gold Coast since 1899, Curling asked for leniency based on the fact that he "did not realize how completely the old order of things was changing and . . . therefore . . . did not look on the matter as seriously as [he] ought to have done."[33] Indeed, he later recounted that Governor Rodger's "undesirable relations" circular was not taken seriously by anyone; rather, he claimed that when it "was issued it was regarded as merely a new whim of a most unpopular Governor and not as having emanated from the Secretary of State."[34]

Curling argued that his relationship with Owusi was far from an anomaly by alleging that between 50 and 75 percent of European government officers engaged in sexual relations with African women. He further defended himself by suggesting that he had been far more discreet than the majority of his colleagues with regard to how they went about procuring sexual access to African women:

> I have the satisfaction of knowing that my relations to any native woman will bear favourable comparison with those of the majority

of the 75% of officials to whom I have referred. I can truthfully say that no one has ever seen a native woman coming to or going from my house or in or about it. That in this way I have never brought a suggestion of discredit on my name and I have been strongly opposed to the prevalent and dangerous habit of sending one's boy to bring in a native woman when required.[35]

Although Curling denied using his male domestics to procure "native women," he conveniently overlooked the fact that he had no need to "send" for women since he already had ready access to his female load carriers, who were supplied to him by his headmen. Nonetheless, in referring to the "prevalent" use of male servants, Curling confirmed a point already made by Marcus Clarke: these kinds of sexual arrangements were frequently brokered by "native" subordinates who were intimately familiar with the private lives and sexual desires of European officers. These relationships were thus always already part of wider networks of cross-racial knowledge and affiliation, what Heike Schmidt calls the "shared spaces" of colonial life worlds, thereby increasing their visibility and potentially their liability to European government officers like Commissioner Curling who participated in them.[36]

As proof of his good moral standing in the wider African and European communities, Curling claimed to be "received as a personal friend at every mission house in my Province and I enjoy the confidence of my Chiefs."[37] Moreover, he vehemently denied the accusation that his relationship with Owusi had affected his judicial and administrative work, describing the claim as "a dastardly attack" on his record of service. Curling's line of defense employed the administration's own rhetoric about the threat posed to the reputation of the colonial service, and consequently its administrative efficiency, when the sexual affairs of its officers resulted in public scandals. Completely missing the point that Rodger's circular was aimed at preventing European officers from being diminished in the eyes of Africans, Curling claimed that he had not been "openly immoral"—meaning he hid his indiscretions from Europeans—and as a result had not blemished his or the service's reputation. It was only after ACP Collins took it upon himself to investigate his private life, contended Curling, that anyone but Owusi and her immediate relatives "had the faintest knowledge that any relationship existed between us." He therefore could not see why he was "selected to appear as the scapegoat of this large section of the community [the 50 to 75 percent of European officers who regularly had sexual relations with African women]."[38]

Unwilling to be the fall guy for the rest of his colleagues, Curling was quick to peel the covers off their private affairs. The first to be exposed was

Dr. Palmer, whom Curling held personally responsible for prompting ACP Collins to investigate the nature of his relationship with the Otibos.[39] In justifying his countercharge of sexual misconduct against Palmer, Curling argued that he was "compelled in self defence to take advantage of the precedent so created . . . and lodge a similar complaint against Dr. Palmer who is keeping a girl of the Lutterodt family at Akuse, and [against] numbers of [other] persons in the Colony. For an isolated case when brought to light stands revealed to the glare of public gaze but when surrounded by numerous companions shares only divided attention."[40] His charge against Dr. Palmer was duly investigated and found to be true. Cornered, Palmer admitted that from May to August 1908, he had "occasional intimate relations with a native woman for personal hygienic reasons in a quite seemly way which I considered at the time brought no disrepute to the Public Service and do not think in my particular case ever has; I have since discontinued the practice."[41] Palmer's rationale tapped into prevailing ideas about the adverse health consequences of sexual abstinence on the part of young men—an argument that might have seemed particularly credible coming from a doctor.[42] Moreover, in emphasizing his discretion, Palmer recognized that the best exculpatory strategy was not to refute the existence of the sexual relationship, but rather to deny that it had brought shame on the administration. Thus, Palmer sought to show that his modus operandi had been in keeping with the spirit of the government's recently articulated concerns over "undesirable relations with Native women," even if he had not strictly abided by the new directive.

In his dispatch to the Colonial Office regarding the Curling and Palmer cases, Governor Rodger argued for leniency. Although Rodger acknowledged that Curling, "as a married man and the chief administrative officer, was specially bound to set a good example in the Eastern Province," he and the Executive Council agreed that mitigation of punishment was warranted on several grounds: "(i) His long and good service; (ii) The former general laxity of relations with native women in West Africa; (iii) The fact that this is the first case dealt with officially since the 1907 Circular was issued."[43] In raising the third point in favor of leniency, Rodger conveniently ignored the fact that Marcus Clarke's case had already been dealt with vis-à-vis his 1907 circular. For our purposes here, however, the second mitigating factor was the most significant because it acknowledged just how at odds the circular was with the sexual practices of European officers as conditioned by the weight of history. With these considerations in mind, Rodger asked that Curling be reduced from the rank of a provincial commissioner to that of a traveling commissioner, with a commensurate salary reduction of £150 as well as a £30 reduction in duty allowance, and that he be transferred to either Asante or the Northern Territories.[44] Most importantly, he did not call for Curling's resignation or dismissal.

As for Dr. Palmer, Governor Rodger found that his case was "a far less aggravated one than that of Mr. Curling" because he was unmarried and had "lived in concubinage with a girl unconnected with the District he was temporarily in administrative charge of." As a result, he recommended that Palmer lose one year's seniority, in addition to being officially censured.[45] Although little is known about the Lutterodt woman Palmer admitted to having had a sexual relationship with, her surname indicates that she was likely a descendant of the once-prominent Afro-Danish Christiansborg (Osu, Accra) merchant family bearing that name. If true, this may help to contextualize her participation in the relationship. Marriages, as well as less formal unions, between European men and local women had for centuries been an integral feature of Christiansborg's trade-based social economy. In the same way that Rodger recognized that history had conditioned officers to think of these relationships as acceptable, many Gold Coasters surely continued to see them in the same way, especially those who hailed from areas where these relationships had a long and concentrated history. Perhaps this Lutterodt woman, or her family, hoped that her relationship with the young British medical officer would materialize into something more permanent, reviving a tradition that had been central to the family's formation. If so, they misapprehended not only Palmer's intentions, or were deceived by him, but also how radically different this new colonial dispensation was from the bygone era of their ancestors.

In both the Palmer and the Curling cases the Colonial Office rejected Governor Rodger's recommendations in favor of harsher penalties. Having just issued his own anticoncubinage circular a few months earlier, Lord Crewe was hardly in a position to act leniently. He ordered Curling's dismissal in light of his influential position in the colony's government and his disregard for Rodger's "undesirable relations" circular. But in view of his long and good service Lord Crewe granted him a compassionate allowance equal to the pension he had earned. Dr. Palmer was allowed to remain in the service, but he was "very severely reprimanded" and lost two years' seniority.[46]

Angered by the disciplinary actions taken against him, Curling soon made good on his threat to reveal more than just Palmer's indiscretions by detailing other cases involving European officers' relationships with African women. Striking close to the pinnacle of power, he accused Governor Rodger's former aide-de-camp, Captain Heincks, of keeping a woman named Abba. Giving some historical depth to his claims about the widespread practice of "keeping" local women, Curling disclosed that Abba was the daughter of a Christiansborg woman named Barkor, who had been the "native wife" of Williams Taylor, a British officer, during his first tour. On his second tour Taylor was said to have kept an Adangbe woman.[47] A previous acting governor openly kept a "native woman" at Accra and "talked freely of her to his subordinates," including Curling.[48] Curling then accused a sitting member of the Executive Council, whom he further identified as a member of the committee of inquiry investigating the charges against him, of having several children by a "native woman." The man in question was Charles Riby Williams, treasurer of the colony and progenitor of the sizable Ghanaian family that today bears his name.[49] Riby Williams was one of the most prominent and long-serving government officers in the colony at the time. Having served there since at least 1884, Riby Williams started his career at a time when cohabitation with local women was not prohibited, even though it was by and large no longer publicly legitimized through marriage. Almost a quarter of a century later such relations were not only officially prohibited, they were the subject of disciplinary proceedings. One can only imagine what an awkward and potentially explosive position Riby Williams was put in when called upon to serve as a member of the committee of inquiry looking into the charges against Curling. Perhaps his presence on the committee helps to explain its decision to curtail the investigation, as well as the more lenient disciplinary action the local colonial government recommended.

In a final blow, Curling returned to the blatant disregard of Rodger's apparently impotent "undesirable relations" circular:

> That the custom was not stopped by the issue of the Circular is evidenced by the fact that Captain Scovell, the Governor's present A.D.C. [aide-de-camp] kept a woman named Tawia during both his tours of service. This woman belongs to the Christiansborg Mantshe's quarter and is a daughter of one Christian Quist. The A.D.C.'s quarters are within a stones throw of the Castle. I have quoted these two officers [Heincks and Scovell] in particular as being most intimately associated with the Governor's person and also because not being Civil Servants they will not be injured by my so doing but they by no means stand alone in Accra. I know of one official who has just had a child by a native woman. I know of another who keeps two. And since the issue of the circular I have

known officials senior to myself who expected their priests to sit at the same table with a native woman.⁵⁰

Curling's numerous references to liaisons between British colonial officials and African women served to reinforce his claim that his relationship with Owusi was part and parcel of a much longer tradition in the Gold Coast of European men "keeping" local women—a tradition that Rodger's circular had clearly not stopped. His disclosures about his well-placed European colleagues also worked to establish that participation in these relationships was not limited to the rank and file of the colonial service; rather, men employed in prestigious positions, including acting governors, aides-de-camp to the governor, treasurers, and Executive Council members, were all actively engaged in relations with African women. Indeed, Curling's and Palmer's respective positions as provincial commissioner and physician in the West African Medical Service demonstrate that these relationships were pervasive across the administrative ranks. As such, Curling was able to position himself as one of many distinguished men who had failed to realize that their relationships with African women were no longer congruent with the racial and sexual politics of the new colonial order, or, to be more precise, he had failed to realize that the "new whim of a most unpopular governor" might actually constitute a new order.

Curling continued to argue that leniency was also warranted on the grounds that he lived "the lonely existence of a man in the bush," in contrast to officers stationed in Accra, "where society and every amusement can be got."⁵¹ Seeking to minimize the potential harm done by his relationship with Owusi, he claimed that he had kept her only "while completely away from other Europeans" during a two-month trek when he knew he would be "lonely and also very anxious to improve my knowledge of the language."⁵² Thus he perceived that a public scandal was contingent upon Europeans, rather than Africans, discovering the existence of the relationship. The Colonial Office rejected his rationale:

> Mr. Curling . . . denies that he brought discredit on himself or weakened his authority or brought his office into disrepute. He did not, he says keep her openly. . . . I presume he means no white fellow officer knew that he kept her.
> It is obvious that the native father and his relations knew, and probably most of the natives knew. His circuit carrier and followers knew and if to keep a native concubine lowers the position of a Commissioner—and the view we hold and are bound to hold as

persons possessing common sense and as responsible for the administration of a Crown Colony is and must be that it does—Mr. Curling's answer is no defense at all.[53]

In a series of file minutes, Whitehall advisers fretted that whatever harm had been done locally to the administration's reputation would pale in comparison to the international scandal if word leaked out. If Narkoyo and her brother were clever enough to solicit Curling's relations in England, it would not be long before they and others began writing to major British newspapers like the *Times* and the *Spectator* to air the colonial service's dirty laundry for all to see. Lamenting the likelihood of this practice becoming widespread, long-serving principal clerk Terence Macnaghten said he had "no doubt that what these papers [regarding the Curling case] establish pretty clearly with regards to the Gold Coast is equally true as regards Sierra Leone and the Nigerias; and it seems almost certain that there will be very unpleasant public revelations on the subject some day soon."[54] These fears were not without precedent—as we shall see in the next chapter—recent events in Kenya had already put colonial officers' sexual misdeeds in the national headlines and on the floor of the British Parliament.

In order to keep a tight lid on Curling's salacious accusations against his colleagues, the Colonial Office did not investigate any of the additional charges he made. It did, however, notify Governor Rodger of Curling's claims against his aides-de-camp, Captains Scovell and Heincks. Heincks had already retired; however, Scovell was still employed by the governor. As Rodger's personal employee rather than an employee of the colonial state, Scovell was not governed by the same set of colonial regulations, including the "undesirable relations" circular, as were European officers. Thus, Scovell's fate was in Rodger's hands, not the Colonial Office's. Scovell was unsuccessful in convincing Governor Rodger that he should not be fired for his admitted intercourse with "native women," but his exculpatory strategy warrants further examination because it underscored the circular's limitations and exemplified the loophole created by its focus on concubinage.

Scovell denied that he had "kept a native woman in the ordinary sense of the word." Rather, he admitted to having "had occasional sexual intercourse with one or more women."[55] In making a distinction between "keeping a woman," a euphemism for concubinage, and casual intercourse with different women, Scovell tapped into the categorical ambiguity of these arrangements. When did occasional illicit acts become habitual? When did habitual intercourse become concubinage? A continuum like this did not lend itself to easy distinctions, a fact that other officers would later try to exploit. Scovell also argued that as the personal employee of the governor, his intercourse with African women did not constitute an official offense.[56] This line of defense highlights the circular's major limitation: it had the power to police sexual relations only between African women and European government officers; traders and other privately employed Europeans were not bound by it. But, as Scovell's fate shows this did not mean that they were free from regulation or censure by their private employers.

The Colonial Office plainly admitted that if investigated the bulk of Curling's charges would be proven true. File minutes attached to Curling's letters offer revealing insight into the Colonial Office's assumptions about the sexual habits of its officers. Responding to Curling's allegations, Alexander Fiddian, now in his second decade at the Colonial Office, expressed little surprise at the nature of his claims:

> I am afraid that this kind of letter is just what may be expected in future. It is natural for a certain type of man who has been visited with what he feels is a disproportionate punishment for a common offence to bring railing accusations of this character. The worst of it is that his specific charges would very likely prove to be true if they were thoroughly sifted, which I hope they will not be.[57]

Seconding Fiddian, another Colonial Office adviser acknowledged the prevalence of such relations among the majority of officers in the African colonies and insisted that the administration avoid vigilantism:

> I earnestly trust that we shall take no notice whatever of "informations" of this kind in future. From what I have heard I believe that if we were to investigate the private life of every officer in the West and East African service we should find that from one half to two thirds of them had sexual relations with native women from time to time. To attempt such an investigation would create an intolerable situation.

A final minute noted, "We should sympathize more with Mr. Curling in his troubles if he refrained from mentioning the names of other officers."[58] Collectively, these comments suggest that more troubling than the accusations themselves was the fact that Curling had made them at all. In short, infrequent sex with African women was expected and could be overlooked if not too egregious or scandal-provoking; gratuitously revealing the sexual affairs of a brother officer could not. Disgruntled European officers like

Curling were not alone, however, in bringing sexual misconduct charges against their colleagues, Native officers did too.

THE F. W. GREIG CASE: REVENGE OR LEGITIMATE GRIEVANCE?

In November 1908 Mr. J. M. Robertson, a Native timekeeper employed at Makongo, in the southern fringe of the Northern Territories, accused his European boss, Mr. F. W. Greig, assistant surveyor of roads, of stealing away his junior wife, Ambah. In a letter to the governor's office, Robertson recounted how Greig "very often troubled and pressed hard on me, to allow my wife to sleep with him," even offering him an incentive of £1 a month for sexual access to Ambah. When he refused the offer, Greig allegedly bypassed him altogether by "frequently send[ing] his cook to my wife, conversing with her, and coaxed her, with money, meat and soft bread."[59] In the face of his continued objections, Greig dismissed Robertson from his job, after which he returned with Ambah to the town of Atebubu, just south of Makongo, where they had previously lived. But this, according to Robertson, did not bring an end to the story.

Shortly thereafter Ambah ran away to Greig, who was now in the town of Prang on the border of Asante. Robertson suspected Greig of secretly agreeing with Ambah to have her join him there. He dispatched a messenger to Greig, demanding the return of his wife, but Greig allegedly refused. According to Robertson, "Without knowing that [Greig] had already had a connection with her at Makongo," he traveled in person to Prang to get Ambah back himself, but the operation failed when Greig "took [Ambah] by force from [his] hand." Robertson contended that Greig "kept [Ambah] with him at Prang 16 days good, and satisfied himself with her."[60]

Outraged by Greig's behavior, but seemingly powerless to stop it by himself, Robertson relayed all of his complaints in person to the Salaga district commissioner, Mr. Berney. Much to Robertson's chagrin, Berney responded by declaring Ambah "free and no longer a slave of Mr. Robertson."[61] While Berney gave Ambah permission to proceed anywhere in the territory she liked, he forbade her to return to Greig.[62] It appears, however, that she did return to him, this time at the government station at Yeji, some distance to the northeast of Prang, where Robertson tried once again to get her back. Although what happened next is unclear, it appears that in the course of trying to regain possession of Ambah, Robertson was jailed by Berney for using force against her. Indeed, Robertson might very well have written his letter to the governor's office detailing these events from his jail cell.

After recounting what had transpired between Ambah, Greig, and himself, Robertson concluded his letter by explaining why he was so aggrieved by the whole affair.

According to his letter, Robertson had invested twenty years in raising his wife, Ambah, who as a four-year-old child had been captured alongside her mother in "Sammore's [sic] war." Ambah and her mother were Dagarti, a northern ethnic group, to which Robertson's first wife also evidently belonged. It was at his wife's behest, he claimed, that he redeemed them from slavery, probably around the late 1880s or early 1890s, when Samori Touré's armies were indeed actively involved in warfare as they attempted to repel French advances. When Ambah's mother died, he took it upon himself to "train her up," and "when she grew fine," said Robertson, "I took her as a wife." Greig, he claimed, knew all of this and still had the nerve to "try his best to run the risk of getting my wife out of my hand to set free, and get chance of her as a wife." He staunchly defended his right to Ambah, saying, "I was not guilty of any crime in my complaint . . . against Mr. Greig, which can cause my wife to be taken away from my hand, to allow Mr. Greig the free chance at her." Robertson then asked, "Is it lawful, that Mr. Greig can take advantage of a poor Blackman, to entice and coax his wife and take her away from him, whilst I am under him as a clerk?"[63]

Returning to Greig's misdeeds, Robertson claimed that he had also "enticed another woman from Yeji, by name of Akoshua Addais, the wife of a certain water policeman, by name of Quablah, who left his wife behind at Yeji, and went on duty at another station."[64] Having levied this final charge, Robertson concluded by making it clear that Greig was taking advantage of his superior position in the colony's racial and administrative hierarchies, as well as his remote location in the Northern Territories, to have his way with the wives of his African subordinates: "Mr. Greig's station is in the field alone, far from any white man to witness the conduct and the bad treatment to the blackmen here and report him. I therefore humbly beg and submit that your honour may be pleased to call his attention to Mr. Greig, and check him in a way that all the labourers under him will not feel discouragement in the discharging of their duty to the satisfaction of the Government."[65] Robertson's closing remarks invoked the threat posed to administrative efficiency by Greig's immoral behavior and in this way echoed the very concerns raised by Governor Rodger in his circular. But he also invoked race as an enabler of Greig's behavior by emphasizing how his own identity and that of Greig's other Native subordinates as "blackmen," in tandem with Greig's racial seclusion from other white men, had empowered him to wantonly abuse his power as a white supervisor.

Although Robertson framed himself as a "poor Blackman" to emphasize his abuse at Greig's hands, there are a number of speculative observations that clue us into who Robertson was. First, he was employed as a timekeeper, considered a skilled position, but one that colonial administrators argued ought to be filled by trained Africans "to avoid the expense of excessive European skilled labour."[66] Given that ethnicity was closely linked to labor hierarchies, Robertson was likely from the coastal zone or Asante, from where the colony drew the vast majority of its skilled workers, while the Northern Territories and adjacent French colonies supplied most of the unskilled manual labor required for the colony's development projects, such as road and railway construction.[67] Since many Gold Coasters adopted Christian or otherwise-Anglicized names, the surname Robertson does not necessarily indicate a European ancestor, but it is indicative of the culturally hybrid character of the growing numbers of educated men who were joining the ranks of the clerical staff of the colonial administration. All of this may help to account for why Robertson, despite describing himself as a "poor Blackman," felt empowered enough to bring such explosive charges against his European supervisor.

If there are only a handful of clues about Robertson's identity, there are even fewer about Ambah's. Yet, we do know that at the very least she was taken at a young age as a war captive, alongside her mother, during a time of great upheaval as Samori Touré's army resisted French occupation. We also know that not long after she was "redeemed" from slavery her mother died, making her an orphan in the care of Robertson and his Dagarti wife. By his own admission, Robertson was grooming Ambah for the role of his junior wife when she came of age. Thus she was completely without kin in a society dominated by kin networks and attached to a man who had earmarked her, as a very young girl, as his future wife and sexual property. Given the frequency of child marriages, in which very young girls were betrothed to older men with the marriage being consummated after menstruation and the performance of nubility rights, Robertson's actions were not without precedent, but it was unusual for husbands to actually raise their wives — most men rendered support to the mothers of their child brides.[68] What this meant for Ambah was that the possibility she might have a say in her marital prospects was foreclosed and in the context of her relationship with Robertson she had to transition from being like his child to being his wife.

Upon receipt of Robertson's letter, Governor Rodger quickly forwarded it to the chief commissioner of the Northern Territories, Lieutenant Colonel A. E. Watherston, for immediate investigation. Watherston subsequently reported that although Greig admitted to the charge of having sexual relations with Akoshua Addais, he was innocent of the charge of having kept Ambah. The guilty parties, according to Watherston, were Robertson and Ambah. Denying the legitimacy of their marital union by referring to Ambah as Robertson's "concubine," Watherston accused them of working as a team to lure men into sex for monetary compensation: "The girl has been in the habit of going with linesmen and clerks, and Mr. Robertson then steps in, and demands money as blackmail."[69] As proof of this allegation, Watherston noted that the Yeji District Office clerk, Mr. J. A. Robinson, had previously written to Mr. Greig asking him "to keep Ambah away from his linesmen, as Robertson was making trouble with them after allowing them to have connection with his wife."[70] Robinson had, in fact, not only accused Ambah and Robertson of getting up to this in Yeji, but also in Atebubu, leading him to conclude that Robertson "generally sets his wife as a trap for people's destruction . . . which is unfair."[71] Thus, multiple sources concurred that Robertson was using the system of adultery compensation to financially profit from his wife's sexuality. The abuse of this system for bald profit was hardly unique to Robertson; rather, it had already come to constitute a much wider phenomenon documented as early 1883 by the queen's advocate who noted that it was rife throughout the colony.[72]

If the claim against Robertson was correct, F. W. Greig was one of many men who had been targeted by the timekeeper. This raises some interesting questions about how the mechanics of adultery compensation might have been reconfigured by the integration of Europeans into the system. Compensation in adultery cases was determined by the rank of the offended husband, with larger payments made to men of high rank, and much smaller payments made to commoners.[73] Robertson typically targeted men to whom he would have been superior in terms of administrative standing, education, and class background. As such, Robertson would have been well placed to demand more than just the "small compensation" paid when such offenses were between commoners.[74] Still, an African linesman's humble salary must have put a cap on how much someone like Robertson could profit from the system, but what about well-paid European officers? Was Robertson inverting the system of adultery compensation—which had already shown itself to be quite malleable—such that the amount payable could be determined by the rank and salary of the European offender, rather than by the rank of the offended African husband? If the system of adultery compensation created room for powerful men to "flaunt their ability to pay for misdemeanours as marks of wealth and position," perhaps Robertson (mis)calculated that Greig would welcome the chance to pay handsomely for his alleged dalliance with Ambah and in the process not only satisfy himself sexually, but also reinscribe his power over Robertson.⁷⁵ Although without clear answers, these questions are important nonetheless because they remind us that Gold Coasters also had recourse to their own systems of sexual regulation as they sought to control and/or profit from European men's sexual access to African women.

Colonial officials characterized Ambah as a willing participant in this scheme, but given the imbalance of power between her and Robertson, it seems far more likely that she was a victim of his exploitative practices—especially when we recall that she was kinless. Her possible victimization at the hands of Robertson might help to explain why she left him on several occasions for Greig. Did she perceive that she could use her purported relationship with Greig to sever her ties with Robertson and regain control over her own sexuality? What role did Mr. Berney's "freeing" Ambah from Robertson play in her understanding of her status with Robertson and other potential male partners? That she followed Greig on more than one occasion—something that multiple witnesses agreed upon—suggests that she saw the relationship with him as presenting enough benefits, whether emotional or material, to warrant severing her ties with Robertson, despite having been associated with him for the previous twenty years. While the exclusion of Ambah's voice from the historical record makes it difficult to answer these questions with certainty, we can at least read her actions as indicating that she was making decisions for herself in what she perceived as her best interest. Moreover, her actions suggest that she was using the domain of interracial sexual relations as a space to contest her gendered and generational subordination to Robertson, which was not buttressed in ways that we have come to expect by colonialism's gendered hierarchy. Indeed, Mr. Berney's intervention served to undermine rather than bolster Robertson's patriarchal authority over her. Thus, while Anne McClintock rightly points out that "colonized women had to negotiate not only the imbalances of their relations with their own men but also the baroque and violent array of hierarchal rules and restrictions that structured their new relations with imperial men," we must not close the possibility that colonized women could use their relations with colonizing men to challenge their subordination to colonized men.⁷⁶

In the end Watherston concluded, "There was no evidence that connects Mr. Greig with any of the charges made by Mr. Robertson as far as the girl Ambah is concerned," although he offered no explanation as to why she had followed him over a fairly wide swathe of territory.⁷⁷ The charges, he said, had been made out of spite against Greig after he had dismissed Robertson for workplace "irregularities." Mitigating Greig's admitted affair with Akoshua Addais, in Watherston's opinion, was the fact that Greig had never seen Rodger's "undesirable relations" circular. The director of public works, Mr. Wilkinson, confirmed that the circular had been distributed in 1907 to all European members of the department, but there was "no record of it being sent to the officers engaged last year."[78] Having pointed out to Greig "the derogatory position he puts himself in, by interfering with native subordinates' wives," Watherston was convinced that the "present charges will bring home to him the undesirability and danger of continuing such practices." Therefore, he urged the governor to "take into consideration his good work, and give him another chance."[79] Persuaded by the facts before him, Governor Rodger once again asked for a lenient punishment by requesting the secretary of state to censure Greig, while allowing him to complete his second tour of duty. Lord Crewe concurred, but added that Greig "will of course not be re-engaged on the expiration of his agreement."[80] In this way, despite having most of his charges dismissed, Robertson was successful in having some measure of punishment exacted against Greig.

The extent to which Robertson's allegations were true or not does not detract from the point that he was unwilling to quietly accept being confined to his subordinate position within the hierarchy of colonial officialdom. In order to redress his grievances, whether stemming from having been fired by Greig or from Greig's actions toward Ambah, Robertson skillfully represented Greig's behavior as an egregious abuse of official position — precisely the kind of abuse that colonial authorities identified as destroying an officer's ability to discharge his official duties because it engendered jealousy and anger and lowered an officer's prestige. Adding an additional layer of complexity to his charges, Robertson argued that Greig was using his elevated position in the colony's racial hierarchy to steal Ambah from him. Even if only partially successful in substantiating his claims, the fact that he went to the authorities at all suggests that he thought he had some chance of turning the tables on his administrative superior.

CONCLUSION

The Curling and Palmer cases demonstrate how personal and professional animus between European officers, and in the Greig case between a European officer and his Native subordinate, were expressed through the levying of sexual misconduct charges precisely because they had attained unprecedented currency in the wake of Rodger's "undesirable relations" circular. The Curling case also offers a particularly dramatic example of how sexual relationships between European government officers and African women were often an outcome of other kinds of cross-racial intimacies and dependencies that characterized the lives of European officers and the African communities they lived and worked among.

While the ban on concubinage came into force partly because Governor Rodger feared that European government officers were abusing their official power to procure sexual relationships with "native" women, these cases also reveal that Africans had their own strategies for wielding power through these relationships, their knowledge of them, or simply their awareness that such relations were now officially prohibited. In reflecting on Greig's case in the spring of 1909, one of Lord Crewe's advisers remarked that "the chief lesson to be drawn from this case is the great danger of encouraging blackmailers if we insist too strictly upon absolute continence in the relations between Europeans and native women."[81] As will be demonstrated in the next chapter, this remark was an early indication of the Colonial Office's realization that its own circular against concubinage, which it had issued just a few months months earlier, would have subversive and unintended consequences. Thus, the Gold Coast cases considered in this chapter provided the Colonial Office with an almost immediate sense of what it could expect as a result of its own efforts to stamp out concubinage. It is to this circular and the wave of disciplinary cases it spawned that we now turn.

4 ~ The Crewe Circular
The Life and Death of a Policy on Interracial Concubinage

JUST AS THE CURLING, PALMER, AND GREIG cases were coming to light in the Gold Coast, events across the continent in the East African Protectorate (Kenya) were similarly forcing administrators there to address scandalous allegations about the sexual affairs of British government officers. In February 1908 an altercation occurred between Hubert Silberrad, an assistant district commissioner, and an *askari* named Mgulla who served under him.[1] The confrontation between the two men was precipitated by Silberrad's cohabitation with three "native women" or "girls," as they were variously called, one of whom Mgulla had also been romantically involved with. Incensed that Nyakayne, the young woman in question, was now living with Silberrad, Mgulla entered the commissioner's compound in Nyeri to rebuke him for stealing her away. Silberrad was so outraged by the affront to his position that he locked Mgulla up in the guardroom and kept him there overnight. The next morning he sent both Mgulla and Nyakayne away. Unfortunately for Silberrad, his neighbors were William Scoresby and Katherine Routledge, British ethnographers who were studying the Kikuyu and had taken a vested interest in the colonial administration's so-called "native policy." As soon as the couple got wind of the altercation between Silberrad and Mgulla, Mrs. Routledge turned up at the commissioner's compound and demanded that he hand over the two remaining girls he was cohabitating with, which he did at once.

Mr. Routledge promptly wrote to the colony's governor, Colonel J. Hayes Sadler, about the incident and requested that Silberrad be removed from Nyeri "as a sign that the Government wishes all natives to see that an official who acts thus does not do so with the approval of the Government."[2] After cautioning Governor Sadler against viewing Silberrad's relations with the "girls" as an isolated incident, he urged him to consider what steps could be taken to ensure that all government officers were "best made to see that intercourse with native girls is associated with evils that seriously detract from their position as administrators."[3] Although Sadler responded by issuing a local circular condemning concubinage, when the government's course of disciplinary action against Silberrad failed to meet with the Routledges' approval, they went public with their concerns.[4] The entire affair snowballed and ultimately landed on the pages of the British press and on the floor of the British Parliament.[5]

With the attention of the British government and public focused on the sexual misdeeds of British officers in the colonies, the Colonial Office took action despite its own expressed disinterest in pursuing these kinds of charges. After extensive consultation and following the precedents set by Governor Rodger in 1907 and Governor Sadler in 1908, it decided to "impress upon members of the whole Colonial Service that such actions [concubinage], all questions of morals apart, are damaging to the public service, and that the gravest consequences must follow from conduct unworthy of a servant of the crown."[6] On 11 January 1909, the secretary of state for the colonies, Lord Crewe, issued a circular prohibiting concubinage between British government officers and "native" women and girls on the grounds that it was "both injurious and dangerous to the public service."[7] Governors and leading officials were instructed by Lord Crewe to "spare no effort to diminish these abuses where they may be found still to exist," and to this end they were "to rely upon the assistance of the senior officers of the districts in which instances of such misconduct may possibly occur." In conjunction with this mandate, senior district officers were empowered, "whenever an instance of [such] conduct . . . comes to their notice, to make it the subject of official action."[8]

In his study of Lord Crewe's 1909 circular, historian Ronald Hyam contends that the decisive factor leading British authorities to take a "hard line on concubinage" was "metropolitan puritanical insistence, backed by bureaucratic preoccupation with preserving racial prestige and social distance," rather than "African demand for it."[9] Hyam's emphasis on metropolitan demand entirely overlooks the leading role that local governments in the colonies, as well as African interests, played in the circular's issue. The very fact that governors Rodger and Sadler issued anticoncubinage circulars in 1907 and 1908, respectively, without seeking the Colonial Office's approval, indicates that the desire to bring interracial concubinage to an end was not simply a matter of "metropolitan puritanical insistence," but rather also reflected local colonial concerns that were marked by a desire to preserve racial prestige and social distance as a way of ensuring administrative efficiency. Others have claimed "the factors that prompted [the circular] were entirely specific" to the Silberrad case in Kenya, but Whitehall advisers were already well aware that these "factors" were a problem elsewhere in the African colonies.[10] Indeed, by the time they drafted the Crewe Circular they not only had a copy of Rodger's 1907 circular in hand, they had also already taken ad-hoc disciplinary action against officers who had caused public scandals as a result of their relations with African women. As such, the Silberrad case represents a tipping point in favor of an official policy against concubinage, rather than its *raison d'être*.

The claim that there was no "African demand" for a policy against interracial concubinage needs reevaluation as well. As early as 1902, sporadic commentary began appearing in the African-owned *Gold Coast Leader* calling for "moral sanitation" among the growing numbers of white men who were coming to the colony. The mining boom at the turn of the century had occasioned "a large influx of male whites of loose and indiscriminate morals into the Colony," lamented one Gold Coast writer, who warned that these men were "an evil and a danger . . . that menaces the people of this country, even at the present moment." He therefore urged the government to attend to the spiritual and moral salvation of the white enclaves in the country. Elsewhere in the paper Africans were cautioned against "selling" their "young, tender, pure virgins to dissolute Europeans," and others similarly complained that marriages between black women and white men in West Africa were "putting a premium on immorality."[11] Although these commentaries were not specific to European government officers, they suggest that metropolitan bureaucrats were neither first nor alone in identifying interracial sexual relations between white men and African women as a festering moral problem. And as we have just seen, the case that most directly spawned Lord Crewe's 1909 circular was triggered by the anger of Mgulla, an African policeman, who believed his European supervisor had stolen away his lover. It appears, moreover, that Mgulla was not the only African upset by Silberrad's behavior—the chief of the nearby village that was home to the three young women Silberrad "kept," had also complained to the Routledges about Silberrad's wantonness actions.[12]

Thus, there is compelling evidence to suggest that a growing number of Africans would have welcomed the ban on interracial concubinage, as well as the mechanisms created by the circulars to redress their grievances. This was something that local and metropolitan colonial authorities explicitly recognized when they acknowledged that interracial concubinage caused "ill-feelings and jealousy" and "serious trouble among native populations," even if they never bothered to consult with Africans prior to the release of the circulars. Hence, the 1909 circular not only fell in line with local colonial policy in the Gold Coast and Kenya, it was also in consonance with an increasingly vocal strain of African opinion that advocated for an end to such abuses. Scholars have tended to more easily recognize how colonial regimes came to regard interracial sexual relations as threatening especially in relation to white prestige, but in the first decades of the twentieth century an increasingly strident group of Africans also began to voice their anxieties in ways that positioned these relations as a threat to their own racial respectability.

While "African demand" must be factored into any assessment of the origins of the 1909 circular, it was the actions of Africans—particularly the ways they manipulated the ban on concubinage to advance their own agendas—that led to the Colonial Office's decision in 1924 to let the circular quietly be forgotten, and then ten years later, in 1934, to officially discontinue its distribution. Thus the circular came equipped with a set of unintended consequences that led to its official end. This chapter goes behind the scenes at the Colonial Office as its advisers deliberated and debated the terms and parameters of the circular. Rather than a ready-made, one-size-fits-all response to the Silberrad controversy in Kenya, the Crewe Circular was formulated in ways that grappled with the diversity and complex social terrain that characterized the British Empire. Hitherto obscured by the fact that the circular has rarely been assessed in a meaningful way beyond its immediate origins in Kenya, this chapter also explores the significant role the Gold Coast played in the life span of the Crewe Circular.

FORMULATING THE CREWE CIRCULAR

The crisp language that the Colonial Office finally delivered its anticoncubinage decree in belies the tedious process that culminated in the Crewe Circular. What kinds of interracial sexual relations should the circular prohibit? What was the appropriate terminology to describe government officers? Where in the British Empire was the circular needed? Far from being settled matters these questions provoked considerable debate among Whitehall advisers who were also charged with deciding how to convey the new regulation to currently employed officers and to future recruits, a problem they solved by issuing two different versions of the circular. Circular A was to be given to "all British officers who in future enter the service of any of the Colonies or Protectorates in which such practices have existed or may still exist at the time when they enter upon their duties," while Circular B was to "be similarly communicated to all British officers at present in the service in those Colonies and Protectorates." Of the two, Circular A was purposely designed to contain the strongest admonition against concubinage so as to make absolutely clear to new recruits the dangers associated with such relations. Finding it unnecessary to dwell on the widely recognized "moral objections to such conduct," the circular's architects emphasized the adverse effects concubinage had on "good administration":

> Gravely improper conduct of this nature has at times been the cause of serious trouble among native populations, and must be strenuously condemned on that account; but an objection even more serious from the standpoint of the Government lies in the fact that is not possible for any member of the administration to countenance such practices without lowering himself in the eyes of the natives, and diminishing his authority to an extent which will seriously impair his capacity for useful work in the Service in which it is his duty to strive to set an honourable example to all with whom he comes in contact.[13]

So as not to impugn the character of incoming officers, but to warn them nonetheless of their fate should they disregard its warning, the circular ended with Lord Crewe stating he was "anxious to make clear that this circular is not intended to cast any reflection upon those who are about to be admitted into the ranks of an honourable profession. Its object is simply to advise those who enter the service of a danger in their path, and to warn them of the disgrace and official ruin which will certainly follow from any dereliction of duty in this respect."[14]

The somewhat shorter Circular B was written such that it politely assumed its recipients shared the same concerns as the Colonial Office regarding the ill effects of concubinage. Accordingly, it encouraged currently employed officers to voice their condemnation of such practices rather than warning against them. Harnessing the power of reverse psychology, Lord Crewe wrote:

> I will not for a moment believe that such practices receive anything but the gravest condemnation from the members of the Service. Their admirable work and excellent conduct are fully appreciated by His Majesty's Government, and I feel sure that this Circular will be accepted by the Service as an appeal for loyal co-operation in vigorously reprobating and officially condemning all such cases of concubinage between Civil Servants and native women whenever and wherever they are detected.[15]

Thus, whereas Circular A made clear that engaging in concubinage would result in "official ruin," Circular B made no such warning. However, in cases where Circular B's more optimistic tone was not regarded as sufficiently driving the point home, senior officers were authorized to use their discretion to issue Circular A to "officers already in the service" who needed "an additional warning." So as not to be constrained by technicalities related to which circular was received by whom, Crewe added a clause that stipulated, "It will . . . be understood that summary punishment for offences of this character may at any time be applied to individual officers, irrespective of whether that Circular [Circular A] has or has not been issued to them, should the facts show such action to be necessary."[16]

In the copious minutes that preceded the final drafting of Circulars A and B, a range of different phrases, including "immoral relations," "immoral practices," "illicit sexual relations," "concubinage," "cohabitation," "misconduct with native women," and "interference with native women," was employed to describe the various sexual arrangements between European officers and local women that were cause for concern. It was, however, soon made clear, and no objections were raised, that the circular was to be drafted "so as to deal with concubinage and not with occasional illicit acts."[17] Adherence to this standard was evident a few months later when Whitehall advisers urged "no notice" be taken of "sexual relations with native women [occurring] from time to time" in response to Commissioner Curling's extensive allegations of sexual misconduct on the part of his colleagues in the Gold Coast.[18] Although strictly speaking these advisers were adjudicating Curling's case based on Governor Rodger's 1907 circular—as the Crewe Circular had been issued after the events recounted by Curling had taken place—the case's file minutes indicate a very clear commitment to punishing only habitual relations.

Discussions both in the colonies and in Britain about the need to bring concubinage between government officers and "native women" to an end had implicitly referred to "European officers." As we have already seen, this designation was problematic because it encompassed officers of different racial backgrounds—most notably, West Indian officers of African descent like Marcus Clarke. The two Colonial Office advisers, Macnaghten and Antrobus, who pressed the hardest for precision in the circular's terminology with regard to government officers, had worked closely on the Clarke case. When Macnaghten seconded the need for "every officer" to receive such a warning, he went back and inserted the word *white* in his official minute so that it read "In future every *white* officer who enters the service of a Crown Colony containing a native population should be personally and explicitly warned as to the grave view which the Government takes of such practices and the danger to the public service inherent in them."[19] When the first draft of the circular came to him, he immediately objected to the appearance of the term "British officer" because, as he put it, "the phrase covers every native or black officer who is a British subject." As such, he again suggested that "White officer" be used.[20] Antrobus concurred with Macnaghten that "it would be better to say 'white' in the circulars," although he acknowledged that in the army at least, the term "British" was understood "to mean 'European' as opposed to 'Native.'"[21] Despite their protests and for reasons not recorded in the archival record, the phrase "British officer" was retained in the final draft of the circular.

Nonetheless, the fact that there was a debate at all over this terminology likely stemmed from Macnaghten and Antrobus's recent encounter with the Marcus Clarke case, and highlights the potentially influential role this case played in the formation of the 1909 policy. It is also suggestive of the different standards of behavior and sexual comportment that were expected of colonial officers of different racial backgrounds. Indeed, one of the mitigating factors that the Colonial Office brought to bear on the Marcus Clarke disciplinary proceedings was his multiracial background—it was not only deemed unfair to expect "the same standard of morals from him" as from a European officer, it was also suggested that as a "mulatto" his actions were simply not capable of producing the same level of scandal as a European.[22]

The West Indian question also emerged in the Colonial Office's discussion of where the circular was to be sent. All of Britain's African Crown colonies (Gold Coast, East African Protectorate, Nyasaland Protectorate, Somaliland Protectorate, Uganda Protectorate, Gambia, Northern Nigeria, Southern Nigeria, and Sierra Leone) received the circular; however, it was not sent to any of Britain's self-governing colonies in Africa, who were administered separately by the dominions department.[23] Nor was it sent to the British West Indies. The Colonial Office argued that it would be "a great blunder" to enforce the circular in a place where "black and white live together, often intermarry, and where you have every shade of colour living side by side in social union."[24] In addition to the idea that race relations, racial demography, and residential geography in the West Indies were such that the circular would impose an inappropriate form of segregation, it was also noted that there were only a few West Indian colonies that had "any indigenous native population," making the term "native women" a misnomer as far as the West Indies were concerned. It had already been decided that the circular would not be issued to Mauritius and the Seychelles, and since it was argued that "the conditions to which the circular refer do not exist in the West Indies any more than in Mauritius and the Seychelles ... [it] should not go to the West Indies."[25] Readily evident in these minuted observations were the ways in which metropolitan policy makers grappled and at times struggled to comprehend the diversity of the empire they managed from the imperial center.

In addition to the nine Crown colonies in Africa, the circular was also sent to Fiji, Western Pacific, Ceylon, Hong Kong, Straits Settlements, and Weihaiwei.[26] These fifteen colonies were regarded as having not yet succeeded in stamping out the practice of concubinage. There was some debate among Whitehall advisers about whether concubinage was more endemic among officers in Africa or in the Eastern colonies. Macnaghten argued that the practice was so widespread in Africa that copies destined for colonies there need not contain a proposed clause allowing the circular to be withheld in cases where a colony's governor could demonstrate to Lord Crewe that officers no longer practiced concubinage. Antrobus countered that he thought the "evil is if anything greater" in the Eastern colonies where, he alleged, "the women are more attractive" than in Africa. In the end, however, the proposed clause was dropped altogether, and a standard version of the circular containing a cover letter, as well as Circulars A and B, was sent to each of the designated fifteen colonies.[27]

The focus on eradicating concubinage in these locales and not in others, like the West Indies and the Seychelles, clarifies the official view that the dangers it posed to the public service were contextually specific. Where a rigid racial hierarchy was regarded as essential to colonial control, concubinage could not be tolerated because it—unlike prostitution—was more likely to (further) embed officers in local communities and practices. In Africa, Asia and the Pacific, where indigenous populations vastly outnumbered white officials, concubinage and other practices that called into question on which side of the dividing line government officers stood were particularly problematic. As colonial administrators in these locales experimented with different methods of securing their grip on power, they focused for a time on concubinage as part of a wider set of ongoing efforts to establish "categories of rule."[28]

"BLACKMAIL FROM A BLACK WOMAN"

When 520 copies of the Crewe Circular arrived in the Gold Coast on 1 February 1909, its aims were all too familiar to Governor Rodger, who was in the middle of adjudicating the Curling, Palmer, and Greig cases. The existence of the three cases is one indication that Rodger's 1907 circular had not succeeded in its mission. In the face of the colony's stubborn concubinage problem, Rodger would have surely welcomed Lord Crewe's circular as both a confirmation and much-needed reinforcement of his own governing instincts. Yet, the existence of both circulars would lead to heightened concerns about European officers' increasing vulnerability to blackmail as local populations got wind of the new rules. Blackmail's emergence as a central component of many of these cases was entirely consistent with the far more global phenomenon of blackmail at this time, which saw its "profitability and frequency" grow in tandem with the rise in "legal and social disapproval of certain forms of sexual behavior."[29] This is an important contextual point to make given that colonial officers and administrators frequently painted blackmail as a predilection of "scheming" Africans. The first case to be investigated in the wake of the Crewe Circular not only highlights blackmail as the circular's unintended consequence, it also illustrates how the domain of interracial sexual relations became a space in which Africans asserted power over one another.

In July 1909, Mr. W. A. Kisseadoo, a Native registrar, complained in a letter to the Western Province's commissioner that he and other officials were daily experiencing "very unbecoming ill-treatment . . . from the hands of Elizabeth Namoo the District Commissioner Dakeyne's native wife."[30] Kisseadoo claimed that Namoo—who was said to be just nineteen or twenty years old—interfered semiofficially with his duties and uttered abusive and slanderous words to him daily, including threats. While acknowledging that he held no personal malice toward Dakeyne, it was with regret that he had to remark "that in spite of his being aware of his wife's conduct towards me [he] shuts his mouth."[31] In reporting Namoo's abusive treatment, Kisseadoo disclosed that she was Dakeyne's "native wife" in order to suggest that her behavior was premised on her privileged position vis-à-vis the district commissioner. Nonetheless, it was Namoo's ill-treatment of Kisseadoo, rather than her relationship with Dakeyne, that Kisseadoo was aggrieved at.

Exacerbating this was Dakeyne's apparent failure to stop his young wife's abusive behavior. Instead, Kisseadoo claimed that he was passively permissive of it. In lodging his complaint, Kisseadoo attempted to restore his position within a gendered and generational hierarchy that Namoo's public dressing-down of him had challenged. This was an early inkling of the kinds of "wayward" behavior that would give way to far more pronounced anxieties on the part of Gold Coast men in the coming decades. In levying these accusations, Kisseadoo was also implicitly challenging an administrative-cum-racial hierarchy by asserting that his European supervisor was unfit for duty. If he could not control his "native wife," how could he possibly be fit to oversee the affairs of a major district?

When Dakeyne was called upon to verify whether the allegations against him were true, he denied that Namoo had interfered with Kisseadoo's work, but admitted to the relationship with her by acknowledging that "there are certain facts not altogether in accordance with Lord Crewe's circular." To this he added, "I have now taken steps which I would have taken on receipt of the circular had I not feared a scandal. I therefore trust the matter will end."[32] Dissatisfied with his response, the Western Province's Comissioner Arthur Philbrick asked Dakeyne for assurance that he had taken every measure possible to sever the relationship with Namoo and asked him to explain why he had disregarded not only Crewe's circular, but also Governor Rodger's 1907 circular.

Not unlike Kisseadoo's portrayal of Dakeyne as passive in the face of Namoo's abuse of his subordinate Native officers, Dakeyne painted himself as helpless in the face of Namoo, whom he described as the aggressor in his account of how they began their relationship: "The native woman [Namoo] was the last of three who on different occasions obtained uninvited access to my quarters at Cape Coast. I turned out the first two but was unwise enough to allow the one in question to remain the night." He claimed that he had not intended to form a permanent arrangement with Namoo and tried to "get rid of her," but was "afraid to use strong measures from fear of disclosure" in the wake of Governor Rodger's circular.[33] Dakeyne would later explain that the 1907 circular had been typewritten in the governor's chancery, and as a result it "soon became generally known amongst the black population."[34] He alleged that Namoo used her knowledge of the circular's contents to induce him to keep her on through threats of blackmail, which he complied with. When his tour came to an end, he gave her money and "hoped that she would go away." However, when he took up his new posting in Sekondi, he claimed that she "persisted in joining me about three or four weeks after my return. Later she followed me to Akwantamra."³⁵ Again, his defense was one that consistently relied on the notion that he was a victim of Namoo's persistence, an argument that drew its intelligibility from prevailing stereotypes that asserted African women were sexually aggressive and promiscuous—a claim he sought to bolster by carefully underlining that Namoo was the third "native woman" to gain "uninvited" access to his private quarters. In another exculpatory letter he added that "she had lived with two Europeans previously," an admission that was clearly designed to paint Namoo as a particularly calculating woman, and himself as a sitting target.³⁶

But how might we productively think about Namoo's alleged behavior? Was she challenging her subordination to both Kisseadoo and Dakeyne? If within the colonial hierarchy Africans were subordinate to Europeans, African women were expected to be subordinate to African men. Did her "unbecoming ill-treatment" of Kisseadoo stem from the power she felt accrued to her through her intimate relationship with a high-ranking European official? If there was some truth to Dakeyne's claims that Namoo was blackmailing him, how did that action reshape the relations of power between them? Certainly, it suggests that the raced and gendered coordinates of power we have come to associate with colonial rule were challenged within the context of their relationship and perhaps more broadly as a result of the two anticoncubinage circulars. And if he was telling the truth about her having previously lived with two other Europeans—presumably men—what does this suggest about the relationship strategies of and options available to women who partnered with white men?

Namoo was a young "Accra girl" living in Cape Coast at the time she met Dakeyne. Perhaps her serial relationships with white men provided her a source of income and support that was otherwise unavailable to her in a town where she lacked familial networks. Or was it precisely the lack of family in Cape Coast, Sekondi, and Akwantamra that made these towns attractive to her? After all, these locales would have offered her greater anonymity as she exercised control over her sexuality and romantic prospects. Or was the serial nature of her involvement in these relationships a result of the fact that as a woman who had already been "deflowered and cast off" by white men, Elizabeth Namoo could never "hope to wed a respectable African"—an idea that was repeated numerous times in the Gold Coast press.³⁷ Whichever was the case, her presence in towns like Cape Coast and Sekondi reminds us of what a misnomer the term "local" can be when describing the African women like Elizabeth Namoo who participated in these relationships. By obscuring the distances she traveled, the challenges she might have endured, and the relationships that were severed as she sought a new life for herself, the term naturalizes her availability—she was local, thus she was there for the taking—making it impossible to see how she may have strategically made herself available in ways that force us to reckon with the muddled middle ground between consent and coercion.[38]

When Dakeyne received Crewe's circular, he warned Namoo that she had to leave him at the end of his current tour, and to this end he "endeavoured to arrange the matter quietly." Things came to a head, however, when Namoo quarreled with Kisseadoo's wife, and according to Dakeyne this was the reason for Kisseadoo's letter, not Namoo's interference with his official duties or insulting behavior toward him, accusations that he contended were false. Still the very fact that Kisseadoo's wife was fighting with a woman who regarded herself and was regarded by others as Dakeyne's "native wife" would have surely been enough to alarm authorities reading his exculpatory letter. Namoo reportedly followed him to Dunkwa, where she demanded "too much money" from him, causing him to "send her away."[39] Their relationship ended there; however, he claimed that Namoo continued to try to extort money from him through a third party. Dakeyne's letter detailing the circumstances of his relationship with Elizabeth Namoo was clearly intended to minimize his culpability in the hopes of keeping his job. He was the victim, she was the perpetrator, but his account undermines this assertion by unwittingly showing that he was an active participant in the relationship, which spanned the course of two tours of duty—approximately three years. He gave her money so that she would not go public with their first affair, but then proceeded to "keep" her during his second tour of duty. Unless Namoo was demanding both money and sex from him in order to keep quiet, it seems more likely that he chose to reengage with her during his second tour, or at least decided that if he had to continue paying her hush money, he would reap the benefits as well.

Unconvinced by Dakeyne's line of defense, and peeved that he initially acknowledged only having violated Lord Crewe's circular, Governor Rodger sent his case to the Colonial Office and recommended that he be dismissed. Although favorably impressed by Dakeyne's record of service, in which he was touted as "a very promising young officer," and convinced that he had not abused his official position to procure his relationship with Namoo, Colonial Office adviser Macnaghten noted that from "a strict official point of view he has only himself to thank for putting himself in *the intolerable position of having to fear blackmail from a black woman.*" He then warned that "if the circulars which have been issued on this subject become generally known amongst the natives in East and West Africa there is certain to be a good deal of blackmailing of government officials." Seconding this fear, another adviser minuted, "I must call attention to the grave danger to which our officers are exposed by the use of the circular as an instrument of blackmail. In this case it (or rather Sir J. Rodger's previous circular) was used to prevent an offender putting away his concubine—but it may equally be used to extort money from the innocent or to induce them to offend."[40] Extorting money seems a likely use to which the circular would have been put, but the suggestion that it might "induce" officers to offend is curious.

Despite the prevailing opinion at Whitehall that there "was some plausibility ... that it was really the Circular which prevented [Dakeyne] from getting rid of the woman sooner; in that he kept her on for fear of the consequences which would follow her denunciation of him," he was dismissed so as not to undermine the ongoing efforts to bring the wider practice of concubinage to an end.[41] Thus, while recognizing that the blackmail of European officers by Gold Coasters was emerging as an unintended consequence of the circulars, the Colonial Office ultimately decided that so far as guilty officers were concerned, being blackmailed was not a legitimate excuse. Here one also sees how little room was left for making allowances after the release of the Crewe Circular even for outstanding officers like Dakeyne, who was otherwise highly regarded.

The extent to which these charges were taken seriously even in the face of chronic shortages of highly skilled officers is made evident by the formation of a committee of enquiry in 1910 to investigate charges of "intercourse with a native woman" made against Dr. Andrew Connal who was being vetted for a position in the Gold Coast branch of the West African Medical Staff. A colleague who had strained relations with Connal during his tenure in Southern Nigeria had made the charges unofficially, but they were nonetheless sifted through until Connal "had entirely cleared himself."[42] Such vigilance says much about the particularly pronounced anxieties surrounding concubinage that followed in the immediate wake of the Crewe Circular. It also says much about the Colonial Office's need to demonstrate its commitment to upholding its own rules.

CONCUBINAGE VERSUS PROSTITUTION

During the drafting of the Crewe Circular, an easy consensus was reached with regard to the circular's aim: to prohibit European officers from engaging in concubinage—defined by Whitehall advisers as an ongoing sexual relationship—with "native women," rather than prohibiting "occasional illicit acts." Precisely because Circulars A and B both used the term "arrangements of concubinage" to describe what had now become a punishable offense, officers were able to exploit the circular's specificity to claim that their sexual affairs did not constitute concubinage and accordingly did not violate the terms of the circular. The next case under consideration exemplifies this exculpatory strategy and in doing so underscores the more lenient attitude administrators took toward prostitution.

On 27 May 1911, Mary Ajeley Charway, a Gold Coast woman, petitioned Major Herbert Bryan, the acting governor of the Gold Coast, on behalf of her son Samuel Andrews Charway, a Native clerk employed by the colonial government. According to Mary Charway, a "miscarriage of justice" had caused her son to be sentenced to a two-year jail term in the Northern Territories on charges of fraud. Sometime after her son had been imprisoned, she received a letter from her nephew, John W. Anum, informing her of irregularities that had led to her son's predicament. She appended Anum's letter to her own and asked the governor to order an immediate and confidential inquiry into her son's case "with a view to bringing the real facts of the case to light so as to relieve a broken-hearted mother from her present troubled state." In a bid to underscore both her own and her son's faithfulness to the Crown, and to induce the Crown's fidelity in return, Charway pledged, "Your Excellency's petitioner is a loyal subject of the British Empire and her son has also been in the Colonial Service for the past eleven years and as such Your Excellency's petitioner entertains the hope that no injustice will be encouraged under Your Excellency's administration without a proper enquiry being made."[43] Her skillfully articulated request resulted in an investigation that revealed a tangled web of intrigue involving a high ranking British officer, his Fulani lover, and several Native clerks. Before turning to it, however, it is worth noting that Mary Charway's and John Anum's actions played the decisive role in bringing this case to light, drawing our attention again to the active involvement of Gold Coasters in these cases and their willingness to challenge the colonial administration when they felt there was a miscarriage of justice.

Samuel Charway was a long-serving government employee who, just prior to his imprisonment, had served as a clerk to Captain H. A. Kortright, the acting provincial commissioner of Tamale in the Northern Territories. According to Charway, Captain Kortright wrongly believed that he was having a relationship with his "mistress," a Fulani woman named Ayambah. Here, for reasons that will become clear later, it is important to note that Charway referred to Ayambah as Kortright's "mistress" and elsewhere as his "native wife," suggesting that their relationship was more seemly than that between a prostitute and her client. Charway had come to know Ayambah through his cousin, John Anum, whom Ayambah visited on a fairly regular basis at the house the two cousins shared. It was well known in Tamale that Ayambah was Kortright's mistress; however, at the time she started visiting Charway and Anum's house, they were under the impression that Kortright no longer "kept" her. By the time Charway discovered otherwise, "it was too late," he lamented, "to stop her coming to our house." Captain Kortright was angered by her presence in their home and reportedly sent his "Fulani boy" to spy on them.[44]

Things became increasingly tense after Ayambah sat in Charway's amateur photography studio to have her portrait taken. Despite the fact that Charway charged Ayambah for his services, a sign that he was not trying to woo her by taking her portrait, Kortright questioned Charway about the event—trying to ascertain whether it was on account of the portrait that Ayambah frequented his house. Charway's insistence that his relationship with Ayambah was strictly professional did not persuade Kortright, who, according to Charway, believed that he and his cousin were both sexually involved with Ayambah. Kortright began expressing his personal hostilities toward Charway in the workplace, and soon others became aware of them too. In his petition Charway noted, "Mr. C. W. Norman, Chief Clerk and Interpreter Northern Territories often joked with me about this Fulani woman saying that Captain Kortright would prosecute me about her . . . but his warning came too late."[45]

Indeed, Kortright soon joined an elaborate scheme hatched by two Native clerks—Mends and Mullens—who were jealous of Charway's rising reputation in the clerical service—to convict him on charges of fraud.[46] Kortright, it seems, was all too eager to believe the charges because of his animosity toward Charway; however, when presented with indisputable evidence that the talented clerk had not engaged in fraud, Kortright was forced to drop the charges. New allegations of accepting bribes quickly followed at the hands of Mends and Mullens, with Kortright stepping in to arrest Charway again. As the trial approached, the acting chief commissioner of the Northern Territories, Arthur Festing, recused himself from hearing the case on the grounds that he had received letters from Charway that might bias his judgment. Festing also barred Captain Kortright from trying the case because of his intimate involvement in it and because of the allegations Charway had made about his relationship with Ayambah. Accordingly, he brought in the district commissioner of nearby Salaga, Mr. Louis Castellain, to preside over the case. Serious irregularities ensued over the course of the trial, including Kortright's presence on the bench with Mr. Castellain.[47] The miscarriage of justice was made complete when a two-year jail sentence was handed down to Charway.

Mary Charway's letter to the governor detailing these events prompted the investigation that led to her son's exoneration and release from prison by C. H. Armitage, the chief commissioner of the Northern Territories. Armitage in turn convicted Mends and Mullens of "fabricating evidence to procure Charway's degradation and imprisonment" and recommended that they be dismissed from the government service.[48] But Armitage's investigation not only revealed the truth about the sham sentence passed against Charway, it also produced some scandalous claims about Major Festing's decision to recuse himself from the trial. Fearful that his own "immoral relations" with African women would come to light, Festing "ke[pt] aloof from the proceedings."[49] Mends and Mullens accused Festing of taking part in orgies with African women and using his clerks to procure women for him. Although the two clerks appear to have disclosed this information in the hopes that it would take some of the heat off them by refocusing attention on Festing's failings, the charges gained traction.[50] In denying them Festing contended that he was unpopular among government clerks, "owing to my having recently punished certain educated malefactors for abducting native girls and establishing brothels in cantonments."[51] Thus, Festing countered the charge of sexual misconduct made against him by positioning himself as an upholder of sexual morality who was being maligned by clerks whom he had deprived of enjoying the pleasures of and profits from prostitution.

Festing was unable to capitalize on the growing concern in the Colonial Office about the proliferation of blackmail and "put-up cases" in the wake of Lord Crewe's circular for the simple reason that the charges Mends and Mullens had made against him were regarded as true. Captain Armitage reported to his Whitehall colleagues that he had no doubt that Festing was guilty, having been informed by a fellow official "that he was addicted to irregular sexual indulgences when he was stationed in Nigeria."[52] Festing tried another strategy instead. Knowing that senior officials were loath to undertake an inquiry into unseemly charges that would require "native" testimony to prove, Festing exploited their fears when he warned them that if he were called upon to defend himself in a formal investigation he would be forced "to bring as witnesses primitive savages to whom the possibility of such charges being made against a white man will come as a revelation."[53] Faced with the realization, again, that investigating these charges was likely to do more harm to the service's reputation than the alleged misdeeds themselves, the administration proposed forgoing an executive council inquiry if Festing agreed to retire on grounds of ill health, an offer he accepted.

As for Captain Kortright, Armitage found that he "behaved badly through the proceedings" and recommended that he not be allowed to return to the

Northern Territories, and certainly not "to act in the responsible position of a Provincial Commissioner."[54] Having been charged only with investigating the legality of Charway's imprisonment, Armitage did not comment on Kortright's alleged relationship with Ayambah. He did, however, forward all of the evidence to the governor's office, including the letter in which Charway exposed Kortright's involvement with her.

Among the irregularities he was made to explain, Governor James Thorburn called upon Kortright to address the charge of "having immoral relations with a native woman."[55] Kortright's exculpatory strategy was dependent on exploiting the Crewe Circular's precision by showing that he had not "kept" Ayambah in the regular sense of the word, which implied concubinage:

> In denying that I kept the woman, I do not deny that she—if the woman I speak of and Ayambah are one and the same person—came to my house frequently, but I deny (i) that she came to my house every night. (ii) That I paid her a fixed sum of money. (iii) That I endeavoured to control her action outside of my house.
>
> ... It was a matter of no concern to me if the woman who came to my house went to Charway's or not. I regarded her as a Prostitute and did not attempt to control her in any way. Had I had the slightest intention of doing so I would naturally have insisted on her being in my house every night.[56]

Charway and Korthright thus presented Ayambah in radically different ways to the authorities. Kortright framed her as a "prostitute" in order to emphasize that their relationship had been irregular and illicit, while Charway called her Kortright's "mistress" and "native wife" in order to emphasize that their relationship involved more than an occasional exchange of sex for money.

Kortright's strategy was successful to a point. Governor Thorburn took him at his word that Ayambah was a prostitute and that he had related to her accordingly. The governor's willingness to accept Kortright's claim about her without asking for evidence is hardly surprising given that he believed prostitution among Africans allowed them to, in his words, satisfy their "natural—even though excessive possibly—inclinations in this regard." Thorburn held this belief so firmly that just a year before, in 1911, he rejected pleas from both Africans and Europeans to strengthen the colony's almost nonexistent antiprostitution laws.[57] But Thorburn held Kortright to a higher standard than Ayambah. "Although Captain Kortright's admitted relationship with this woman may not amount to concubinage so as to come within the scope of Lord Crewe's Circular," he wrote, "it is I think sufficiently discreditable to merit severe disapprobation, as an officer in Captain Kortright's position could hardly expect to maintain the dignity of his post or to enjoy the respect of the natives in such circumstances."[58] Thorburn asked the secretary of state for permission to remove Kortright from the Northern Territories and to deprive him of two years' seniority. Kortright was also warned that "any future lapse on his part [would] entail immediate dismissal." Thus, sexual misconduct falling outside the terms of the circular could be punished when it brought the administration into disrepute.

Thorburn's recommendation that Kortright be dismissed should he again engage in prostitution ruffled feathers in the Colonial Office.[59] Here the tension turned on the question of occasional versus habitual illicit relations. Pragmatically speaking, Whitehall advisers realized the impossibility, and frankly the inadvisability, of investigating and punishing officers who, on occasion, engaged in illicit sexual intercourse with African women. Whatever minor threat infrequent intercourse, particularly with a sex worker, posed to the administration, provided it was undertaken discreetly, was offset in the minds of Whitehall advisers by the advantages gained when officers refrained from participating in concubinage. As such, officers were rarely if ever punished for occasional intercourse. A case in point is Captain Wingrove of the Gold Coast police, who was caught in 1927 with prostitutes in his room in the European police quarters in Accra. While he was reprimanded for "taking loose women into official quarters," it was the director of criminal investigations, George Brewer, who was slammed by the administration for acting "in a reprehensible manner" and showing "no consideration for his brother officers" by spying on him.[60]

Habitual illicit intercourse, however, was a different matter precisely because it was characterized by its recurrence and thus was far more susceptible to being discovered and in turn creating a public scandal—which was almost always the litmus test for deciding whether disciplinary action had to be taken. This proved to be the case for a government locomotive fitter, Mr. M. J. Houghton, who was described as an "incorrigible libertine" who frequently spent his nights in Sekondi's "Accra Town native quarter," when not entertaining different African women in his government-appointed bungalow.[61] The railway general manager, W.E. Smith, was scandalized to discover "that practically the whole of the second-class men have known all along of Houghton's conduct," leading him to conclude that "the conspiracy of silence and indifference to the respectability of the Railway service is discreditable in the extreme."[62] The manager's disappointment that most officers kept their brother officers' secrets underscores the circular's irreconcilable impulses: it demanded discretion in disclosure, but not easy acceptance of offenses. Smith's "conspiracy of silence" remark is also suggestive of just how little impact the circulars were having not only on the behavior of individual men, but also on the wider culture of acceptance that the circulars had set out to change. Although Houghton apparently stopped bringing women to his quarters after being punished for disregarding the Crewe Circular, he continued to be "a constant visitor to the native town."[63] Ultimately it was the public visibility of his sexual antics that led to the government's decision in 1911 not to reengage Houghton at the expiration of his contract, even though by all reports he was "a very good workman."[64]

Like Houghton's case, the outcome of Kortright's case turned on the questions of public scandal and sexual excess. Even though his actions fell outside the terms of the circular, the Colonial Office decided to punish Kortright because "he had allowed his relations with the woman Ayambah to become a public scandal and so to destroy the confidence in the impartiality of British officers which is the foundation of our rule." His intercourse with Ayambah had not been "occasional," for while he may have regarded her as a prostitute, he had become habitually involved with her. His case was also held to exemplify how habitual sexual relations with women belonging to subject populations could bias an officer in the execution of his duties. Indeed, it was widely accepted in the Colonial Office that Kortright had "deliberately endeavoured to ruin Charway and that in order to do so he brought charges against him. . . . The reason [for this] was that he was jealous of Charway's supposed relations with the woman Ayambah."[65] In short, bringing the administration into disrepute, "circular or no circular," as one adviser put it, was grounds enough to discipline an officer.[66]

Yet, when looked at comparatively, Kortright received a far more lenient punishment for "habitual relations" with a woman whom he successfully portrayed as a prostitute than did District Commissioner Dakeyne, who had "kept" one woman—and was regarded by the authorities as partly doing so under duress. This discrepancy and the inverse moral order it seemed to uphold were not lost on the Colonial Office's staff. One adviser noted that he found "regular concubinage less objectionable from all points of view than constant and open commerce with a notorious prostitute."[67] Several other staff members recorded similar sentiments. Given this consensus, it is difficult to understand why Kortright was not dismissed. Perhaps a provisional answer lies in the fact that while the Colonial Office's advisers regarded, at a visceral level, habitual intercourse with a prostitute as more repugnant than regular concubinage, in practice the former still retained a power differential that was more consistent with the power hierarchy of colonial rule than regular concubinage. In entering into arrangements of concubinage with Gold Coast women, European officers were participating in a recognized social institution that had its own meaning, and attendant rights and responsibilities, within a local context in which increasing numbers of women were opting for concubinage not just with Europeans but also with African men because it gave them greater control over their choice in partner.[68] While concubinage with European officers certainly did not confer African women with the same kinds of rights as did marriage, it could further open up spaces for them, and their families, to exert influence over European officers, thereby creating an inverse set of power relations, which posed a threat to the administration. For this reason it was banned; but making concubinage a punishable offense arguably did more to undermine British authority than it did to preserve it.

ALLOWING "PANIC LEGISLATION" TO "DIE A NATURAL DEATH"

Between 1912, when the Kortright and Festing cases had come to an end, and 1924, there was only one Crewe Circular case prosecuted in the Gold Coast. That case involved Mr. A. C. Allen, a telegraph foreman who had violated the circular, and continued to do so after being warned repeatedly of the consequences. Allen received the circular when he first arrived in the colony in 1914, but by 1915 reports already showed that his work was suffering on account of "the freedom of his relations with native women."[69] At the conclusion of his first tour of duty, he was warned about this behavior and told that his agreement would be terminated if he continued to have relations with African women when he returned from leave. He repeatedly violated the circular upon returning to the colony, but his misdeeds were only brought to the attention of the governor after Allen had completed his second tour of duty. As a result, he was not dismissed from the service; instead, it was decided that he would not be reengaged for a third tour.

Although no further details about Allen's relations with Gold Coast women appear in the records, his case is important for two reasons. First, it demonstrates one spectrum in the range of actions taken against officers who violated the circular. Despite contravening the circular in the face of repeated warnings about his behavior, he continued his associations with Gold Coast women and was allowed to complete two tours of duty. Although several supervisors were aware of Allen's misconduct they failed to bring it to the government's attention during his first tour. It was only after Allen's second tour had come to an end that an official report on his conduct and work, containing the allegations, was submitted to the governor's office. All of this suggests that the culture of silence that W.E. Smith condemned in the Railway Department was rife elsewhere in the government service. His case is important for a second, simpler reason: it indicates that at least in 1914, the Crewe Circular was still being issued to some incoming officers. Fast-forward a decade, and there is no evidence to suggest that the circular was in circulation anymore, a development that was not unique to the Gold Coast.

In 1924 the governor of Nigeria, Sir Hugh Clifford, reported to the Colonial Office that the distribution of the Crewe Circular had not continued regularly there. After 1909, when all of the existing employees were provided with a copy of Circular B, incoming employees were not always given a copy of Circular A, Clifford explained.[70] His attention had been drawn to the irregular distribution of the circular by a recent case in which a European officer had been charged with violating the circular, but pleaded that he had in fact never received a copy of it. While eager to bring the contents of the circular to the attention of all current and future officers, Clifford warned that "the local distribution of these circulars is attended by grave risks. . . . If through the carelessness of an individual officer a copy comes into the possession of unscrupulous natives, attempts may be made either to blackmail or to intimidate officers by threats that charges will be brought against them which will cause their official ruin."[71] Accordingly, he suggested that in future officers should be made aware of the circular's contents in England, prior to departing to the colonies.

Clifford's dispatch reawakened the issue of concubinage and more specifically concerns over the ramifications of the Crewe Circular's existence, matters that had been relatively dormant for many years at the Colonial Office. Only a few of the Whitehall advisers who had assisted in drafting the Crewe Circular and worked on the spate of concubinage cases that were prosecuted in its wake were still working at Whitehall. As such, it was a new crop of men who were charged with understanding the original circumstances that led to the circular's issue and determining the Colonial Office's policy on the circular now that it was widely assumed that most colonies no longer regularly distributed it. At the onset of their investigation, Colonial Office advisers made clear that decisions about the circular's fate should not be premised on the belief that "most or even many officers indulge in 'immorality' of the kind referred to in the circulars." Instead, it was the probability that "a conspiracy could be engineered or that a casual indiscretion would be made to form the basis of an accusation that an officer had entered into arrangements of concubinage" that ought to guide their discussions.[72]

With this is mind they undertook a comprehensive review of past cases with a view to isolating those that illustrated the primary problems associated with the circular's issue: the tendency toward using it for purposes of blackmail or revenge, and its improper application to casual intercourse.

Of the seven cases that were identified as best exemplifying these problems, four were from the Gold Coast; of the remaining three, one was from Nigeria, one was from another (unnamed) West African colony, and the other was from N. Rhodesia. In each of the cases either blackmail or spite was held as the motivating factor behind the charges, some of which were regarded as false accusations. Moreover, among these cases Whitehall advisers regarded F. W. Greig's case as the classic example of all that could go wrong as a result of the circular. Also cited as emblematic of the "revengeful motives" trend were the C. N. Curling and H. T. Palmer cases, with the latter also held to exemplify the "casual indiscretion" trend. The Dakeyne case was regarded as an example of how blackmail was used by a woman to force a man who wanted a one-night stand into "entering into an arrangement of concubinage." Thus, past sexual misconduct cases from the Gold Coast were front and center in the Colonial Office's deliberations about the Crewe Circular's future.

With the negative repercussions of the circular's distribution in the colonies clearly laid out, the Colonial Office's Africa hands turned their attention toward debating the usefulness of the circular. One adviser quickly pointed out that officers could and in fact had been punished for such offenses prior to the circular's issue. Two cases, one occurring in 1903 in N. Rhodesia, which resulted in a "grave scandal," and a second occurring in 1908, in which a European doctor employed by the Sierra Leonean government purchased the wife of a Native prison warder and "paraded her in public," were cited as resulting in the officers' dismissal. Thus, as one adviser put it, "there is plenty of ground for the view that when such cases become public scandals the officer involved is liable to dismissal or lesser punishment," and accordingly concluded that "the circular is not really necessary as an officer can be charged with 'bringing the public service into disrepute.' "[73] It was further argued that the existence of the circular made it difficult to "be lenient—or even fair—because a plain warning will have been disregarded."[74] Failing to uphold its own rules would result in the administration appearing weak. Another adviser pointed out that the circular's existence provided loopholes through which officers could seek to exculpate themselves; specifically, he argued that "to disseminate a circular is to encourage culprits to plead that their attention was not specifically called to it;

or that they thought it was merely routine; or that it does not exactly cover their case or any one of the hundred disingenuous excuses that guilty men find when their guilt can be made to turn on a document."[75]

Others pondered whether the situation in Africa presented unique concerns that still warranted the circular:

> Conditions do differ [in Africa]. An officer might conceivably keep a concubine in a back street, in say Port of Spain [Trinidad], for years without untoward results for the Government service. The presence of a black mistress in official quarters or in the compound in Africa must always have bad results for the Government service, for our prestige, and for the welfare of the native. The element of public scandal must always be present in these cases in countries with a large indigenous uncivilized population. There is therefore something to be said for a special circular for Africa.[76]

Tempering this, however, was a prevailing feeling that the increase in the number of European women coming to the colonies as officers' wives had raised "the general tone of European society in West Africa."[77] The assertion that white women occasioned the end of interracial fraternizing in the colonies has been shown to be a hollow claim, but so too was the assertion that the number of white women in West Africa had significantly increased. Just three years earlier, in 1921, the Gold Coast census showed that 46 percent of British men were married, and of this number 17 percent were accompanied by their wives.[78] While this represented a jump from 7 percent as recorded by the 1911 census, this statistic is less impressive when looked at in the context of the overall number of British men in the colony. In 1921 there were a total of 1,464 British men residing in the Gold Coast, which means that of this number approximately 123—that is to say, only 8 percent—were actually accompanied by their wives. Government officers made up only a fraction of this number and thus only a handful of officers' wives were in the colony. Whatever Colonial Office staffers imagined these women could do to raise the tone of European society in the colonies was clearly not something that local administrators valued enough to reverse their long-standing refusal to allow officers, with few exceptions, to bring their wives out with them.

Still, it was the perception of Whitehall advisers that mattered most in these deliberations. In the end they agreed that while "greater severity in dealing with irregular connections with non-Europeans is justified in Africa," it did not constitute "so strong a case in favour of warning officers as to justify us in disregarding the very real dangers of blackmail and 'put-up' cases against unpopular officers." Having created more problems than it solved, the Crewe Circular was deemed "a piece of panic legislation and like other such legislation," agreed the advisers, it should "be allowed quietly to die a natural death."[79] To this end no plans were made to formally withdraw it; instead, it was hoped that it would just "fade into oblivion."[80] The Colonial Office even refrained from answering Governor Clifford's dispatch in favor of verbally communicating their decision to him in London so as not to chance reviving the issue in the colonies.

SEXUAL MISCONDUCT ALLEGATIONS AFTER THE CREWE CIRCULAR'S DEMISE

Because the Colonial Office decided in late 1924 not to inform the colonies that it was allowing the Crewe Circular to lapse, it is not possible to comment on how the Gold Coast government reacted to this decision. The existence of sexual misconduct allegations in the post-1924 period, however, suggests that while the circular's distribution may have petered out, the strategy of leveraging sexual misconduct charges to redress grievances did not. For instance, in late 1926 at the behest of her husband, ex-Native superintendent of police Imoru Grunshi, also known as Omar, a Hausa woman named Kachina presented an affidavit to her district commissioner claiming that the assistant commissioner of police, Mr. E. F. L. Penno, was forcing her to divorce her husband so that he could have her for himself.[81] Penno, she claimed, had in fact already slept with her. When Penno got wind of their allegations, he arrested and imprisoned the couple for criminal libel. They were subsequently tried in early January 1927 in the chief commissioner's court of Asante.

In her testimony in front of circuit judge Joseph Yates, Kachina wove a complicated narrative about her multiple associations with three men who were all linked together as members of the colony's police force. According to her, Penno sent her a letter demanding that she leave her husband, Omar, and threated to get her into trouble if she refused. Penno's orderly then came to her house and informed her that he "wanted me at his house." Kachina recorded the events that followed as such: "I and the orderly and a child all went to Mr. Penno's house. I went upstairs into his bedroom. His Orderly prepared me a bed on the floor and Mr. Penno had connection with me. I stayed till 1st cock crow and then returned. The child had gone home when I got down stairs."[82] Later the next day she said she was called to Penno's office, where escort police constable Mala Kanjarga, who worked for Penno, was waiting. Kanjarga had previously cohabited with Kachina, prior to her Mohammedan marriage to Omar. Kachina, of her own free will, had apparently left Kanjarga for Omar, the former having never paid the necessary "marriage fees" to her family, and therefore did not have a legitimate claim on her. According to Kachina, "Mr. Penno in my presence gave [Kanjarga] £1.2/- as divorce fees to take to Sariki Zongo's Court to dissolve my marriage with 2nd accused [Omar], he [Penno] did so because he said I was the wife of [Kanjarga] — but I know very well Mr. Penno wants to marry me himself."[83] The fact that she would have gone to this particular court to have her divorce presided over by the chief of the Hausa community in the Kumasi *zongo* suggests that Kachina was most likely a Hausa immigrant form the Northern Territories or beyond who had settled in the bustling urban center of Kumasi.

During her cross-examination, she further explained that when she reached Penno's bedroom, his orderly told her "that the whiteman love me very much and that is why he wanted my marriage to be dissolved."[84] While she said that she loved Penno too, Kachina told the court that she made the charge against him because he was trying to forcibly separate her from Omar before she had been given the chance to decide which of the two men would make the most suitable husband for her: "I love Mr. Penno if he allowed me to go to my husband I would not have made this complaint. I love my husband too. I love the one best who can keep me best and bring forth children for me. I still love Penno and if he had not tossed me here and there I would not have brought this complaint."[85] Her testimony is telling because it mirrored the same kind of thinking that had likely inspired her to leave Kanjarga, who, as a member of the escort police, occupied the lowest rank of the colony's civil police force and consequently would have been paid much less than Omar, who held the rank of native superintendent of police.[86] If indeed she was an immigrant from the north, Kachina surely would have struggled to make a life for herself in Kumasi and thus it makes sense that in choosing a husband she was looking for the man who could "best" keep her.

Judge Yates found that Kachina's claims were true and accordingly acquitted her and Omar without calling the latter to testify.[87] On 29 January 1927, the *Gold Coast Independent* ran an article about the case and the couple's acquittal. Alarmed by the bad publicity the charges had stirred up, Governor Guggisberg quickly called upon the colony's attorney general and inspector general of police (IGP) to investigate the lurid accusations circulating in the "native" press about one of the highest-ranking European police officials in the colony. The attorney general was of the opinion that the allegation that Penno "had possessed and wished to possess Kachina" was untrue, but he found that Penno had acted improperly in attempting to broker a divorce between Kachina and Omar against their will as a favor to his constable, Mala Kanjarga, who wished to recover possession of Kachina from Omar.[88] The IGP concurred that the claims of sexual relations with Kachina were most likely false. To substantiate himself, he disparaged Omar as an "unsavoury" character who was regularly involved in "many palavars."[89] In short, the investigation found that the illicit intercourse and attempted wife-stealing charges were made against Penno in revenge for his attempting to return Kachina to Kanjarga. While Governor Guggisberg was prepared to terminate Penno had the investigation confirmed the court's ruling, he was persuaded by the report's findings and opted to reduce Penno's salary to his initial grade as punishment for his indiscretion in intervening in the marital affairs of his Native subordinates and his abuse of power in bringing an action for criminal libel against the couple without the authority of the IGP.

Even if the charge of sexual relations with Kachina was false, this does not diminish the fact that Penno was interfering in her marital affairs, and the couple challenged this intrusion by filing an affidavit with their district commissioner. Perhaps they calculated that their case would be more persuasive if they alleged that his interference reflected his own sexual interest in Kachina, rather than his interest in defending Mala Kanjarga's claim to her. Yet it is precisely his defense of his lowly escort policeman's heartstrings that makes this case so compelling because it speaks directly to the affinity, affection, and intimacy that the two men must have shared. After all Penno was not only familiar with Kanjarga's romantic affairs, he was also willing to personally intercede on his behalf in a messy love triangle, even going so far as giving Kanjarga the money he needed to pay for Kachina's divorce fees — activities that would otherwise appear inexplicable for a police commissioner to undertake. Penno's actions and even Captain Kortright's strange intrigues with his clerks Mends and Mullens further expand our understanding of intimacy across the colonial color line beyond sex by revealing how the quotidian encounters between Africans and Europeans in the workplace bred other kinds of familiarity and connection that were arguably more intimate and involved than sex itself.

The Penno case indicates that even after the Crewe Circular's heyday had long since passed, Gold Coasters still found that levying sexual misconduct charges, whether true or false, could be a useful strategy for challenging the power that Europeans exercised over them. There is some evidence suggesting that European officers also continued to use sexual misconduct charges to advance their own agendas. In 1929 a disgruntled European officer, Drake Brockman, retaliated against the termination of his probationary appointment on the grounds that he "was not temperamentally suited for the duties of an Administrative Officer," by alleging that several of his colleagues were involved in "illicit liaisons with native women and continue to live with them openly." Brockman hoped he could convince the administration to reverse his termination by pointing out that despite these liaisons, his fellow officers had been reported on favorably. This, he argued, proved that reports on an officer's performance "are not always strictly accurate and contain no little personal bias," and by extension the negative reports on his own service could be flawed.[90] Brockman's strategy only confirmed the administration's initial assessment of his temperamental unsuitability for government work. Governor Alexander Slater noted that he found it "deplorable that Mr. Drake Brockman should have sought to bolster up his case by traducing his brother officers."[91] Making matters worse for Brockman was Slater's discovery that he had engaged in concubinage too, a fact that came out when it was revealed that Brockman had fathered a child with Agnes Okutu.[92] When Okutu and her "illegitimate child" died, their caretaker, Salome Brabo, was forced to sue Brockman to recover the cost she incurred paying for their funerals. Slater presented Brockman with copies of the court proceedings as proof of his sexual misconduct, "the truth of which he readily admitted."[93]

While the Penno and Brockman cases suggest that the strategy of levying sexual misconduct allegations remained current among both Africans and Europeans, it is perhaps more significant that throughout the 1920s only these two sets of allegations, along with the Wingrove case mentioned earlier, made their way through the administrative hierarchy. While the Wingrove and Penno cases demonstrate that interracial sexual misconduct allegations did not have to involve concubinage in order to be investigated, it seems fairly clear that by the 1920s the administration's policy toward these cases was to take action only when a public scandal had been created. The government's attitude was perhaps best summed up in 1927 by Governor Gordon Guggisberg, who, in commenting on the Wingrove case, noted that "irregular relations between European officers and native women in a tropical country form a fruitful source of trouble. In my view, while I expect Heads of Departments to set an example, and to advise their juniors, it is not advisable to pry too closely into the lives of officers so long as they can do their work efficiently and do not cause a scandal." While Guggisberg concluded that a scandal had been caused, he was of the opinion that "it was only indirectly caused by Captain Wingrove" and "directly due to the harsh and indiscreet methods of Mr. Brewer."[94] Wingrove was lightly punished for the offense, a course of disciplinary action that was consistent with the administration's tradition of acting more leniently in instances involving prostitution or casual intercourse. Implicit in Guggisberg's warning about the inadvisability of "pry[ing] too closely into the lives of officers" was an admission that the probable outcome would be the discovery that most officers continued to engage in interracial sexual relations, some of which amounted to concubinage and others that skirted the line. Thus the paucity of cases investigated did not signal the triumph of efforts to bring concubinage to an end; instead, it represented their success in creating a culture of secrecy around both concubinage and the even less seemly sexual exchanges that were promoted as preferable alternatives to it. This pattern was replicated in Nigeria where "discretion" in "keeping" local women and "reticence" about disclosing participation in such affairs went hand in hand in the decades after the release of the Crewe Circular.[95]

By the 1920s it was only the rare officer, like Brockman or Brewer, who stirred the sexual misconduct pot. Had both Brockman and Brewer not been motivated by revenge to tattle on their fellow officers, it is likely that the cases they reported would have gone undiscovered. This begs the question, how many colonial officers had relations with Gold Coast women, but belatedly or never came to official attention? Colonial authorities, for instance, became aware of the fact that assistant government printer Alfred Johnson had fathered a child in 1933 with his underling Miss Kate Easmon, a Native bookbinder, only after he had retired from the colonial service and returned to England. Johnson was found out when Easmon petitioned the Colonial Office for help in obtaining child support from him.[96]

It was not until 1934 that the Colonial Office officially addressed the question of concubinage again on an imperial scale. That year the Gold Coast government received a confidential circular from the secretary of state for the colonies, Sir Philip Cunliffe-Lister, officially announcing that the distribution of the Crewe Circular was "no longer necessary or desirable and should be discontinued."[97] Although it was deemed unnecessary because of an alleged "decrease in actual instances of concubinage," this misstated the case. The decrease was in the frequency with which concubinage cases were brought to official attention. The reasons given for the undesirability of the circular's continuation were all those identified in 1924 by the Colonial Office: its misuse as a tool of blackmail and intimidation; an improper widening of its scope from concubinage to casual intercourse; and, providing guilty officers with the ready-made excuse that they had not received the circular. In short, the unintended outcomes of Crewe's circular were regarded as more problematic than concubinage itself.

None of this, however, was communicated to any of the colonies until 1934. Having been queried by an official in the Straits Settlements as to whether the circular was still to be issued to newly appointed officers, the Colonial Office finally decided that it should issue clear instructions in order to ensure procedural uniformity. The 1934 circular made clear that while the Crewe Circular's distribution was being officially terminated, concubinage was still considered a punishable offense. Accordingly, Cunliffe-Lister affirmed that his decision "implies no condonation of the offences against which [Lord Crewe's] circular was directed. Nor does it imply that there should be any hesitation in taking appropriate disciplinary action against officers whose conduct in this respect is such as to bring discredit upon the Service and to impair their efficiency." To this he added, "I am confident, however, that the reprobation of such conduct may properly be regarded as inherent in the standards of behavior which the traditions of the Service demand and that the co-operation of senior officers in ensuring the maintenance of those standards may be more effective than the promulgation of official warnings."[98]

CONCLUSION

Why by the turn of the century did concubinage between European government officers and African women present a threat to the administrative efficiency of Britain's African colonies? The answer to this question is to be found in the changing practice of colonialism, characterized as it was by the onslaught of alien political rule, which depended on force and compulsion rather than on reciprocity and compromise. Paradoxically, with greater imbalances in power between Europeans and Africans as colonial rule formalized and entrenched itself came greater insecurity on the part of Europeans about how best to maintain their grip on power. Anything that threatened to destabilize the tenuous nature of colonial rule, by necessity, had to be controlled. The more interracial sexual relations came to be perceived as a potent source of destabilization, the more they came under attack; first in the Gold Coast in 1907, in Kenya in 1908, and finally throughout a much wider sphere of the British Empire in 1909 with the issue of Lord Crewe's anticoncubunage circular. Less than two decades later, however, the Colonial Office did an about-face, even going so far as calling the Crewe Circular "a piece of panic legislation." While that phrase might have reflected what Whitehall advisers genuinely regarded as an overreaction on the part of their predecessors, the copious minutes that led up to their decision to allow the circular to "quietly die away" suggest that the real motivating factor was the unintended and adverse consequences brought on by the circular itself. Intended to shore up British colonial authority, in reality it did the reverse. In the years following its release, when it had the most visibility, the circular had been used by Africans to accomplish a range of different goals: addressing workplace grievances by disclosing to authorities that a European officer was in violation of the circular; using it as a tool to extort money; blackmailing officers in order to prevent them from bringing an end to an arrangement of concubinage, et cetera. And when European officers used the circular against one another the results were no better. Perhaps its irregular distribution not long after it was first issued was a response to the fact that the circular quickly caused more problems than it solved. Turning a blind eye, as Guggisberg suggested, avoided the problems associated with investigating these charges, but his admonition and the willingness on the part of the Colonial Office to allow the circular to lapse in 1924 and then to officially discontinue it in 1934 should also be viewed in light of the different colonial moment the interwar years represented.

While the financial toll of the war put an even greater premium on retaining control of the colonies, it also gave way to a new emphasis on making them more profitable, which led to numerous colonial welfare and development programs throughout British Africa during the interwar years. Although such programs were clearly meant to enrich Britain, they were at least partially successful in staving off demands for full political independence until after World War II. Arguably, then, the supremacy of British rule during the interwar years was far less in doubt than it was in 1907 and 1909, when Governor Rodger and Lord Crewe issued their circulars. In the Gold Coast, Governor Guggisberg's long tenure as governor (1919–1927) saw the expansion of education and major development projects, as well as the creation of greater opportunities for African employment in the civil service. Although his governorship was not without its controversies and confrontations with the colony's educated elites, during the interwar years Gold Coasters largely articulated their demands for colonial reforms and greater autonomy within the bonds of empire, not outside them. While a forceful critique of the moral legitimacy of British colonial rule, which drew its strength from the illicit nature of sexual relationships between European men and African women, emerged during this time period, colonial authorities seemed little concerned by it. Apparently they believed their hold on power could withstand the denunciation of "immoral whites" in the pages of the colony's indigenous press, at least as long as fingers were not pointed directly at European government officers. Colonial administrators' attention to interracial concubinage waned throughout the interwar years, but their anxieties were stoked again in 1945, just over a decade after the Crewe Circular was discontinued, when four European officers married African women in the Gold Coast. It is to these unprecedented interracial marriages and the firestorm they ignited that we now turn.

5 ～ "A Manifestation of Madness"
The Gold Coast's Interracial Marriage "Epidemic"

IN THE SUMMER OF 1945, the governor of the Gold Coast, Sir Alan Burns, wrote in a panic to Gerald Creasy, the Colonial Office adviser who would replace him as governor two years later. Governor Burns told Creasy that he had just received the "distressing news that another of my District Commissioners, one Knight, is about to marry an African woman with whom he has apparently been living for the past year and has had a child." This, according to Burns, would make the second district commissioner who was marrying his African "concubine," in addition to two doctors who "have done the same thing." Eager to confer with the Colonial Office about what could "be done to stop this sort of thing," he suggested that while it was clearly impossible to distribute a circular warning officers against intermarriage, it might be possible to "issue a revised [Crewe] Circular . . . warning men against living with African women, and adding . . . that the discovery that a man has been living in sin is not going to be over-looked just because he has made an honest woman of her." He closed his worried note by emphasizing that he was "not very keen on this, as I do not consider that the morals of my officers are my business, provided that they do not create a public scandal or affect the efficiency of the Service."[1]

Governor Burns believed that the cause of the interracial marriage "epidemic," as he put it, was a combination of a restriction on home-leave and the shortage of European women in the colony resulting from wartime travel difficulties. While his use of the term "epidemic" to describe the four marriages, which had occurred between 1944 and 1945, implicitly evoked the imagery of contagious disease, it was not long before these unions were explicitly pathologized. In justifying why reviving the Crewe Circular in a modified form was futile, one Whitehall adviser contended that "this particular type of conduct is a form of madness, and no amount of warning is going to prevent people from becoming unbalanced."[2] He even went so far as to say that he was quite sure that "the usual reaction of a brother officer is that these cases are a manifestation of madness." European officers would react with pity toward their mentally unstable colleagues, but there was "no excuse," he said, "for cluttering up the Service with people who are quite definitively mad." Drawing on the oft-repeated claim that such unions were particularly offensive to white women, he added that the wives of European officers would take a "far less charitable and much more emphatic" stance against officers who married African women.[3] By proceeding leniently, the government might appear to condone such marriages, he warned, and would invite nothing but utter contempt from its officers' European wives.

But advisers at the Colonial Office found themselves in a predicament. On the one hand, if the existence of these marriages became rapidly known throughout the service, the general public, and spread to other colonies, they feared the reputation of the Gold Coast service would be permanently tarnished. To avoid such a scandal the officers' "immediate removal" seemed warranted. On the other hand, if the officers in question were terminated, trouble was certain to come from those who "would be horrified at official action to penalize marriage after a period of living with an African woman whereas no penalty at all has been imposed in the much more frequent case of an officer living with an African woman without marriage."[4] Implicit here was recognition of the continuing practice of concubinage and an affirmation that colonial officials continued to regard marriage as the greater offense. The alternative to acting swiftly was "eventual removal when, as is bound to happen sooner or later, inefficiency can provide the excuse."[5]

Whitehall advisers soon agreed that the four officers would be hindered in discharging their duties as a result of their marriages. Not only was it suggested that an officer could not take "his proper place in the life of his district in such circumstances," it was also argued that nonadministrative officers, like the two doctors Governor Burns mentioned, would be unable to command the respect and confidence of their junior officers. These doctors, it was said, "would be at a disadvantage if placed in authority of a staff of [white] Nursing Sisters." Rather than dismissing the officers in question, Whitehall adviser P. A. Tegetmeier recommended that they be called upon to retire "on the grounds of public interest or on the grounds that their efficiency and their value to the government has been impaired."[6] In the end it was decided that the government had been justified in making an offense of concubinage, but it was quite another matter to make an offense of marriage, especially when sanctioned by the church or state—as was the case in the marriages under consideration here. Accordingly, the Colonial Office resigned itself to leaving each officer in question "to wrestle with the social problems he has created for himself."[7] Action would be taken only if and when the efficiency of the officers was impaired, and it was to be taken only on those grounds. The Colonial Office cleverly worked its way around the catch-22 by leaving a space open for itself to discipline officers who married African women, but to do so on supposed professional, rather than racial, grounds.

A WARTIME PHENOMENON?

In blaming the interracial marriage "epidemic" on the shortage of European women in the colony caused by wartime travel restrictions, Governor Burns was essentially suggesting that these were situational intermarriages induced by the temporary lack of marriageable European women. Apart from completely discounting the possibility that these marriages were a product of genuine love, Burns's rationale conveniently overlooked the fact that there had always been a lack of European women in the colony, but this had never given way to publicly recognized intermarriages. Moreover, in attributing the low numbers of European women to wartime travel difficulties, Burns also conveniently glossed over the fact that the colonial government's longstanding policy, dating back to the early 1900s, favored single candidates and prevented all but a select few married candidates from bringing their wives to the colony with them. In short, the demographics had long been ripe for intermarriage, but the racial prescripts of formal colonial rule had militated against it with such great effect that these four publicly recognized interracial marriages were completely unprecedented.

The panicked response to these marriages is all the more notable for revealing the great degree to which colonial authorities had come to accept the continuing practice of cohabitation between European officers and African women. As late as 1945 the "problem" was not sex across the color line; it was still, as Ann Stoler argues, "its public legitimation in marriage."[8] The truth of this observation is made clear not only by the tacit acceptance of concubinage, but also by the colonial government's slow response to the rampant interracial prostitution occasioned by World War II between foreign servicemen—both (white) American and European (primarily British)—and West African sex workers, many of whom were trafficked into the Gold Coast from Nigeria. Although prostitution and the spread of venereal disease had long been a concern of African authorities, as well as members of the colonial service who were familiar with the adverse consequences these diseases had on the health of local populations, the Gold Coast government had a track record dating back to 1911 of rejecting calls to strengthen its extraordinarily lax antiprostitution legislation.[9] The onset of World War II, however, brought the Gold Coast government's decades-long legislative intransigence on the question of prostitution into sharp relief as the flow of sex workers from Nigeria into the colony increased dramatically to meet the demand for commercial sex by thousands of newly arrived European and American military personnel, as well as African troops undergoing predeployment training.

In the spring of 1941, Accra and the deepwater harbor town of Takoradi witnessed an influx of thousands of white American and European military personnel, as these two locales became strategic nodes in the Allied forces' network of bases for the North African and Middle East war theaters.[10] Their presence had a profound impact on the cities' social life and sexual economies. As Nate Plageman notes with regard to Accra, "The city's foreign servicemen . . . had deep pocketbooks and a penchant for making heavy drinking, commercial sex, and illicit activities regular components of their free time."[11] Much the same was the case in Takoradi, where entrepreneurial young men known as "pilot boys" served as middlemen between sex workers and foreign servicemen looking to buy sex. It was not long before police authorities declared the sudden rise in the number of foreign military men in the colony the cause behind an "increase in the number of women who earn their living by prostitution with Europeans."[12] Commensurate with the increase in prostitution was an escalation in the number of European and American military personnel infected with venereal diseases, which alarmed medical authorities and impaired the war effort.[13] In the view of the colony's chief of police, E. C. Nottingham, sex workers posed "a danger to health [and] should be removed from the immediate vicinity of the large camps housing European personnel." Not surprisingly, he singled out Accra and Takoradi, where the largest populations of military men were based, as the cities in which "the conduct of these women is causing embarrassment."[14] Typical of contemporaneous gendered discourses on prostitution, the behaviors of johns were never identified as factors in the prostitution epidemic, nor were their actions considered punishable offenses or a public health threat.

Although Nottingham persistently petitioned the colonial government to increase police authority to crack down on prostitution, and outraged Gold Coast citizens condemned the public spectacle of open prostitution in the streets of Accra and Takoradi in the pages of the colony's press, the government remained impervious to the situation. It would take over a year of police pestering and another year of legislative debate before new laws were finally enacted in the summer of 1943 to curb the sex trade.[15] Sir Alan Burns, who had taken over the governorship in the previous year, approved this legislation. At first glance it would seem to make sense that the governor who reacted so frantically to the four interracial marriages was also the one who responded to rampant wartime interracial prostitution by bringing the colony's long-standing refusal to tighten its antiprostitution laws to an end. Perhaps all forms of sex across the color line offended Governor Burns, but the scale and consequences of wartime interracial prostitution dwarfed the interracial marriage "epidemic"—yet it was the latter that caused Governor Burns and his colleagues to imagine dire scenerios of government ruin. These discrepant responses underscore a consistent pattern in official attitudes toward interracial marriage and prostitution—the former was deemed so unthinkable that when a handful of European government officers finally did marry across the color line, they were written off as "lunatics," while prostitution was tolerated as long as it did not create a public scandal. But what could have been more public or scandalous than white men in uniform on the streets of Takoradi and Accra procuring sex from West African sex workers? The answer, evidently, was four European men publicly wedding their African wives.

While the realization that these men could not be overtly penalized without adverse consequences for the administration led to their retention in the colonial service, the alarmists in the Colonial Office assumed it would be only a matter of time before the men brought about their own demise. While to different degrees these men faced some career challenges in the wake of their marriages, they were not as dire as predicted. In fact, all four of the officers remained in the employ of the colonial government through the transition to independence. Two of their number, moreover, remained in government service long after independence, while a third went into private practice in Ghana shortly after decolonization. Only one, Donald S. Turner, left the country shortly after independence with his Ghanaian wife, Gladys Adzo Chapman. As the four following biographical sketches suggest, the professional challenges and disapproval these men encountered as a result of their marriages occurred alongside varying degrees of career advancement and support from Africans and Europeans alike. The fifth and final biography of Hans and Mercy "Kwadua" Roth helps illuminate the often similar circumstances that privately employed European men and African women had to navigate as they strived to legitimize their relationships.

GLADYS ADZO CHAPMAN AND DONALD S. TURNER

Born in Keta, the colony's most eastern coastal city, Gladys Chapman married Donald Turner, the Eastern Province's assistant district commissioner, on March 22, 1944. Close in age, Donald was twenty-six and Gladys twenty-seven at the time of their marriage before the registrar of the Ho-Kpando District.[16] Within a week of their marriage Donald was transferred to Axim, on the opposite end of the colony's coastline in the Western Province, where he and Gladys both took up residence.[17] No reason is provided in Donald's personal file for his sudden transfer, but the fact that it happened in the immediate wake of his marriage suggests a correlation, especially if we recall that administrators tended to more harshly sanction officers who were intimately involved with women from their own districts. Donald himself would later convey to the colony's acting colonial secretary that "certain personal and domestic matters . . . have been the subject of personal comment by a superior officer," which had in turn caused him "great and continuing distress." Although he did not wish the "particulars of these matters to be officially recorded," it is clear that he believed his marriage to Gladys played a part in his disputed promotion to district commissioner in 1949.[18]

But it is also evident that Donald did not allow the disapproval of his peers to deter him from acknowledging his marriage or ensuring that Gladys was given the rights and privileges owed to her as the wife of a colonial officer. Immediately after their nuptials, the couple filed the paperwork necessary to comply with the Pensions Ordinance so that in the event of his death Gladys would be his beneficiary.[19] He also applied for a separation allowance for her when he was forced to go on an early sick leave to Britain shortly after their marriage. His request could have been easily rejected on the grounds that the allowance was intended for (presumably white) wives left behind in the United Kingdom. Indeed, one official bluntly noted that in 1942, when the circular explaining the terms of the separation allowance "was drafted, it was not considered that there was a possibility that a European officer . . . would marry a Lady of African descent."[20] But local officials also agreed that Turner's "unique" case required an "ad-hoc decision," especially since they wished to avoid the "very understandable objections" to his bringing Gladys to the United Kingdom with him, and so they approved the allowance.[21] These objections were the colonial government's, not the Turners', since on all of his subsequent leaves the couple traveled together to Britain. Donald was subsequently promoted in 1954 and again shortly after independence in April 1957. During those years the couple had their first child, a son named Ian Leslie Obeng Turner.[22] On 30 March 1959, Donald retired at the grade of administrative officer class I.[23] That it took almost two decades to reach this class is in keeping with the time it took other colonial officers, suggesting that his marriage did not adversely affect his career to the degree predicted fifteen years earlier by members of the Colonial Office.[24]

Although it is not possible to comment specifically on this couple's integration into the social circles of late colonial society, both European and African, it is worth noting that as the first (recorded) interracial civil marriage between a British officer and an African woman in the colony during this time period, the Turners were breaking new ground in a society that had long been structured by various forms of racial segregation, even if such boundaries were less strictly maintained by the mid-1940s. The couple's long-term residential fate was determined by the course of African independence, as the timing of Donald's retirement from government service and the couple's subsequent departure from Ghana suggests that they left as a result of the ongoing Africanization of the civil service, which had started prior to independence but was ramped up in the years immediately following it. According to Gladys's contemporary and friend Felicia Knight, the couple relocated to England in the face of the increasingly limited number of government jobs available to Europeans in Ghana.[25] The couple settled in Manchester, where they raised their two sons. Donald died in 1983, followed by Gladys at the age of ninety in 2007.[26]

MARGARET MARY BARETTE AND ALBERT JOSEPH HAWE

In the remaining three cases, each officer served throughout the duration of the colonial period and continued to live and work in Ghana long after independence. Albert Hawe was an Irish-born doctor who came to the Gold Coast in 1928 to serve in the West African Medical Service. In 1944 he married Margaret Mary Barette, herself the daughter of a Fante woman named Essie Mansah and a British trader only remembered by the name Barette. Born in 1905, Essie Mansah was from Cape Coast and began her career as a trader at an early age. Although it is not clear how she met the trader Barette, their relationship was brief, and in May 1919, at the age of fourteen, she gave birth to their daughter. Faced with having to raise Margaret Mary without the support of Barette, who had already left the Gold Coast, Essie Mansah placed her in the St. Mary's Convent School in Cape Coast.[27] Because Essie lived near the convent, she was able to regularly visit her daughter and bring her food. Margaret, in turn, was allowed to see her mother at home, and the two remained extraordinarily close throughout Essie's life. After completing her education in the convent, Margaret went on to pursue teacher training but gave that up when she married Albert. By 1947 Margaret had given birth to the couple's three children—Muriel, Francis, and Cathleen—who were all sent to boarding school in England at a young age.

In the years prior to independence Margaret was excluded from some of the social pastimes of her husband, who frequented the "Accra Club" without his wife because it barred Africans from membership. Fortunately for Margaret, her anger at being racially excluded from her husband's social world was tempered by the fact that she had a thriving social life of her own among the nationalist set in Accra. In the years right before independence Kwame Nkrumah frequently visited Essie Mansah at her Cape Coast home with Margaret. After independence the Hawes often socialized with Kwame and Fathia Nkrumah, and Margaret and Fathia eventually became close friends.[28] The Hawes' daughter Cathleen fondly recalls her summer holidays in Ghana as a time when she and her siblings regularly joined their parents for tea with the Nkrumahs at Flagstaff House.[29]

Albert Hawe's medical career does not seem to have been adversely impacted by his marriage to Margaret. By the time they married in 1944 he had already been working in the colony for sixteen years and had garnered a reputation as one of its best doctors. In recognition of his medical services, he was awarded the Order of the British Empire (OBE) in 1953, and then in 1959 he was given the additional honor of the Commander of the British Empire (CBE).[30] In 1965 Hawe's alma mater, the Liverpool School of Tropical Medicine, awarded him the prestigious John Holt Medal for "meritorious work in the tropics."[31] The *Liverpool Echo*'s coverage of the award ceremony noted that Hawe had married his wife while serving in the Gold Coast and prominently featured a picture of the couple with Albert attired in suit and tie and Margaret Mary donning distinctly West African couture. Little did the *Echo*'s readers know that had cooler heads not prevailed in the Colonial Office decades earlier, the Hawes' decision to marry in 1944 might very well have eclipsed Albert's storied medical career, which included serving as Kwame Nkrumah's personal physician after independence. Indeed, Nkrumah expressed his pride in Hawe's accomplishment in a letter to the dean of the Liverpool School of Tropical Medicine, Professor B. G. Maegraith, shortly following his receipt of the John Holt award.[32] While it is tempting to assume that Hawe's selection as Nkrumah's personal physician was based solely on his prodigious medical skills, Nkrumah's personal relationship with Dr. Hawe was an extension of his friendship with Margaret, and thus it was Margaret that brought her husband into Nkrumah's inner circle, not the other way around.[33]

Although the Hawe children were raised primarily in England, their birth in the Gold Coast and the couple's long tenure there clearly weighed on Albert's and Margaret's minds, prompting them to seek clarification on the nationality status of Margaret and the children in a letter to the Nationality Division of the Home Office (Britain) in 1963.[34] Margaret's citizenship status was governed by that of her husband's, and she therefore retained her British citizenship at independence, but the Hawe children lost theirs under the British Nationality Act (1958) because the year before they had become citizens of Ghana under the Ghana Nationality and Citizenship Act (1957). In order to regain their British citizenship, which they did, they had to apply for special consideration as laid out by the British Nationality Act of 1948. Having secured the family's British nationality, one might imagine that as the personal physician to Kwame Nkrumah, Dr. Hawe would have relocated back to Britain in the wake of the 1966 coup that overthrew Nkrumah. It is a testament to the deeps roots the Hawes had planted in Ghana that they remained there until Albert fell seriously ill with cancer in 1979. Shortly after returning to their English family home in Maidenhead, he died at the age of seventy-eight. Margaret returned to Accra in the late 1990s, where she lived until her death in 2007.

MARTHA GLADYS OWUSU AND CHARLES BOWESMAN

On 5 May 1945, Martha Gladys Owusu and Charles Bowesman married at the African Methodist Episcopal Zion Church in Keta, where Charles worked as a doctor in the town's hospital.[35] Two notable things occurred immediately prior to their marriage. Martha retired from her position as a well-regarded Junior Civil Service second division nurse in charge of the surgical theater at the Kumasi hospital, where the couple first met during Charles's tenure there (1943–1944).[36] It seems likely that she retired in order to join him in Keta, but this certainly came at the loss of an esteemed position. As a trained African nurse, Martha was one of only a handful of African women to be employed by the colony's medical service after successfully completing training in human anatomy and physiology, surgical and medical nursing, and first aid.[37] While their marriage was preceded by a career sacrifice on Martha's part, just days before they wed the Colonial Office approved Charles's promotion to surgical specialist.[38] The timing could not have been better, since confirmation of his promotion reached the colony after their wedding had taken place.

In his memoir Charles notes that both Africans and Europeans attended their nuptials, with Keta's district commissioner, Tom Mead, serving as best man, and a Mr. Aggrey giving away the bride.[39] "My wedding to an African lady was resented by some and praised by others," writes Charles, but even those who disapproved could not challenge the marriage's legitimacy, since "on official grounds no valid complaints or disciplinary action could be taken."[40] The very fact that his own district commissioner acted as his best man suggests the wide gulf in opinion that existed within the colonial service. While some officials were ready to consign men like Charles Bowesman to the lunatic asylum, others were actively supportive of their colleagues' decisions to marry across the color line. Support among Europeans also came from the church: the couple's marriage was officiated by Reverend James Taylor and attended by André van den Bronk, who would later become the bishop of Kumasi's Roman Catholic Church. Both men traveled from Kumasi to be at the wedding.[41]

Like Donald Turner, Dr. Bowesman immediately notified his superiors in the medical service of his marriage so that Martha would be his recognized beneficiary of the Widows and Orphans Pension Scheme.[42] A year later, in 1946, the couple went on leave by air to Charles's native Ireland. Shortly after their arrival, Bowesman wrote to the director of medical services to express his appreciation "for the Government's leniency in allowing [Martha] to proceed to the United Kingdom with me, a privilege afforded to a limited number of Africans." But the purpose of his letter was also to request that Martha be granted a priority passage so they could travel back to the colony at the same time. In Charles's words, "As her home is not England she would have great difficulty in remaining there ... after my return to the colony."[43] Although this request might have reflected real concerns about Martha's ability to cope in Britain alone, it was likely calculated to boost her limited chances as an African of receiving a priority passage, an elevated ticket status typically reserved for those traveling on official business. To further bolster her eligibility, Charles noted that Martha would return to nursing if required to by the government. The official responses are telling. The acting director of medical services agreed that it would be "a matter of difficulty" for Martha to remain alone in England, but he also saw the granting of the priority passage as an opportunity to regain the services of a "very competent nurse."[44] Another local official unsympathetically responded that "Dr. Bowesman was responsible for taking his wife home to U.K. and cannot ... expect special treatment on these grounds." He was, however, favorably persuaded that Martha's services as a nurse were valuable enough to the colony to warrant an upgraded passage.[45] To ensure this outcome, Martha was asked to sign a promissory note swearing to undertake nursing duties if given a priority passage. The couple returned to the Gold Coast together in October 1946 and subsequently traveled to and from England on numerous occasions throughout Charles's career in the colonial service.

In 1946 Charles was stationed at Accra's Korle Bu Hospital, where he helped train Dr. Charles Odamtten Easmon, the first Ghanaian to qualify as a surgical specialist. His confidence in Easmon and the other African students he trained is suggested by his calling upon their expertise to jointly tackle the surgical needs of high-profile patients, such as Asantahene Otumfo Nana Osei Tutu Ageyman Prempeh II, as well as his loved ones, including Martha's own mother.[46] Later he was transferred to Sekondi and then in 1951 to Kumasi, where a few years later he designed the Kumasi Central Hospital with Albert Hawe, who had also garnered a reputation for training young African medical students.[47] Given that Martha was born in the town of Kyikyiwere in Asante's Mampong District, not far from Kumasi, this posting afforded the couple an opportunity to be closer to her family.

In late 1956, shortly before independence, Charles tendered his resignation to take effect in the spring of the following year. In a letter explaining his decision, he said that he wanted to devote his time to completing "a text book on Surgery in the Tropics," a project he had been working on for more than twenty years.[48] But he also intimated that he would consider seeking reemployment in Ghana after completing the book, which he did indeed do. After a two-year stint in Lewisham, a district in southeast London, where he completed his thousand-page tome, *Surgery and Clinical Pathology in the Tropics*, Charles and Martha returned to Kumasi, where he established a private medical practice in 1960.[49] Bowesman would later write in his memoir that as a nonnational, his limited chances of being permitted to go into private practice were, he believed, greatly enhanced by his marriage to a Ghanaian woman, along with his medical expertise.[50] With a thriving medical practice, the couple adopted two Ghanaian newborn girls whose mothers had died during childbirth.[51] In 1976, when the Kumasi Central Hospital was converted into a teaching hospital (now the Komfo Anokye Teaching Hospital), Charles was appointed professor of surgery and thereafter remained actively involved in the training of young African medical students. According to his obituary, he contracted quartan malaria in 1987 during an epidemic that killed well over a million people. He emerged out of a five-month coma only to fracture his hip later that year. Consigned to a wheelchair until his death in 1993 at the age of eighty-six in Kumasi, Charles was survived by Martha and their two daughters.[52]

His long and distinguished career, which included being awarded an OBE in 1958, suggests that, like Donald Turner and Albert Hawe, Charles's professional advancement was not curtailed by his marriage to Martha, although it does appear that along the way he may have endured the disapproval of some of his colleagues.[53] His memoir briefly alludes, as well, to "private storms" with his sister as a result of his marriage to Martha.[54] Unfortunately, much less is known about Martha, apart from the fact that she appears to have reentered the nursing profession after her marriage and that she joined her husband at his various postings. It does, however, seem clear that the couple shared a close relationship during their forty-two-year marriage, regularly traveling abroad together during Charles's leaves and ultimately choosing to stay in the region of Martha's birth instead of resettling in the United Kingdom.

FELICIA AGNES AND BRENDAN KNIGHT

The final of the four couples to wed in the year spanning mid-1944 to mid-1945 was Brendan and Felicia Agnes Knight. Felicia was born in Amanokrom, in the colony's Eastern Province, in 1927. After completing Standard 6, she left school at the age of fifteen in order to relocate to Kumasi, where she lived with her aunt Mercy and trained as a seamstress. Mercy's husband, Kwabena, was a clerk in the Kumasi district commissioner's office, where he first met Brendan, who had been stationed there since 1943. Brendan had joined the Gold Coast colonial service in 1940 at the age of twenty-three. The son of a prominent diplomatic family, he was born in Greece where his father, W. L. C. Knight, served as consul general at Salonika. His father was later stationed in Egypt among other North African, Mediterranean, and Middle Eastern locales. While Brendan's early childhood was nomadic, at the age of seven he went to boarding school, along with his three siblings, in England. Shortly after earning his degree from Cambridge University's Christ's College, which offered courses in colonial administrative services, he arrived in the Gold Coast, never to take a post elsewhere in the British Empire.[55]

As an entry-level assistant district commissioner, Brendan was charged with numerous administrative tasks that involved interacting directly with African officers and clerks, including Felicia's uncle Kwabena. When Kwabena was transferred to an administrative station outside Kumasi, Mercy and Felicia went with him. Brendan regularly visited Kwabena's station to pay African police officers and other workers. Although he had known Kwabena in Kumasi, it was during these visits that he first met Felicia—a testament, once again, to the fact that interracial relationships were frequently forged through preexisting affiliations that European government officers had with Gold Coasters. After a yearlong courtship, Brendan asked Mercy and Kwabena if he could marry Felicia by customary law. Brendan, Felicia recalls, was keenly interested in "native" customs and traditions and insisted on correctly carrying out the protocol for their customary marriage, which took place in Kumasi in the spring of 1944. It was after their customary marriage, Felicia says, that local administrators became aware of their relationship and started to pressure Brendan to dissociate himself from her. When he refused he was transferred to the small town of Juaso in May 1944, a move that the couple interpreted as a willful attempt to break them apart.

At the end of 1944, Brendan went on leave to England with the intention of securing his parents' permission to marry Felicia in a church wedding. According to Felicia, Brendan's father was less concerned with the question of her race and more interested in his son's feelings for her.[56] Convinced by his sincerity, the Knights gave Brendan their blessings. Pregnant with their first son, one can imagine how stressful this period of separation and uncertainty must have been for Felicia, who was just eighteen years old. Although her family had come to know and respect Brendan, they feared he would not return to fulfill his promise of a church marriage to Felicia. Her family's emphasis on a church wedding, even after the couple had wed in accordance with customary law, suggests that they believed legitimacy could be conferred on their union only if it was publicly recognized by church and state. The prevailing view, according to Felicia, was that girls who "went around with white men" were involved in illegitimate relationships. Apart from the question of social stigma, the family was justifiably concerned about the financial strain that would accompany the birth of the child if Brendan did not return. In the end their fears did not materialize.

In April 1945 Brendan returned to the colony and traveled to Amanokrom, where Felicia had gone to stay with her mother during her pregnancy. Having conveyed the good news that his parents had agreed to support the couple's desire to marry, Felicia and Brendan returned to Kumasi and began planning their wedding. According to Felicia, local colonial administrators renewed their efforts to sabotage their relationship, including abruptly transferring Brendan to Sunyani on the day in late May 1945 that they were to wed in Kumasi.[57] After settling in Sunyani, the couple was finally able to pull off their marriage. A simple affair, Felicia wore a kente cloth wrapper and a white blouse for the ceremony officiated by two white Catholic priests and attended by Felicia's family. That evening they held a small party attended by Charles and Martha Bowesman and a few other friends.

Despite the hostility the couple faced from members of the administration, their life proceeded apace with the birth of five children between 1945 and 1951. Martha Bowesman delivered each of the Knight's five children at home, a sign of the trust and closeness forged between the women and their families. In January 1946 the Knights were transferred to Wenchi and then later that year back to Juaso. Finally, in 1948 Brendan was promoted to district commissioner, a class III administrative officer. In the decade that followed he was subsequently promoted to a class I position, and the family eventually settled in Accra. Although his advancement through the administrative ranks was in keeping with other officers, Felicia believed wholeheartedly that Brendan's career aspirations were thwarted by those who disapproved of his marriage to her.[58] He may have ended his career in the colonial service as a class I officer, but he might have risen more quickly and even higher had he not courted the disapproval of his superiors. Felicia's ruminations seem less like speculation if we recall that it was Brendan's marriage, in particular, that set off the firestorm about intermarriage. If it was not simply the straw that broke the camel's back, perhaps the son of such a distinguished diplomatic family choosing to intermarry unsettled the authorities to a degree that compelled them to officially respond, even if in the end they did not take formal action.

While the Knight family carved out a niche for themselves in late colonial society, it was largely due to Felicia's willingness to challenge the racially segregated landscape they lived in, an indication of which were the numerous social clubs in the colony that excluded Africans from membership. At the late date of 1956 there were still dozens of clubs across the colony that were for "Europeans only."[59] Felicia recalls going to both the European club and the hospital in Kumasi and insisting that she and her children be admitted. In one particular instance she arrived at the European hospital with one of her children who was sick at the time and pressured the staff until her child was treated.[60] But those painful memories are balanced by happier ones of their relations with Felicia's family and the wider African community. Equally so, the couple and their children were extraordinarily close with Brendan's family. During his annual leaves the entire family traveled with him to his parents' home in Brighton. On one of their earliest visits Brendan returned after his three-month leave was over, but Felicia and the children stayed on for an additional three months.

During that time Brendan's mother enrolled Felicia in etiquette classes in order to help her establish and maintain a European-style home in the colony. One can imagine that Felicia might have justifiably taken umbrage at this, but her memories of her mother-in-law are of a woman who was kind, affectionate, generous, and, like her son and father-in-law, very much interested in other cultures. In the early 1950s her in-laws traveled to the Gold Coast to visit them. Felicia fondly recalls that when they came to Amanokrom to meet her family, the entire town came out to greet them. Set against the hierarchies of race and class that separated these families even in the waning days of the British Empire, one cannot help but appreciate what an extraordinarily rare event this meeting in Amanokrom was. It neatly symbolizes the familial support the Knights had and the integral role it must have played in helping the young couple navigate the racial politics of late colonial society.

If, to varying degrees during the colonial period, Charles Bowesman, Albert Hawe, and Brendan Knight were disparaged for marrying across the color line, in the postindependence period their marriages to Ghanaian women were critical to their retention in government service, and in the case of Dr. Bowesman, his ability to establish a private practice in Ghana. Like Doctors Bowesman and Hawe, Brendan Knight stayed on after independence as the principal assistant secretary in the Ministry of Justice. But on 30 December 1960, three years after Ghana's independence in 1957, Knight received a letter notifying him that his employment would soon be terminated as part of the ongoing Africanization of government service. As recounted in the opening pages of this book, it was this news that propelled Felicia out of the confines of her comfortable upper-middle-class home in Osu to the gates of Flagstaff House, where she launched a one-woman protest to save her husband's job and by extension to ensure the viability of her family's life in Ghana. Felicia was able to persuade Nkrumah that her husband was committed to her and to raising their five children as Ghanaians. This was an argument that must have resonated with Nkrumah, since in subsequent government correspondence about the decision to grant Knight a special dispensation allowing him to remain in the civil service it was noted that "Mr. Knight is married to a Ghanaian and has five children with her all of whom have been brought up as Ghanaians."[61] At the time the Knight children ranged in age from ten to sixteen, and although they had regularly gone on holiday with their parents to England they were by all accounts reared for a life in Ghana.

Although Felicia notes that the postindependence period ushered in an era of slightly more relaxed social relations with expatriate Europeans in

Ghana, she still found the greatest comfort among Ghanaians, as well as her tiny and very tight-knit community of relatively privileged, legally married interracial friends, which included the Bowesmans and the Hawes. In 1962, encouraged by her husband who had an abiding interest in Ghanaian cultural practices and traditions, Felicia became the first female chief of Amanokrom under the title Nana Tetkyi Ampong I, a position she held for close to eight years. Felicia cites her enstoolment as proof of the fact that her interracial marriage did not alienate her from Ghanaians. In fact, her selection, she says, was a result of the fact that others saw her as powerful precisely because she was willing to challenge convention. For his part, over the four decades that Brendan lived and worked in Ghana, he acquired a tremendous knowledge of the region's history and culture, including becoming fluent in Twi. In order to secure his family's future in Ghana, he invested his earnings there instead of sending them back to Britain. Although he eventually returned to England, Felicia remained in Ghana until her death in 2012, supported in part by the rental income she earned from the block of flats that Brendan had built on the parcel of land he purchased for their family home in Osu.

MERCY "KWADUA" KWAFO AND HANS ROTH

European government officers were not the only white men pursuing relationships with African women in the Gold Coast. As early as the turn of the century, the subject of sexual relationships between privately employed European men, especially the large number of miners who came to work in the colony's lucrative mining industry, and local women had garnered the attention of concerned Africans, missionaries, and members of the colonial administration. Yet the government had no powers of prescription when it came to the sexual affairs of privately employed Europeans, whose numbers steadily increased over the decades. Some of the European-owned trading firms did, however, have clauses in their employment contracts that forbade their expatriate employees from engaging in sexual relationships with local women. These clauses, as one Swiss trader noted in his memoir, "essentially forced encounters with the local beauties 'underground.'"[62]

Like government officers, privately employed Europeans faced difficult choices when they wished to act honorably toward their African partners. Hans Rudolf Roth, a young Swiss man who came to the Gold Coast in the late 1940s to work for the Swiss African Trading Company Limited (SAT) firm in Kumasi, quickly found this out when he began courting Mercy "Kwadua" Kwafo. Given that Switzerland had no colonial territories in

Africa, Swiss men like Hans were generally privately employed if not part of the large Swiss missionary presence associated with the Basel Mission. Africa had long been the object of Hans's childhood fascination, and when he learned about a vacancy in SAT's Gold Coast branch, he immediately applied for it.[63]

After traveling by plane to Accra, Hans boarded a train to his final destination, Kumasi. Seated next to the new recruit was Asimaku Idun, an elderly businessman and cocoa farmer, with whom Hans enjoyed a lively conversation. Within a few minutes of his arrival at the Kumasi train station, however, Hans had his first brush with colonial racism. Awaiting him at the station were his Swiss coworkers Erwin Scheitlin and Koni Bertschi, who refused to shake Idun's hand when Hans introduced them to the "distinguished looking gentleman."[64] After they had departed Idun's company, Scheitlin warned him, "If you want to stay here, you better forget to 'Sir' such bloody gentlemen-niggers like Idun. These chaps are no damn good" (*BK*, 18). But the real lesson for Hans was the duality of colonial racism, which allowed white men like Scheitlin to disrespect Africans, while "keeping" African women as sexual companions. Indeed, the first local woman Hans met after settling into his quarters at the SAT residential compound was Mary, Scheitlin's African girlfriend. As Hans put it, "When they went home in the evening they sought the comfort which these women gave," but that did not mean that by day such men were models of racial egalitarianism.[65] Hans nonetheless suggests that there was real affection between Mary and Scheitlin, even if it required her to ignore his "rough talk and allusions to 'keeping blacks in their proper place'" (*BK*, 28). Anti-African racism was clearly flexible enough to accommodate these kinds of intimate relationships, if not manifesting itself through the sense of sexual entitlement white men had toward African women. Still Hans's recollections point to the fact that affective ties could and often did grow within the unequal power dynamics and prejudices that structured these relationships.

Not long after his arrival in Kumasi, a colleague invited the firm's European bachelors to a dance party with local "creatures of paradise," as Hans put it (*BK*, 30). It was on that occasion that Hans first met Mercy "Kwadua" Kwafo. Kwadua was born on 21 May 1926 in Dunkwa-on-Offin in the Central Province not far from the border with Asante, to an Akwapim father and an Asante mother. Her father, a railway man, died at an early age, leaving Kwadua, the second oldest of nine children, to help her mother, a farmer, care for the large family. In the mid-1940s she trained as a nursing assistant and was subsequently posted to Tamale, where she entered into her first romantic relationship with an "expatriate friend" (32). Kwadua gave up her job, but soon found herself devoid of support when the man suddenly returned to Europe. She then decided to move to Kumasi, where she learned how to sew and was quickly able to grow her business, providing her with a means of supporting herself and continuing to help her mother and younger siblings.

Although self-sufficient, Kwadua still yearned "to find someone who would take care of her," an impulse she attributes to having lost her father at such an early age. Her father's philandering and that of other men she grew up around, however, made her "distrustful of getting involved in binding relationships with men of her own race."[66] Instead, Kwadua availed herself of opportunities to socialize at interracial gatherings in Kumasi, like the one she met Hans at in late 1948. The couple has been together ever since, but over the years they have faced and surmounted many challenges.

SAT employees like Hans understood that the company's prohibition of sexual relations with local women was a measure intended to keep up good appearances rather than one that was strictly enforced. While men were expected not to cohabitate, there was an unspoken rule that women could spend the night provided their presence at the SAT compound did not attract attention and that they left before daybreak. Hans's description of the compound "as something of a roost, with pretty birds of varying shades and shapes coming evenings and weekends, and disappearing quietly at dawn," attests to the relative sexual freedom these men enjoyed while also underscoring its limits (*BK*, 29). SAT employees, it seems, were also aware of the presence their managing director Werner Hintermann, and his Swiss wife, who lived adjacent to the compound. Given the flow of women in and out of the compound, this was "too close for comfort" (29). Hintermann's subordinates may have wished for greater privacy because they suspected that their activities were a painful reminder to Mrs. Hintermann of her husband's own infidelities, which included fathering three children with his long-standing African mistress. Indeed, it was this fact that provoked Hans to tender his resignation when Hintermann rebuked him for cohabiting with Kwadua in an SAT flat in Accra, where he had been temporarily transferred. Hintermann persuaded Hans not to resign by assuring him that he did not object to his relationship with Kwadua, but rather to the fact that it had become the subject of "gossip all over Accra." He advised Hans "to rent a room for your sweetheart," and to that end Hintermann increased his salary (73).

It was not only among Europeans that the couple had to navigate unpredictable reactions toward their relationship. Hans recalls that the couple's long motorcycle rides around Accra used to elicit "occasional jeers and abuses from pedestrians who resented the sight of a black woman perched on the back seat of a whiteman's bike" (*BK*, 57). Although Kwadua ignored these slights, Hans believes they were at the root of her unease about riding on his bike.[67] When asked what provoked such hostility, the couple says that the push toward independence brought "big tensions between black and white," which were particularly acute in Accra's jumpy political climate.[68] Kumasi, in comparison, seemed a more hospitable place to them.

The couple's first major challenge arose when Kwadua became pregnant in late 1951. Although pleased at the thought of fathering a child with her, Hans "feared the consequences" for his career (*BK*, 88). A number of his SAT colleagues, including Hintermann and Scheitlin, had children with African women, but that did not mean he would not face censure. Early in their relationship they had married by customary law, but Hans still regarded this as a temporary measure until they could wed in a civil ceremony and Kwadua could be officially recognized as his wife under Swiss law. But given SAT's policy against cohabitation, he knew there was no question of his being able to publicly wed Kwadua any time soon. Making matters worse, the few colleagues that he confided in questioned Kwadua's character by asking Hans whether he was sure the child was really his. Kwadua, however, was determined to have the baby, and after rebuffing his request that she "do something about it," she told him that she would return to her mother's village to have the baby if he was going to abandon her (88). This was inconceivable to Hans. He quickly accepted the fact that he would soon be a father, and in early September 1952 the couple welcomed their first son, Henry. A month later Hans went on leave to Europe, and while he did not have the courage to tell his parents about Kwadua and Henry, he did inquire with officials at UAC—now the parent company of SAT—about marrying Kwadua, to which they replied it "was out of the question" (92). They did, however, hint that with Ghana's independence in sight, it was likely that things would change. Still, the general tone about these matters was made evident to Hans when he learned that Erwin Scheitlin had been reprimanded for taking his girlfriend Mary to Switzerland without the company's permission, a request that was unlikely to have been granted had he asked (93).

It was not until the birth of their second child in 1956 that Hans felt confident enough to marry Kwadua. Having by then secured his parents' blessing, he informed SAT of his impending nuptials, knowing that should they fire him he could find gainful employment elsewhere. One indication that the company's views had already changed was the fact that prior to their marriage, a heavily pregnant Kwadua was allowed to move into Hans's bungalow on the SAT estate in Kumasi. When an official note of congratulation arrived from his superiors, the last barrier to marriage had been lifted. Hans surmises that he "was probably the first expatriate within the UAC Group of Companies in the Gold Coast who was going to marry a local girl and keep his job" (*BK*, 124). Indeed, Kwadua and Hans were the only interracial couple living on the SAT estate. Although the family enjoyed good relations with their mostly Swiss and British neighbors and their children played together, the couple's social circle also comprised Ghanaians.

Hans and Kwadua were together for almost a decade before they wed in a civil ceremony on 5 January 1957, just a few short months before Ghana's independence. For Hans it was this ceremony that conferred the mark of respectability on Kwadua and their union that he had long wished for. Kwadua, for her part, views their 1957 nuptials as their "official marriage," but regards their earlier customary marriage as equally valid. Their wedding reflected the couple's ties to both the Ghanaian and the expatriate European communities. The ceremony was presided over by the Kumasi town clerk, Alex Kyeremateng, and attended by Africans and Europeans alike. Kwadua's mother, uncles, and extended family "came dressed in their very best, the men wearing rich Kente cloth, the women even more colourful in traditional attire." Although most of the Europeans came dressed in Western attire, they soon jettisoned their suit jackets and made their way to the dance floor where the mixed crowd danced to Ghanaian highlife and ballroom music (*BK*, 126).

The bucolic description of their wedding day renders normal an event that was actually still quite extraordinary. Many if not most of Hans's colleagues engaged in interracial liaisons. Others fathered children with African women. They did not, however, seek to legitimize these relationships in marriage, and some men refused to acknowledge their children. When Werner Hintermann died of a heart attack in 1954, the three children he fathered with his African mistress were still officially unrecognized and left out of his will, despite the fact that he had financially supported them throughout their lives, including sending them abroad for school. It was only at his wake-keeping, which his Swiss wife and daughter did not attend, that rumors about "Hintermann's African wife and children" were publicly confirmed when two of his children showed up (*BK*, 107). Hans's colleague Erwin Scheitlin recognized the child he fathered with Mary, his longtime girlfriend, but when he left Ghana for Switzerland he made arrangements to have only their son join him there, leaving Mary behind. Thus, even while the era of decolonization witnessed small numbers of interracial couples like the Roths, Bowesmans, Hawes, and Knights marrying and settling in

FIGURE 5.1. Hans Rudolf Roth and Mercy "Kwadua" Kwafo on their wedding day in Kumasi, 5 January 1957. (Photograph from the personal collection of Hans and Mercy Roth, Rombech, Switzerland.)

Ghana, many if not most of these relationships continued to be informal and to follow a pattern that had been established centuries before: they were "for the coast only."

CONCLUSION

The colonial period in West Africa was generally a time fraught with hostility and uncertainty for interracial couples, but the foregoing sketches suggest that attitudes and room for maneuver did not remain uniform across the decades spanning the late nineteenth to the mid-twentieth centuries. Indeed, the very fact that these marriages took place at all suggests that the late colonial period created an opening for European colonial officers to push the government's racial boundaries in unprecedented ways where their own personal and marital affairs were concerned. Had these marriages occurred in the early decades of the twentieth century instead of the mid-1940s, it is highly unlikely that the officers in question would have been retained at all by the colonial service. But the government's panicked response, tied as it was to the idea that news of the marriages would spread like a virus "throughout the Service, the general public, and . . . to other colonies," destroying the administration's reputation in the process, also says much about the tenuousness with which administrators in the colonies and in London regarded their hold on power at this particular moment in time.

World War II was coming to a close, and Britain was reckoning with not only the destruction of its infrastructure and economy at home but also its signature to the Atlantic Charter, which recognized the right to self-rule for colonial territories—a clause that Britain did not intend to honor given how vital it believed the African colonies were to the rehabilitation of its postwar economy.[69] Therein lied Britain's problem, it had just fought a devastating war against the Nazis and their virulently racist doctrines but it was not yet ready to fully reckon with the political implications of its own colonial racism. Instead, it opted for "developmental colonialism," which sought to deracialize the "grounds on which a convincing case could be made for the exercise of state power over people who were 'different.'"[70] Viewed in this context, the pragmatic decision not to terminate the four officers for marrying African women is consistent with the postwar colonial state's realization that it could no longer act in an overtly racist manner if it hoped to keep its grasp on the colonies. One small but telling sign that perhaps best hints at the changed tenor of race relations in the postwar period and its implications for interracial couples is the disappearance of the term "native wife" to describe the women in question. They were now referred to as African women who had married European men.

The short-lived but dramatic panic that ensued over the Gold Coast's interracial marriage "epidemic" was in fact the second of two panics provoked by marriages that crossed the colonial color line. Part 2 of *Crossing the Color Line* shifts its focus back to the interwar period when anxieties over interracial concubinage between European government officers and African women were superseded by a new threat: working-class African men who wished to settle in British West Africa with their white wives. Colonial authorities prevented them from doing so because they regarded these couples as unmitigated threats to the racial hierarchy that organized colonial society and upon which its stability was assumed to rest. Hastily implemented measures put into place in the wake of the race riots that swept through the British ports in the summer of 1919, when black men first began requesting repatriation to the colonies with their white wives, were increasingly formalized in the face of sustained efforts by these couples to settle in the colonies over the course of the next two decades. But the viciousness of the race riots and their underlying sexual politics triggered something else of consequence: outraged Gold Coasters began to publicly point out that white men in West Africa had nearly unfettered sexual access to black women, while black men were beaten in the streets of Liverpool and Cardiff for their relations with white women. What began as a critique of sexual hypocrisy, however, was quickly transformed by early Gold Coast nationalists into a provocative rhetorical strategy for challenging the moral legitimacy of British colonial rule.

PART TWO

Metropole and Colony

6 ～ "The White Wife Problem"
Intermarriage and the Politics of Repatriation to Interwar West Africa

IN OCTOBER 1933 ENA PARKER, an Englishwoman, pleaded with Britain's registrar general of shipping and seamen to be jointly repatriated to the Gold Coast with her African husband, John Akok Parker. John was suffering from severe tuberculosis and had been warned by his doctor that he would not live through another winter in Manchester, where the couple eked out a precarious existence. As Ena's repatriation request made clear, the risks to John's fragile health were compounded by the constant threat of homelessness the couple lived under:

> In addition to his illness, we have been knocked about and hounded from one house to another. As soon as we get the tenancy of a house and they find out my husband is a coloured man we have to move. . . . There is nothing against my husband's character only that he is a coloured man.

Anxious to avoid the shame of becoming "chargeable to the Guardians," a prospect Ena knew would "mak[e] my husband's condition worse," she urged the registrar "to try and see your way clear to send both myself and my husband back to his home in the West Coast of Africa."

In a final desperate appeal for assistance, Mrs. Parker closed her letter by drawing attention to John's service in World War I, which included being torpedoed on the *Foylemore* in 1917: "He fought for his country in the war [and] now his country offers no shelter.... We have only till November 6th before we are thrown on the streets. So I beg you please try and use your influence to get us to Africa."[1] Her request, having been forwarded by the registrar general to the Colonial Office, fell on deaf ears. Ena was told that repatriation would be considered for her husband only.[2] Undaunted, she continued to press the Colonial Office until it relented and sent her request to the governor of the Gold Coast, Sir Shenton Thomas, who in turn agreed to fund John Parker's repatriation provided Ena did not accompany him.[3] She emphatically refused to be separated from her husband. We do not know whether John Parker lived through the winter of 1933–1934.

The Parkers' quest to resettle in the Gold Coast was thwarted because colonial authorities feared that a white woman living in "native fashion" with her working-class African husband would grossly undermine European prestige and destabilize colonial race relations. Indeed, in Ena's case it was specifically noted that "the conditions under which she would have to live would be most unsuitable." Here "unsuitable" referred to the fact that John Parker's hometown, Apowa, was a small fishing village in the Western Province where it was doubted "there is a single iron roofed home in the place."[4] In short, colonial authorities regarded Ena's potential living conditions, especially the physical home she would inhabit in her husband's village, as racially inappropriate for a white woman and an affront to the prestige of all white women in the colony with adverse consequences for good governance. Such concerns were at the root of the unwillingness of colonial authorities to repatriate not only the Parkers, but also numerous other interracial couples who made similar requests for repatriation to British West Africa during the interwar years.[5] Thus, this period saw a marked shift from concubinage between European officers and African women to marriage between West African men and white women as the primary source of colonial anxieties around interracial sex. If colonial confidence in the Gold Coast was robust enough to turn a blind eye to the discrete sexual affairs of European officers, it was certainly not regarded as strong enough to withstand the presence of working-class black men married to white women.

This chapter traces the evolution of colonial policies used to prevent Ena Parker and countless other white wives from taking up residency in British West Africa to the end of World War I and the social and economic upheaval it brought. Black men from Britain's overseas colonies and their white wives and lovers came to embody the fears and anxieties gripping Britain's economically depressed port cities.[6] Black men were accused of taking jobs from white British men and stealing *their* women. White women who partnered with black men, as Laura Tabili notes, "were denounced in gendered and class-specific terms as disruptive, deficient, 'of a very low type.'"[7] Press reports and port officials regularly characterized them as depraved and immoral traitors who selfishly prioritized their own sexual and material desires above the good of the nation.[8] Working-class interracial couples became targets of abuse on the increasingly tense streets of Britain's port cities, and when a series of violent race riots erupted in the summer of 1919, they were largely blamed for their outbreak.[9] White mobs, ranging in size from a few hundred into the thousands, indiscriminately attacked black men, harassed and assaulted their white partners, and destroyed the multiracial settlements they called home.

In the wake of the riots, some of these couples attempted to leave their hostile environs for the British colonies, most notably in West Africa and the West Indies, where many of the men in question came from. Their desire to take up residency in the colonies, however, led to a watershed moment in the regulation of colonial interracial sexual relations: for the first time metropolitan and colonial state authorities explicitly agreed to keep white women married to working-class black men out of the colonies. In the prewar period, colonial social conventions and their attendant racial taboos were the primary mechanisms that, at the very least, kept European women and black men from openly fraternizing in the colonies, but after World War I events in the metropole required new and progressively more rigorous state authorized methods of control to ensure the colonies were kept free of such couples. Thus what started as a policy response to the 1919 race riots continued to guide colonial authorities' decision-making processes throughout the interwar years as West African seamen who lived in Britain and were married to white women sought joint repatriation as their economic positions worsened during this time.

Given that British women like Ena Parker retained their citizenship upon marriage to British colonial subjects, they were simply denied entry to the colonies and were expected to stay in Britain with or without their husbands. Faced with this difficult choice, some couples separated upon the man's return to West Africa, while others, like the Parkers, remained together in Britain. During the interwar years, the Colonial Office confronted several cases involving British West African men married to mainland European women who were facing deportation. The women in question had gained by marriage their husbands' status as British subjects or protected persons. While it has been argued that the distinction between British subjects and protected persons was "little more than a technical one," it had a significant bearing on the outcome of these cases.[10]

By way of example, Michael Egali, who was born in the Protectorate of Nigeria rather than the colony, and his German-born wife, Elisabeth, were forcibly separated in 1933 when German authorities deported Egali to Nigeria. This outcome was the result of Egali's status as a British protected person, which did not entitle him to domicile in Britain, leaving British domestic authorities in an ironclad position to refuse the couple permission to enter Britain. Meanwhile, in a dramatic display of the way in which British nationality law could be superseded by colonial anxieties, colonial authorities refused Elisabeth permission to enter Nigeria, even though she was technically a British protected person by virtue of her marriage to Michael.[11] So keen were they to avoid her being sent to Nigeria that colonial authorities even entertained plans to have Elisabeth maintained in another part of the British Empire, at the Nigerian government's expense, if the Germans insisted on their "right to . . . deport her from Germany."[12] Unwilling to resign themselves to their fate, on the eve of Michael Egali's deportation the couple stowed away on the *M. V. Dunkwa*, an Elder Dempster ship headed for Nigeria. Before the ship set sail, German police discovered Michael and Elisabeth, who was disguised as a man, and took them ashore, where they were detained in separate facilities.[13] Elisabeth was released only after Michael was put on another Nigeria-bound ship. Although German authorities were eager to "dispose of Mrs. Egali at the same time as her husband," in the end they allowed her to remain in Germany.[14] Her fate in Nazi Germany is unknown. Had deportation to Britain been an option for this couple, the tragic outcome of the Egali case would have likely been much different.

While far less common, these complex dual nationality cases became the battleground upon which British metropolitan, colonial, and foreign authorities most vigorously fleshed out their anxieties about where interracial couples should be permitted to settle. The second half of this chapter focuses on the case of the Annan family to illuminate how concerns about race, sex, gender, class, nationality, religion, and spatiality informed the contested politics of repatriation to British West Africa during the interwar years. These disputes also offer a glimpse into the social world of the West African diaspora in Britain and mainland Europe during the interwar years and provide valuable insight into the challenges faced by many interracial couples as they carved out an existence for themselves in a world that was hostile to their unions. During the interwar years, metropolitan racism, gendered citizenship laws that penalized European women for marrying foreign men, and racialized labor competition compelled some of these working-class families to fight—albeit in vain—for the right to live in the colonies.

Ultimately, domestic anxieties over the way in which Britain's empire was remaking the metropole were trumped by acute fears that European women living in "native fashion" with their working-class African husbands would turn the colonies' racial hierarchy on its head.

While competing tensions between the domestic and the overseas organs of the British state dominate the archival records of these cases, we must bear in mind that it was the mundane longing for home on the part of interracial couples that provoked such intense debates about where they should be allowed to settle. To more fully understand the very real impact these deep-seated anxieties about interracial unions had on black men and white women during the interwar years in Britain, this chapter undertakes the difficult work of documenting the voices of some of the "women and men who negotiated their personal and sexual relationships in the face of a barrage of both official and cultural hostility," while paying particularly close attention to "their experiences, the impact of prejudice upon them, and their strategies of survival and support."[15] In highlighting their actions and voices when and where they emerge in the archival record, these couples speak for themselves in ways that underscore the extent to which they challenged and defied—to the best of their abilities—the colonial state's determination to keep them out of Africa.[16]

A handful of wealthy West African men who were able to demonstrate to colonial authorities that they could maintain their white wives at a standard deemed suitable to European womanhood were, however, allowed to make the colonies home. This caveat underscores the importance of class in the decision-making processes of colonial authorities. It also demonstrates that in contrast to the settler colonial regimes of Southern Rhodesia and South Africa, the administered colonies in British West Africa stopped short of implementing the most draconian forms of sexual segregation through the use of antimiscegenation laws and barbaric extralegal measures such as lynching. Rather, to keep the colonies free of all but a handful of wealthy interracial couples, colonial authorities used a combination of strategies, including denying passports to the white wives of working-class African men, refusing to pay the cost of their passage to West Africa, and later classifying them as "undesirable immigrants" under the provisions of the colonies' Immigration Restriction Ordinance. These strategies followed earlier but comparatively less vigilant efforts on the part of colonial administrators to bring an end to the far more frequent occurrence of sexual relationships between European colonial officers and African women through the use of the official anticoncubinage circulars previously discussed in part 1. When viewed together, these efforts underscore the importance of attending to the spectrum of colonial anxieties that accompanied the gendered, racial, and spatial configurations of interracial couples, as well as the forms (illicit, casual, marital) their relationships took. Indeed, if we are to use panic and bureaucratic strong-arming as yardsticks, preventing European officers from cohabiting with African women was a far less pressing issue than keeping lawfully married working-class black men and white women out of the colonies.

By extending its analysis of colonial interracial sexual relationships to the metropole, this chapter exposes the geography of interracial sexual relationships and its raced and gendered coordinates. We already know that relationships between black women and white men were a common if frowned-upon facet of life in the colonies during the interwar years. This chapter makes clear that during this time period, with few exceptions, relationships between black men and white women were confined to the metropole. The extraordinary measures that colonial authorities took to keep it this way underscore that in this instance sexuality was managed in ways that determined the demographics of European expansion, not the other way around.[17] If white women generally faced restricted access to the colonies even as the wives of white men, what this chapter helps elucidate is that such women were excluded altogether from the colonies when they were the wives of working-class black men. By extension, the demographics of places like Liverpool, Cardiff, and London were also influenced by the ways in which interracial sexuality was managed in the colonies. These port cities were home to high numbers of interracial couples, in part because they were denied the right to settle in the colonies. By bringing colony and metropole into a single analytic frame, the deeply entangled nature of these seemingly geographically distinct histories of interracial sex comes into sharp focus.

RIOTS, REPATRIATION, AND THE POLICY OF PREVENTION

Although black communities and interracial marriages in Britain long predate World War I, during the war itself increasing numbers of black seamen came to its ports from different parts of the empire to fill the labor vacuum in the shipping industry that resulted from the drafting of white British men into the military.[18] The majority of these seamen originated from Britain's colonies in the West Indies and West Africa, as well as from India, the British Somaliland Protectorate, and Aden. While seamen from India, known as lascars, had always made up a significant number of the colonized labor hired on British vessels, the contracts they were hired under restricted their ability to reside in Britain.[19] As a result, settlement rates were higher among seamen from the West Indies, West Africa, Somaliland, and Aden. Ethnic settlement patterns differed from port to port: West Indians and West Africans were more populous in Liverpool, while Cardiff had a higher percentage of men from Aden and Somaliland. The multiracial and multiethnic makeup of Britain's ports also resulted from seamen's resistance to the maritime industry's discriminatory wage system, which sought to exploit colonized labor by paying men who signed on in the colonies significantly lower wages than those who signed on in British ports.[20] This served as an incentive for West African seamen to jump ship in Britain, where they waited until they could sign on to another ship at the higher metropolitan rate, and explains, in part, why many of them chose to establish residences in British ports. At the close of the war in late 1918, most of these seamen, along with sizable numbers of demobilized soldiers from the colonies, remained in the country's seafaring districts. Together, they competed with white British men for an increasingly limited number of maritime jobs.

Economic hardship in the ports, created by the postwar depression and racialized job competition within the shipping industry, offers a compelling explanation of the underlying cause of the 1919 race riots. In the six-month-long series of smaller riots that preceded the outbreak of major rioting in June, racial violence was in each instance a direct result of competition over jobs.[21] Moreover, the initial incidence of racial violence that led to the outbreak of major rioting in Liverpool in June was attributed to tensions between black seamen and white foreign labor, in this case Scandinavians, who were in direct competition with one another for jobs not already taken by white British seamen.[22] Yet, it was the notion that black men were consorting with white women that garnered the most attention from the press and local and national authorities, as well as everyday observers. The "sex problem," as one newspaper dubbed it, became a primary explanatory framework for understanding, and in many cases rationalizing, the impetus behind the riots.[23]

Shortly after the riots had started in Liverpool, the city's assistant head constable informed the Home Office that "the trouble has been caused between the citizens and the Blacks, mainly on account of the Blacks interfering with white women [and] capturing a portion of the labour market."[24] Although wrong in his assertion that blacks were not also citizens, the constable's false dichotomy undergirded and exacerbated wider tensions over interracial sex. His elevation of sex over job competition was mirrored in press coverage of the riots. Commenting on the riots in Cardiff and Liverpool, an editorialist for the *Sunday Express* noted, "It is naturally offensive to us that coloured men should consort with even the lowest of white women.

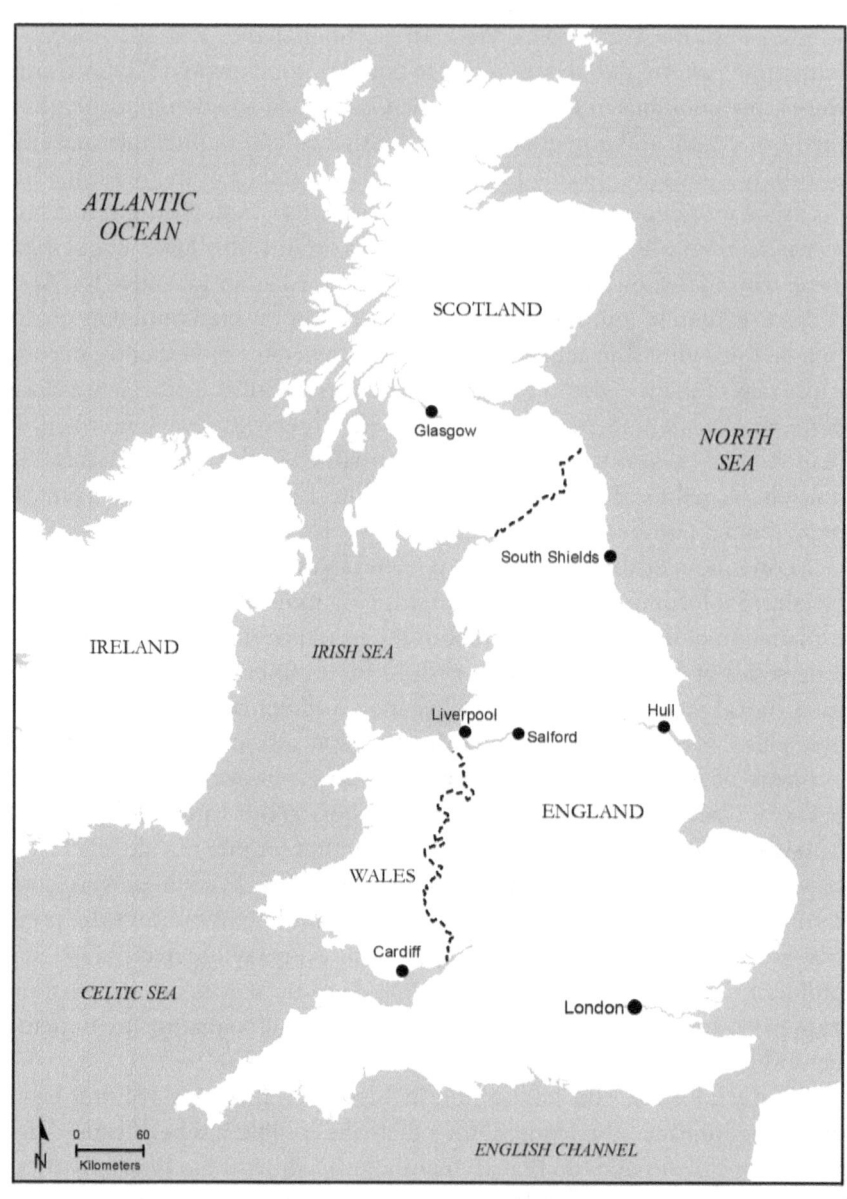

MAP 6.1. Map of the United Kingdom, indicating riot-stricken port cities, ca. 1919. (Map by Brian Edward Balsley, GISP.)

Racial antipathy is always present, the sex jealousy inflames it to a violent, unreasoning wave of emotion. To add to the resentment, it is suggested that the Black men are holding white men's jobs.[25] Even in articles that discussed a variety of causal factors and gave primacy to job competition, interracial sexual relations received a disproportionate amount of coverage. The lead article in the *Western Mail* on the thirteenth of June listed job competition first among the reasons for the riots, with the "resentment aroused by the consorting of Black men and white women" second, followed, respectively, by a general feeling of postwar popular unrest and the hot weather. Yet, the "sex problem" received most of the article's attention.[26] Some press reports ignored all other possible factors, choosing to focus on sex alone. The *Daily Mail*, a popular nationwide paper, simply reported that "the riots have arisen out of the growing feeling of hostility towards the Blacks mainly because of their association with white girls and women."[27] Cardiff's chief constable, who informed the Home Office that the white rioters were "alarmed at the association of so many white women with the coloured races," apparently shared this monocausal view.[28]

Thus, the unprecedented level of violence perpetrated against black men during the riots was naturalized through the discourse of "sexual jealousy" on the part of the white rioters. One measure of that violence was the lynching of Charles Wootton, a twenty-four-year-old West Indian who had served as a fireman in the navy during the war. Chased to his death by a lynch mob of more than two hundred rioters, Wootton's murder was the first officially reported lynching in Britain.[29] While we must be careful to distinguish between incidences of lynching in Britain like Wootton's and the cultures of lynching that existed in the southern United States and in the settler colonies of southern Africa, a cautious comparison reveals that across time and space, horrific acts of violence against black men have often been justified through accusations of interracial sex, particularly between black men and white women.[30] While scholars have focused on the link between lynching and rape accusations, the 1919 race riots in Britain underscore that consensual interracial unions could also be a foil for intense racial violence.

Despite the fact that the white rioters were generally regarded as the aggressors and the "sex problem" as the cause of their hostility, police authorities simultaneously undermined their claim of white culpability by attributing the "racial feeling" in the ports to the grievances of the black community. In the view of Cardiff's chief constable:

> The coloured men resent their inability to secure employment on ships since the Armistice as they're being displaced by white crews;

> They are dissatisfied with the action of the Government;
> They regard themselves as British subjects;
> They claim equal treatment with whites and contend that they fought for the British Empire during the war and manned their food ships during the submarine campaign.[31]

Arrest ratios offer further evidence that the police disproportionately targeted black men for punishment, despite identifying whites as the instigators of violence: out of twenty-one arrests made during two days of rioting in Cardiff, only four "Britishers" were apprehended, the remaining seventeen arrestees were all black men.[32] Others were bolder in their pronouncements of black culpability and white innocence: Liverpool's head constable placed blame squarely in the corner of black men, who, he stated, were the aggressors in "nearly all cases." His assertion, however, was undercut by his own report, which documented only one instance of unprovoked black-on-white violence.[33]

While black men's grievances were used to deflect blame from the white rioters, they were nonetheless real. As such, black men's fierce response to the violence perpetrated against them should be viewed as both a matter of immediate self-defense and a wider defense of their place in British society, as well as an active assertion of the rights owed to them as a result of their participation in the war.[34] Fola Thomas, a demobilized soldier from West Africa, aptly stated this in his protest letter to the House of Commons: "Ain't these men have the right of obtaining their daily bread under the Flag they have the proud to belong[?] And who they have . . . fought for[?]"[35] Thomas went on to call into question the unethical way black men in Liverpool were being treated in the wake of the riots—treatment that he claimed was far worse than what the British had inflicted upon their German enemies. Plans to intern the city's black population in vacated military camps on the outskirts of town prompted Thomas to ask with sardonic wit, "Are these men German subjects or British subjects[?]"[36] The proposed internment scheme had grown out of the massive numbers of black men and their families who had either sought police protection or had been rounded up by the police and taken into protective custody, ostensibly for their own safety.[37] As the number of black men and their families in police custody quickly dropped, internment plans were abandoned, and the authorities turned their attention toward a massive repatriation scheme.[38]

Within days of the major outbreak of violence in June, local and national authorities began drawing up plans to send black men back to the colonies of their birth in an attempt to restore calm and (racial) order to the port cities. Liverpool's assistant head constable put it bluntly when he said he wanted "to remove this Black population, some 2000 to 3000 by compulsory repatriation or otherwise."[39] The Colonial Office, however, feared that if the repatriations were handled inappropriately, disgruntled men would return to the colonies to stir up trouble. Disturbances had already broken out in Sierra Leone as early as July 1919 over the ill-treatment of black men in the British ports.[40] How much more unrest could be expected if the victims of the riots, many of whom participated in the war effort, were forcibly returned to the colonies?

The Colonial Office quickly quashed these locally initiated repatriation schemes, but the damage had already been done.[41] Police in Cardiff reported that some West Indians and West Africans had agreed to repatriate for the sole purpose of "creating racial feeling against white people domiciled in their country."[42] Most West Africans and West Indians, however, refused to return to the colonies.[43] In the view of Cardiff's chief constable, these men had "made the United Kingdom their home, they have formed attachments with white women and are prepared to stubbornly defend what they call their rights."[44] While domestic British authorities were concerned that marriage to white women would deter West Africans and West Indians from consenting to be repatriated, colonial authorities were alarmed by precisely the opposite: there were some West Africans and West Indians who wanted to be repatriated with their white wives.

Rioting had barely come to a stop in June 1919 when the Colonial Office decided that "there can be no question of providing passage at Government expense for the European wife of a coloured man."[45] Given that the men in question had no funds to repatriate themselves, let alone their wives, by refusing to pay passage fees, British authorities effectively made it impossible for black men who desired joint repatriation to return to the colonies with their white wives. On 30 July 1919 this policy of prevention was solidified during a meeting at the Ministry of Labor, which had assumed responsibility for the repatriation scheme. At the special insistence of the Colonial Office, the Ministry of Labor instructed the local committees charged with carrying out the repatriations in the seven main ports (Salford, Liverpool, Cardiff, Glasgow, Hull, South Shields, and London) not to repatriate black men with their white wives.[46] The "white wife problem," as one Whitehall adviser later put it, was as the phrase suggests particular to white women.[47] The government paid the cost of transporting the black wives of men like Joseph Queashie from the Gold Coast back to the colonies.[48]

It is difficult to ascertain the exact number of West Africans and their white wives who were adversely affected by this policy, but the statistical information available suggests that their numbers were by no means negligible. In a survey conducted by the Liverpool police shortly after the riots had come to an end, a total of 188 men from British West Africa were identified as residing in Liverpool. While the police suspected that the actual number was much higher, they explained the lower number reported as the result of "an exodus of negros [sic] from the city to inland towns since the question of repatriation arose."[49] Of the 188 West African men identified, twenty-one were married. Of this number, eighteen were married to white women resident in Liverpool and three to African women who resided in West Africa. Eleven of the eighteen interracially married men were willing to be repatriated back to West Africa *only* if joined by their white wives.[50]

The willingness of well over half of the surveyed married West Africans to accept repatriation compared to 47 percent of single West Africans indicates that the authorities were wrong in believing that marriage to white women created ties to the metropole that could not be broken as easily as those of single men. Rather, it was the authorities' policy of prevention that kept these men in Britain because it barred them from returning to the colonies with their wives. Thus, if we are to understand the range of different imperatives that shaped the unwillingness of West Africans to be repatriated and that ultimately led to the scheme's widely recognized failure, we must acknowledge that in addition to unsatisfactory remuneration packages and the desire to remain in Britain, for some West Africans the policy of prevention was also a major factor.[51] A representative from the Local Government Board said as much when he expressed his belief that "the white wife constituted a big difficulty."[52]

The Colonial Office's refusal to repatriate West Africans with their white wives contrasts sharply with its concession to allow black men primarily from the West Indies to return home with their white wives at the government's expense.[53] According to Jacqueline Jenkinson, by September 1919 the government had reverted to its preriot scheme, in which "repatriation for white wives and families was to be considered and granted on receipt of proof that a marriage had taken place, and that the sailor was in fact, from the colony to which he wished to return." Although the reintroduction of this nonrestrictive scheme is referred to broadly as a "concession by the government [to allow] the white wives and families of Black men to be repatriated with them," Jenkinson's evidence is limited to West Indians and one black Canadian.[54] Colonial Office records indicate that this concession was never contemplated for West Africans, nor is there any evidence to suggest that the preriot scheme for white wives was ever applied to the West African colonies. What is abundantly evident is that immediately following the 1919 riots a clear policy of prevention emerged, which remained focused on the West African colonies for several years before expanding to incorporate other parts of British Africa.

While not completely enthusiastic about its concession, implicit in the Colonial Office's decision to repatriate West Indians with their white wives was its belief that a different set of racial politics was at work in the West Indies, where it imagined that the region's long history of intermixture between Europeans, Africans, and surviving indigenous peoples had created more racially tolerant societies. This myth and its repercussions on colonial policy were not new. As explained in part 1, a decade earlier the West Indian colonies were intentionally excluded by the Colonial Office from its widely distributed anticoncubinage circular on the grounds that enforcing such a directive "where black and white live together, often intermarry, and where you have every shade of colour living side by side in social union, would be a great blunder."[55] Similarly, the Colonial Office felt that race relations in the West Indies could withstand the presence of working-class black men married to white women. It is critical to note, however, that local colonial authorities vehemently disagreed and tried to convince the Colonial Office not to repatriate interracial couples to the West Indies.[56] Here we have another example of the different perspectives and agendas that characterized the colonial project as it was carried out in the metropole and in the colonies, and the kinds of "tensions of empire" that could arise between those who wielded their power from imperial centers and the "men on the spot."

Thus, the Colonial Office pursued very different strategies in its management of interracial sexual relations throughout its diverse empire. In fact, it explicitly acknowledged "the case of West Africans with white wives was on a somewhat different footing from white wives of natives of the West Indies." In support of this assertion, Alexander Fiddian cited the system of residential racial segregation in some parts of the West African colonies as a major obstacle. Using Nigeria as a case in point, he noted that "in various Nigerian townships a white woman would be supposed not to live in the native reservation and a native not to live in the European reservation unless he did so as his wife's servant!"[57] The irony here is that although residential segregation ordinances were enforced primarily on health grounds, it was hoped that they would help curb the far more common occurrence of sexual relations between European men and African women in the colonies.[58] Yet they were now being used as an excuse to exclude legally married African men and European women from making the colonies home. While Fiddian made recourse to legalities in order to justify his claim of West

African exceptionalism, the reams of correspondence produced by these requests reveal that colonial officials refused to repatriate Africans and their white wives because they steadfastly believed that a European woman living with a working-class African would obliterate European racial prestige — that talisman invested with the power of "keeping the natives in their place" and ensuring the stability of colonial rule. The Colonial Office, in the words of one of its advisers, was simply not willing "to face the consequences of letting an Englishwoman . . . go to West Africa as the wife of a black man."[59] In short, the decision to allow West Indians but not West Africans to be repatriated with their white wives must be read against the particular dynamics of race, sex, and class relations in each of these colonial spheres, and more specifically read against the way in which the Colonial Office, situated in the metropole, read (or misread) such relations in its overseas colonies.

REPATRIATION POLICY DURING THE INTERWAR YEARS

While the Colonial Office's policy of prevention kept the West African colonies free of working-class interracial couples in the immediate aftermath of the 1919 race riots, it did not stop West Africans and their white wives from petitioning for repatriation during the interwar years. Before turning to a particularly dramatic case in point, I want to extend this chapter's purview to the Somaliland Protectorate in order to make some important observations about the policy of prevention's geographic and temporal expansion, as well as its formalization in the early 1920s.

In January 1923, faced with the impending arrival of Ismail Noor, a Somali, and his English wife, Edith, the protectorate's governor, Colonel Gerald Summers, hurriedly enacted legislation to prohibit the entry of the white wives of Somali men on the grounds that they were "undesirable non-natives." This legislation was not limited to the protectorate, but rather "effectively exclud[ed] European wives from all of British East Africa."[60] Reflecting on this legislative development, Laura Tabili concludes "it was a colonial government with an immediate stake in local social and political relations, not metropolitan empire-builders, who initiated debate regarding 'the desirability of allowing European women married to natives to proceed to Tropical Africa.'"[61] The evidence discussed earlier, however, indicates that "metropolitan empire-builders" in London's Colonial Office were the first to initiate this debate during the summer of 1919. What was precedent-setting about events in the Somaliland Protectorate, however, was that they marked the first time *formal* colonial legislation was used to exclude the white wives of African men from the colonies. The original incarnation of the policy of prevention, conversely, depended on nonlegislative measures, namely, refusing to pay the passage fees of interracial couples to the colonies. Its success in the immediate postriot period was made possible by the fact that these couples were typically working class, if not impoverished, and could not fund their own travel. As a measure designed in response to the riots and the repatriation schemes that followed in their wake, the policy of prevention clearly did not anticipate the possibility that interracial couples could or would make it to the colonies on their own.

Indeed, in the case of the Somaliland Protectorate, the government's hand was forced when Ismail and Edith Noor financed their own travel from Cardiff to Aden before being detained by British authorities in January 1923. In less than a week the protectorate's governor had enacted shotgun legislation barring Edith's entry. This marked the geographic expansion of the intention behind the policy of prevention from West Africa to East Africa, its temporal expansion beyond the immediate postriot period, and the policy's formalization into legislation.[62] It also foreshadowed what would take place in West Africa during the late 1920s and 1930s with regard to the deployment of legislative measures to meet the challenges of increasingly complex repatriation cases, and the more active role local colonial governments would begin to play in these matters.

Like the immediate postriot period, most interwar cases involved British colonial subjects married to British women, whose citizenship status remained unchanged upon marriage. Given that these women were entitled to remain in Britain, as were their husbands, requests for joint repatriation from such couples were quickly rejected and generally left little documentation. Yet, as the story of Ena and John Parker has already demonstrated, these couples often faced tremendous hardships and difficult choices when denied the right to settle in the colonies. In rejecting the Parkers' request, colonial authorities cited the possibility that Ena Parker would live in her husband's fishing village in "native fashion," as one bureaucrat put it, without the modern amenities that the colony's urban European enclaves offered European women. To live in "native fashion" was to "go native"—no other transgression frightened colonial administrators more, especially when it involved European women.

THE ANNAN FAMILY IN GERMANY

The kinds of colonial anxieties generated by white women who "violated imperial sexual categories and spatial boundaries, not only by marrying implicitly 'downwards' across the colour line, but also by seeking to move geographically and culturally 'backwards' from metropole to colony," were on full display in the case of Frieda Annan, the German wife of Gold Coaster Alfred Annan. The couple's case was distinguished by the fact that they resided in Germany and that she was a German citizen. Upon marriage to a foreign national, Frieda lost her German citizenship and was no longer entitled to domicile in Germany, nor was her husband, a British subject, or their children.[63] Their story vividly illustrates the additional risks involved for women who married across national, religious, and race lines.[64] Unwanted in Germany, the Annans by virtue of British nationality law were British subjects with the right to domicile in Britain or the Gold Coast, but neither wanted to accept the family on their soil. Their fate became the subject of intense diplomatic and legal wrangling, which in turn produced voluminous archival records that chart their struggles to settle in Alfred's birthplace, the Gold Coast. These records also reveal the complications occasioned by his presence as a British subject in Germany, reminding us that the diasporic routes forged during the age of new imperialism were not always neatly contained within imperial spheres, but often cut across them in ways that confronted imperial regimes and colonial subjects with unprecedented challenges.[65] These challenges increasingly required colonial authorities to clarify and formalize the grounds on which they could legally prohibit the white wives of all but a few wealthy West Africans from taking up residency in the colonies.

Our first glimpse of the Annans occurs in September 1927 when Alfred Annan, having been denied assistance by the British consulate in Berlin because he had no papers that could prove his status as a British subject, wrote to the Colonial Office requesting that his family be repatriated to the Gold Coast. Born in 1888 in Christiansborg, Accra, Annan had apparently come to Germany in 1901 as the personal servant of a "coloured man" named Robert Larsen, who eventually died. Annan subsequently became a seaman working in the German merchant marines. While his whereabouts during the First World War are unclear, Annan eventually returned to Germany. After a courtship of at least two years he married twenty-three-year-old Frieda Meyer in early 1927 and the couple settled in Hamburg, where Alfred occasionally found employment as a singer and step-dancer at Busch Circus.[66] By August of that year they had two children, a girl and a boy. As his family grew they became increasingly impoverished, a condition Annan hoped to ameliorate by settling in the Gold Coast, where he said his family was waiting to receive them. Once the Colonial Office had ascertained that Annan was a "native" of the colony and that his wife was white, it instructed the

Foreign Office to have the consulate in Berlin inform him that "it is not possible to give any assistance towards his repatriation if his wife and family accompany him to West Africa, but . . . if he is willing to return to the Gold Coast without them, the Secretary of State will be prepared to refer his case to the Government of the Gold Coast for consideration."[67]

Nothing more was heard from the Annans until the early fall of 1930, when they came into the hands of German authorities seeking to deport them. The radical change in the family's position can be explained in relation to two major interrelated events. First, the Great Depression, which started in 1929, wreaked havoc on the German economy and led to several calls for the expulsion of foreigners. Second, and equally important, was the increasing popularity of the Nazi Party, which became the second-largest political party in Germany during the September 1930 elections, the very month the Annans were targeted for deportation. While the different länder (administrative divisions) devised their own policies to deal with "unwanted" foreigners, it is fair to say that across Germany as a whole, a family like the Annans would have felt increased hostility. Hitler scorned interracial couples and their progeny in *Mein Kampf*, which by 1930 was a best seller in Germany. While referring specifically to German women and their children fathered by African soldiers who garrisoned the Rhineland as part of the French occupation after World War I, Hitler no doubt cast aspersions on all German women who were interracially married and their children. That Frieda Annan was also Jewish compounded an already tense situation. Little surprise, then, that both the Annans and the German state were looking to part ways.

With the German government now eager to deport the entire family to the Gold Coast at its own expense, Alfred returned to the British Consulate in Berlin to renew his application for a passport. Although the British authorities had not changed their position, the German government's intervention in the case posed a new challenge. As Lord Passfield remarked, "If the German Government is prepared to provide the necessary funds for the repatriation of the whole family, it will hardly be possible to prevent their embarkation."[68] Up until this point colonial authorities had prevented white women from accompanying their working-class African husbands to the West African colonies by refusing to pay their passage fees. The policy succeeded in achieving its goal because these couples did not have the financial means to repatriate themselves. The exception to this de facto rule occurred in 1922 when Mr. Samuels, a Gold Coaster employed by the government as a prison instructor, returned from Europe with his Irish wife at their own expense. The couple, having made their own way to the Gold

Coast, was accepted into the colony. However, within a year of their arrival Mr. Samuels died, leaving his wife destitute and forcing the government to pay the cost of her repatriation back to England. The outcome of the Samuelses' case heightened colonial authorities' concerns about the class status of interracial couples seeking residency in the colonies. After all, if a case involving a fairly well-paid Gold Coaster employed in the government service ended in the destitution of his European wife, what would become of a woman like Frieda Annan, the wife of a working-class African?

Given the German government's intention to deport the family and the Colonial Office's uncertainty about how to prevent their embarkation, the Gold Coast government launched its own investigation into what it could do to prevent the Annans from being sent to the colony. The colony's attorney general, Mr. Sidney Abrahams, plainly admitted that there was no way Alfred could be refused permission to enter the Gold Coast, but he contended that Frieda and the children could be refused under several sections of the Immigration Restriction Ordinance. In particular, section 5(6) of the ordinance allowed immigrants to be excluded on the grounds of their entry being "undesirable." While Abrahams argued that it was "obviously undesirable in the interests of the wife and children themselves that they should come here particularly at a time of economic stress," his real concern was the social stability of the colony.[69] In a rebuke to his colleagues for apparently failing to see things the same way, Abrahams warned:

> Undue emphasis is laid upon the interests of the Annan family, and the possibility of their becoming a financial burden on the colony, and insufficient emphasis upon what in my opinion is the only factor for consideration, namely whether the residence in the Colony of a European woman under conditions to which this woman would probably be forced to live is undesirable in the interests of the Colony.[70]

In short, while the Annan family's entry into the colony posed a number of potential hazards, Abrahams contended that these threats formed a hierarchy of danger, at the top of which was the intensely subversive nature of Mrs. Annan's presence in the colony as the white wife of a destitute African man. Like Edith Noor, the case of Frieda Annan "illustrates the apparent threat a woman out of place could pose, symbolically and materially, to the stability of imperial rule, a power system to which racial but also gendered and class, spatial and sexual boundaries remained integral."[71]

Following his attorney general's advice, Governor Slater prohibited the entry of Frieda and her children as "undesirables" unless or until Alfred could prove that he had "means sufficient to maintain her in a manner not altogether unbefitting a European woman and to make reasonable provision for her and her children in case of his death."[72] There was some debate, however, over how high to set the sum Annan was asked to meet. Attorney General Abrahams not only felt that the sum originally proposed might be interpreted as being purposely prohibitive, he also thought it unnecessarily high for "the type of European woman who would marry an 'illiterate African sailor,'" since such a woman "would hardly expect a refined standard of life and probably has never enjoyed a substantial measure of comfort." He then added, "German women of the lower order are notably frugally-minded."[73] Although incorrect in his assumption that Frieda had "never enjoyed" a life of comfort—she was in fact the daughter of a solidly middle-class Jewish family in Leipzig—his comments are suggestive of the role played by nationality and class, as well as race and gender, in the decision-making processes of colonial authorities in these kinds of cases. In their view Frieda's nationality, presumed class background, and gender combined to transform her into an impoverished penny-pincher who could justifiably be provided with a more modest standard of living.

The stipulated amount of £20 per month for maintenance and a £300 death insurance policy that Annan was required to provide was still prohibitively high, but it cleverly allowed the Gold Coast government not to appear completely unreasonable in its decision-making process. With a legal solution now in place, vis-à-vis the Immigration Restriction Ordinance, Governor Slater's response to the Colonial Office was crafted to dramatically highlight why Frieda and her children could not be admitted to the colony. Having used the Samuels case as an example of the fate that had befallen the white wife of a gainfully employed African civil servant, Governor Slater went on to paint a frightening picture of the even greater consequences of a European woman living in "one room of a house crowded by Africans of the labouring class" in the "native quarter" of Accra:

> It is not difficult to conceive of the tragic conclusion to such a ménage, very possibly with repercussions on public peace and good order. Nor can I view without disquiet the effect upon the less cultured majority of Africans of a European woman living the life of an African labourer; I regard it as thoroughly undesirable in the

interests of the colony that a European woman should be perceived to be living in a state of social degradation.[74]

Whereas the repatriation of Mrs. Samuels back to England after her husband's death had rid the colony of the sight of a European woman living in destitution, Governor Slater further argued that if a similar situation were to occur, the government would be unable to deport Frieda back to Germany, as she had lost her German citizenship upon marrying Alfred. As a result, Governor Slater predicted that "her residence on the Gold Coast would be continued in the same depressed and degraded condition."[75] She would in effect become the permanent liability of the Gold Coast government. Slater's description illustrates how the presumed subversiveness of Frieda Annan's presence in the colony was constituted through not only race and gender, but also class and spatiality. After all, some white women were already living in the colonies at this time, but most of these women were, as Tabili points out, "wives of British colonial functionaries who inhabited a hermetic all-European society as the dependents of colonizing men, affirming gendered and racial as well as colonial hierarchies between men and women, colonisers and colonized."[76] Frieda's home, in sharp contrast, was likely to be located in a bustling "native quarter," thereby allowing working-class Africans to see and participate in her "social degradation." Worse yet, a fearmongering Governor Slater conjured up the specter of "black peril" to dramatize the risks to all white women posed by Frieda's potential proximity to black men. Resorting to such alarmist measures is but one indication of the acute anxieties that the so-called "white wife problem" produced in colonial authorities. In violating the colony's racial geography, which by the 1930s had been set into place by the creation of European residential segregation areas in the major towns and cities with large European populations, the purported location of Frieda's home would physically transgress the divide between colonized and colonizer that was so essential to colonial rule. While colonial stability was overtly tethered to "keeping the natives in their place," it was arguably more dependent upon keeping Europeans in *theirs*.

The Gold Coast government was well aware that its determination to keep the Annans out of the colony would put it at odds with British domestic authorities, who were also loath to accept the family. The colony's attorney general summed things up without mincing his words:

> This is an ugly situation. It looks as if German patience has been exhausted and that these wretched people will be landed in England

and there taken in according to international understanding. But I think we must stick to our guns and refuse to accept them as long as we can. It may be hard on England but in a way it would be worse for the Gold Coast and we can . . . justify exclusion by our law. It may be that the Home Office will press the Colonial Office to force our doors open, but until then we should refuse to open.[77]

THE ANNAN FAMILY IN HULL, ENGLAND

The attorney general's prediction turned out to be true. After nearly two years of diplomatic wrangling, the Germans deported the Annans, now a family of five, in March 1932 to the British port city of Hull. Adamant about refusing the family entry to the Gold Coast, the Colonial Office prepared itself for "a squabble with the Home Office." In the words of one of its advisers, the Home Office was "certainly not in a position to compel us to raise a finger, certainly not to send a white woman to West Africa with a black man, even if he is her husband."[78]

The extent to which the Home Office and local authorities continued to pressure the Colonial Office to repatriate the family to the Gold Coast is unknown; however, the numerous letters that Alfred sent to the colonial authorities made clear that life was so miserable for them that they continued to press for repatriation. Upon arrival the family was placed into separate workhouses in Hull: Frieda and the children went to the Beverly Road Institution and Alfred was sent to the Anlaby Road Institution. In a letter written from Anlaby Road to the secretary of state for the colonies, Alfred lamented the family's separation; a fact that he said was making Frieda ill. To this he added, "I am left here in a strange town, with a wife and five children. I don't want to hang about here, I want to get back home, to Accra, Gold Coast, so if you could assist me in any way I should be extremely obliged to you."[79] Five years later, in September 1937, with two more children born to the couple, Annan wrote directly to Governor Arnold Hodson of the Gold Coast in the hope of securing a better outcome. In his letter he recounted his family's increasing destitution and the indignities they were subjected to at the hands of local authorities: "On account of unemployment I was imprisoned for 6 months by this English Government and my poor 7 children were kicked about and beaten. During these 6 months the government has sold all my furniture and cloth, so now I stand naked with my poor children."[80] In another letter, sent a few years later to the Colonial Office, Annan again requested to be repatriated with his family in order to escape being harassed by Hull authorities at the onset of World War II:

> Send me and my family home. I think I could live more better at home than in England.... Why I am not satisfied is because my children are being neglected.... Now my name in Britain is called Foreign as people assault me by calling us German spies also the Hull government. I am under a British colony therefore I am neither, my wife is a Russian Jew and the people put down she is a spy.... I can see this great day every body should not consult people to assault people, but the Hull Government follow such low down people themselves detectives keep coming and upsetting my home about us being spies for any reason at all. They also brought soldier with a gun and threatened them [his children] about mum and dad being a spy and did they know anything.[81]

In closing his letter, Annan sought to ensure the Colonial Office that his wife would be able to adjust to life in the Gold Coast, just as he had adapted to life in Europe: "My wife understands African food although she is a jew. Never mind African people walk barefooted but not in England." That Frieda Annan was Jewish redirects our attention to the additional factor of religion, in addition to race, class, gender, and nationality, as a source of marginalization and persecution for the Annans, particularly as the linked phenomena of anti-Semitism and Germanophobia intensified in the context of wartime Europe. Throughout the letter Alfred drew attention to the relentlessness with which local authorities in Hull disturbed, indeed, invaded his home, rendering it a site that he needed to flee from. In stark contrast, Alfred imagined his home in the Gold Coast as a place where he could protect, feed, and clothe his wife and children. Home was where he and Frieda would cease being "foreigners" and "spies."

The last trace of the Annan family in the colonial archive appears in the form of a Colonial Office minute dated 20 January 1941. The minute recounts an emotionally fraught visit Frieda Annan made to the Colonial Office days earlier, on Friday, 17 January. The purpose of her visit was to follow up on her husband's most recent application for repatriation to the Gold Coast. Upon hearing that the Gold Coast government had once again rejected their request, Frieda reportedly "alternated between tears, rage and threats."[82] The cause of her distress, she explained, was the impending removal of their children by the Hull magistrate, who had accused the Annans of neglecting to provide the children with appropriate material provisions. Having previously been separated from their children on the same charge, a fact that Alfred had lamented in an earlier letter to the governor of the Gold Coast, Frieda was desperate to comply with the magistrate's order that the couple prove their ability to properly care for their seven children within a fortnight.[83] Making matters worse, she said, Alfred had declared to the magistrate that he was planning to leave on the next available ship, never to come back.

With their hopes of being sent to the Gold Coast dashed once again, Frieda pleaded for help in providing winter clothing for her children. Her fear of being separated from them was so great that she reportedly threatened to commit murder if "anyone attempted to remove the children."[84] Frieda's hour-and-a-half visit to the Colonial Office failed to yield any winter clothing for her children and ended with a vague invitation to resubmit their repatriation application so that it could "be considered from the point of view of seeing whether there were any grounds on which we could write to the Governor of the Gold Coast again."[85] Essentially, it was an invitation to restart what had long proven to be a futile process. On these grounds alone, we might conclude that the end of the Annans' colonial correspondence was hastened by their sheer frustration with a system that was committed to keeping them out of the Gold Coast.

THE ANNAN FAMILY IN CARDIFF, WALES

Interviews with three of the four surviving children of the Annan family provide a different explanation, however, for the cessation of their parents' long-standing efforts to repatriate to the Gold Coast. In the wake of their failed repatriation application in early 1941, the couple knew they had to take drastic measures to improve their situation, not least because of the intensifying German air raids on Hull.[86] Encouraged by another Gold Coaster, in the late spring of 1941 Alfred relocated his family to Cardiff, where he hoped they would be safer.[87] One might also surmise that relocating to Cardiff put the family at a distance from the surveillance of Hull's municipal authorities. After lodging briefly with Alfred's compatriot, Frieda was able to secure a sizable corner home for the family on Railway Street in Splott, Cardiff, through a connection she had with a Jewish landlord, who had known Frieda's family in Leipzig.[88] Once the family was settled into their new home, Alfred went back to sea in early May 1941, serving as a fireman and trimmer on the *Graiglas*, a newly built merchant steamer.[89] Part of one of the war's earliest transatlantic convoys (ON 005), the *Graiglas* finally departed from Clyde on 6 August 1941 for Father Point on the Atlantic coast of Canada.[90] As had been the case when the family lived in Hull, Alfred was away at sea for many months, returning in late February 1942.

Three short weeks later, Frieda and the couple's eldest daughter, Ellen, accompanied Alfred down to the docks for his second, and last, wartime voyage. Although in her eighties now, Ellen vividly recalls the day of his departure: "I remember the exact moment. I remember every word he said because I never ever forgot it. We got to the docks and we couldn't go on the ship, we had to stand to the side. And he [Alfred] was talking to my mother, but I never really paid attention until he said, 'Ooh! I saw a rat crossing [over there]! Frieda, I don't think I'm coming back. That's bad luck.' I swear to God. And that's the last time I saw him . . . he never came back."[91] Frieda, Ellen says, was in tears. That was 17 March 1942, and Alfred, in his capacity as a fireman and trimmer, had joined the crew of the SS *Cape Corso*, a Merchant Navy steamship that was part of the PQ 15 convoy bound for the Soviet ports of Murmansk and Arkhangel'sk, laden with wartime supplies.[92] The convoy made its way to Reykjavik, Iceland, in late April and continued farther north where it came under intense fire by German torpedo bombers on 2 May 1942. Upon being hit, the SS *Cape Corso*'s large cargo of munitions exploded with great force, sinking the ship almost instantaneously and taking fifty of its fifty-six passengers to their deaths.[93] Alfred Annan was among the dead.[94]

Branded in Ellen's memory, too, is the moment she learned of her father's death. She had just been to the movies with her friend, Grace Bassey (sister of the famous Welsh-Nigerian singer Dame Shirley Bassey), and as they rounded the corner Ellen spotted a police car in front of her house. As they hurried toward the house, "I heard my mother scream. I mean the scream was unbelievable. And I ran then, and Grace behind me. And the Catholic priest was there, and the police. They gave my mother the news that my father had been killed."[95] Although Frieda and her children had grown accustomed to Alfred's long absences away at sea, he had always come home and had, to the best of his abilities, provided for the maintenance of his family. In the immediate wake of his death Ellen says the family was buoyed by other Africans: "I remember they [Africans] came from everywhere. They weren't even living in Cardiff, but they knew him and the word got around that he'd been killed, and they all came . . . checked to see my mother had enough for the children. They were just fantastic."[96]

But it was ultimately Frieda, alone, who was charged with caring for her seven children: Ellen, then just one month shy of her sixteenth birthday; Max Heinz Joachim, fourteen years old; Wilson, thirteen years old; Eduard, twelve years old; George Alfred, ten years old; Robert, eight years old; and Kate, seven years old. The image of Frieda as a fiercely protective mother that emerges in colonial correspondence is one that resonates with her children, before and after Alfred's death. At the time of the family's arrival in Cardiff the city was still predominantly white, with a visible

Muslim minority population of primarily Yemenis and Somalis, and its own history of racial antagonisms, partly rooted in anxieties over relationships between white Welsh women and Muslim men.[97] Frieda's efforts to shield her children from prejudice are evident in George and Robert Annan's account of an incident in which two neighbors, elderly white women, taunted them with racial epitaphs. As soon as Frieda got wind of what was happening, she rushed from her home and "raised Cain." Having not mastered the English language, Frieda's vitriol came forth in a mixture of German and English, but the women got the point and were quickly sent "running to their house."[98]

Her solidarity with the plight of black people was not limited to her own children. During the war, upwards of 130,000 African American soldiers were deployed to Great Britain and Northern Ireland—a substantial number of whom were stationed in Cardiff.[99] Frieda became well known to a platoon of African American soldiers after she interceded on behalf of two of their number who were being publicly berated by two white men. She brought the beleaguered men home to cool off, telling them, in the words of her son Robert, "As long as you are here, you are always welcome here [in my house]." Their house in Splott became a hub for members of the platoon, so much so that the military police often came to the Annan house first when they were looking for a missing soldier. Her loyalty to them was repaid in the form of regular deliveries of canned food, which allowed Frieda to keep her cellar stocked with luxuries like pineapple, chicken, peaches, corn, and cigarettes, despite the rations. Robert further recalls that on the morning that the platoon was leaving for home they marched from their base in Sully, some seven miles southwest of Cardiff, to the Annan house on Railway Street to bid Frieda farewell. "They all stood outside of the house," according to Robert, "and they went in one by one to say goodbye to her."[100]

Although vocal when it came to racism and fiercely protective of her children, by all accounts Frieda was a deeply private person who rarely shared her feelings with her children. Nonetheless, as her eldest daughter, Ellen, says, "her mind was always going . . . you could see her mind was just going, she was thinking. But I don't know what she was thinking about."[101] Perhaps Frieda's thoughts drifted back in time to the loss of her natal family. Upon marrying Alfred, her father had disowned her, and although her mother secretly kept in contact with her, Frieda's relationship with her family was severed for good when she and Alfred, along with the children, were deported from Germany in 1932. Having been pushed out of Germany, only to be harassed and disappointed by British authorities, one can imagine that the cruel irony of losing Alfred to a German torpedo while he was serving on behalf of the British war effort was not lost on Frieda. Sitting on her favorite rocking chair in front of the fire in their Splott home, perhaps Frieda dwelled silently on how differently their lives might have turned out had they been repatriated to the Gold Coast. If in her moments of silence she still contemplated a life in West Africa, she never mentioned anything to her children about their thwarted efforts to resettle in their father's homeland. Nor did she ever make contact with the Colonial Office again, either to seek assistance or to request that the family be sent to the Gold Coast. Alfred's death closed that chapter in her life. She spent the next three decades living in Cardiff, until her death in 1974. Her presence there, as both a German and a Jew, reminds us that the "white side of black Britain" was diverse in terms of its national and religious makeup.[102]

THE CLASS CAVEAT

A caveat to the colonial authority's policy of prevention allowed the white wives of wealthy African men who could demonstrate that they could maintain their wives in a standard suitable to European womanhood to proceed to the colonies at their own expense. While the economic requirements African men were forced to meet in order to receive this dispensation severely limited the number of these couples in West Africa, those who did meet them appear not to have been actively discouraged from entering the colonies. There are six documented cases of this type for the Gold Coast, Nigeria, and Sierra Leone combined, and in each case the husband was extremely well off. Among them a wealthy barrister, Mr. Akerele, and his white wife settled in Lagos after the government of Nigeria raised no objections to their arrival in the colony.[103]

Likewise, in 1936 the Gold Coast government raised no objections to Dr. Isaac Boaten Asafu-Adjaye's plans to bring his white wife and her nine-year-old daughter from a previous relationship to Kumasi, where he intended to establish a medical practice.[104] Asafu-Adjaye hailed from a wealthy and politically influential Kumasi family, who had groomed their sons, Isaac and his younger brother Edward, to become part of the Asante elite. The two brothers were among the first Asantemen to qualify in medicine and law, and both men went on to become prominent figures in Asante and in nationalist politics.[105] In 1922, at the age of twenty-one, Isaac traveled to London to study medicine at University College. By 1927 he was in an established relationship with an Englishwoman named Dorothy, which is borne out by their shared address and details given on the 1927 birth certificate of Dorothy's daughter, Olive. Isaac is listed as Olive's biological father, but this was a fiction. During the early years of their relationship Dorothy had been married to a (white) British man, and when Olive was born it became obvious that Isaac was not the father of this "clearly caucasian" child.[106] Nonetheless Isaac and Dorothy stayed together and he raised Olive as his own. Two years later, in 1929, they married.[107] Although a complicated and extraordinarily unconventional relationship, especially given the time period, Isaac's course of action suggests real love and affection for Dorothy.[108]

In 1933 he qualified for Membership of the Royal College of Physicians and Membership of the Royal College of Surgeons, but instead of immediately returning home, as was expected of him, he set up a medical practice on Kensington Park Road. It was there that he met another Englishwoman, Jenny Davies (née Lewis), who had brought her young son, Gerald, to Dr. Asafu-Adjaye for treatment. Despite the fact that they were both married, with Jenny separated from her husband, they became lovers. On 22 December 1936 Jenny, known to be a strong-willed and fiercely independent woman, gave birth to their daughter Janice, Isaac's firstborn child. His name, however, did not appear on Janice's birth certificate. At the cost of her own reputation, Jenny deliberately left the "Father's Name" section of the certificate blank, thus saving Isaac from any possible charge of professional misconduct for breaking the bounds of the patient-doctor relationship. It was around this time that Isaac was "summoned home" to Kumasi, where he was expected to put his medical training to use.[109] Perhaps his desire to father his own biological children, something he had been unable to do with Dorothy, helps to explain why he asked the seemingly unthinkable of Jenny: Would she come with him to the Gold Coast with little Janice and Gerald *and* with Dorothy and Olive? She refused, and so the colonial authorities were never confronted with a request that they certainly would have rejected. Jenny did, however, agree to let Isaac take Janice home with him. In February 1936, when Janice was just six weeks old, he came to collect her, but by then Jenny had a change of heart and refused to let her go. Not long after, Isaac left England with Dorothy and Olive. Upon returning to the Gold Coast, he acknowledged the existence of Janice to his family, but he never saw her or Jenny again.[110] Isaac, Dorothy, and Olive settled into life in Kumasi, but the couple remained childless, and he eventually took a young Asante woman as a second wife, with whom he went on to have six children. Quite apart from the fact that this was in violation of the law, Isaac failed to appreciate that Dorothy was not willing to tolerate a polygamous union. She and Olive, now in her late teens, returned to London, although they remained on cordial terms for the rest of Isaac's life.[111]

FIGURE 6.1. Janice Noble (née Davies) with her mother, Jenny, and cousin Jean in London, ca. 1939. (Photograph from the personal collection of Janice Noble, London, England.)

Dorothy Asafu-Adjaye's departure from the Gold Coast avoided stoking colonial anxieties about the threat to British womanhood and white prestige posed by British women who married men from corners of the empire where polygamy was practiced and unwittingly ended up in polygamous unions.[112] Had her case come to official attention, it would have almost certainly confirmed colonial administrators' belief that they were right to worry about the fate of the white wives of even the most highly educated Africans. Indeed, where any doubt lingered about the probable class status of an interracial couple, the colonial authorities erred on the side of extreme caution. By way of example, in 1935 a young doctor, Mr. M. O. Phillips, who had recently finished his medical studies in Britain, was not allowed to return home to Nigeria with his white wife and their child. Instead, the Colonial Office advised him to return alone, and if "he was successful in finding work and in a position to support [his family], the question might then be considered whether [they] might join him."[113]

Notwithstanding the stringent criteria employed by the Colonial Office, this caveat further amplifies the importance of class considerations in the decision-making processes of colonial authorities as they determined the eligibility of interracial couples to establish homes in West Africa. Race and class were mutually constitutive, and, as far as the colonial authorities were concerned, the European community's racial prestige would be obliterated by the presence of a European woman living in "native fashion" with her African husband. On the other hand, the white wives of wealthy African men were afforded the kinds of lifestyles deemed racially appropriate for European women. The European wives of extremely wealthy Africans arguably enjoyed even more comfortable lifestyles than the wives of European government officers who often lived on modest budgets. We might also consider whether the presence of one or two wealthy African men living with their white wives per West African colony may have worked in favor of colonial officials, who wished to portray themselves as not entirely unreasonable where matters of race were concerned. Indeed, it was not uncommon for colonial advisers to reference the few interracial couples that had been allowed to make the colonies home when justifying why they barred others from doing the same.[114]

More practically, colonial authorities had no legal grounds on which they could prevent these couples from entering the colonies provided they could fund their own passage and could show that they had adequate resources at their disposal to prevent them from being deemed "undesirable immigrants." Still, with the exception of a handful of wealthy couples, the colonial administration's policy of prevention was successful in stopping the vast majority of interracial couples from taking up residency in British West Africa precisely because they generally lacked the financial resources necessary to fund their own repatriation and to meet the requirements of the Immigration Restriction Ordinance. This policy, therefore, provides an important key to understanding why it was not until the era of independence that larger numbers of African men resided in West Africa with their white wives, a story we will return to.

CONCLUSION

The rarity of relationships between black men and white women in the African colonies has generally been understood as the result of colonial social conventions. Within British West Africa's expatriate societies, as Barbara Bush notes, "powerful sexual taboos policed white female sexuality, which could only be broken covertly."[115] Indeed, if and when such relations occurred, they were shrouded in secrecy and therefore rarely made their way into the archival record. The exception that proves the rule is the unique case of Annie Muller, a European woman whose nationality could not be determined by colonial authorities. After being deserted in the Gold Coast by her European husband in 1913, Muller began openly liaising with African men. Her behavior was regarded as so aberrant that it contributed to her certification as insane and to her subsequent confinement in a lunatic asylum in Accra for twenty years. Described as "singularly repulsive" by the colony's acting attorney general, her lengthy confinement created such a public scandal that the Gold Coast government was forced to pay for her relocation to and maintenance in a mental institution in Britain in 1933.[116] Muller's case stands unparalleled in the colony's archival record.

We know now, however, that taboos were not the only mechanism through which the colonies were kept free of the "white wife problem." The colonial state exercised its power through the use of both legislative and nonlegislative measures to accomplish this goal as well. As Joel A. Rogers succinctly put it in his three-volume series on sex and race, "Africa was no place for the white wife of a black man," and increasingly draconian measures were taken during the interwar years to keep it that way.[117] But as the Annan family history poignantly demonstrates, such couples did not passively resign themselves to this fate—rather, with vigor and passion they fought to keep their families united. From the Gold Coast to Germany to Hull and then to Cardiff, their fraught journey reminds us that this story is not just about metropole and colony, nor just about Africans and Britons, it is truly a global narrative.

The 1919 race riots set off the chain of events that culminated in the formation of policies and the use of formal legislation to keep all but a handful of white women married to West African men out of the colonies. But the riots sparked something else of consequence: shortly after news of the violent outbreaks filtered back to the Gold Coast, the colony's most politically radical indigenous newspaper, the *Gold Coast Leader,* was awash with fiery commentaries criticizing the hypocrisy of white rioters who were beating black men for marrying or cohabiting with white women in the British ports, while white men had for centuries been having their way with African women in the colonies. White men, they argued, were the real sexual menace. As Gold Coast writers began articulating the need to protect *their* women from "immoral whites" whose sexual licentiousness rendered them unfit overlords, they were drafting a provocative rhetorical strategy for questioning the moral legitimacy of British colonial rule. The next chapter explores these critical commentaries to show how colonized populations' own concerns about interracial sex and their political uses of those concerns provide a deeper understanding of the role of sex across the color line in spurring anticolonial nationalism in the Gold Coast. Chapter 8 then turns its attention toward the political and social milieus of postwar Britain in order to explore how intimate relationships between West African men and white British women contributed to and complicated the work of decolonization.

7 ⤳ "White Peril"/Black Power
Interracial Sex and the Beginning of the End of Empire

IN THE SUMMER AND FALL OF 1919, the African-owned Gold Coast press was awash with news stories and impassioned commentary about the race riots that had recently devastated Britain's port cities. Angered by the sexual politics underlying the race riots, Gold Coast commentators were quick to point out that the ports' white rioters were not the only ones aggrieved by interracial sexual relations. Atu, a regular columnist for the *Gold Coast Leader*, responded to news that black men were targeted for repatriation after being attacked on the ports' streets for "consorting with white women" by reminding his readers "that in their own country white men freely consort with coloured women, forming illicit alliances, and in many cases leaving on the coast abandoned offspring to the precarious protection of needy native families."[1] He continued, "It does not require much skill to diagnose the canting hypocrisy underlying" the riots, but the question now was, "[Could] any sensible man suppose that these men will return to their homes to view with complacency the spectacle of white men associated with coloured women?"[2] In a few short lines Atu vivified the "tensions of empire" created by the movement of African men between metropole and colony, and their different systems of raced and gendered sexual access.[3]

Not long after, the *Leader* published a series of commentaries under the provocative title "Immoral Sanitation." The unnamed author of the series' first installment declared that unseemly sexual liaisons between African women and European men had transformed the "social life" of Sekondi into "a condition of depravity." Elsewhere in the colony, "a woman who boldly acknowledges herself the kept mistress of a European is thrown out of society and virtually looked down upon by men and women of respectability," claimed the writer. In the bustling coastal town of Sekondi, however, he accused "energetic advocates of this dishonourable mode of life" of enticing young women into sexual relationships with European men, whose "carnal lust" was causing the moral deterioration of the town's womenfolk.[4] The claims made in the "Immoral Sanitation" series, argued *Leader* columnist Atu, were more broadly applicable to "other parts of the country where this traffic," which he likened to "prostitution on the part of African women by a class of white men of a low caste," was carried on.[5]

These lurid tales of illicit relationships between profligate white men and debauched African women were not altogether new. Scattered commentaries in the *Leader*, from as early as 1902, suggest that unseemly interracial sexual relations had periodically piqued public criticism in the press for at least two decades.[6] This discontent, as we have already seen, was expressed in other ways too. Gold Coasters who found themselves adversely affected by European officers' sexual misdeeds occasionally addressed their grievances by filing official complaints with the colonial government. With the appearance of the "Immoral Sanitation" series and like-minded commentaries, however, this simmering discontent boiled over into full-blown condemnation of interracial sexual relations in the colony. Drawing on these rare primary sources, this chapter argues that a diverse group of politically marginalized, yet highly politicized Gold Coast men from the colony's embattled intelligentsia, along with disillusioned demobilized soldiers and seamen in post–World War I Britain, used these illicit relationships to challenge the moral legitimacy of British colonial rule.[7] On the one hand, by portraying African women as either immoral race traitors or innocents in need of protection from predatory Europeans, these men were able to claim a leadership role as moral stewards of the nation. On the other hand, by casting European men as sexually promiscuous interlopers, they challenged the very idea that Europeans were morally suited to rule the colonial world.

Implicit in colonizing powers' various efforts to control the domain of interracial sex, like those explored in previous chapters, was a keen awareness of its potential to destabilize hierarchies of rule. Given this, it is remarkable that scholars of colonialism and anticolonial nationalism have not paid greater attention to how colonized populations politicized their own anxieties over interracial sex. This lacuna is all the more notable given the numerous instances in which interracial sexual relations fomented anticolonial discontent and/or became a staple feature of anticolonial rhetoric across a wide swath of the colonial world. From Canton, Kabul, and Indonesia to German Southwest Africa, Kenya, Nigeria, Sierra Leone, South Africa, and Madagascar, the sexual abuse and exploitation of indigenous women by European men provoked deep resentment, outbreaks of violence, and anticolonial sentiments and struggles.[8] Frances Gouda has pointed out more broadly that anticolonial intellectuals in Asia and Africa used the rape of "native" women by white men as a metaphor for colonial violence and domination writ large.[9] The metaphor's rhetorical power surely flowed from the actual fact of sexual exploitation and violence. Gold Coasters also made these connections in their public writings. One such writer framed Africa as Europe's "mistress . . . milked for the larder of others," while another used the figure of a young African girl who, abused and discarded by her European lover, died of a broken heart, to describe the asymmetrical and destructive relationship between Europe and Africa.[10] When read in isolation, such examples run the risk of being dismissed as anecdotal evidence, but collectively they reveal the connective tissue between the domain of interracial sex and anticolonial nationalism, which, as the Gold Coast case suggests, was being forged well before the heyday of political nationalism in the late 1940s and 1950s across much of Africa and Asia.[11] Shifting focus from the myriad meanings of interracial sexual relations for the colonizer to illuminating what they meant for the colonized expands our understanding of these relationships beyond their role in the formation of empire by demonstrating how they are implicated in its dissolution.

Gold Coasters responded to the changing prescriptions and practices that shaped interracial sexual relationships during the early twentieth century in ways that illustrate how gender and sexuality intersected with race to influence the rise of anticolonial nationalism in the Gold Coast. Partha Chatterjee's theorization of anticolonial nationalism as a multisited and multistaged process that "creates its own domain of sovereignty within colonial society well before it begins its political battle with the imperial power" is particularly helpful in understanding these developments.[12] Like Chatterjee's India, the deeply interventionist and paternalistic nature of British colonialism in the Gold Coast, as elsewhere in Africa, sought to transform African cultures and societies, with particular emphases on women, the family, sexuality, and religion. It is hardly surprising, then, that the "inner domain of national culture" emerged as the first battleground of nationalism throughout much of the continent.[13] What is significant about the Gold Coast case study is that in decrying "white peril"—used here to refer to the sexual threat, both real and perceived, that white men posed to black women—anticolonial nationalists did more than claim their own inner domain of sovereignty over the colony's women, they also challenged the very grounds upon which British colonialism legitimized itself by drawing attention to the gap between the civilizing mission's moral rhetoric and the sexual immorality of white men in the colony. In this way we might productively think of the domain of interracial sexual relations as one of the spaces in which anticolonial nationalism begins to make its transition from an inward-looking process of (re)consolidating masculine power to an outward-looking one that is readying itself to lay claim to political power. While control over women remained central to both stages, with few exceptions women were marginalized from the articulation of anticolonial nationalism in the Gold Coast.[14]

"WHITE PERIL"

In an ongoing historical moment in which press reports in diverse corners of the globe were rife with inflammatory tales of the sexual threat black men posed to white women, the proverbial "black peril," Gold Coasters turned this popular narrative, which they were clearly familiar with, on its head by asserting that white men were the real sexual menace.[15] That they did so without ever deploying the term "white peril" exemplifies how the rhetoric of sexual peril retained its power even when "unlabeled."[16] Gold Coast writers were, however, explicit about what it meant in practice. Their fears were provoked by sexual relationships between young African women and European men, which they regarded as exploitative and transgressive, but consensual insofar as the women in question were viewed as willing participants.

The line between consent and coercion, particularly in the context of unequal power relations inflected by race, gender, class, and generation, is difficult to discern, but extant sources do not suggest that fear of rape and other forms of sexual violence prompted this outbreak of anxieties over interracial sex in the colony. Sexual corruption rather than sexual violence constituted the threat white men posed to the colony's young women at this particular moment. Indeed, it was the seemingly consensual nature of many of these relationships that provoked such alarm among commentators who believed that once young women were enticed by the prospects of monetary and material gain, they were despoiled by their voluntarily sexual liaisons with European men. Worse yet, "with their fashionable vices and genteel appearances," they encouraged other "young ladies in town" to cavort with "whitemen . . . from [whom] they can get all necessaries of life."[17] In doing so, they corrupted other women and failed to represent their race with honor and respectability.

Given the integral role that racial respectability played in demonstrating fitness for self-rule, politically ambitious Gold Coast men saw their nationalist aspirations thwarted by these young women.[18] While female sexual libertinage emerged as an obstacle for early Gold Coast nation builders, these men held their European counterparts, the "promoters of such immoral habits," responsible for destroying female virtue, subverting gender norms, and interfering with their patriarchal prerogatives.[19] But white men's sexual licentiousness not only imperiled young women, and hence the collective future of the Gold Coast nation, it also imperiled white colonial power. By laying bare their sexual predations, Gold Coast writers identified white men as the real source of sexual peril, while also giving the lie to the claim that Europeans' moral superiority endowed them with the right to rule over Africans and other subject populations.

Although penned with dramatic flare, Gold Coasters' "white peril" commentaries reflected a series of truths about the changing practice and perception of sexual relationships between European men and African women, as well as changing ideas about marriage in the colony. In earlier centuries marriages between African women and European men were a recognizable phenomenon, but as we have already seen, by the early twentieth century the deeply entrenched racial prescripts of formal colonial rule had rendered them a thing of the past. The decline in intermarriage was plainly evident to Rudolf Asmis, a visiting German colonial authority from neighboring Togoland, who commented approvingly, "Thanks to the healthy race feeling of the British such marriages are extremely uncommon."[20] Three years later, *Leader* columnist Atu lamented the passing of "Dutch times" when "marriage relations between black and white [were] honest."[21] Also writing in the pages of the *Leader*, the prolific "literary gent" and British palm-oil trader John Moray Stuart-Young observed in 1922 the absolute rarity of marriages "in the legal and religious sense" between black women and white men in British West Africa.[22] In twenty years on the coast, Stuart-Young claimed, he had encountered only six such marriages. At the same time, growing numbers of Gold Coasters from the literate elite and newly literate classes, who were typically Christian converts, not only condemned concubinage and polygyny, they also eschewed the institution of customary marriage. Instead, they placed a premium on the practice of Christian marriage, as institutionalized by the 1884 Marriage Ordinance, and the closely allied notion of companionate marriage.[23] For this group of Gold Coasters, the growing expectation for ordinance marriage and the actual practice of it, where European men and African women were concerned, were at odds.

Yet ideas about marriage were by no means uniform. Many elite men, despite in most cases being Christian themselves, defended the institution of customary marriage. They denounced the imposition of ordinance marriage and its ill effects on gender relations, which they blamed for inciting wifely insubordination and fomenting moral decay.[24] But even proponents of customary marriage, by the first decades of the twentieth century, doubted the legitimacy of such unions when contracted between European men and African women. As one writer for the *Leader* put it, customary marriages between Africans "are sacred to us," but when contracted across the color line "the evil result" is that our "daughters becom[e] temporary wives to Europeans."[25] Thus, regardless of which side of the contentious "marriage question" Gold Coasters fell on, neither camp believed that sexual relationships with European men conferred respectability on the African women who participated in them.

Governor Rodger's and Lord Crewe's efforts, in 1907 and 1909, respectively, to stamp out interracial concubinage only pushed these relationships further into the recesses of colonial society, where they undoubtedly appeared all the more unseemly. The order of the day was discretion rather than abatement of the practice. Despite their potential professional and social consequences, European officers and privately employed Europeans continued to pursue these liaisons. The fates of European officers like C. N. Curling, H. Palmer, F. W. Greig, and N. H. Dakeyne, who were punished for "keeping" local women, underscore the persistence of concubinage despite official prohibition. Even French officers stationed in neighboring Ivory Coast reportedly circumvented indigenous prohibitions there against "temporary marriages" by crossing into the Gold Coast to find "native wives."[26] Liaisons between local women and European men employed by expatriate trading firms remained commonplace, even though some firms expressly forbade them.[27]

As had been the case in earlier centuries, Gold Coasters, typically lineage heads or other male relatives and in some instances mothers, brokered relationships between young women and European men. During the first half of the twentieth century, a new class of men, often stewards employed by Europeans, as well as entrepreneurially inclined young men in new urban centers, like Takoradi's "pilot boys," acted as middlemen on behalf of Europeans looking for commercial sex.[28] And as women in the colony increasingly sought greater control over their marital arrangements and sexual lives, some of their number independently formed alliances with

European men. Thus, despite the colonial state's efforts, when the "Immoral Sanitation" series ran in early 1920, sexual relationships between European men and African women were still an ever-present feature of colonial life. The series and like-minded commentaries, however, marked a decisive moment in the long local history of these relationships by making them more than just the subject of fleeting public criticism; they were now the source of anticolonial agitation.

BLACK ATLANTIC CONNECTIONS

The politicization of indigenous opposition to sexual relationships between white men and African women in the Gold Coast occurred within the wider set of Black Atlantic developments discussed in the preceding chapter. For many Gold Coasters at home and abroad in postwar Britain, late 1919 and 1920 was a time of turmoil characterized by a reappraisal of their position within the British Empire, even as they continued to affirm their place in it. This was especially the case for men drawn from the educated elite and the growing class of sub-elites, including maritime laborers.[29] Despite their service to Britain in the Great War, West African seamen and soldiers, educated in the ways of the world through their travels but largely of working-class origin, became the target of unprecedented violence during the race riots that swept the British ports in the summer of 1919. As chapter 6 showed, instead of heeding black men's calls for equal treatment and fair employment opportunities, local authorities responded to the riots by quickly drawing up plans to forcibly repatriate them to the colonies.[30]

While some black commentators quietly called attention to events taking place in Britain and their repercussions for the colonies' white residents, others boldly declared that the riots and repatriation schemes were stoking anticolonial agitation.[31] A self-identified "British coloured soldier" gave voice to his anger by calling for the reciprocal return of white colonials to Europe in the *Liverpool Post*. "All your people who is out there making their living must come back home and make theirs here," he demanded.[32] A representative of the Anti-Slavery and Aborigines' Protection Society echoed this sentiment in the pages of Liverpool's *Evening Express* when he reminded the British public that its empire was "coloured" and "legislation resting solely on colour is unthinkable, *except at the risk of dissolution of the Empire*." To this he added, "You cannot prevent the Black man from coming here, because this is the centre of his Empire."[33]

Black men in the ports were well aware that the violence directed at them stemmed not only from competition over jobs, but also from their associations with white women. In a letter published in the *Leader*, representatives of the Black Seamen in Liverpool organization explained that white rioters were angered that "black men [were] co[ur]ting their girls."³⁴ Others were quick to point out that while black men were being attacked in Britain, Europeans were busy fathering children with African women in the colonies. Fola Thomas, the demobilized West African soldier whom we heard from in chapter 6, called attention to this double standard in his protest letter to the House of Commons: "I beg to ask who are the fathers of those half castes estimated to be over 13,000 molatoes [*sic*] in 1908 in the West Coast of Africa[?] Wasn't their fathers whites and their mothers black?" His invocation of the progeny of these relationships was an astute strategy employed by others to illustrate white men's sexual promiscuity and their lack of paternal responsibility. Eager to indicate that the sexual license of European men in the colonies did not go unnoticed, Thomas posed the rhetorical question, "Ain't the negroes in Africa have their own feelings as the whites here today[?]" Thomas concluded his letter by noting that despite their unease, Africans had not *yet* allowed their jealousies to be enflamed to the point of violence.³⁵

While the "canting hypocrisy," as Atu put it, evident in the riots embodied a wider set of grievances over unequal access to the rights and privileges black men believed they were owed as loyal British subjects, it is instructive that these grievances found such powerful expression in a discourse about unequal access to black and white women's bodies and contested masculinities.³⁶ As a result, the riots focused the attention of West African seamen and demobilized soldiers, who formed a vocal stratum of the sub-elite, and the colony's intelligentsia on the question of interracial sexual relations at home and abroad.³⁷ From their shifting locations in the Atlantic world, this group of highly politicized and mobile Gold Coast men authored a trenchant critique of the sexual politics of empire. That the transoceanic circuits of the Atlantic feature so prominently in this story alerts us to the continuing centrality of Africa to the formation of the Black Atlantic world in the twentieth century. Much of the literature on the Black Atlantic consigns its engagement with Africa to the transatlantic slave trade, or portrays it primarily as an object of the diaspora's gaze. Indeed, Paul Gilroy's foundational text, *The Black Atlantic: Modernity and Double Consciousness*, marginalized Africa in these very ways.³⁸ Yet, (male) Gold Coasters, in their roles as seamen, soldiers, political activists, union members, writers, pressmen, and consumers of news from around the black world, were far from marginal actors in the dynamic networks that constituted the early twentieth-century Black Atlantic. Their lived realities and political aspirations suggest a symbiotic relationship between black Atlanticism and nationalism, rather than the antithetical one Gilroy proposes.[39]

"WHITE PERIL" COMMENTARIES IN THE GOLD COAST LEADER

In the wake of the 1919 race riots, the Gold Coast press brimmed with vivid reports of the violence perpetrated against black men.[40] As the colony's robust reading public quickly became aware of what was happening in the British seaports, they glimpsed the hardships faced by the scores of men who left each year to work aboard the shipping lines that plied the Atlantic.[41] The dramatic stories of racism endured by black men in Britain must have resonated with the colony's educated elites, who once served at the highest levels of the local colonial administration but were pushed out of power through a confluence of factors. Late nineteenth-century advances in tropical medicine increased the numbers of Europeans employed on the coast, while assertions of African racial inferiority were used to justify the imposition of formal colonial rule.[42] As noted in chapter 2, these factors made it physically possible and ideologically necessary to exclude Africans from high office.[43] Meanwhile, the system of indirect rule, introduced at the turn of the century and intensified during the 1910s, endowed the colony's "natural rulers," rather than the intelligentsia, with the right to preside over "native" affairs.[44] To challenge these exclusions, many educated elites carved out alternative spheres of power and influence through the creation of their own political and social organizations and by harnessing the power of the Gold Coast press.[45] During the opening decades of the twentieth century, as Audrey Gadzekpo has observed, "the chief advocates of social and political reform ... could be found within the ranks of the politician/journalist."[46] Indeed, many of the men who formed part of the early nucleus of the nationalist movement in the Gold Coast, including J. E. Casely Hayford, Samuel Richard Brew Attoh Ahuma, F. V. Nanka-Bruce, Thomas Hutton-Mills, and James Hutton Brew, were closely associated with indigenous newspapers, either as founders, editors, or investors.[47]

Among the colony's numerous newspapers, the *Gold Coast Leader* was undoubtedly the most politically radical. Founded in 1902, the *Leader* was exceptional for its thirty-year print run and its invitation to all sectors of society to contribute to its pages, whether in the form of reportage, commentary, or letters to the editor.[48] One measure of its influence was its sizable print run, estimated annually at 57,200 in 1912, more than double what it had been just a decade earlier.[49] During his long tenure as its most prominent editor, from

1919 to 1930, the famed nationalist figure J. E. Casely Hayford helped forge the paper's Pan-African sensibilities and its unrelenting critical engagement with the colonial state.[50] The *Leader* was inevitably closely associated with the National Congress of British West Africa (NCBWA), the region's earliest nationalist organization, which Casely Hayford cofounded in 1920, the very same year the "white peril" commentaries ran in the paper.[51] In an era when government censorship of the indigenous press was less restrictive than it would later become, a wide range of grievances with the colonial state was aired in the pages of the *Leader*.[52] Newspaper commentaries registered concerns over increased European immigration to the colony, the exclusion of Africans from higher posts in the colonial service, and race-based differences in pay scales for African and European civil servants.[53] A significant cluster of these grievances also involved colonial incursions into the "inner domain of national culture." Many nationalists regarded acts such as the 1884 Marriage Ordinance and the 1892 Native Customs Ordinance, as well as the institutionalization of indirect rule, as unwanted encroachments on native institutions that fomented social chaos. In the immediate postwar period, in particular, demands for political reforms and fuller enfranchisement in recognition of the critical wartime support rendered by the colony to Britain were also a common feature of press commentary. These demands, as Stephanie Newell notes, were made within "the discourse of imperial loyalty," which continued to frame political agitation throughout the 1920s.[54] In this sense, for many Gold Coast nationalists, national independence within the British Empire was the goal at hand.[55]

Significantly, it was grievances over interracial sexual relations that broke this mold by provoking disenfranchised yet highly politicized Gold Coasters to question whether their interests would be better served outside the bonds of empire. In the wake of the 1919 race riots, this group of men used the *Leader* not only to decry attacks against black men in Britain for cohabiting with or marrying white women, but also to declare that the sexual appetites and mores of European men were corrupting local women and thereby threatening the moral fiber and future of the nation. In this moment, affirmations of their own fitness for self-rule were newly coupled with assertions of European men's lack of fitness for colonial rule.

The *Leader*'s columnists and letter writers agreed that in corrupting female virtue, interracial liaisons imperiled their nationalist aspirations. Nowhere was this strain of thinking better exemplified than in the three-part "Immoral Sanitation" series, which formed part of a larger body of late nineteenth- and early twentieth-century newspaper writing in the Gold Coast that "advocated that education be directed at preparing girls towards a cultured companionate marriage that would make them good intelligent mothers and wives that could benefit the nation."⁵⁶ The commentaries under consideration here also foreshadowed the tensions that emerged more widely in gender relations throughout the colony in the late 1920s and 1930s as women sought various means of resisting increased infringements on their freedom, and more specifically on their labor, marital prospects, and sexuality.⁵⁷ One of the ways in which they did this was to choose lives as unmarried women, or "spinsters" as they were then called, but some women chose concubinage over marriage because it allowed them to partner with men of their choosing without being constrained by the financial demands associated with contracting a customary or ordinance marriage. Thus the choice of concubinage was hardly unique to interracial relationships. While these developments fit into the larger body of scholarship on "wicked women," a stigmatizing label often given to women in colonial Africa who "push[ed] the boundaries of 'acceptable' behavior," it departs in one critical way.⁵⁸ Rather than collaborating with colonial authorities to reassert patriarchal control over the colony's "wayward" young women, the male writers in question used the women's sexual libertinage as proof of the demoralizing influences of European men, and by extension colonial rule, in order to bolster their own patriarchal claims to power.

The title "Immoral Sanitation" satirized the colonial government's acute concerns about sanitation, which were used to legitimize the policy of residential segregation and other much-hated measures to regulate the behavior and movement of Africans.⁵⁹ Insalubrious white men were cleverly rendered as the source of moral squalor as they pulled black women into their beds with one hand while hypocritically using the other hand to push Africans out of their "sanitary" white enclaves. In the series' first installment, the *Leader*'s Sekondi correspondent painted an alarming picture of unruly African women and "immoral whites" recklessly pursuing their selfish desires with no regard for their deleterious effects on society. The correspondent claimed that women, even those who were educated, ended up in the "whiteman's bungalow" after engaging in "gross moral vices" during their youth such that no respectable African man would marry them. These "ladies in silk hats, dainty diaphanous frocks and shining boots about the streets of Seccondee" were, in turn, accused of deceiving their innocent younger counterparts into believing that "advantages [were] derivable under the beneficent care of the Europeans."⁶⁰ The correspondent's detailed description of the young women's Western attire not only confirms Anne McClintock's observation that "the intense emotive politics of dress" stem from the fact that "for male nationalists, women serve as the visible markers of national homogeneity," it also highlights the care and intention with which these young women comported themselves in an effort to please themselves and presumably the men they hoped to attract.[61]

But these women and their fancy apparel were not the only problems; the correspondent criticized their mothers, too, describing them as "poor wretched women [who] in their blind folly . . . prefer gold to the virtue of their daughters." Ultimately, however, as "the promoters of such immoral habits," he blamed European men for the depraved condition of Sekondi's social life. White men of lower economic standing, he said, "seize these opportunities to satisfy their carnal lusts at a cheap rate" because they cannot afford to "bring their wives out with them, or often have none." European men were even held accountable for introducing polyandry into the colony by allowing their female consorts to become the lovers of their male colleagues.[62] Nowhere was it ever suggested that African men played a role in brokering these relationships—an omission that implicitly absolved them of complicity in this "traffic," while obscuring the degree to which they continued to place their female relatives, dependents, or associates with European men, even as some of their number decried the practice.

The first installment of the "Immoral Sanitation" series was certainly descriptive, but it was also prescriptive. Women who liaised with Europeans were portrayed as opportunistic "gold diggers," who would never find true love in their serial romances despite their purported claims of being "content and jolly in whitemen's company."[63] Instead, the Sekondi correspondent praised the merits of companionate marriage: "We advise the young ladies that a man and a woman can have in their true relationship, only as two fond and faithful lovers, each finding in the other father, mother, friend, riches and felicity." He implored the town's "inexperienced and unwary" young girls to shun the company of "night wanderers . . . for the future of this country depends on its womanhood."[64] While this was obviously meant to warn young women against engaging in a life of "vice" with white men, and hence an attempt to regulate female sexuality, it must also be read as an expression of male anxiety about the loss of patriarchal authority over Gold Coast women, and in turn the nation. Portrayed as irreverent, these women used their sexuality to assert their independence by accruing for themselves the material benefits of their connections with European men and encouraging other women to do the same. Whatever money they earned, argued another writer, was promptly exchanged for "expensive clothing" at European-owned stores. In this way "the morality of the country," he

FIGURE 7.1. While Sekondi had been integrated into Atlantic trade networks since the seventeenth century, when the Dutch and English established trading forts there, its urbanization was catalyzed by the 1903 completion of a railway linking the resource-rich hinterland to the town's natural harbor. With its rapidly expanding male and female migrant population, as well as a sizable, largely male European population, Sekondi's infrastructure developed in response to the city's commercial life and to its diverse residents' recreational and material desires. The city was home to a prominent business district, with numerous European-owned trading firms and shops, as well as to a variety of social clubs, drinking spots, and dance venues. After the completion of neighboring Takoradi's deepwater harbor in 1928, Sekondi's regional dominance waned, but as the illuminated building pictured here suggests, it still retained some of its grandeur in subsequent decades. ("Illuminated Building, Sekondi," 1937. Colonial Office 1069/39/11, The National Archives of the United Kingdom.)

continued, was being reduced "in inverse ratio to the rate of advance of the whiteman's profits."[65] Thus, the pleasure and profit of European men was had at the expense of the nation, and by extension the men who rightfully belonged at its helm.

The Sekondi correspondent portrayed these women as "gold diggers," but he did so without providing a sense of the socioeconomic context in which they were living and making decisions.[66] Sekondi provides a stark example of how the forces of colonial urbanization created the particular circumstances that made sexuality a key resource for female capital accumulation.

FIGURE 7.2. Foregrounded in this image are two of the colony's young women shopping for patent-leather high heels at the fashionable Czech-owned Bata shoe store in Sekondi. Donning Western-style frocks and wearing imported hats, the two women are assisted by an African clerk. Almost imperceptible at first glance, the mirror lining the shoe rack contains the reflection of a European man, likely the store manager, peering over the front counter with a wide grin on his face. The image unwittingly conjures the link between female capital accumulation, consumerism, especially of Western goods, sexual corruption, and European plunder that Gold Coasters made in the pages of the *Leader* during the 1920s and 1930s. ("Sekondi: Bata Store, October 1938." Gold Coast, Ref. No. QU-30.003.0489, Basel Mission Archives/Basel Mission Holdings.)

The colonial government's creation of an important railway terminus in Sekondi in 1903 transformed the small fishing village, with its natural harbor, into a busy commercial center that linked gold- and timber-producing sites in the hinterland to the Atlantic economy. To satisfy labor demands, colonial policy makers encouraged immigration, which resulted in the rapidly growing town's largely male African population, as well as a sizable population of European men. This, in turn, drew female migrants, who "came to play a crucial role as retailers of food and drink, and providers of recreation and domestic comforts, including the sale of sex."[67] These entrepreneurial endeavors, as Emmanuel Akyeampong notes, "provided women with the opportunity to make money outside the confines of kinship and marriage."[68] With a limited range of opportunities for income generation, strategic partnerships, whether stable or serial, with comparatively financially prosperous men could dramatically enhance young women's access to resources, both financial and material, as they struggled to make new lives for themselves in the colony's old and new urban enclaves.[69] While women in Sekondi were surely brokering financially lucrative arrangements with African men as well, it was their relationships with European men that first catalyzed alarm among Gold Coasters about the sexual corruption of female virtue. Underscored here, then, is not only the heightened visibility of these relationships due to their interracial character, but also the ways that female independence and sexual autonomy constituted *transgressions* in need of eradication when practiced by Gold Coast women with European men and *aberrations* in need of correction when practiced with African men.

In the series' second installment, its anonymous author wrote of his shock at the "allegation of polyandry on the part of our young girls" and expressed discomfort with its inversion of traditional gender norms. "Polygamy is not strange to the male African but polyandry is a new thing in the history of our country," bemoaned the writer, who attributed it to "the introduction here of Western civilization and Christianity which like veneers cover a lot of sins."[70] Turning the West's civilizing discourse on its head, the author lambasted Europeans for morally corrupting Africans. Lamenting the "sad fate of the country" should this evil go unchecked, he concluded, "It is a pity that our girls, the future mothers of the country, should yield to the temptations of the white man who should know better."[71] Atu, the *Leader*'s "Scrutineer" columnist, went a step further by pointing to "the growing numbers of mulattoes which some members of the [European] race are fostering in the country" and to reports of rampant sexual promiscuity in Europe in order to urge Europeans to examine their own moral shortcomings instead of making "unwarranted attacks on our Race."[72]

It was Atu as well who responded to the "Immoral Sanitation" series with an ardent call for the cessation of these sexual liaisons. "History," he warned, "supplies instances of the decay and fall of nations having been preceded or even hastened by their giving themselves up to licentiousness." To guard against this, he invited his readers to join him "in a crusade to ostracise" the African paramours of European men, whom he described as a "disgrace to the race":

> They are a social evil in themselves and a source of danger to others since they may lure innocent girls from the path of rectitude. They should be treated as social pariahs and refused admission into decent society or other social gatherings and they should be given the cold shoulder whenever encountered.[73]

Here the connection between sexuality and nationalism is made explicit and bears out Joane Nagel's observation that

> the moral economy of nationalism is gendered, sexualized, and racialized. National moral economies provide specific places for women and men in the nation, identify desirable and undesirable members by creating gender, sexual, and ethnic boundaries and hierarchies within nations, establish criteria for judging good and bad performances of nationalist masculinity and femininity, and define threats to national moral and sexual integrity.[74]

During a period in Gold Coast history when one variant of nationalism in the colony tended toward localization and mapped more closely onto ethnic identities, most famously in the rise of Fante nationalism in Cape Coast at the turn of the century, the terminology Gold Coasters employed in their "white peril" commentaries consistently pushed beyond the narrowly ethnic: "nation," "country," "African women," and "black women" were staple terms, not "Fante nation," "Asante women," or similarly ethnic-specific terminology.[75] Indeed, anxiety over sexual relationships between white men and African women in the Gold Coast became a locus of provocation for anticolonial nationalist sentiments that trumped ethnicity as Gold Coast men, from both the literate elite and the newly literate classes, shared a sense of being collectively imperiled by a common racial other—in this case "immoral whites." These published opinions suggest that it was not just imperial powers who viewed interracial sex and sexual morality as pivots around which the fate of the empire turned and around which they could mobilize their political ambitions; so, too, did the colonized. As the Gold Coast's "white peril" scare played itself out in the pages of the colony's newspapers, it opened up a space for some Gold Coast men to position themselves as the moral stewards of the nation and its women, in contradistinction to dissolute white men.

Despite Atu's ominous exhortations, there is no evidence to suggest that the "white peril" commentaries resulted in acts of violence against European men or their African paramours. It would, however, be a mistake to assume that unforgiving public opinion like Atu's about the women involved in interracial liaisons did not have adverse consequences on at least some of their lives. By way of example, in 1934 when Miss Kate Easmon petitioned the Colonial Office for help in obtaining support from her infant child's father, Alfred Johnson, who had retired from government service and returned to England during her pregnancy, she pleaded that "on account of [his] betrayal,

[my] parents and relatives have refused all support."[76] Prior to the birth of her child, Easmon had been employed as a government bookbinder, a respectable position that she could not have obtained without a considerable measure of education, which was also evident in her eloquently written letter to the secretary of state for the colonies, Sir Cunliffe-Lister. Indeed, she might very well have been a member of the prominent Easmon family, in which case her fall from grace would have constituted an embarrassing departure from the picture of professional and civic excellence that had become synonymous with the Easmon name in the Gold Coast.[77] While her firsthand account of being ostracized by her family is unique, at least in the archives, it does suggest the high social and emotional price that African women and their multiracial children could face when abandoned by European men.

Yet, the example of another woman, Dorothy Lloyd, suggests that not all women found their prospects for a respectable life and honorable marriage to African men diminished by their relations with European men. Lloyd was a multiracial Fante woman who, it seems, was abandoned by her own white father, said to have been a British district commissioner in Dixcove at the time of her birth in 1898.[78] Raised by her Fante mother, Sarah, and fully integrated into her matrilineage, Lloyd customarily wed George William Yates, a British mining accountant who worked as a paymaster for the Broomassi mines in the early 1910s. Dorothy gave birth to their son, Harry Phillip Yates, in 1915, and the couple raised him in their Broomassi home until 1917 when George Yates left the Gold Coast. Despite all of this, Dorothy went on to marry Frank Vardon, a prominent member of Sekondi's tight-knit community of educated African elites, who served as the registrar of the city's divisional court and was a patron, alongside J. E. Casely Hayford, of Sekondi's Optimism Club.[79]

How do we account for Dorothy Lloyd's incorporation into elite society after her relationship with George Yates came to an end, while Kate Easmon was arguably excluded from it? The key here seems to be the nature of the two relationships. We must also remember that Dorothy's family had already accepted her mother's brief liaison with a European man, and was thus unlikely to reject her relationship with George, especially considering that it was by all accounts regarded as a respectable marriage.[80] As a privately employed European, George probably had greater flexibility in acknowledging his relationship with Dorothy, but this should not minimize that the visible way the couple set up their Broomassi home and lived as publicly recognized man and wife was unheard of even for privately employed Europeans. Alfred Johnson, on the other hand, was a government employee who likely would have been severely punished had his relationship with Easmon come to official attention. The fact that he left her in such a vulnerable position and ignored her appeals for child support suggests that his intentions were hardly honorable, but even if they had been, it would have been at his professional peril to acknowledge his relationship with her, let alone paternity of their child. Perhaps eager to ensure that his misdeeds on the coast did not chip away at his pension, he retired and left in a hurry, leaving Easmon to reckon with the social stigma of being an unwed mother—a situation compounded by her family's dashed expectations about her chastity and presumably its consequences for their social standing, which seemingly led them to disown her.

While rejecting "fallen" women might have been a strategy for protecting family honor, preserving racial respectability, and reasserting male authority locally, Gold Coasters simultaneously chipped away at the veneer of European moral superiority that underpinned the legitimacy of the colonial project by formulating an explicit critique of the sexual immorality of European men. One of the Gold Coast's earliest and most prominent anticolonial nationalists, Kobina Sekyi, who alongside Casely Hayford cofounded the NCBWA, contended that European sexual immorality posed a formidable threat to British rule. In describing what he regarded as "the English colonial's heaviest handicap," namely, the "Anglo-Saxon form of colour prejudice," Sekyi noted that it was distinguished by an "extraordinarily intense" disdain for foreigners, but even this, he suggested, could be trumped by sexual desire:

> The Englishmen's contempt for foreigners—even in the intensified form which is known as colour prejudice—absolutely vanishes when he is under the domination of the sexual impulse in a foreign land—no Englishman can pretend to abhor the Negress who is his paramour or his lawful wife according to Native Customary Law, whilst he is in a state of sexual or erotic excitement in the presence of such Negress.[81]

While today it is widely acknowledged that access to sex is often a correlate of racial domination, and that the presence of interracial sexual desire does not indicate an absence of racism, Sekyi's remarks remind us that observers in the early twentieth-century Gold Coast were already linking these two impulses together, albeit in very different ways.[82] By suggesting that British racism was often selectively put on hold to allow for the "congregation of white men and black women by night and in some cases even in broad daylight," Sekyi displayed an awareness of racism's malleability, if not its multiple manifestations. More than that, his observations reveal that colonial authorities were by no means alone in recognizing that the sexual license of

European men and their access to colonized women were both products of colonial power and threats to its maintenance.

Sekyi made it absolutely clear that he found interracial relationships repugnant, whether between white men and African women or African men and white women, and in this way he sympathized with the feelings of disgust that motivated white port dwellers to "blindly and unthinkingly take the law into their own hands." What he found egregious, however, was the arrogance of Anglo-Saxons, which he believed prevented them from comprehending that many Africans shared their feelings of revulsion and were just as capable of viewing Europeans as sexually immoral:

> It is very difficult for the average Englishman to believe that there are even now in Africa men and women who consider it the worst possible disgrace for a respectable woman to be seen in frequent association with white men and that such men and women consider white people most immoral and disrespectful in their attitude towards women, seeing how very freely they mix with their women at social gatherings, and seeing that in the ballroom their customs permit such liberties to be taken with other people's wives, as if taken by black men with black married women, would not very long ago, in these parts have resulted in successful suits for *ayi-fer* or seduction.[83]

By foregrounding African perspectives on the sexual behavior of British men and women in the colony and contrasting their sexual libertinage with what he deemed the stricter codes of sexual morality governing interactions between African men and women, Sekyi unpinned an integral part of the "civilizing mission's" rhetoric. Elsewhere he contended that if there was a lack of sexual morality among Africans, it was due to ongoing processes of "general Europeanisation."[84] In short, Sekyi positioned Europeans as obstacles to civilization, not bearers of it.

In decrying the sexual corruption of Gold Coast women by European men in the colony and the violent attacks against black men who cohabited with or married white women in Britain, Gold Coasters in the early decades of the twentieth century were calling for equality. To this end Sekyi declared that Gold Coasters would "remain in the Empire" only if "we are treated as freemen but not as helots to be exploited either in the sphere of industry or in the political and social sphere."[85] While this is in keeping with the well-documented demand for greater parity and autonomy within the British Empire that followed World War I, what has not been significantly appreciated is that colonized subjects, even at this early stage, were calling for the end of empire should they fall short of achieving equality.[86] One Gold Coaster summed up this revolutionary caveat when he noted that "the funny part of the [riots] is that the same white men who in their country cannot bear the presence of the black, take . . . black women [as] wives with whom they breed when they come out to the black man's country. . . . If the world would like to enjoy peace and goodwill towards men, there must be brotherhood unlimited by race, colour, or creed, *or, in the alternative, the colour line must be drawn everywhere—white men keeping to their countries and the blacks to theirs.*"[87]

These rare press commentaries from 1919 and 1920 provide a decidedly male set of perspectives that reflect the predominantly male authorship of Gold Coast newspapers at the time. It would be a mistake to assume that concerns over interracial sex in the 1920s and earlier were the sole preserve of the colony's men; however, without a similar corpus of writing attributable to women for this time period, it is difficult to gauge how closely their concerns mirrored those of their male counterparts.[88] By the 1930s, a small group of highly educated elite Gold Coast women was writing openly in the indigenous press, and they often used their columns to promote companionate marriage and moral uplift among the colony's female population.[89] The most prolific of these women, Mabel Dove, is best known for her columns written under the pen name of Marjorie Mensah in Accra's *West Africa Times* (1931–1934), founded by nationalist leader J. B. Danquah.[90] A playwright as well, in the final year of her tenure at the *West Africa Times* she serialized *A Woman in Jade*, a play that provides a fictional account of scandalous sexual relationships between local women and European men in the colony from the rare perspective of an African woman. *A Woman in Jade* attests to the fact that the moral-cum-racial-purity concerns articulated in the "white peril" episode in 1920 were not fleeting. Like male nationalists before her, Dove painted a bleak picture of where young African women's sexual adventures took them. In the tragic figure of Baake, a "frock girl" who sabotages her marriage prospects to a respectable native lawyer in search of romance and adventure with European men, Dove renders such women beyond rehabilitation, consigning them instead to life in the "whiteman's bungalow."[91]

Dove's harshest criticism, however, was reserved for European men. Through the figure of a sixteen-year-old multiracial girl, Beryl, whose white father abandoned her African mother upon learning she was pregnant, Dove inverts the classic colonial trope of the African seductress who lures her European lover into a downward spiral of moral-cum-racial descent. "Dove's version of the 'white man on the West African Coast' narrative," as Stephanie Newell argues, "[lays] the blame for immorality . . . squarely

FIGURE 7.3. Departing from the dominant narrative about white men who abandoned their multiracial offspring, Basel Mission catechist William Timothy Evans raised his two daughters in the mission community in Accra and Akropong after his Ga wife, Emma Evans (née Reindorf), died during childbirth in 1900. Evans is pictured here with his daughters Mary Emma and Elizabeth. ("Seminary House Father Evans 1909," Gold Coast, Ref. No. QD-30.112.00067, Basel Mission Archives/Basel Mission Holdings.)

at the feet of the colonial man who dallies with local women and refuses to take responsibility for the outcome."[92] If white men were unwilling or unable to care for their own offspring, how could they be regarded as morally fit guardians of the colonial world? By raising this question, Dove, like Atu and numerous other Gold Coasters before her, challenged colonialism's paternalistic ideology while expressing her own concerns about the reproductive consequences of these illicit relationships for native families on the coast who were left to shoulder the responsibilities shirked by absentee white fathers.

But Dove did not limit her critique to interracial relationships between African women and European men. Writing as Ebun Alakija in 1936, she railed against "our supposed intelligent men" who return from abroad with European wives because, in her words, "marriage with another race is pure disintegration and it is viewed by intelligent Europeans and Africans with contempt."[93] Instead, she commended marriage across ethnic lines among

Africans—or as she put it "intertribal marriages"—as an essential ingredient of African unity, development, and pride. Given how few West African men were allowed to return to the British colonies with their white wives during the interwar years, Dove's comments underscore the extraordinary visibility of interracially married African men even though they formed a tiny minority of the colonies' elite intelligentsia. As was the case for Dove's male counterparts in the previous decade, the domain of interracial sex provoked nationalist sentiments that trumped ethnicity. Echoing Marcus Garvey, she concluded her column by calling for an end to interracial marriages: "African men for African women and European men for European women, for the salvation of the race lies in its purity."[94] By condemning both illicit unions *and* legitimate marriages, Dove and Sekyi articulated a far more radical opposition to interracial sex, which moved beyond critiquing its frequently illegitimate nature to positioning even lawful intermarriage as a threat to the viability of the African race. When set against Joseph Renner Maxwell's 1891 treatise on the benefits of "lawful miscegenation brought about in accordance with the Divine and moral laws" for the survival and "physical improvement of the negro race," the decades-long shift in thinking among the colony's most educated elites about interracial relationships could not be more evident.[95] Powerfully hinted at here is the way that some Gold Coast nationalists came to believe that the progeny of these relationships embodied what was most threatening about them in ways that mirrored colonial discourses about the dangers of *métissage* in the French empire and even elsewhere in the British Empire, but never in the Gold Coast itself.

CONCLUSION

Dove might have been the earliest nationalist figure to express anxieties about African men who went abroad to Europe and returned with white wives, but she would not be the last. After the war, a growing number of men from the colonies came to Britain to prepare themselves, through education and political action, for independence. While there, many of these men formed intimate relationships, some fleeting, others lasting, with white women. While some African nationalists and intellectuals in England questioned whether intimacy with white women was commensurate with the work of African nationalism, others came to see and respect these women as an important source of emotional and practical support. Kwame Nkrumah was among the latter.

8 ⇝ WASU, White Women, and African Independence

BY THE TIME Kwame Nkrumah arrived in London in 1945, his youth in the Gold Coast followed by his decade-long stint in the United States had seemingly conditioned him to think of white women as untouchable. His reserve around them was immediately noticeable to members of the London-based West African Students Union (WASU). His one-time friend and political comrade, Joe Appiah, recalls that at WASU social functions "Nkrumah was reluctant or too shy to talk to white girls or to dance with them or even to get too close to them." Nkrumah, he said, "looked on embarrassedly" as his friends cuddled with their white girlfriends. To disabuse him of the "dread of white women that the United States had instilled in him," his WASU friends set out to find him a white girlfriend.[1] Although Nkrumah's relationship did not endure with Diana P., the revolutionary Marxist English-born daughter of a Russian émigré, who was also an avid supporter of WASU activities, he felt sufficiently at ease with her as both a companion and a comrade to take her with him to the 1945 Pan-African Congress in Manchester. He went on to form at least one other significant romantic relationship with an English woman, Florence Manley, during his stay in London.[2] The colonial government later aired details of his relationship with Manley in a crass attempt to discredit him during the Watson Commission hearings convened to ferret out the cause of anticolonial unrest in the Gold Coast in 1948. As this brief account makes clear, the romantic affairs of a man like Nkrumah were not just personal, they were also political and politicized. This final chapter brings the political and the personal together to explore the place of interracial relationships between black men and white women in the making of African independence.

WASU

Despite episodic racial tensions over interracial relationships between white women and black men in Liverpool, London, Cardiff, and other British port cities, these cosmopolitan locales still presented African men like Nkrumah with far greater access to white women, as friends, political comrades, and lovers. London, in particular, also offered men from different corners of the British Empire unprecedented opportunities for political organizing as they flocked to the imperial center in search of the university educations and the intellectual and activist networks that would help prepare them for independence.

For young West Africans arriving in the colonial metropolis during and after World War II, WASU was the heart of anticolonial political action in Britain. Nigerian Ladipo Solanke, a graduate of Sierra Leone's prestigious Fourah Bay College, and Herbert Bankole-Bright, the Nigerian-born descendant of Saro immigrants, founded WASU in 1925 while studying law and medicine, respectively, in Britain.[3] By the late 1930s, WASU had overcome years of internal disputes to become the go-to organization for West African students looking for political and social camaraderie and the practical support the organization offered African students, such as housing at its Camden Town hostels.[4] While primarily meant to serve the interests of West African students, WASU became an important institution for Africans from elsewhere on the continent and from the diaspora. In addition to fostering its members' intellectual and political ambitions, WASU catered to their social needs. It frequently held dances and other gatherings that were open to the public in an effort to promote interracial understanding. These events provided a space for white British women and African men to socialize and form romantic relationships. The ubiquity of these relationships was in part a product of the gendered social and political milieu that African men found themselves in as they prepared for African independence in Britain and elsewhere in Europe. Indeed, the lopsided gender ratios that characterized the predominantly male European presence in West Africa were mirrored in the African presence in Britain: African men far outnumbered African women.

Most of these men studied and worked in Britain or elsewhere in Europe while they were still quite young and typically, but not always, unmarried.

The small number of men who were married generally did not bring their wives to Britain with them. As such, they more commonly mixed with white women, who far outnumbered their black counterparts, even as the population of African women in Britain grew after World War II.[5] But skewed gender ratios offer only a partial explanation for this trend. Black women in London complained that even in their presence their male counterparts preferred the company of white women.[6] This is an important point, since assumptions about the gendered demographics of the African presence in Britain may obscure other factors, ranging from personal preferences and pragmatic considerations to more psychoanalytic explanations, that influenced African men to select white women as their partners while abroad.

Unlike the colonies where these relationships remained taboo, unions of varying degrees of formality between black men and white women were a common although contentious feature of cosmopolitan late imperial centers, like London and Paris, where African men resided during the years leading to independence. Liberal-humanitarian social and political movements that had taken an interest in race relations in Britain since the 1930s coalesced into organizations such as Racial Unity by the early 1950s and provided ideal settings for fostering interracial social contact. As historian Barbara Bush points out, British women were prominent participants in these movements, thereby increasing opportunities for more intimate kinds of relationships to develop amid political organizing.[7] But as ubiquitous as these relationships were, they could also be a source of concern for black men from the colonies who wrestled with their ideological implications.

These tensions were discernible to (John Gibbs) St. Clair Drake, the famous African American scholar who later became a close adviser to Kwame Nkrumah. During his fieldwork in Britain during the mid-1940s, Drake observed that most relationships between black men and white women were characterized by an element of pragmatic dependence on the part of black men. Only a few, he thought, fit the affectionless "pimping for the race" model, in which some race leaders and agitators married or successively lived with one or more white women whom they financially exploited in support of "the cause."[8] But as Marc Matera points out, the very idea that the "pimping for the race" model existed at all is instructive. "Some African and Afro-Caribbean men equated sexual freedom or the exploitation of British women with anticolonial resistance and colonial liberation," says Matera, or "they embraced the former in lieu of a fuller realization of the latter."[9] Others have made this link, including Susan Miller, who argues that "the ultimate expression of authority on the part of the colonizers, and of liberation on the part of the colonized, was the sexual possession of the women of the other."[10] But Africans and other colonized men did not have to politicize their relationships with white women in this way in order for the imperial establishment to regard them as a form of anticolonial resistance. Long-standing colonial prescripts that rendered sex between white women and black men taboo ensured that these relationships were subversive by default, even if they occurred with increasing frequency in the metropole.

There was, however, significant disagreement among Africans about whether these relationships were commensurate with the work of anticolonial nationalism and African independence. In addition to objecting to the callous and parasitic treatment of goodwilled white women, some feared that "overreliance on white women transformed black revolutionaries into ineffectual dependents."[11] Others argued that these relationships tended to confirm rather than counter racist stereotypes about African hypersexuality used to exemplify that Africans were not ready for self-rule. To combat this, Ladipo Solanke and his Nigerian wife, Opeolu Obisanya, who served as the warden and matron of WASU's Africa House, made it a priority to ensure that its residents' relationships with white women did not tarnish the organization's reputation or the image of West Africans more generally through "the inculcation of proper sexual mores."[12] Yet even critics of interracial sexual relationships (the Solankes aside), observes Matera, were often partnered or otherwise involved with white women, dramatically illustrating just how ubiquitous these relationships were to metropolitan anticolonial nationalist social and political networks.[13]

While there is no indication that Ghanaian nationalists like Kwame Nkrumah and Joe Appiah were ever financially dependent on white women, both men acknowledged that the political, emotional, and physical camaraderie white women shared with Africans in Britain helped sustain the anticolonial struggle. "To the women of Britain, in particular, we owe a special debt of gratitude," wrote Appiah in his autobiography, "for their clerical help, their comforting words of hope in times of frustration and despair and, above all, their love and human affection so freely given, often in the face of opposition from families, friends and workmates."[14] Testifying to the widely shared nature of his sentiment, WASU vowed that at independence each country would erect monuments "to the eternal honor and memory of (a) the white women of Europe, for making our stay in Europe possible and (b) the Almighty Mosquito, for saving our lands from the settlement of colonial usurpers."[15]

Nkrumah also used his autobiography to pay tribute to the white women in Britain, like Florence Manley, who assisted his work at the West African National Secretariat. Nkrumah makes evident the practical and emotional support these women rendered when he explains, "Even if we had difficulty in warming our bodies round a fire, our hearts were constantly warmed by the ever ready offer of help by several English girls." Keen to dispel the persistent myth that white women who associated with black men were "of a low type," as the saying went, Nkrumah noted that "most of them [come from] good class families" and donated their services for free.[16] Nkrumah's and Appiah's recollections confirm that far from being a salacious footnote in the history of anticolonial nationalist struggles, the role that white women played in the push toward independence as political comrades, friends, and sometimes as lovers to many of the African men who had come to the imperial center to wrest control of the colonies from Britain was sustained and meaningful.

For members of the colonial establishment in postwar Britain, the site of young, educated, middle- and even upper-class white British women seemingly working together with African nationalists toward the dissolution of empire must have provoked an acute sense of national betrayal, not unlike that felt decades earlier by early Gold Coast nationalists when they witnessed young Gold Coast women liaising with European men. British authorities seemed painfully aware of this reality and not only carefully monitored sites of interracial congregation and political activity, but also used their knowledge of the interracial romantic affairs of African nationalists to discredit them. As alluded to earlier, colonial authorities hoped they could use Nkrumah's relationship with Florence Manley, a British divorcée whom he had met during his stay in Britain during 1947, against him.[17] A love letter from Manley was produced in an attempt to blight Nkrumah's character during the Watson Commission hearings. While the letter confirmed that their relationship was very close, it clearly did not adversely affect the public's opinion of Nkrumah as colonial authorities had hoped.[18] Perhaps Gold Coasters were savvy enough to realize that this information was disclosed as part of a smear campaign, or perhaps it was a moot point given the relationship did not result in marriage.

Despite falling flat with Gold Coasters, British authorities were still contemplating the significance of Nkrumah's relationship with Manley several years later. In late 1951 Sir Thomas Lloyd, assistant principal at the Colonial Office, dispatched a "personal and secret letter" to Sir Charles Arden-Clarke, then governor of the Gold Coast, to ascertain the veracity of a rumor that Nkrumah planned to wed Manley. The timing of the letter was not accidental—Nkrumah by then had emerged as the leading nationalist figure and within a few months would become prime minister. Arden-Clarke replied in an equally confidential manner that this rumor had indeed been circulating in the Gold Coast, but that Nkrumah was "at pains to deny this publicly."[19] Moreover, according to the governor, Manley was "reluctant to marry Nkrumah for fear of ruining his political career," although she proposed "to visit the Gold Coast with her child to test African reaction and judge the position for herself." While suggesting "the probable effects of such a marriage on [Nkrumah's] political career must give him pause," Arden-Clarke plainly admitted that Nkrumah was not the type to be swayed by such concerns.[20] Still, the episode is suggestive of the kinds of political considerations men like Nkrumah, as figureheads of independence, had to wrestle with in arranging their romantic affairs.

GOLD COAST NATION BUILDERS AND INTERMARRIAGE

The considerable extent to which Nkrumah's relationship with Florence Manley was the subject of political maneuvering and transatlantic gossip should not overshadow the fact that for other Gold Coasters, marriage to white women was not nearly as great an obstacle to the work of African nationalism in Britain or to the task of nation building in Ghana. Two of WASU's most prominent Gold Coast members, Frederick Kankam-Boadu and Joe Appiah, married across the color line while living in London and actively presiding over the affairs of WASU. Kankam-Boadu was born in 1913 in the southeastern Gold Coast town of Mamfe-Akwapem. One of a select few young men in the colony to receive an education at the prestigious Mfantsipim Secondary School in Cape Coast, he graduated with a Cambridge Overseas School Certificate in 1934. Five years later, as the war broke out, Frederick traveled to London to study law at Cambridge's Selwyn College. Upon completing his law degree in 1943, he was appointed visiting lecturer in the Twi language at the London School of Oriental and African studies. As the years progressed, Frederick's involvement with WASU shifted from being a beneficiary of its resources to supervising its operations. He oversaw the students who lived at WASU's Camden Square Africa House hostel; served as chairman of the editorial board of the organization's information organ, *Wasu*; and sat on the executive committee, alongside Kojo Botsio and Joe Appiah, during the presidency of Ebenezer Ako-Adjei in the mid-1940s. Together these men represented WASU at the Fifth Pan-African Congress in Manchester in 1945.

Presided over by W. E. B. Du Bois, the 1945 Congress was a watershed moment for African participation, which saw the likes of Kwame Nkrumah, Jomo Kenyatta, and Peter Abrahams assume prominent positions of leadership.

FIGURE 8.1. West African Students Union (WASU) social gathering in London, ca. 1947. Frederick and Erna "Miki" Kankam-Boadu are pictured in the middle of the photograph, and Joe Appiah is the bespectacled man in the lower left-hand corner. (Photograph from the personal collection of Miki Kankam-Boadu, Accra, Ghana.)

Nkrumah and Kenyatta, in particular, laid "valuable groundwork for independence movements" during the Congress.[21] Frederick Kankam-Boadu was in the thick of WASU's vibrant political activities on the international stage and at home in his Primrose Hill Gardens residence in Hampstead, which he shared with Appiah and two other prominent WASU members, Nigerians Bankole Akpata and Afolabi Odebiyi. It was their house that Kwame Nkrumah would increasingly frequent during his 1945–1947 sojourn in London, where he forged the political ties with fellow Gold Coasters, West Africans, and other Africans, including those from the diaspora, that would further shape and later become the hallmark of both his nationalist and his Pan-African sensibilities.[22]

While living in Primrose Hill Gardens, Frederick was introduced to Erna "Miki" Cohn by a mutual German friend. Erna's own life experiences had instilled in her a deep openness to people different from herself. Growing up under the increasingly dark shadow of racism and anti-Semitism in Nazi

FIGURE 8.2. Frederick and Erna "Miki" Kankam-Boadu enjoying an excursion in the English countryside with friends, ca. 1950. (Photograph from the personal collection of Miki Kankam-Boadu, Accra, Ghana.)

Germany and then fleeing to Britain where she and her sister were the only family members to survive the Holocaust, Erna encountered an entirely new language and culture. A constant theme in her life was that of difference and alienation and this enabled her to sympathize with Africans and others who were similarly situated because despite being white, she deeply understood herself to be a member of an oppressed group. At the same time she longed for the security of family, but was unencumbered by any particular notion of what that family should look like. When she and Frederick began their relationship, it was Erna's friends who awakened in her an awareness of how unusual their pairing was: a German Jewish woman and a West African man in London. But none of that mattered to Erna; she was happy with her choice.

Following a yearlong courtship they wed in 1947. Erna joined Frederick in the Primrose Garden house with their first child, Akua. Although they had a room to themselves, the small family continued to share the house with the rest of Frederick's WASU comrades. While obviously a site of anticolonial political activity, their residence was also home to interracial social gatherings that eventually fostered a tightknit community of interracial couples who rendered mutual support, camaraderie, and aid to one another in good times and bad.[23]

Six years later, in July 1953, Erna and Frederick sat in the pews of St. John's Anglican Church in London with their good friends Ruth and Seretse Khama seated next to them. The two couples had come to witness the nuptials of their close friends Joe Appiah and Enid Margaret Cripps, better known as Peggy. Frederick and Miki's daughter, Akua, was the flower girl. The relationship between budding nationalist and scion of the Asante aristocracy Joe Appiah and Peggy Cripps, the well-heeled daughter of the British Labour politician Sir Stafford Cripps, chancellor of the exchequer (1947–1950), illustrates how some white women came to be romantically linked with African men through their own progressive political leanings and organizational affiliations. Peggy's introduction to the WASU community came through her involvement in the movement for interracial cooperation, which promoted friendship and understanding across color lines and was very much an extension of her extraordinarily cosmopolitan upbringing. Her childhood travels and early work experience during the Second World War exposed her to life in Burma, China, India, Iran, Jamaica, and Russia. Shortly after the war's end, her commitment to working toward racial integration found concrete expression in her membership in the World Assembly of Youth, which "articulated interracial respect as a crucial part of its mission."[24] It was also visible in a secretarial job she took in 1952 with Racial Unity, a newly formed organization that sought to raise awareness of racial discrimination and to promote "a moral concern about race through the wider knowledge of different societies and races."[25] During her tenure at Racial Unity she met Joe Appiah, who was then president of WASU, and their love for each other quickly blossomed, but not without some hesitation about what "the reaction of the color-conscious Britons to such a marriage" might be.[26] With the blessing of both families, however, the couple's only delay in wedding was the death of Peggy's father in 1952. But even that served as Joe's public entrance into Peggy's family, when Lady Cripps invited him to join their procession at Sir Cripps's memorial service. The Appiah family in Kumasi reciprocated by organizing an elaborate two-month visit to the Gold Coast for Peggy so she could see firsthand what her life in West Africa would be like.[27]

The Appiahs' 1953 nuptials sent the British press into overdrive and also drew considerable coverage in the Gold Coast and elsewhere around the world.[28] Yet, the media spectacle sensationalized what was actually not

FIGURE 8.3. Joe Appiah and Enid Margaret Cripps's London wedding in 1953 drew international attention. The image here was featured in the 30 July 1953 edition of the popular African American magazine *Jet*. Below the picture is the original caption that United Press Photo prepared for distribution with the image.

altogether uncommon. Many African independence leaders were interracially married or had significant relationships with white women while abroad—albeit most did not have Peggy Appiah's aristocratic upbringing. Jomo Kenyatta (Kenya); Eduardo Mondlane (Mozambique); Leopold Senghor (Senegal); Agostinho Neto (Angola); and Seretse Khama (Botswana) all married white women. At independence, the white wives of Senghor, Neto, and Khama became the first ladies of Senegal, Angola, and Botswana, respectively. Nigeria's Nnamdi Azikwe and Malawi's Hastings Banda also had long-standing affairs with British women. Banda's lover, Merene French, even accompanied him to Ghana on the eve of its independence where he set up a medical practice, and she had a bird's-eye view of the political machinery of African independence.[29] When Banda left Ghana to lead Malawi to independence, he also left Merene behind. Of all these relationships, however, it was the 1948 marriage of Seretse and Ruth Khama that proved most controversial, because it struck right at the heart of the racial politics of settler colonialism in southern Africa.

Khama married his British wife, Ruth Williams, to the utter dismay of his Bamangwato ruling family and to the horror of both South Africa's newly inaugurated National Party apartheid government and Southern Rhodesia's settler colonial regime. For its part, the British government was less concerned with the fact of Khama's interracial marriage than it was with its political implications for the southern African region. Although the Khamas would eventually enjoy a happy ending, with Seretse assuming the presidency at independence in 1966 with Ruth by his side, it was during the firestorm over their marriage and subsequent exile in London (1952–1956) that the Khamas, Appiahs, and Kankam-Boadus were all part of a tight-knit community of interracial couples. Indeed, a few months after attending the Appiahs' 1953 wedding, Seretse Khama served as best man for J. Halcro Ferguson, a (white) British journalist, who wed Joyce Dorthea Thompson, a Jamaican nurse, in London. Three decades later the Appiah's daughter, Isobel, married her Norwegian husband in Botswana, in the home of Ruth Khama, who had been recently widowed. The bonds of family and friendship formed in 1950s London clearly endured.[30]

The Khamas and Appiahs regularly joined Erna and Frederick Kankam-Boadu for Sunday lunch at their Primrose Gardens home, and it was during these intimate gatherings that Erna says she palpably felt the incredible pressure that Seretse and Ruth were under. As she encouraged them to remain steadfast in the face of their critics and foes, Erna sensed how different her reality was being married to a West African. There had been no public or private outcry over their nuptials, no government or familial intervention. Avid press interest aside, even her friends Peggy and Joe Appiah, both the offspring of prominent political families, had not faced the barrage of criticism and pressure that the Khamas were made to endure.[31] This gave Erna an early indication of the more hospitable social and political climate that awaited her in the Gold Coast. In 1954 Frederick was the first West African appointed to the post of deputy managing director of the Gold Coast Cocoa Marketing Co. Ltd., the London-based subsidiary of the Gold Coast Cocoa Marketing Board, charged with handling the sale of the colony's cocoa crops.[32] That same year their first son, Quasi, was born. A year later Frederick was appointed chairman of the Accra-based Gold Coast Cocoa Marketing Board, and the family prepared to move to the Gold Coast. Although Erna did not know exactly what to expect, she was confident that she would not face the opposition and hatred that Seretse and Ruth encountered both in Britain and in southern Africa.

While the romantic interracial relationships that men like Frederick Kankam-Boadu and Joe Appiah formed in London during and after their school days were by no means a new phenomenon—working-class African seamen in British ports had long partnered with white women—what was new was the fact that these men were taking their white wives home with them unencumbered by the late colonial state, which, in its prime, had acted vigorously to prevent such couples from making the African colonies home. One might surmise that this had to do with the class and educational status of men like Kankam-Boadu and Appiah, but even affluent Gold Coasters were subjected to screening in previous decades, and those who held credentials as lawyers and doctors were refused permission to bring their white wives with them until they could demonstrate financial stability upon their return to the colonies. Even just a few decades earlier, a man with Kankam-Boadu's educational background but untested financial stability would have likely been denied the right to settle in the colonies with his white wife. But in 1955 the sunsetting British colonial government was far less preoccupied with such questions than it was with choreographing its exit from the imperial stage and stewarding "the winds of change," to borrow British prime minister Harold Macmillan's famous phrase. What this meant for Erna and Frederick, and the many other interracial couples that began making their way to the colony at this time, was that their entry into the Gold Coast was not hindered by colonial authorities, although it was likely monitored by them.[33] But that was hardly the audience that mattered. Far more important to the young family as they carved out a niche in Accra on the verge of independence was the reception and the perception of Ghanaians. If history is any measure, the Kankam-Boadus did more than carve out a niche, they settled in the place that would become home for the rest of their lives. Frederick passed away in 2005. Erna, now in her eighties, still lives in Accra.

One other marriage warrants discussion here. When Kwame Nkrumah finally married in December 1957, just months after Ghana's independence, his choice of bride could not have carried more political symbolism. Nkrumah's son, Gamal, has written openly about the fact that his father chose to marry a young Egyptian student, Fathia Rizk, in order to cement a Pan-African alliance: "It was a political union between Mediterranean-oriented North Africa and the rest of the continent, often pejoratively termed sub-Saharan or Black Africa."[34] For this reason, the marriage alarmed both British and American authorities, who exchanged a flurry of diplomatic correspondence about it.[35] Their marriage also sowed controversy in Ghana. "At first, many Ghanaian women did not take kindly to the idea of Kwame Nkrumah marrying a foreigner," says Gamal, who notes that "the militant women's league of the ruling Convention People's Party was especially galled that the national hero had married a 'white woman,' even though Father explained to them that his bride was an African despite her fair skin."[36] The furor soon died down and Fathia Nkrumah emerged as the much beloved first "first lady" of Ghana. With extraordinary visibility and grace, she joined her husband in building the new nation until 1966 when Nkrumah was overthrown in a military coup while en route to Hanoi. That it was Fathia and her three children who endured the terror of the coup before being evacuated to Cairo on a plane sent by Egyptian president Gamal Abdel Nasser seems a poignant reminder of what a national figurehead she became in her own right.

CONCLUSION

Anticolonial nationalism succeeded in bringing an end to British rule, but it did not stop nationalists' concern over the sexual exploitation of Ghana's young women by European men from resurfacing in the years after independence. In 1963, President Nkrumah received a letter from a distressed Ghanaian civil servant who was, in his own words, "becoming increasingly concerned about the way expatriate personnel treat our women in this country."[37] Echoing some of the complaints of the "Immoral Sanitation" series four decades earlier, the civil servant claimed that "throughout the country," Europeans "court our girls freely, some have babies by them, and eventually throw them overboard without so much as making a provision for the maintenance of the children much less for the mother." Such behavior "smacks of racial superiority which is intolerable in our present age," said the civil servant, who exhorted Nkrumah to implement "drastic" measures to stop it. Signaling that these claims were taken seriously, Nkrumah's minister of justice advised the drafting of legislation broadly aimed at protecting school-age girls from sexual exploitation and out-of-wedlock impregnation, as well as ensuring the maintenance of any child born out of wedlock.[38] With the exception of a clause rendering expatriates "liable to deportation," the proposed legislation was applicable to men of all races and nationalities, including Ghanaians. Nkrumah's government saw the need to protect the morality and sexual integrity of the new nation's young women from the predations of expatriate and Ghanaian men alike, yet the provocation remained the domain of interracial sex.

Conclusion
Sexuality's Staying Power

INTERRACIAL SEXUALITY
AND MULTIRACIAL LIVES AFTER EMPIRE

"The sexual habits of British colonists in West Africa at the turn of the century will be discussed before a High Court judge in an attempt to prevent the Home Office deporting a man to Ghana."[1] So read the opening lines of an article that appeared in Britain's *Guardian* newspaper on 7 April 1982. The man in question was Reggie Yates, the grandson of British mining accountant George William Yates and Dorothy Lloyd, a multiracial Fante woman. This was not the first time Reggie Yates had been on the verge of deportation. In 1979 he had successfully avoided being sent back to Ghana for overstaying his visitor's permit by arguing in front of a magistrate's court that "since his grandfather was British he could justifiably claim to be a patrial," with the right of abode in Britain per the Immigration Act of 1971.[2] As the *Young Socialist* newspaper reported, the court "gave [Reggie] an absolute discharge forcing the Home Office to recognize his right of settlement in Britain."[3] But this did not stop Britain's immigration machinery from hounding him.

Facing deportation again in 1981, Yates appeared in front of an immigration appeals tribunal. Beside him was his father, Harry Philip Yates, who, for the first and only time in his life, flew from Ghana to London to vouch for his son's status as a patrial. Harry Yates presented a sworn affidavit stating that both his father and his grandfather "were born in England of English parents."⁴ But none of this seemed to matter to the tribunal's chairman, P. N. Dalton, who rejected Reggie's case on the grounds that his grandparents did not have a valid marriage, thereby rendering his paternal ancestry "illegitimate" and in the process invalidating his status as a patrial. In an unlucky twist of fate for Reggie, Dalton had served as a colonial administrator in the Gold Coast during the late 1930s, and thus said he spoke with authority when judging it "extremely unlikely" that either George or Dorothy could have believed that they were "entering into a valid marriage."⁵ While he doubted that Dorothy gave the legitimacy of their union "any thought at all," Dalton explained away George's participation as "the custom of the time in the Gold Coast." Men like George, he asserted, "entered into relationships with [local] women" simply because "[white] wives seldom came out to stay."⁶ With his appeal denied, Reggie returned to Ghana to avoid the indignity of deportation.

In early 1982 he returned to London to join his wife, Felicia, and their newborn daughter. Reggie, however, was subjected to invasive immigration surveillance that was halted only after the liberal-leaning Lord Avebury and the London Immigration Action Group intervened on his behalf. They asked a high court judge "to grant leave for a judicial review of the appeal refusals," based on Reggie's belief that his grandparents "had a settled relationship and that [Dorothy] believed herself to be a respectable married woman."⁷ While the review process dragged on, major changes in British nationality law ultimately resolved the Yates family's immigration nightmare.⁸ By virtue of section 6(2) of the British Nationality Act of 1981, which came into force on 1 January 1983, Reggie was now able to apply for naturalization as a British citizen based on his marriage to Felicia, a Ghanaian-born British citizen. Prior to the act, only British husbands could confer this right on their foreign national wives. As one of Reggie's supporters aptly observed, "His case is a classic example of both racial and sexual discrimination."⁹ Fortunately for Reggie Yates, the gender-based discrimination that had for so long characterized British nationality law was remedied precisely at the moment that its racially exclusive character was further ramped up under the conservative leadership of Margaret Thatcher. It was a legal respite that came just in time.

Reggie Yates's immigration battle and the recourse to colonial history that became such a crucial part of its adjudication dramatically illustrate what Jordanna Bailkin calls "the afterlife of empire"—that is, "the impact of [decolonization] upon metropolitan life, and the ways in which the empire continued to be lived in Britain after it appeared to come to an end elsewhere."¹⁰

Reggie, like many others, fell victim to Britain's rapid retreat from the broadly inclusive way it sought to secure its postwar international influence by reconstituting its dwindling empire into the British Commonwealth. It did this by passing the 1948 British Nationality Act (BNA), which in theory put all British subjects, regardless of their place of residence, color, or creed, on equal footing by granting them "full and unimpeded rights to enter and settle in the United Kingdom." This was a "cherished illusion" given the manifold ways that British politicians and lawmakers curbed these rights with subsequent pieces of legislation in the 1960s and 1970s, but it remained powerful enough to require a final retreat from in the form of the aforementioned 1981 BNA.[11] The act symbolized Britain's repudiation of the ways in which decolonization had and continued to change its racial makeup by severing, once and for all, its national identity from that of its former empire.

As legal scholar David Dixon observes, the purpose of the act's translation of "immigration law into nationality [was] 'finally to dispose of the lingering notion that Britain is somehow a haven for all whose countries [it] once ruled.'"[12] It did this, in part, by replacing the category Citizen of the United Kingdom and the Colonies (CUKC) with that of British citizen "for those who are 'closely connected' to Britain," a move that further enshrined patriality, and thus direct racial descent from a white British father or grandfather, as the primary determinant of immigration rights and nationality.[13] In practice, patriality was "no more than a corollary of a racist definition of those who did not 'belong.'"[14] Caught in the middle were people like Reggie Yates, who were black and patrials, a combination that defied the racially coded ways in which immigration and nationality law were wedded to each other in increasingly exclusionary ways. His immigration battle vividly highlighted these racist practices, helping to explain why his case received so much attention from both the progressive press and Britain's immigration machinery, which sought to rectify his incongruous identities by arguing that he was not the legitimate offspring of a British forefather.

Nowhere was this more evident than in the arguments made by immigration appeals tribunal chairman P. N. Dalton. In a stunning display of how "empire continued to be lived in Britain after it appeared to come to an end elsewhere," Dalton brazenly reprised his role as a British officer capable of controlling the destiny of his colonial subjects by invoking his knowledge of interracial sexual relations in the Gold Coast to counter Reggie's assertions about the legitimacy of his paternal ancestry. Dalton's claims about the nature of Dorothy and George's relationship rehearsed colonial thinking about interracial sexual relationships between European men and African women; namely, that these relationships were illegitimate and occurred primarily because of the small number of white women in the colony. Colonial thinking at the time, as well as Dalton's regurgitation of it a half century later, however, failed to acknowledge the ways in which colonial policies and racist attitudes were largely responsible for making it all but impossible for interracial couples to publicly legitimize their unions. Also conveniently overlooked was the fact that colonial policies kept the number of white women in the colony intentionally small. Altogether dismissed was the possibility that European men might actually prefer African women to white women—for a range of different reasons—rather than viewing them as consolation prizes.

More importantly, Dalton's historical reading rendered couples like Dorothy and George, and others, like the Knights, Hawes, Bowesmans, and Turners, who challenged the conventions of their times, invisible. Dorothy and George's marriage, after all, was not just legitimized by customary law, it was also publicly recognized by Dorothy's family, and African and European members of the Broomassi mining town where they visibly set up a home and raised their infant son, Harry, until 1917 when George left the Gold Coast. Although the fact that he was already married to an Englishwoman with whom he had several children complicates how we might otherwise understand his relationship with Dorothy, what is germane here is that for approximately half of George's decade-long stay in the Gold Coast he and Dorothy enjoyed a "settled relationship," and Dorothy regarded herself and was regarded by others as George's wife, and Harry as their son. The "respectability" of their union is further attested to by the fact that Dorothy went on to marry a prominent Gold Coaster, something that would have been unlikely had she been seen as nothing more than a discarded "white-man's toy," as one Gold Coast writer mockingly called local women who casually liaised with European men. Dalton's unwillingness or perhaps inability to see Dorothy and George's relationship as something other than the insalubrious "custom of the time" speaks to the staying power of colonial discourses that disparaged interracial relationships as inherently immoral.

Thus it was only after the breakup of the British Empire that multiracial Ghanaians like Reggie Yates came to constitute a "problem" in ways that prompted responses reminiscent of those enacted by French colonial officials and jurists in the early twentieth century that linked citizenship status in part to the legitimacy of paternal recognition, in order to deal with the "*métis*" problem."[15] The primary difference between these efforts was that in the case of the French, legitimacy came to be constituted through proof of filiation to a French father, among other considerations, but was not contingent on birth occurring in wedlock. In the case of the British, both paternal filiation and legitimate birth mattered, and the absence of the latter was enough to invalidate the former for purposes of granting patriality until the late date of 2006.[16] The purpose of continuing to bar British men from conferring patriality on their illegitimate offspring with non-British women, long after children born out of wedlock to British women were given automatic patriality, was to avoid the problem of "fraudulent recognitions" that had so vexed officials throughout the French Empire almost a century earlier.[17] Clearly, like empire itself, its afterlife was no respecter of national boundaries.

In contrast to the progressively exclusive way that British nationality law was rewritten in the decades after the empire's end, since its inception Ghana's nationality law has been broadly inclusive and increasingly so in more recent decades. The Ghana Nationality and Citizenship Act of 1957 established three different criteria by which Ghanaian citizenship could be obtained: by birth, descent, and registration. For our purposes here, the most important thing to note is that the act did not confer or deprive citizenship based on racial or ethnic qualifications. Most multiracial Ghanaians, like most other Ghanaians, received their citizenship by birth because they were born in Ghana and had at least one parent or grandparent who was also born in Ghana. Those born abroad were able to claim citizenship based on ancestry, provided they had a parent who was born in Ghana. The 1957 act also allowed non-Ghanaian wives of Ghanaian husbands to register for citizenship.

Although multiracial Ghanaians in Ghana had little difficulty receiving Ghanaian citizenship, the loss of British citizenship (CUKC) did pose some challenges, which were met with different responses and solutions. As we have already seen, Reggie Yates had to endure a lengthy immigration battle before he was granted the right of abode in Britain. Dr. Albert Hawe (chapter 5) successfully petitioned the Home Office in 1963 for his children to regain their British citizenship per the British Nationality Act of 1948. The Hawe children, at the time, were already schooling in Britain, where they went on to establish their lives, so the change in their citizenship status was in line with the reality of their lives. Hawe and his Ghanaian-born multiracial wife, Margaret Mary, by contrast, were resident in Ghana. By virtue of their marriage, Margaret Mary was entitled to her husband's citizenship, and thus both remained British citizens after independence. At that time there was no legal mechanism for Ghanaian women to confer their citizenship on their non-Ghanaian husbands, so it was fortunate that the couple did not wish to become Ghanaian citizens. Subsequent changes to Ghana's citizenship law eased this restriction and others. The 1992 Constitution of Ghana included a gender-neutral provision allowing Ghanaian women and men to confer citizenship on their non-Ghanaian spouses by registration.[18] The Constitution, however, did not recognize dual citizenship and thus militated against the acquisition of Ghanaian citizenship by registration for foreign national spouses because it required them to renounce their own citizenship—an act that most would have been loath to do given that Ghana was just emerging from decades of political instability.

Progressive amendments made it even easier to claim citizenship by birth, including a provision incorporated into the 1979 Constitution that conferred citizenship by birth to those born outside of Ghana, provided they had a parent who was a citizen of Ghana, irrespective of how that citizenship was acquired.[19] By virtue of the 1992 Constitution, citizenship by birth could be conferred regardless of whether birth occurred in or outside of Ghana, provided the recipient's parent or grandparent was a citizen of Ghana.[20] While not retroactive, these increasingly inclusive provisions contrast sharply with the way in which British nationality law dramatically narrowed entitlements to citizenship based on patriality. The inclusionary and exclusionary impulses of Ghana's and Britain's nationality and immigration laws are of course deeply intertwined. Ghana hopes to stem the tide of out-migration and promote new streams of potentially lucrative return migration, while Britain and other European countries continue to be committed to keeping out all but a handful of highly skilled Ghanaian immigrants.[21]

More recently, the terms of the citizenship debate for multiracial people and families in Ghana has shifted toward the question of dual nationality and enhanced residency rights. As a result of the initiative taken by the International Spouses Association of Ghana (ISAG), the Immigration Act 2000 (Act 573), which entitles the foreign national spouses of Ghanaians to "Indefinite Residence" status with the automatic right to work, among other privileges, was enacted in February 2000.[22] This act lifts the onerous burdens and restrictions that prior legislation placed on foreign spouses. Previously, female foreign spouses were eligible for only one-year residence permits that had to be renewed annually accompanied "by a letter from the Ghanaian partner confirming that he wished his spouse to remain in the country."[23] Gendered discrimination against Ghanaian women was also enshrined in the law, which barred their foreign male spouses from applying for residence permits based on marriage. The only way such men could obtain these permits was as "investors or quota workers."[24] The right to work for foreign spouses has thus remained an important issue since the early days of independence, when British men like Brendan Knight saw their prospects for gainful employment diminished by the Africanization of government service. The Citizenship Act 2000 (Act 591), which ISAG also lobbied for on behalf of the offspring of these unions, removed remaining barriers to dual citizenship that were present in previous legislation.[25]

Some of the terms of the acts, as well as the delays and difficulties in implementing them, however, speak to the precariousness that continues to characterize the lives of those whose fate hangs in the legislative balance. After Act 573 was passed in 2000, foreign spouses waited more than two years before the necessary forms to apply for indefinite residency were printed and made available. Act 591 expanded the number of sensitive high-ranking offices that dual citizens are barred from holding, an indication that the state regards such persons as potentially disloyal.[26] Although former Ghanaian president J. J. Rawlings, who is of Ewe and Scottish descent, has held only Ghanaian citizenship, one has to wonder whether the expansion of prohibited posts was in part a response to the popular misgivings that many Ghanaians expressed about the appropriateness of having a multiracial president. An article appearing in the *Free Press*, an avowedly anti-Rawlings paper, summed up these kinds of racially informed objections in the lead up to the 1992 presidential elections with the following pronouncement: "In the first place the half Ghanaian blood said to be running in Rawlings veins hardly shows him out as a Ghanaian. Rawlings is not a Ghanaian in terms of culture, physical outlook, as regards language, skin color, hair and character. . . . It would be disgraceful for Ghanaians to elect him as their president."[27] The terms of the *Free Press*'s criticisms suggest that questioning candidates' ethnic or racial credentials remains a politically expedient way of delegitimizing claims to power, not unlike an earlier period when multiracial Gas found their "ethnic credentials" challenged by those who wished to keep them out of stool politics. Although still popular in some quarters, there can be no doubt that Rawlings's long and controversial time in power has dramatically altered the political possibilities for other multiracial Ghanaians.

Finally, even though Act 591 allows multiracial children who are citizens of another country to obtain Ghanaian citizenship, parents have reported difficulty in applying for this in practice. In a particularly telling case, a Dutch mother, Maria, and a Ghanaian father, Kwame, applied for Ghanaian citizenship for their children, who were already Dutch citizens, but their request stumped the Ghanaian Embassy in the Netherlands. According to Maria, the embassy "found it very strange, because if the children have Dutch citizenship, why would you want them to have another citizenship with it?" For Ghanaians in the Netherlands, she said, "Dutch citizenship is sort of a prize. . . . If you have that, you have made it."[28] The embassy, it turns out, was so used to Ghanaians renouncing their Ghanaian citizenship in order to win the "prize" of Dutch citizenship that it wrongly assumed Dutch law did not recognize dual citizenship at all.

The Ghanaian Embassy's befuddlement at Maria and Kwame's desire to claim Ghanaian citizenship for their children points to a broader phenomenon. With multifaceted crises facing the postcolonial state in Africa and the rise of "fortress Europe," Ghanaians and other Africans in ever-increasing numbers are literally dying to get out of Africa. Harrowing reports of capsizing boats taking hundreds of migrants to their deaths are now an almost weekly if not daily phenomenon. Even those who do not die in pursuit of a life in Europe are willing to encounter a social death of sorts. According to Ghana's Ministry of the Interior in 2013, 817 Ghanaians renounced their citizenship, while only a paltry 39 foreigners applied for it. All but two of those Ghanaians were applying for citizenship in European countries.[29] That most multiracial Ghanaians enjoy far less obstructed paths to European or American citizenship and are shielded from the intense poverty that drives African migrants to risk death in search of better lives in Europe underscores a theme that has been present in the history of interracial relationships in Ghana from its early beginnings. Namely, familial connections, through marriage and birth to Europeans have often been conduits for enhanced access to wealth, education, and influence. Indeed, the belief that marriage to a foreigner, especially a white one, can lead to a prosperous life abroad motivates many young urban Ghanaians to spend long hours at Internet cafés in pursuit of foreign contacts.[30] Yet, these modern-day cyber romances rarely have fairy-tale endings. Like their precolonial and colonial counterparts, they are shaped by the fraught intersection between race, sex, gender, and power, even as they have largely ceased being the taboos they once were.

INTERRACIAL HETEROSEXUALITY, HOMOSEXUALITY, AND STATES OF PANIC

Over the years it has taken me to complete this book, I have annually marked the anniversary of *Loving v. Virginia*, the 1967 landmark Supreme Court decision that deemed the prohibition of interracial marriage unconstitutional. Today a new battle rages in the United States for a different kind of marriage equality that would give same-sex couples the legal right to marry. Many contemporary observers have made the link between the two struggles, but none more eloquently than Mildred Loving, who, on the fortieth anniversary of the *Loving* decision, issued the following statement:

> I believe all Americans, no matter their race, no matter their sex, no matter their sexual orientation, should have that same freedom to marry. . . . I am still not a political person, but I am proud that Richard's and my name is on a court case that can help reinforce the love, the commitment, the fairness and the family that so many people, black or white, young or old, gay or straight seek in life. I support the freedom to marry for all. That's what *Loving*, and loving, are all about.[31]

While gay Americans fight for marriage equality supported by allies from an earlier civil rights struggle, in many African countries such imperatives give way to more pressing concerns, like the threat of prosecution, violent attack, and death that many LGBT Africans increasingly face. Over the last several years the spike in church-sponsored and state-sanctioned repression and brutality against the LGBT community in a number of African countries has led to the deaths of prominent gay-rights activists, including Cameroon's Eric Ohena Lembembe, Uganda's David Kato, and South Africa's Noxolo Nogwaza, while countless others have been terrorized into silence. Attempts to intensify colonial-era legislation criminalizing homosexuality have made the daily lives of many LGBT Africans increasingly perilous. The irony is that while antigay fearmongers like Presidents Robert Mugabe (Zimbabwe) and Yoweri Museveni (Uganda) assert that homosexuality is a Western import, it is the criminalization of homosexuality in Africa that has its roots in Western-cum-colonial jurisprudence—a fact that Western human rights campaigners would do well to remember.

This calls to mind the deeper colonial history of regulation and prohibition that homosexuality and interracial heterosexuality share, but also points to the very different trajectories these rights struggles have taken. In their brilliant introduction to *Love in Africa*, Jennifer Cole and Lynn Thomas assert that the management of sexuality and "ideologies of affect have been an integral part of the disciplinary regimes through which imperial and liberal governments have sought to regulate their subjects and citizens." They go on to note that these "regimes have worked in part by marking certain intimate relations—namely, those premised on the heterosexual monogamous couple—as more valuable and, hence, more worthy of political recognition than others."[32] But the valorization of heterosexual monogamous unions was racialized. This was most evident in places like the United States and South Africa, where interracial marriage was legally prohibited, but it was also evident in administered colonies in Africa where heterosexual marriages contracted across the color line elicited panicked responses and were subject to de facto forms of prohibition. The language of pathology used to characterize the Gold Coast's interracial marriage "epidemic" in 1945 as "a form of madness" is hardly distinguishable from the lexicon of pathology applied to homosexuality. Not unlike the rationale often given for why white men turned to other men for sexual fulfillment in the colonies, Governor Burns believed that the cause of the interracial marriage "epidemic" was a combination of the shortage of European women in the colony resulting from wartime travel difficulties and restrictions on home-leave. Thus, the notion of situational homosexuality found its counterpart in situational interracial marriage.

Meanwhile, "heterosexual unions based on concubinage and prostitution across the colonial divide were defended as a 'necessary evil' to counter those deemed more dangerous still—carnal relations between men and men."[33] By its very exclusion from this prophylactic equation, intermarriage is figured in the colonial imagination as homosexuality's coeval. This is not to say that the colonial pecking order of sexual danger was stable. Sexual arrangements like concubinage, which were valorized in earlier centuries for acculturating European men and stabilizing the colonial presence in new parts of the empire, were by the turn of the twentieth century denounced as sources of racial and cultural contamination and colonial instability.[34] Despite the reversal in colonial thinking, concubinage and managed prostitution continued to be preferred over homosexuality *and* interracial marriage. But in the waning years of colonial rule, intermarriage between European men and African women in the Gold Coast and between African men and European women in Europe was not only on the rise, it was also a phenomenon that colonial administrators had to reckon with in a more measured fashion, even if they were horrified by its occurrence. By the late 1950s and early 1960s, interracial marriages were an increasingly visible social facet of the early independence era in Ghana. The very fact that prominent Gold Coast politicians like Joe Appiah and Frederick Kankam-Boadu were married to white women, and former British colonial officers like Brendan Knight and Charles Bowesman were married to African women and gainfully employed in independent Ghana, indicates the evolution in opinion and social practice regarding intermarriage.

But the link between sexuality and political power remains very much intact in postindependence Africa. A growing number of African governments today seem to be invested in legitimizing themselves and laying claim to power through discourses that link sexuality to nationalism. This is not always a bad thing. Postapartheid South Africa was the first country in the world to outlaw discrimination based on sexual orientation and the first African country to legalize same-sex marriage—a move intended to bolster the legitimacy of the new South Africa by demonstrating that bias of any kind was unacceptable. But the rampant violence meted out to LGBT South Africans and the state's failure to curb these hate crimes illustrates the wide gap between prescription and practice. Still, the South African state's recognition that one form of oppression cannot be resisted by embracing another one underscores the interdependent, rather than antithetical, nature of the struggles against racial and sexual discrimination.

By way of contrast, in other countries the link between sexuality and nationalism has rendered homosexuality a form of national and cultural betrayal and homophobia a misguided expression of anti-imperialism and ethnic, cultural, racial, and/or national authenticity.[35] Zimbabwe's and Uganda's ossifying presidents, Mugabe and Museveni, regularly whip up antigay hysteria in order to foster nationalist fervor amid and often in response to pressing social, economic, and political issues—not unlike the effect that "black peril" scares had on white settlers in colonial Zimbabwe during the early decades of the twentieth century. In Ghana, government minister Paul Evans Aidoo urged citizens in 2011 to "round up" suspected homosexuals in an effort to "get rid of these people in society."[36] Aidoo's remarks are eerily reminiscent of an earlier moment in Ghana's colonial history when "spinsters" were rounded up because of the moral threat, represented by prostitution and venereal disease, that male patriarchs believed unmarried women—who were conflated with prostitutes—posed to social order in their districts.[37] The year 2014 opened with the passage of draconian legislation in Nigeria and Uganda that prescribes much harsher punishments than ever before for homosexuality. In their wake, the language of "moral sanitization"—seemingly lifted from the pages of the *Gold Coast Leader*—has been deployed in an effort to rally support for "root[ing] out, imprison[ing] and punish[ing] gays" across Nigeria.[38] When viewed through this lens, homophobia's seemingly sudden and violent appearance in a number of African countries is actually part of a much longer history in which sexuality is made to serve as a register for social dis-ease and is used to legitimize the tightening of patriarchal and state power and the closing of ranks through the policing of cultural and national boundaries.

While there are complicated factors at work, the recent escalation of state- and church-sponsored homophobia in a number of African countries is part of a wider global past and present. Far from being exceptional, what is happening in places like Uganda, Nigeria, and South Africa mirrors our own recent history in the United States and elsewhere. Less than two decades ago Matthew Shepard, a young American, was sadistically murdered in an antigay hate crime in Wyoming—a killing that many describe as a turning point in America's confrontation with its own culture of homophobia. While the US government has made gay rights a sticking point of its international diplomacy and aid agreements with African governments, the gap between foreign and domestic policy is made evident by attempts in Kansas and Arizona in 2014 and in Indiana in 2015 to introduce legislation that would make it legal for businesses and government employees to deny service to same-sex couples.[39] In Russia, the government came under international fire for tightening antigay legislation ahead of the 2014 Winter Olympics, while the mayor of Sochi made headlines after declaring that the game's host city had no homosexuals.

Homophobia, then, is clearly not unique to Africa. I would suggest, however, that its recent appearance in a number of African countries is rooted in the racialization of sexuality and the ways in which this process historically marked out Africa as the site of unbridled sexuality and Africans as hypersexual. As Marc Epprecht has pointed out, "'African sexuality'—the idea that Africans share a common sexual culture distinct from people elsewhere in the world—has had numerous incarnations over the centuries," but in each instance African sexualities are collapsed into a singular pathologized entity.[40] One response to this stigmatizing representation has been to juxtapose an alternate version of a singular African sexuality characterized by heteronormative conservatism against a sexually corrupt(ing) Western sexuality. Not unlike the response of African Americans, and particularly African American women, to centuries of racialized sexual abuse and exploitation that was so often legitimized through similar kinds of discourses asserting black promiscuity, many Africans have tied racial respectability to conservative notions of sexual morality.[41] But the "rhetoric of patriotic heterosexuality" is more than a flawed attempt to right the wrongs of colonial racism; it is creating a new template for African authenticity that hinges on a "morally conservative African nationalism" that leaves little room for acknowledging, let alone accepting, the range of sexual practices and cultures that exists across the continent.[42]

The consequences of these essentializing practices have been dire, ranging from delayed and ineffective responses to the HIV/AIDS epidemic—government efforts gained momentum only after the epidemic was delinked from homosexual transmission—to the criminalization of same-sex practices and the rise of violent homophobia. This situation has only been made worse by the way in which external calls for reform by the United States and European countries have been interpreted—not without reason—as cultural imperialism and resistance to such calls as anti-imperialism, thereby interjecting the vexed questions of both cultural and national sovereignty into an already racially fraught debate. As the fate of LGBT activists in Africa makes evident, this binary leaves little room for maneuvering between rhetoric and reality. Meanwhile, racist stereotypes about African sexuality show few signs of waning. Thus the historic interplay between the denigration of African sexualities and the self-articulation of a narrowly defined conservative African sexuality continues into the present. Studies like this one may not bring this vicious cycle to an end, but they offer an opportunity to better understand the circumstances that have produced this particular response. More importantly, I hope that in making the connection between the historic regulation and denigration of both homosexuality and interracial heterosexuality, *Crossing the Color Line* will encourage those who regard the struggles for racial equality and LGBT rights as unrelated to see them as interdependent.

SEXUALITY, RACE, POWER

Michel Foucault famously observed that sexuality is an "especially dense transfer point for relations of power ... endowed with the greatest instrumentality: useful for the greatest number of maneuvers and capable of serving as a point of support, as a linchpin, for the most varied strategies."[43] Although Foucault ignored race, it is plainly evident that sexuality has been an incredibly dense transfer point of racial power, particularly white supremacy. The iconic American film *The Birth of a Nation* makes the point cinematically. That white men sexually victimized and exploited colonized women with impunity is a widely accepted fact. But this phenomenon was more than a quotidian reality of colonialism and other regimes of racial oppression—slavery, Jim Crow, and apartheid among them—it was also a constitutive part of the political movements that brought these regimes to an end.[44] The case of the Gold Coast suggests that even when interracial rape and other forms of overt sexual terror were not involved, sexual exploitation had political consequences.

Racialized sexual exploitation was one part of the story, but so too were intimate relationships that withstood the challenges of their times. These loving relationships—while not free of racial baggage—presented their own revolutionary ways of moving forward. Like *Loving v. Virginia* and the fight for marriage equality today, they challenged and transformed received wisdom about who has the right to form a family and how family formations impact state and society.

I want to end with a seemingly uncharacteristic disclosure by Frantz Fanon in *Black Skin, White Masks*: "Today I believe in the possibility of love; that is why I endeavor to trace its imperfections, its perversions."[45] A statement affirming the possibility of love across the color line contained in the landmark study of the dehumanizing psychological impact of colonial racism ought to make even the most skeptical reader pause and take note. But Fanon was neither delinking love from racism nor posing them as mutually exclusive phenomena. Rather, he sought to show how love and power, sentiment and demand, desire and domination, and intimacy and oppression coexist—rendering love imperfect and perverse, while at the same time humanizing both racism and colonialism. Fanon's brilliance is evident in the ways that he employed Manichaean dichotomies—black skin/white masks, woman of color/white man, man of color/white woman—to demonstrate the relational and contingent nature of racial domination and resistance to it, and to show how such practices are articulated in spaces of real and imagined intimacy. *Crossing the Color Line* has endeavored to do the same, finding abuse and coercion, advantage and gain, and affection and love, running through and across the color line in colonial Ghana, Britain, and beyond.

Notes

Abbreviations used throughout notes:

ADM	Administration Files
BT	Board of Trade
CO	Colonial Office
CSO	Colonial Secretariat Office
HO	Home Office
PF	Personal Files
PRAAD	Public Records and Archives Administration Department (Ghana)
SEK	Sekondi
TNA	The National Archives (United Kingdom)
WRG	Western Region

INTRODUCTION: THE STAKES OF STUDYING SEX ACROSS THE COLOR LINE IN COLONIAL GHANA

1. A. L. Adu to B. W. A. T. Knight, Ministry of Justice, 30 December 1960, Public Records and Archives Administration Department (hereafter, PRAAD. All PRAAD files are from the Accra branch unless otherwise noted), PF 1/38/242.

2. Felicia Agnes Knight, interview, Accra, Ghana, 18 June 2007.

3. Illegible signature, Secretary of the Cabinet to Hon. Tawia Adamafio, Minister for Presidential Affairs, 2 February 1961, PRAAD, PF 1/38/242.

4. Governor Alan Burns to Gerald Creasy, Colonial Office, 9 June 1945, "Concubinage with Native Women," The National Archives of the United Kingdom (hereafter TNA), CO 850/218, no. 20901.

5. The Colonial Office was housed in central London's Whitehall, along with several other government departments, including the Home Office. In order to avoid constant repetition, I use Whitehall as a metonym for only the Colonial Office. Illegible signature, file minute, 17 July 1945, "Concubinage with Native Women," TNA, CO 850/218, no. 20901.

6. Ibid.

7. P. A. Tegetmeier, file minute, 16 July 1945, "Concubinage with Native Women," TNA, CO 850/218, no. 20901.

8. File minute, 17 July 1945, "Concubinage with Native Women," TNA, CO 850/218, no. 20901.

9. "European officer" was the term that the Gold Coast government used to refer to all non-Native officers. While most of the men who fell into this category were white and British, it also included white officers from other European countries, as well as officers of various racial backgrounds from other parts of the British Empire, especially the West Indies. While "British" and "European" are not used interchangeably, it should be understood that when an officer is described as "British," it is because he was a "European officer" of British origin.

10. "Immoral Sanitation," *Gold Coast Leader*, 7–14 February 1920.

11. On the centuries-long history of formal interracial unions between African women and European men and the families they produced in the Gold Coast, see Natalie Everts, "'Brought up Well According to European Standards': Helena Van Der Burgh and Wilhelmina Van Naarssen: Two Christian Women from Elmina," in *Merchants, Missionaries and Migrants: 300 Years of Dutch-Ghanaian Relations*, ed. Ineke van Kessel (Amsterdam: KIT Press, 2002), 101–9; Harvey M. Feinberg, *Africans and Europeans in West Africa: Elminans and Dutchmen on the Gold Coast during the Eighteenth Century* (Philadelphia: American Philosophical Society, 1989), 85–92; Pernille Ipsen, *Daughters of the Trade: Atlantic Slavers and Interracial Marriage on the Gold Coast* (Philadelphia: University of Pennsylvania Press, 2015); Margaret A. Priestley, "The Emergence of an Elite: A Case Study of a West Coast Family," in *The New Elites of Tropical Africa*, ed. Peter C. Lloyd (London: Oxford University Press, 1966), 87–99; Priestley, *West African Trade and Coast Society: A Family Study* (London: Oxford University Press, 1969); Ty M. Reese, "Wives, Brokers, and Laborers: Women at Cape Coast, 1750–1807," in *Women in Port: Gendering Communities, Economies, and Social Networks in Atlantic Port Cities, 1500–1800*, ed. Douglas Catterall and Jodi Campbell (Leiden: Brill, 2012), 300–307; Ulrike Sill, *Encounters in Quest of Christian Womanhood: The Basel Mission in Pre- and Early Colonial Ghana* (Leiden: Brill, 2010); Randy J. Sparks, *Where the Negroes Are Masters: An African Port in the Era of the Slave Trade* (Cambridge, MA: Harvard University Press, 2014), 80–86. For a popular account of the interracial sexual economy of Cape Coast Castle, which primarily focuses on marriage practices, but also gestures toward less formal and more exploitative sexual relations, see William St. Clair, *The Door of No Return: The History of Cape Coast Castle and the Atlantic Slave Trade* (New York: BlueBridge, 2007), chap. 6.

12. See Pernille Ipsen, "'The Christened Mulatresses': Euro-African Families in a Slave-Trading Town," *William and Mary Quarterly* 70, no. 2 (2013): 371–98; Adam

Jones, "Female Slave-Owners on the Gold Coast: Just a Matter of Money?" in *Slave Cultures and the Cultures of Slavery*, ed. Stephan Palmié (Knoxville: University of Tennessee Press, 1995), 100–111; Larry W. Yarak, "West African Coastal Slavery in the Nineteenth Century: The Case of the Afro-European Slaveowners of Elmina," *Ethnohistory* 36, no. 1 (1989): 44–60.

13. Atu, "Scrutineer," *Gold Coast Leader*, 4–11 December 1915.

14. Ato Quayson, *Oxford Street, Accra: City Life and the Itineraries of Transnationalism* (Durham, NC: Duke University Press, 2014), 117.

15. Ann L. Stoler, *Carnal Knowledge and Imperial Power: Race and the Intimate in Colonial Rule* (Berkeley: University of California Press, 2002), 49–54.

16. Passing references to interracial concubinage and prostitution in the precolonial Gold Coast can be found in Feinberg, *Africans and Europeans in West Africa*, 89; Jennifer L. Morgan, *Laboring Women: Reproduction and Gender in New World Slavery* (Philadelphia: University of Pennsylvania Press, 2004), 45–46; John Vogt, *Portuguese Rule on the Gold Coast, 1469–1682* (Athens: University of Georgia Press, 1979), 234n63. For a lengthy examination of precolonial and colonial prostitution among the Akan that includes a discussion of interracial prostitution, see Emmanuel Akyeampong, "Sexuality and Prostitution among the Akan of the Gold Coast c. 1650–1950," *Past and Present*, no. 156 (1997): 144–73.

17. On rape and sexual coercion during the Middle Passage, see Bukola Adeyemi Oyeniyi, "Rape and Sexual Abuse," in *Encyclopedia of the Middle Passage*, ed. Toyin Falola and Amanda Warnock (Westport, CT: Greenwood Press, 2007), 315–18; Marcus Rediker, *The Slave Ship: A Human History* (New York: Viking, 2007). On the inclusion of rape in the narratives of tour guides at Elmina and Cape Coast, see Bayo Holsey, "Transatlantic Dreaming: Slavery, Tourism, and Diasporic Encounters," in *Homecomings: Unsettling Paths of Return*, ed. Fran Markowitz and Anders H. Stefansson (Lanham, MD: Lexington Books, 2004), 171; Holsey, *Routes of Remembrance: Refashioning the Slave Trade in Ghana* (Chicago: University of Chicago Press, 2008), 188, 192–93; Sandra L Richards, "What Is to Be Remembered? Tourism to Ghana's Slave Castle-Dungeons," *Theatre Journal* 57, no. 4 (2005): 625–27.

18. See Rebecca Shumway, "Castle Slaves of the Eighteenth-Century Gold Coast (Ghana)," *Slavery and Abolition* 35, no. 1 (2013): 92–93; and Simon P. Newman, *A New World of Labor: The Development of Plantation Slavery in the British Atlantic* (Philadelphia: University of Pennsylvania Press, 2013), 147–48.

19. Wendy Wilson-Fall, "Women Merchants and Slave Depots: Saint-Louis, Senegal and St. Mary's, Madagascar," in *Paths of the Atlantic Slave Trade: Interactions, Identities, and Images*, ed. Ana Lucia Araujo (Amherst, NY: Cambria, 2011), 274–75.

20. For an excellent analysis of the consent/coercion binary, its limits, and the ways in which a range of scholars and writers have engaged it in their readings of the relationship between Sally Hemings and Thomas Jefferson, in particular, and the kinds of ideological work rape and romance narratives of interracial sex have been made to do in constructing different visions of American history, see Salamishah Tillet, *Sites of Slavery: Citizenship and Racial Democracy in the Post–Civil Rights Imagination* (Durham, NC: Duke University Press, 2012), 19–50. For a similar set of observations about colonial India, see Durba Ghosh, *Sex and the Family in Colonial India: The Making of Empire* (Cambridge: Cambridge University Press, 2006), 23–25.

21. Atu, "Scrutineer," *Gold Coast Leader*, 4–11 December 1915; W. Asmis, "Law and Policy: Relating to the Natives of the Gold Coast and Nigeria," *Journal of the African*

Society 12, no. 45 (1912): 48; J. M. Stuart Young, "Miscegenacious Unions," *Gold Coast Leader,* 29 April 1922.

22. "Immoral Sanitation," *Gold Coast Leader,* 3–10 January 1920.

23. Shirley Zabel, "The Legislative History of the Gold Coast and Lagos Marriage Ordinance: III," *Journal of African Law* 23, no. 1 (1979): 20.

24. J. Murray, "An Address by Dr. J. Murray: The Social Position of West African Women," *Gold Coast Leader,* 13 December 1902 (emphasis in original).

25. Stoler, *Carnal Knowledge and Imperial Power*; Ghosh, *Sex and the Family in Colonial India*; Emmanuelle Saada, *Empire's Children: Race, Filiation, and Citizenship in the French Colonies,* trans. Arthur Goldhammer (Chicago: University of Chicago Press, 2012); Owen White, *Children of the French Empire: Miscegenation and Colonial Society in French West Africa, 1895–1960* (New York: Oxford University Press, 1999); Julia A. Clancy-Smith and Frances Gouda, eds., *Domesticating the Empire: Race, Gender, and Family Life in French and Dutch Colonialism* (Charlottesville: University Press of Virginia, 1998); and Frederick Cooper and Ann L. Stoler, eds., *Tensions of Empire: Colonial Cultures in a Bourgeois World* (Berkeley: University of California Press, 1997).

26. W. E. B. Du Bois, *The Souls of Black Folk: Essays and Sketches* (Chicago: McClurg, 1907), 13.

27. Chouki El Hamel, *Black Morocco: A History of Slavery, Race, and Islam* (Cambridge: Cambridge University Press, 2013); Jonathon Glassman, *War of Words, War of Stones: Racial Thought and Violence in Colonial Zanzibar* (Bloomington: Indiana University Press, 2011); Bruce S. Hall, *A History of Race in Muslim Africa, 1600–1960* (Cambridge: Cambridge University Press, 2011); Eve Troutt Powell, *A Different Shade of Colonialism: Egypt, Great Britain, and the Mastery of the Sudan* (Berkeley: University of California Press, 2003); and Terence Walz and Kenneth Cuno, eds., *Race and Slavery in the Middle East: Histories of Trans-Saharan Africans in Nineteenth-Century Egypt, Sudan, and the Ottoman Mediterranean* (Cairo: American University in Cairo Press, 2011). For a historically minded anthropological study of the vexed politics of race and blackness in modern-day Ghana, see Jemima Pierre, *The Predicament of Blackness: Postcolonial Ghana and the Politics of Race* (Chicago: University of Chicago Press, 2012).

28. Karen Tranberg Hansen, *Distant Companions: Servants and Employers in Zambia, 1900–1985* (Ithaca, NY: Cornell University Press, 1989); Elizabeth Schmidt, "Race, Sex, and Domestic Labor: The Question of African Female Servants in Southern Rhodesia, 1900–1939," in *African Encounters with Domesticity,* ed. Karen Tranberg Hansen (New Brunswick, NJ: Rutgers University Press, 1992), 221–41; Lynette A. Jackson, "'Stray Women' and 'Girls on the Move': Gender, Space, and Disease in Colonial and Post-Colonial Zimbabwe," in *Sacred Spaces and Public Quarrels: African Cultural and Economic Landscapes,* ed. Ezekiel Kalipeni and Paul T. Zeleza (Trenton, NJ: Africa World Press, 1999), 147–67; Jackson, "'When in the White Man's Town': Zimbabwean Women Remember Chibeura," in *Women in African Colonial Histories,* ed. Jean Allman, Susan Geiger, and Nakanyike Musisi (Bloomington: Indiana University Press, 2002), 191–215.

29. Selected readings on southern Africa's "black peril" scares include Gareth Cornwell, "George Webb Hardy's *The Black Peril* and the Social Meaning of 'Black Peril' in Early Twentieth-Century South Africa," *Journal of Southern African Studies* 22, no. 3 (1996): 441–53; Norman Etherington, "Natal's Black Rape Scare of the

1870s," *Journal of Southern African Studies* 15, no. 1 (1988): 36–53; Dane K. Kennedy, *Islands of White: Settler Society and Culture in Kenya and Southern Rhodesia, 1890–1939* (Durham, NC: Duke University Press, 1987); Jock McCulloch, *Black Peril, White Virtue: Sexual Crime in Southern Rhodesia, 1902–1935* (Bloomington: Indiana University Press, 2000); John Pape, "Black and White: The 'Perils of Sex' in Colonial Zimbabwe," *Journal of Southern African Studies* 16, no. 4 (1990): 699–720; Oliver Phillips, "The 'Perils' of Sex and the Panics of Race: The Dangers of Interracial Sex in Colonial Southern Rhodesia," in *African Sexualities: A Reader*, ed. Sylvia Tamale (Oxford: Pambazuka Press), 101–15; Charles Van Onselen, *Studies in the Social and Economic History of the Witwatersrand, 1886–1914* (Johannesburg: Ravan Press, 1982).

30. Antoinette Burton, *At the Heart of the Empire: Indians and the Colonial Encounter in Late-Victorian Britain* (Berkeley: University of California Press, 1998), 1.

31. Barbara Bush, *Imperialism, Race, and Resistance: Africa and Britain, 1919–1945* (London: Routledge, 1999), 86.

32. Jean M. Allman, "Of 'Spinsters,' 'Concubines' and 'Wicked Women': Reflections on Gender and Social Change in Colonial Asante," *Gender and History* 3, no. 2 (1991): 176–89; Allman, "Rounding up Spinsters: Gender Chaos and Unmarried Women in Colonial Asante," *Journal of African History* 37, no. 2 (1996): 195–214; Penelope A. Roberts, "The State and Regulation of Marriage: Sefwi Wiawso (Ghana), 1900–1940," in *Women, State and Ideology: Studies from Africa and Asia*, ed. Haleh Afshar (Albany: State University of New York Press, 1987), 48–69.

33. Studies that foreground the collaboration between colonial authorities and African male traditional authorities to (re)assert control over African women include: Elizabeth Schmidt, "Patriarchy, Capitalism, and the Colonial State in Zimbabwe," *Signs* 16, no. 4 (1991): 732–56; Marjorie J. Mbilinyi, "Runaway Wives in Colonial Tanganyika: Forced Labour and Forced Marriage in Rungwe District, 1919–1961," *International Journal of the Sociology of Law* 16, no. 1 (1988): 1–29; Martin Chanock, "Making Customary Law: Men, Women, and Courts in Colonial Northern Rhodesia," in *African Women and the Law: Historical Perspectives*, ed. Margaret J. Hay and Marcia Wright (Boston, MA: Boston University African Studies Center, 1982), 53–67; Samwel Ong'wen Okuro, "Our Women Must Return Home: Institutionalized Patriarchy in Colonial Central Nyanza District, 1945–1963," *Journal of Asian and African Studies* 45, no. 5 (2010): 522–33. Also see contributions to Dorothy L. Hodgson and Sheryl McCurdy, eds., *"Wicked" Women and the Reconfiguration of Gender in Africa* (Portsmouth, NH: Heinemann, 2001).

34. Luise White, *The Comforts of Home: Prostitution in Colonial Nairobi* (Chicago: University of Chicago Press, 1990); Janet M. Bujra, "Production, Property, Prostitution: 'Sexual Politics' in Atu," *Cahiers d'Etudes Africaines* 17, no. 65 (1977): 13–39; Benedict B. B. Naanen, "'Itinerant Gold Mines': Prostitution in the Cross River Basin of Nigeria, 1930–1950," *African Studies Review* 34, no. 2 (1991): 57–79; Akyeampong, "Sexuality and Prostitution"; Emmanuel Akyeampong, "'Wo pe tam won pe ba' ('You like cloth but you don't want children'): Urbanization, Individualism and Gender Relations in Colonial Ghana, c. 1900–39," in *Africa's Urban Past*, ed. David Anderson and Richard Rathbone (Oxford: Currey, 1999), 222–34; and Allman, "Of 'Spinsters,' 'Concubines' and 'Wicked Women.'" For a historically mindful anthropological study of the fraught interracial sexual economy that some Malagasy women aspire to join, which makes compelling arguments about the longer historical arc in which such women's choices

and challenges are situated, see Jennifer Cole, *Sex and Salvation: Imagining the Future in Madagascar* (Chicago: University of Chicago Press, 2010).

35. Jennifer Cole and Lynn M. Thomas, eds., *Love in Africa* (Chicago: University of Chicago Press, 2009), 8.

36. Rachel Jean-Baptiste, *Conjugal Rights: Marriage, Sexuality, and Urban Life in Colonial Libreville, Gabon* (Athens: Ohio University Press, 2014), 13.

37. Ghosh, *Sex and the Family in Colonial India*, 9–10.

38. The term "Native officer" is used here to denote the official administrative category that African employees of the colonial administration were grouped in. The term's capitalization signals its categorical rather than descriptive function. When not referring to the African officers employed by the colonial government or quoting from original source material, I have opted to place the term "native" in quotes to signify my awareness of its problematic connotations and its deep embeddedness in the lexicon of colonial racism and policy making. Nonetheless, judicious use of the term serves as an important reminder of the categories that framed discussions of interracial sexual relationships in the colony. On African employees as lynchpins of colonial rule, see Benjamin N. Lawrance, Emily L. Osborn, and Richard L. Roberts, eds., *Intermediaries, Interpreters, and Clerks: African Employees in the Making of Colonial Africa* (Madison: University of Wisconsin Press, 2006), 340.

39. The obvious exception is South Africa's 1949 Prohibition of Mixed Marriages Act, passed the year after the National Party, the architect of apartheid, came to power.

40. Stoler, *Carnal Knowledge and Imperial Power*, 2, 212.

41. Robert Aldrich, *Colonialism and Homosexuality* (London: Routledge, 2003); Ronald Hyam, *Empire and Sexuality: The British Experience* (Manchester: Manchester University Press, 1990).

42. Notable works in this vein include Stephanie Newell, *The Forger's Tale: The Search for Odeziaku* (Athens: Ohio University Press, 2006); Neville W. Hoad, *African Intimacies: Race, Homosexuality, and Globalization* (Minneapolis: University of Minnesota Press, 2007); Marc Epprecht, "The 'Unsaying' of Indigenous Homosexualities in Zimbabwe: Mapping a Blindspot in an African Masculinity," *Journal of Southern African Studies* 24, no. 4 (1998): 631–51; Epprecht, *Hungochani: The History of a Dissident Sexuality in Southern Africa* (Montreal: McGill-Queen's University Press, 2004); Epprecht, *Heterosexual Africa? The History of an Idea from the Age of Exploration to the Age of AIDS* (Athens: Ohio University Press, 2008); Epprecht, *Unspoken Facts: A History of Homosexualities in Africa* (Harare: Gays and Lesbians of Zimbabwe, 2008); T. Dunbar Moodie, *Going for Gold: Men, Mines, and Migration* (Berkeley: University of California Press, 1994); Stephen O. Murray and Will Roscoe, *Boy-Wives and Female Husbands: Studies in African Homosexualities* (New York: St. Martin's, 1998); Brenna M. Munro, *South Africa and the Dream of Love to Come: Queer Sexuality and the Struggle for Freedom* (Minneapolis: University of Minnesota Press, 2012).

43. Stoler, *Carnal Knowledge and Imperial Power*, 51. Also see Ann L. Stoler, "Carnal Knowledge and Imperial Power: Gender, Race, and Morality in Colonial Asia," in *Gender at the Crossroads of Knowledge: Feminist Anthropology in the Postmodern Era*, ed. Micaela di Leonardo (Berkeley: University of California Press, 1991), 60–61.

44. Penny Edwards, "Womanizing Indochina: Fiction, Nation, and Cohabitation in Colonial Cambodia, 1890–1930," in Clancy-Smith and Gouda, *Domesticating the Empire*, 117–18.

45. Alice L. Conklin, "Redefining 'Frenchness': France and West Africa," in Clancy-Smith and Gouda, *Domesticating the Empire*, 70. The French colony of Guinea appears to have been exceptional in its efforts to officially ban concubinage. See Martin A. Klein, "Review of *Children of the French Empire: Miscegenation and Colonial Society in French West Africa, 1895–1960*, by Owen White," *Journal of Interdisciplinary History* 32, no. 1 (2001): 153–54.

46. White, *Children of the French Empire*, 53.

47. Saada, *Empire's Children*, 16; White, *Children of the French Empire*, 2. This shift echoed what occurred in France's first colonial empire in the Caribbean more than two and a half centuries earlier when, as Doris Garraway points out, "legislation ostensibly intended to curb relations between free men and slave women began to focus on the problem of bastardy." See Garraway, *The Libertine Colony: Creolization in the Early French Caribbean* (Durham, NC: Duke University Press, 2005), 201.

48. Among Britain's Asian colonies, Burma acted even earlier, in 1867, to clamp down on concubinage. For events in Burma, see Radhika Mohanram, *Imperial White: Race, Diaspora, and the British Empire* (Minneapolis: University of Minnesota Press, 2007), 78–79; Kwasi Kwarteng, *Ghosts of Empire: Britain's Legacies in the Modern World* (London: Bloomsbury, 2011), 189–90; and for discussion of the Burma circular in relationship to the Colonial Office's 1909 anticoncubinage circular, see Sadler to Crewe, 21 May 1908, TNA, CO 533/44, no. 21793.

49. For Governor Rodger's 1907 circular, see Rodger to Elgin, 10 August 1907, enclosed Secretariat Circular, 25 March 1907, TNA, CO 96/459, no. 31137. Also see PRAAD, ADM 12/3/14. Prior to 1911 the Gold Coast administration did not retain copies of the appended enclosures to outgoing dispatches from the Gold Coast governor to the secretary of state; rather, only a copy of the dispatch itself was retained. As a result, all pre-1911 dispatches and enclosures are housed in the United Kingdom's National Archives (TNA), whereas only the dispatches can be found in the ADM 12/3 series at PRAAD.

50. Stoler, *Carnal Knowledge and Imperial Power*, 79–80.

51. Diane Frost, *Work and Community among West African Migrant Workers Since the Nineteenth Century* (Liverpool: Liverpool University Press, 1999), 193–96; Jacqueline Nassy Brown, *Dropping Anchor, Setting Sail: Geographies of Race in Black Liverpool* (Princeton, NJ: Princeton University Press, 2009), chap. 8; Paul B. Rich, "Philanthropic Racism in Britain: The Liverpool University Settlement, the Anti-Slavery Society and the Issue of 'Half-Caste' Children, 1919–51," *Immigrants and Minorities* 3, no. 1 (1984): 69–88; Mark Christian, "The Fletcher Report 1930: A Historical Case Study of Contested Black Mixed Heritage Britishness," *Journal of Historical Sociology* 21, nos. 2–3 (2008): 213–41. For the original report, see Muriel E. Fletcher, *Report on an Investigation into the Colour Problem in Liverpool and Other Ports* (Liverpool: Association for the Welfare of Half-Caste Children, 1930).

52. Atu, "Scrutineer," *Gold Coast Leader*, 26 July 1919.

53. See Slater to Passfield, 21 August 1929, PRAAD, PF 2/16/17, enc. 9B; and Northcote to Cunliffe-Lister, 22 September 1934, PRAAD, ADM 12/3/61, enc. 1.

54. For métis mutual aid societies and other community formations in Francophone Africa, see Hilary Jones, *The Métis of Senegal: Urban Life and Politics in French West Africa* (Bloomington: Indiana University Press, 2013); White, *Children of the French Empire*, 151; and Rachel Jean-Baptiste, "'Miss Eurafrica': Men, Women's Sexuality, and *Métis* Identity in Late Colonial French Africa, 1945–1960," *Journal of the History*

of Sexuality 20, no. 3 (2011): 568. For British Central Africa, see Christopher J. Lee, *Unreasonable Histories: Nativism, Multiracial Lives, and the Genealogical Imagination in British Africa* (Durham, NC: Duke University Press, 2014); and Juliette Milner-Thornton, *The Long Shadow of the British Empire: The Ongoing Legacies of Race and Class in Zambia* (New York: Palgrave Macmillan, 2012). For India, see Noel P. Gist and Roy D. Wright, *Marginality and Identity: Anglo-Indians as a Racially-Mixed Minority in India* (Leiden: Brill, 1973), 95–112.

55. For government attempts to stop African Americans from settling in the Gold Coast, see Governor Slater to Bonar Law, Colonial Secretary, 21 June 1915, PRAAD, ADM 12/3/21; and "Settlement of American Negroes in W.A.," 1934, TNA, CO 554/95/8.

56. For Garvey, see Acting Governor Maxwell to the Duke of Devonshire, Colonial Secretary, 17 May 1923, PRAAD, ADM 12/3/39; for Du Bois, see Governor Guggisberg to L. S. Amery, Colonial Secretary, 24 March 1927, PRAAD, ADM 12/3/47; for Dusé Mohamed, see Walter Long, Colonial Secretary, to Governor Clifford, 24 January 1918, PRAAD, ADM 12/1/40.

57. Governor Guggisberg to Amery, Colonial Secretary, 31 March 1925, PRAAD, ADM 12/3/42; James Maxwell, Acting Governor, to Amery, 29 April 1927, PRAAD, ADM 12/3/45; and Governor John Maxwell to Amery, 25 April 1928, PRAAD, ADM 12/3/48.

58. Rodger to Elgin, 10 August 1907, enclosed Secretariat Circular, 25 March 1907, TNA, CO 96/459, no. 31137.

59. Crewe to the Officer Administering the Government of the Gold Coast, 11 January 1909, PRAAD, ADM 12/1/31.

60. T. C. Macnaghten, file minute, 16 December 1908, TNA, CO 533/52, no. 45005.

61. In positing the significance of non-sexual forms of cross-racial intimacy I am not suggesting that all such forms of intimacy produced the kinds of sentimental attachments that have often become fodder for colonial nostalgia. Rather, my intention is to draw attention to the range of other ways that Africans and Europeans came to have intimate knowledge of one another that were not sexual, but that often had a bearing on interracial sexual relations. My thinking about the fraught terrain of such intimacies draws on the work of Ann Stoler and Karen Strassler in their essay "Memory-Work in Java: A Cautionary Tale," in Stoler, *Carnal Knowledge and Imperial Power*, 162-203.

62. Asmis, "Law and Policy," 43.

63. File Minute, 31 December 1924, TNA, CO 583/127.

64. A selection of these studies not already cited include Ann L. Stoler, "Rethinking Colonial Categories: European Communities and the Boundaries of Rule," *Comparative Studies in Society and History* 31, no. 1 (1989): 134–61; Stoler, "Making Empire Respectable: The Politics of Race and Sexual Morality in Twentieth-Century Colonial Cultures," *American Ethnologist* 16, no. 4 (1989): 634–60; Lora Wildenthal, "Race, Gender, and Citizenship in the German Colonial Empire," in Cooper and Stoler, *Tensions of Empire*, 263–83; Kenneth Ballhatchet, *Race, Sex and Class under the Raj: Imperial Attitudes and Policies and Their Critics, 1793–1905* (New York: St. Martin's, 1980). A notable exception to the focus on European empires is the work that has been done on race and sex in the context of US imperialism in places like Puerto Rico and Southeast Asia. See Eileen J. Suárez Findlay, *Imposing Decency: The Politics of Sexuality and Race in Puerto Rico, 1870–1920* (Durham, NC: Duke University Press, 1999); Laura Briggs, *Reproducing Empire: Race, Sex, Science, and U.S. Imperialism in Puerto Rico* (Berkeley: University of California Press, 2002); Susan Zeiger, *Entangling*

Alliances: Foreign War Brides and American Soldiers in the Twentieth Century (New York: New York University Press, 2010); Mire Koikari, "Gender, Power, and U.S. Imperialism: The Occupation of Japan, 1945–1952," in *Bodies in Contact: Rethinking Colonial Encounters in World History*, ed. Tony Ballantyne and Antoinette Burton (Durham, NC: Duke University Press, 2005), 342–62. The literature on so-called "comfort women" is also helping to shed light on the sexual exploitation of colonized women in the context of Japanese imperialism in Asia and the Pacific. See Yoshiaki Yoshimi, *Comfort Women: Sexual Slavery in the Japanese Military during World War II*, trans. Suzanne O'Brien (New York: Columbia University Press, 2000); Yuki Tanaka, *Japan's Comfort Women: Sexual Slavery and Prostitution during World War II and the US Occupation* (London: Routledge, 2002); George L. Hicks, *The Comfort Women: Sex Slaves of the Japanese Imperial Forces* (Singapore: Heinemann Asia, 1995); Hyun Sook Kim, "History and Memory: The 'Comfort Women' Controversy," in Ballantyne and Burton, *Bodies in Contact*, 363–82.

65. For notable examples of scholarship that foregrounds African perspectives on these relationships during the colonial period, see Hilary Jones, "From *Mariage a La Mode* to Weddings at Town Hall: Marriage, Colonialism, and Mixed-Race Society in Nineteenth-Century Senegal," *International Journal of African Historical Studies* 38, no. 1 (2005): 27–48; Rachel Jean-Baptiste, "'A Black Girl Should Not Be with a White Man': Sex, Race, and African Women's Social and Legal Status in Colonial Gabon, c. 1900–1946," *Journal of Women's History* 22, no. 2 (2010): 56–82; Jean-Baptiste, *Conjugal Rights*; Jeremy Rich, "'Une Babylone Noire': Interracial Unions in Colonial Libreville, c. 1860–1914," *French Colonial History* 4, no. 1 (2003): 145–69; Rich, "Gabonese Men for French Decency: The Rise and Fall of the Gabonese Chapter of the Ligue Des Droits De l'Homme, 1916–1939," *French Colonial History* 13, no. 1 (2012): 23–53; Milner-Thornton, *Long Shadow of the British Empire*; Ruth Iyob, "Madamismo and Beyond: The Construction of Eritrean Women," *Nineteenth Century Contexts* 22, no. 2 (2000): 217–38; Guilia Barrera, "Colonial Affairs: Italian Men, Eritrean Women, and the Construction of Racial Hierarchies in Colonial Eritrea (1885–1941)" (PhD diss., Northwestern University, 2002); Sandra Ponzanesi, "The Color of Love: *Madamismo* and Interracial Relationships in the Italian Colonies," *Research in African Literatures* 43, no. 2 (2012): 155–72.

66. David Beriss, "If You're Gay and Irish, Your Parents Must Be English," *Identities: Global Studies in Culture and Power* 2, no. 3 (1996): 191.

67. Animus between colonial officers was hardly unique to the Gold Coast. Heike Schmidt has found that animosities between German officers in German East Africa often found expression in attacks on one another's honor, among which "accusations of same-sex desire constituted a particularly serious affront." Schmidt, "Colonial Intimacy: The Rechenberg Scandal and Homosexuality in German East Africa," *Journal of the History of Sexuality* 17, no. 1 (2008): 26.

68. Anjali R. Arondekar, *For the Record: On Sexuality and the Colonial Archive in India* (Durham, NC: Duke University Press, 2009), 3.

69. Rosemary Weatherston, "When Sleeping Dictionaries Awaken: The Re/Turn of the Native Woman Informant," *Post Identity* 1, no. 1 (1997): 118–19.

70. As Ann L. Stoler has recently argued, reading along the archival grain, when done carefully and critically, does more than regurgitate colonial knowledge, it offers an opportunity to reverse the ethnographic gaze back onto the colonial state. See Stoler, *Along the Archival Grain: Epistemic Anxieties and Colonial Common Sense* (Princeton, NJ: Princeton University Press, 2010).

71. Stoler, *Carnal Knowledge and Imperial Power*, 39.
72. Burton, *At the Heart of the Empire*, 1.

CHAPTER 1: FROM INDISPENSABLE TO "UNDESIRABLE"

1. Horatio Bridge, *Journal of an African Cruiser*, ed. Nathaniel Hawthorne (London: Wiley and Putnam, 1845), chap. 17.

2. On the term "country marriage," see George E. Brooks Jr., *Eurafricans in Western Africa: Commerce, Social Status, Gender, and Religious Observance from the Sixteenth to the Eighteenth Century* (Athens: Ohio University Press, 2003), 210; Brooks, "The Letter Book of Captain Edward Harrington," *Transactions of the Historical Society of Ghana* 6 (1962): 76–77; Margaret A. Priestley, *West African Trade and Coast Society: A Family Study* (London: Oxford University Press, 1969), 106.

3. Pieter de Marees, A. van Dantzig, and Adam Jones, *Description and Historical Account of the Gold Kingdom of Guinea (1602)* (Oxford: Oxford University Press, 1987), 217.

4. Brooks, *Eurafricans in Western Africa*, 28. For more on the integration of Europeans into this system, see Vernon Dorjahn and Christopher Fyfe, "Landlord and Stranger: Change in Tenancy Relations in Sierra Leone," *Journal of African History* 3, no. 3 (1962): 391–97; Anne Haour, *Outsiders and Strangers: An Archaeology of Liminality in West Africa* (Oxford: Oxford University Press, 2013), 61. Joanna Davidson rightly cautions against overgeneralizing the idea that all West African coastal societies were "hospitable to strangers and eager and willing to incorporate them," by showing how exclusionary practices were also part of landlord-stranger relations. Davidson, "Rotten Fish: Polarization, Pluralism, and Migrant-Host Relations in Guinea-Bissau," in *States of Violence: Politics, Youth, and Memory in Contemporary Africa*, ed. Edna G. Bay and Donald L. Donham (Charlottesville: University of Virginia Press, 2007), 60, 83–85. Also see Jacqueline Knörr and Wilson Trajano Filho, eds., *The Powerful Presence of the Past: Integration and Conflict along the Upper Guinea Coast* (Leiden: Brill, 2010).

5. Brooks, *Eurafricans in Western Africa*, 28.

6. In the context of transatlantic commerce, these relationships were of course hardly unique to the Gold Coast. For Lusophone West-Central Africa, see Mariana P. Candido, *An African Slaving Port and the Atlantic World: Benguela and Its Hinterland* (New York: Cambridge University Press, 2013); Candido, "Concubinage and Slavery in Benguela, c. 1750–1850," in *Slavery in Africa and the Caribbean: A History of Enslavement and Identity Since the Eighteenth Century*, ed. Olatunji Ojo and Nadine Hunt (London: Tauris, 2012), 65–84. For Lusophone and Francophone West Africa, see George E. Brooks Jr., "A *Nhara* of the Guinea-Bissau Region: Mau Aurelia Correia" (paper presented at the African Studies Association, Philadelphia, 1980); Brooks, "The *Signares* of Saint-Louis and Gorée: Women Entrepreneurs in Eighteenth-Century Senegal," in *Women in Africa: Studies in Social and Economic Change*, ed. Nancy Hafkin and Edna G. Bay (Stanford, CA: Stanford University Press, 1976); Michael Marcson, "European-African Interaction in the Pre-Colonial Period: Saint Louis, Senegal, 1758–1854" (PhD diss., Harvard University, 1975); Peter Mark, "*Portuguese*" *Style and Luso-African Identity: Precolonial Senegambia, Sixteenth–Nineteenth Centuries* (Bloomington: Indiana University Press, 2002); Walter Rodney, *A History of the Upper Guinea Coast, 1545–1800* (Oxford: Clarendon, 1970); James F. Searing,

West African Slavery and Atlantic Commerce: The Senegal River Valley, 1700–1860 (Cambridge: Cambridge University Press, 1993); and Wendy Wilson-Fall, "Women Merchants and Slave Depots: Saint-Louis, Senegal and St. Mary's, Madagascar," in *Paths of the Atlantic Slave Trade: Interactions, Identities, and Images*, ed. Ana Lucia Araujo (Amherst, NY: Cambria 2011), 273–303.

7. Thomas C. McCaskie, "Cultural Encounters: Britain and Africa in the Nineteenth Century," in *The Oxford History of the British Empire: The Nineteenth Century*, ed. Andrew Porter (Oxford: Oxford University Press, 2004), 688 (emphasis in original).

8. Elliott P. Skinner, "Strangers in West African Societies," *Africa* 33, no. 4 (1963): 309.

9. Brooks, *Eurafricans in Western Africa*, 28.

10. George E. Brooks Jr., *Landlords and Strangers: Ecology, Society, and Trade in Western Africa, 1000–1630* (Boulder, CO: Westview Press, 1993), 38.

11. Sandra E. Greene, "Crossing Boundaries/Changing Identities: Female Slaves, Male Strangers, and Their Descendants in Nineteenth- and Twentieth-Century-Anlo," in *Gendered Encounters: Challenging Cultural Boundaries and Social Hierarchies in Africa*, ed. Maria Grosz-Ngate and Omari H. Kokole (New York: Routledge, 1996), 26. Gold Coast intellectual and anticolonialist Kobina Sekyi similarly noted the tendency of Gold Coasters to betroth enslaved women to Europeans in "The English Colonial's Heaviest Handicap," *Gold Coast Leader*, 5–12 June 1920. For this practice on the Upper Guinea Coast see Walter Rodney, *A History of the Upper Guinea Coast, 1545–1800* (Oxford: Clarendon, 1970), 220. Regarding the Ga refraining from this practice, see Pernille Ipsen, *Daughters of the Trade: Atlantic Slavers and Interracial Marriage on the Gold Coast* (Philadelphia: University of Pennsylvania Press, 2015), 185n21.

12. The quantitative significance of this point is further underscored by the fact that women comprised the majority of the enslaved population in the Gold Coast. See Trevor Getz, *Slavery and Reform in West Africa: Toward Emancipation in Nineteenth-Century Senegal and the Gold Coast* (Athens: Ohio University Press, 2004), 25-26.

13. Greene, "Crossing Boundaries/Changing Identities," 27.

14. Bruce L. Mouser, "Accomodation and Assimilation in the Landlord-Stranger Relationship," in *West African Culture Dynamics: Archaeological and Historical Perspectives*, ed. B. K. Swartz and Raymond E. Dumett (The Hague: Mouton, 1980), 495.

15. Ty M. Reese, "Controlling the Company: The Structures of Fante-British Relations on the Gold Coast, 1750–1821," *Journal of Imperial and Commonwealth History* 41, no. 1 (2013): 116.

16. For instance, a 1529 record of the Portuguese inhabitants of Elmina lists only four Portuguese women who worked in the infirmary and in the kitchen. John Vogt, *Portuguese Rule on the Gold Coast, 1469–1682* (Athens: University of Georgia Press, 1979), 46–47, 51. Feinberg suggests for the eighteenth century that only a few European women came to the Gold Coast; of those who did, most were the wives of European officials. Harvey M. Feinberg, *Africans and Europeans in West Africa: Elminans and Dutchmen on the Gold Coast during the Eighteenth Century* (Philadelphia: American Philosophical Society, 1989), 36. During the mid-nineteenth century, the number of European women rarely exceeded ten, according to Mary McCarthy, *Social Change and the Growth of British Power in the Gold Coast: The Fante States, 1807–1874* (Lanham, MD: University Press of America, 1983), 62n21.

17. Rebecca Shumway, "Castle Slaves of the Eighteenth-Century Gold Coast (Ghana)," *Slavery and Abolition* 35, no. 1 (2013): 92–93.

18. John M. Sarbah, *Fanti Customary Laws: A Brief Introduction to the Principles of the Native Laws and Customs of the Fanti and Akan Sections of the Gold Coast, with a Selection of Cases Thereon Decided in the Law Courts* (London: Clowes and Sons, 1897), 42–43.

19. Gayle Rubin, "The Traffic in Women: Notes on the 'Political Economy' of Sex," in *Toward an Anthropology of Women*, ed. Rayna R. Reiter (New York: Monthly Review Press, 1975), 174. For an excellent analysis of the analytical limits of Rubin's essay, see Pamela Scully, "Malintzin, Pocahontas, and Krotoa: Indigenous Women and Myth Models of the Atlantic World," *Journal of Colonialism and Colonial History* 6, no. 3 (2005): ¶¶16–19.

20. Feinberg, *Africans and Europeans in West Africa*, 88; Marees, Dantzig, and Jones, *Description and Historical Account*, 217.

21. C. R. Boxer, *Race Relations in the Portuguese Colonial Empire, 1415–1825* (Oxford: Clarendon, 1963), 11; Feinberg, *Africans and Europeans in West Africa*, 88.

22. Vogt, *Portuguese Rule*, 7–8.

23. Ibid., 57.

24. Elmina's vicar wrote to King João III complaining of the "shameful things" occurring in the fort, including the retaining of fifteen "Negresses" by the Portuguese soldiers for use as prostitutes. The fact that he had to write to the king to try to curb this practice suggests that local authorities did not share the vicar's objections. Ibid., 234n63. What the vicar witnessed may have been an adaptation of an existing indigenous model for meeting the sexual needs of unmarried men. According to Emmanuel Akyeampong, it was not uncommon in the precolonial southern Gold Coast for Akan elites to acquire female slaves, who were invariably ethnic outsiders, for the specific purpose of providing sexual services to local bachelors as a way of alleviating sexual pressures among this group. Akyeampong uses the term "public women" to describe this group of sex workers, but he acknowledges that most contemporary European observers who documented their existence referred to them as prostitutes. See Akyeampong, "Sexuality and Prostitution among the Akan of the Gold Coast c. 1650–1950," *Past and Present*, no. 156 (1997): 146–49.

25. Vogt, *Portuguese Rule*, 121.

26. Feinberg, *Africans and Europeans in West Africa*, 89.

27. Ibid., 88.

28. Ibid., 89.

29. J. T. Lever, "Mulatto Influence on the Gold Coast in the Early Nineteenth Century: Jan Nieser of Elmina," *African Historical Studies* 3, no. 2 (1970): 253n3.

30. Feinberg, *Africans and Europeans in West Africa*, 91.

31. For a brief period during the seventeenth century, the Danes also occupied Fort Fredericksborg in Cape Coast, but unable to keep their footing in the region's trade, they sold the fort to the British in 1685 and turned their full attention eastward. Thorkild Hansen, *Coast of Slaves* (Accra: Sub-Saharan Publishers, 2002), 12.

32. As Sandra Greene points out, the establishment of the fort in Keta by the Danes was the result of fierce competition and in certain cases military engagement between the Dutch, French, British, and Danes to retain their presence, and exert the right to trade exclusively, in the area. Greene, *Gender, Ethnicity, and Social Change on the Upper Slave Coast: A History of the Anlo-Ewe* (Portsmouth, NH: Heinemann, 1996), 37.

33. Pernille Ipsen, "Intercultural Intimacy in Danish Guinea, 1680–1740," *Historie Netmagasinet* 16 (2005): 2.

34. Ibid., 5–6; John Parker, *Making the Town: Ga State and Society in Early Colonial Accra* (Portsmouth, NH: Heinemann, 2000), 33; Paul Erdmann Isert and Selena Axelrod Winsnes, *Letters on West Africa and the Slave Trade: Paul Erdmann Isert's Journey to Guinea and the Caribbean Islands in Columbia (1788)* (Oxford: Oxford University Press, 1992), 156; Peter A. Schweizer, *Survivors on the Gold Coast: The Basel Missionaries in Colonial Ghana* (Accra: Smartline, 2000), 19; John Parker, "*Mankraloi*, Merchants and Mulattos—Carl Reindorf and the Politics of 'Race' in Early Colonial Accra," in *The Recovery of the West African Past: African Pastors and African History in the Nineteenth Century*, ed. Paul Jenkins (Basel: Basler Afrika Bibliographien, 1998), 34; Georg Norregard, *Danish Settlements in West Africa, 1658–1850* (Boston, MA: Boston University Press, 1966), 166; Ludvig Ferdinand Romer, *A Reliable Account of the Coast of Guinea (1760)*, trans. and ed. Selena Axelrod Winsnes (Oxford: Oxford University Press, 2000), 185, 234.

35. The amount of allowance paid to the female partner of a Danish officer was determined by her race—a "mulatto" woman was paid two thalers a month, while a "black" woman was paid one thaler a month. These women had recourse to the Danish administration if their husbands failed to pay them their monthly salary. Isert and Winsnes, *Letters on West Africa and the Slave Trade*, 156.

36. Parker, "*Mankraloi*, Merchants and Mulattos," 33.

37. Isert and Winsnes, *Letters on West Africa and the Slave Trade*, 156.

38. Norregard, *Danish Settlements*, 167.

39. Schweizer, *Survivors on the Gold Coast*, 19.

40. Norregard, *Danish Settlements*, 167.

41. Ipsen, "'The Christened Mulatresses': Euro-African Families in a Slave-Trading Town," *William and Mary Quarterly* 70, no. 2 (2013): 396.

42. Isert and Winsnes, *Letters on West Africa and the Slave Trade*, 156–57.

43. Ipsen, "'Christened Mulatresses,'" 373.

44. Ibid., 377, 381, 395.

45. McCarthy, *Social Change and the Growth of British Power in the Gold Coast*, 40–41; Margaret A. Priestley, *West African Trade and Coast Society: A Family Study* (London: Oxford University Press, 1969), 106.

46. Priestley, *West African Trade and Coast Society*, 106.

47. McCarthy, *Social Change and the Growth of British Power in the Gold Coast*, 44.

48. Ibid., 42.

49. Ibid., 41.

50. Ibid., 43, 47. Also see R. Porter, "The Cape Coast Conflict of 1803: A Crisis in Relations Between the African and European Communites," *Transactions of the Historical Society of Ghana* 11 (1970): 30.

51. McCarthy, *Social Change and the Growth of British Power in the Gold Coast*, 43–44, 47.

52. Ibid., 44–45.

53. While the rumor that Maclean's wife, Letty, a famous London poet, was driven to suicide or killed by her husband's African mistress, spurred great interest in trying to determine if he did indeed have an African lover, a definitive answer has never been reached, suggesting that if such a liaison existed, it was a well-guarded secret. George E. Metcalfe, *Maclean of the Gold Coast: The Life and Times of George Maclean, 1801–1847* (London: Oxford University Press, 1962), 237.

54. Historical treatments of unions forged between African women and European men during the precolonial period populate two larger overlapping historiographies on the development of the region's coastal societies. The first focuses on areas that were epicenters of commercial activity, and includes but is not limited to the following selection of sources: Larry W. Yarak, "A West African Cosmopolis: Elmina (Ghana) in the Nineteenth Century" (paper presented at the Seascapes, Littoral Cultures, and Trans-Oceanic Exchanges, Library of Congress, Washington, DC, 2003); Edward Reynolds, *Trade and Economic Change on the Gold Coast, 1807–1874* (London: Longman, 1974); John Parker, "*Mankraloi*, Merchants and Mulattos"; Ray A. Kea, *A Cultural and Social History of Ghana from the Seventeenth to the Nineteenth Century: The Gold Coast in the Age of the Trans-Atlantic Slave Trade* (Lewiston, NY: Mellen, 2012); Kea, *Settlements, Trade, and Polities in the Seventeenth-Century Gold Coast* (Baltimore, MD: Johns Hopkins University Press, 1982); Susan B. Kaplow, "The Mudfish and the Crocodile: Underdevelopment of a West African Bourgeoisie," *Science and Society* 41, no. 3 (1977): 317–33; Roger Gocking, *Facing Two Ways: Ghana's Coastal Communities under Colonial Rule* (Lanham, MD: University Press of America, 1999); Raymond E. Dumett, "African Merchants of the Gold Coast, 1860–1905"; Rebecca Shumway, *The Fante and the Transatlantic Slave Trade* (Rochester, NY: University of Rochester Press, 2011).

The second body of literature more squarely focuses on the establishment and growth of the European presence in these coastal areas prior to the imposition of formal colonial rule. See, for example, Christopher R. DeCorse, *An Archaeology of Elmina: Africans and Europeans on the Gold Coast, 1400–1900* (Washington, DC: Smithsonian Institution Press, 2001); Feinberg, *Africans and Europeans in West Africa*; Thorkild Hansen, *Coast of Slaves* (Accra: Sub-Saharan Publishers, 2002); Mary McCarthy, *Social Change and the Growth of British Power in the Gold Coast: The Fante States, 1807–1874* (Lanham, MD: University Press of America, 1983); Georg Norregard, *Danish Settlements in West Africa, 1658–1850* (Boston, MA: Boston University Press, 1966); Peter A. Schweizer, *Survivors on the Gold Coast: The Basel Missionaries in Colonial Ghana* (Accra: Smartline, 2000); Avelino Teixeira da Mota and Paul E. H. Hair, *East of Mina: Afro-European Relations on the Gold Coast in the 1550s and the 1560s* (Madison: University of Wisconsin Press, 1988); Albert Van Dantzig, *Forts and Castles of Ghana* (Accra: Sedco, 1980); Vogt, *Portuguese Rule*; Kwame Y. Daaku, "The European Traders and the Coastal States, 1630–1720," *Transactions of the Historical Society of Ghana* 8 (1965): 11–23; and Daaku, *Trade and Politics on the Gold Coast, 1600–1720: A Study of the African Reaction to European Trade* (London: Clarendon, 1970).

55. Passing reference to the increasing unacceptability of interracial sexual relationships between African women and European men in the Gold Coast and elsewhere in British West Africa can be found in Lewis H. Gann and Peter Duignan, *The Rulers of British Africa, 1870–1914* (Stanford, CA: Stanford University Press, 1978), 240–42, 386–87n55; Henrika Kuklick, *The Imperial Bureaucrat: The Colonial Administrative Service in the Gold Coast, 1920–1939* (Stanford, CA: Hoover Institution Press, 1979), 122–25; Parker, "*Mankraloi*, Merchants and Mulattos," 37; Bush, *Imperialism, Race, and Resistance*, 88–89; Helen Callaway, *Gender, Culture, and Empire: European Women in Colonial Nigeria* (Urbana: University of Illinois Press, 1987), 48–50.

56. Nikos Papastergiadis, "Tracing Hybridity in Theory," in *Debating Cultural Hybridity: Multi-Cultural Identities and the Politics of Anti-Racism*, ed. Pnina Werbner

and Tariq Modood (London: Zed Books, 2000), 257; Robert J. C. Young, *Colonial Desire: Hybridity in Theory, Culture, and Race* (London: Routledge, 1995), 18.

57. On the discovery of quinine and the imperial moves it enabled, see Fiammetta Rocco, *The Miraculous Fever Tree: Malaria and the Quest for a Cure That Changed the World* (New York: HarperCollins, 2003). On the myth and reality of the "white man's grave," see P. D. Curtin, "'The White Man's Grave': Image and Reality, 1780–1850," *Journal of British Studies* 1, no. 1 (1961): 94–110.

58. Appendix AA, "Extract from the Annual Medical Sanitary Report of the Gold Coast Colony for the Year Ended 1891," Gold Coast Census, 1891, PRAAD, ADM 5/2/1.

59. Appendix P, Form B, "Census of the Colony of the Gold Coast and the Protected Territories, 1891, Sixteen Principal Towns," Gold Coast Census, 1891, PRAAD, ADM 5/2/1. The sixteen principal towns were: Accra, Ada, Adjuah, Akuse, Anamaboe, Appam, Axim, Cape Coast, Chama, Dixcove, Elmina, Kwitta (Keta), Pram Pram, Saltpond, Sekondi, and Winneba.

60. Gold Coast Census, 1901, PRAAD, ADM 5/2/2. See subsection titled "Races."

61. Appendix T, "Census of the colony of the Gold Coast, 1901—Principal Town," Gold Coast Census, 1901, PRAAD, ADM 5/2/2.

62. Appendix L, "White Races in the Various Districts According to Sex and Nationality—Colony," Gold Coast Census, 1911, PRAAD, ADM 5/2/3.

63. Ibid.

64. Appendix I, "Occupations of White Races—Colony," Gold Coast Census, 1911, PRAAD, ADM 5/2/3.

65. Ibid.

66. Appendix L, "Ashanti," Gold Coast Census, 1911, PRAAD, ADM 5/2/3. The statistics for Asante were not broken down by gender.

67. Appendix I, "Occupations of White Races—Colony," Gold Coast Census, 1911, PRAAD, ADM 5/2/3. The 1911 census reports just three British women being employed in government service.

68. Ulrike Sill, *Encounters in Quest of Christian Womanhood: The Basel Mission in Pre- and Early Colonial Ghana* (Leiden: Brill, 2010), 132, 135.

69. Hans Buser, *In Ghana at Independence: Stories of a Swiss Salesman* (Basel: Basler Afrika Bibliographien, 2010), 33.

70. Hans R. Roth, *Because of Kwadua: Autobiography of Hans Rudolf Roth* (Accra: Afram, 2008), 29.

71. "Alleged Depravity amongst Mine Labourers," 31 July 1902, ADM 96/408, no. 28327; Atu, *Gold Coast Leader*, "Scrutineer," 26 July 1902; "Hooliganism in the Bush," 7–14 February 1903; "Editorial Notes," 4 July 1903; "Sekundi," 23 April 1904. For the high rate of venereal disease obtaining among European miners, see Raymond E. Dumett, "Disease and Mortality among Gold Miners of Ghana: Colonial Government and Mining Company Attitudes and Policies, 1900–1938," *Social Science and Medicine* 37, no. 2 (1993): 231.

72. Michel Doortmont, ed., *The Pen-Pictures of Modern Africans and African Celebrities by Charles Francis Hutchison: A Collective Biography of Elite Society in the Gold Coast Colony* (Leiden: Brill, 2005), 137.

73. *Gold Coast Leader*, "Editorial Notes," 2 February 1918.

74. Parker, "*Mankraloi*, Merchants and Mulattos," 37n29.

75. Ibid., 37.

76. Lesley A. Hall, *Sex, Gender and Social Change in Britain Since 1880* (New York: St. Martin's, 2000), 10.

77. Barnes, originally from Cape Coast, studied at the Crystal Palace School of Engineering in London. He returned to the Gold Coast and took up a career as an architect and civil engineer. His greatest architectural achievement was the Anglican Trinity Church on High Street, Accra, which can still be seen today. He was also a fellow of the National College of Music of Great Britain, associate member of the Institute of Civil Engineers, and captain of the Gold Coast Rifle Volunteer Force. Doortmont, *Pen-Pictures*, 120.

78. Governor Maxwell to Secretary of State Chamberlain, 26 February 1897, PRAAD, ADM 12/3/6.

79. Regardless of whether they hailed from the Kru ethnic group, "Krooboys" was the generic term given to men and boys who came from the coastal areas of Sierra Leone and Liberia to work as domestics in the Gold Coast. For the Leonard case, see Governor Rodger to Secretary of State Lyttelton, 5 October 1904, TNA, CO 96/420, no. 37043, enc. 5. On the imperative of containment in the context of cases in which (German) colonial officers were being charged with homosexual acts, see Heike I. Schmidt, "Colonial Intimacy: The Rechenberg Scandal and Homosexuality in German East Africa," *Journal of the History of Sexuality* 17, no. 1 (2008): 25–59.

80. Governor Rodger to Secretary of State Lyttelton, 5 October 1904, TNA, CO 96/420, no. 37043, sub-enc. 2 of enc. 5.

81. Governor Rodger to Lord Crewe, 23 July 1910, PRAAD, ADM 12/3/16.

82. See Governor Nathan to Secretary of State Chamberlain, 16 June 1903, "Termination of Appointment: W. G. McGill, Foreman of Works," TNA, CO 96/408, no. 25037; Governor Rodger to Secretary of State Lyttelton, 17 March 1904, "Dismissal of Railway Foreman, T. Richardson for insobriety and misconduct," TNA, CO 96/417, no. 11876.

83. Ann L. Stoler, "Making Empire Respectable: The Politics of Race and Sexual Morality in Twentieth-Century Colonial Cultures," *American Ethnologist* 16, no. 4 (1989): 635.

84. Stoler, *Carnal Knowledge and Imperial Power*, 79–80.

85. Governor Rodger to Secretary of State Crewe, 19 October 1909, PRAAD, ADM 12/3/16.

86. Gold Coast Government, *The Laws of the Gold Coast Colony: Containing the Ordinances of the Gold Coast Colony and the Orders, Proclamations, Rules, Regulations and Bye-laws Made Thereunder in Force on the 31st Day of December, 1919, and the Principal Imperial Statutes, Orders in Council, Letters Patent and Royal Instructions Relating to the Gold Coast Colony* (London: Stevens and Sons, 1920), 788. For the application of the ordinance to multiracial people, see W. Asmis, "Law and Policy: Relating to the Natives of the Gold Coast and Nigeria," *Journal of the Royal African Society* 12, no. 45 (1912): 43.

87. *Report of the Census of the Gold Coast Colony for the Year 1891*, Appendix P, PRAAD, ADM 5/2/1.

88. *Report on the Census for the Year 1901*, Section 21, "Races," PRAAD, ADM 5/2/2.

89. The need for a shift in terminology from "White Races" to "Non-African Races" was articulated in the 1921 census and implemented in the 1931 census. *Census Report, 1921, for the Gold Coast Colony, Ashanti, the Northern Territories, and the Mandated*

Area of Togoland, 47, PRAAD, ADM 5/2/5; The Gold Coast Census, 1931, PRAAD, ADM 5/2/8.

90. Christopher J. Lee, *Unreasonable Histories: Nativism, Multiracial Lives, and the Genealogical Imagination in British Africa* (Durham, NC: Duke University Press, 2014); Lee, "'A Generous Dream, but Difficult to Realize': The Anglo-African Community of Nyasaland, 1929–1940," *Society of Malawi Journal* 61, no. 2 (2008): 19–41; Lee, "*Jus Soli* and *Jus Sanguinis* in the Colonies: The Interwar Politics of Race, Culture, and Multiracial Legal Status in British Africa," *Law and History Review* 29, no. 2 (2011): 497–522; Lee, "The 'Native' Undefined: Colonial Categories, Anglo-African Status and the Politics of Kinship in British Central Africa, 1929–38," *Journal of African History* 46, no. 3 (2005): 457. Also see Ibbo Mandaza, *Race, Colour and Class in Southern Africa: A Study of the Coloured Question in the Context of an Analysis of the Colonial White Settler Racial Ideology, and African Nationalism in Twentieth Century Zimbabwe, Zambia and Malawi* (Harare: SAPES Books, 1997).

91. David Kimble, *A Political History of Ghana: The Rise of Gold Coast Nationalism, 1850–1928* (Oxford: Clarendon, 1963), 463.

92. Augustus L. Casely-Hayford, "A Genealogical History of Cape Coast Stool Families" (PhD diss., University of London, 1992).

93. Kimble, *Political History of Ghana*, 93–109.

94. See, for example, Ann L. Stoler, "Sexual Affronts and Racial Frontiers: European Identities and the Cultural Politics of Exclusion in Colonial Southeast Asia," in Cooper and Stoler, *Tensions of* Empire, 198–237; and Saada, *Empire's Children*, 67–241.

95. "British Nationality: Summary," https://www.gov.uk/government/uploads/system/uploads/attachment_data/file/267913/britnatsummary.pdf, 10 December 2013.

96. "British Nationality Bill," House of Commons Debate, 28 January 1958, *Hansard* 581, cols. 279–312, here 279–280.

97. For a concise overview of British nationality law before and after the 1948 British Nationality Act, see Randall Hansen, "The Politics of Citizenship in 1940s Britain: The British Nationality Act," *Twentieth Century British History* 10, no. 1 (1999): 67–95.

98. For discussion of the 1925 order in the broader context of British immigration and nationality law and state-sanctioned racism, see Ian R. G. Spencer, *British Immigration Policy Since 1939: The Making of Multi-Racial Britain* (London: Routledge, 1997), 10–12; and Laura Tabili, "The Construction of Racial Difference in Twentieth-Century Britain: The Special Restriction (Coloured Alien Seamen) Order, 1925," *Journal of British Studies* 33, no. 1 (1994): 54–98.

99. Christopher J. Lee provides an excellent analysis of the intersection between British nationality law, racial descent, and native versus nonnative status in Nyasaland and elsewhere in British central and eastern Africa in "*Jus Soli* and *Jus Sanguinis* in the Colonies." On the racial despotism of indirect rule see Mahmood Mamdani, *Citizen and Subject: Contemporary Africa and the Legacy of Late Colonialism* (Princeton, NJ: Princeton University Press, 1996).

100. For an excellent study of this process, see Kathleen Paul, *Whitewashing Britain: Race and Citizenship in the Postwar Era* (Ithaca, NY: Cornell University Press, 1997). Marilyn Lake and Henry Reynolds offer fascinating analyses of similar developments in a slightly earlier time period and in a more global context in *Drawing the Global Colour Line: White Men's Countries and the Challenge of Racial Equality* (Cambridge: Cambridge University Press, 2008).

101. Michel Doortmont, "Producing a Received View of Gold Coast Elite Society? C. F. Hutchison's *Pen Pictures of Modern Africans and African Celebrities*," *History in Africa* 33 (2006): 476.

102. These marriage patterns are evident in the family genealogies of the prominent coastal elites that Michel Doortmont has documented in his annotated edition of Charles Francis Hutchison's classic work. Doortmont, ed., *The Pen-Pictures of Modern Africans and African Celebrities by Charles Francis Hutchison: A Collective Biography of Elite Society in the Gold Coast Colony* (Leiden: Brill, 2005).

103. Natalie Everts, "Cherchez la Femme: Gender-Related Issues in Eighteenth-Century Elmina," *Itinerario* 20, no. 1 (1996): 45–57; and Magnus Huber, "Lingua Franca in West Africa? An Evaluation of the Sociohistorical and Metalinguistic Evidence," in *Gradual Creolization: Studies Celebrating Jacques Arends*, ed. Rachel Selbach, Hugo Cardoso, and Margot van den Berg (Amsterdam: Benjamins, 2009), 269.

104. J. T. Lever, "Mulatto Influence on the Gold Coast in the Early Nineteenth Century: Jan Nieser of Elmina," *African Historical Studies* 3, no. 2 (1970): 253.

105. John Parker, "*Mankraloi*, Merchants and Mulattos—Carl Reindorf and the Politics of 'Race' in Early Colonial Accra," in *The Recovery of the West African Past: African Pastors and African History in the Nineteenth Century*, ed. Paul Jenkins (Basel: Basler Afrika Bibliographien, 1998), 45–46.

106. Raymond E. Dumett, "African Merchants of the Gold Coast, 1860–1905: Dynamics of Indigenous Entrepreneurship," *Society for Comparative Studies in Society and History* 25, no. 4 (1983): 669.

107. For India, see Noel P. Gist and Roy D. Wright, *Marginality and Identity: Anglo-Indians as a Racially-Mixed Minority in India* (Leiden: Brill, 1973), 11–15; and Dane Kennedy, *The Magic Mountains: Hill Stations and the British Raj* (Berkeley: University of California Press, 1996), 138. For Africa, see Gustave Hulstaert, "Le Problème des Mulâtres," *Africa* 15, no. 3 (1945): 129–44; Hulstaert, "Le Problème des Mulâtres," *Africa* 16, no. 1 (1946): 39–44; and White, *Children of the French Empire*, 77–89. For the French empire more broadly, see Saada, *Empire's Children*, 49–59.

108. Kimble, *Political History of Ghana*, 88–89.

109. For the history and outcome of these commissions of inquiry, see Juliette Milner-Thornton, *The Long Shadow of the British Empire: The Ongoing Legacies of Race and Class in Zambia* (New York: Palgrave Macmillan, 2012), 131–62.

110. Stoler, *Carnal Knowledge and Imperial Power*, 65.

111. Ibid., 2 (emphasis in original).

112. Rodger to Elgin, 22 November 1906, TNA, CO 96/474, no. 46038.

113. Gold Coast Colony Census of the Population, 1911, PRAAD, ADM 5/2/3. This figure included both official and nonofficial British men, thereby bringing the actual percentage of British officers accompanied by their wives below the recorded figure of 7 percent. These percentages shifted only slightly when other European or "white" races were added to the figure: 45 percent of all white men in the colony were married, and of this number 11 percent were accompanied by their wives, suggesting that the British had lower rates of accompaniment than other Europeans or whites.

114. Ulrike Sill, *Encounters in Quest of Christian Womanhood: The Basel Mission in Pre- and Early Colonial Ghana* (Leiden: Brill, 2010), 186.

115. Joseph Renner Maxwell, *The Negro Question; or, Hints for the Physical Improvement of the Negro Race with Special Reference to West Africa* (London: Fisher Unwin, 1891), 98.

116. *Gold Coast Leader,* "Moral Sanitation," 20 December 1902.
117. Ibid. Also see *Gold Coast Leader,* "An Address by Dr. J. Murray: The Social Position of West African Women," 13 December 1902.
118. *Gold Coast Leader,* Nigeria, "One Thing and Another," 20 April 1907.

CHAPTER 2: "UNDESIRABLE RELATIONS"

1. Rodger to Elgin, 1 September 1907, TNA, CO 96/459, no. 33570, enc. 2.
2. Rodger to Elgin, 10 August 1907, TNA, CO 96/459, no. 31137, enc. 2.
3. Ibid.
4. Ibid., enc. 7.
5. Ibid.
6. This procedure was in keeping with the Colonial Office's general guidelines for handling disciplinary matters. See John W. Cell, *British Colonial Administration in the Mid-Nineteenth Century: The Policy-Making Process* (New Haven, CT: Yale University Press, 1970), 63.
7. This system of categorization was in effect throughout British West Africa as indicated by the pension forms that were distributed to these colonies, which identified officers either as a "European" or as a "Native of West Africa." Consequently, on both of Clarke's pension forms he is identified as a "European." On the portion of the form filled out by the applicant, the instructions stipulate that "in the case of an Officer serving on the West Coast of Africa, a statement is to be added whether he is a native of that Coast." In parentheses next to Clarke's name he wrote, "I am not a native of West Africa." Marcus Clarke, Confidential File, PRAAD, PF 1/15/24.
8. Rodger to Crewe, 19 October 1909, PRAAD, ADM 12/3/16.
9. Ibid.
10. Frederick Cooper and Ann L. Stoler, eds., *Tensions of Empire: Colonial Cultures in a Bourgeois World* (Berkeley: University of California Press, 1997), 10.
11. Nemata A. Blyden, *West Indians in West Africa, 1808–1880: The African Diaspora in Reverse* (Rochester, NY: University of Rochester Press, 2000), 46.
12. Ibid., 166n9.
13. Ibid., 42.
14. Ibid., 57.
15. Ibid., 42.
16. That West Indians continued to be hired in nonadministrative posts is indicated by the fact that at the turn of the century, the government of Sierra Leone approved the employment of West Indian drivers for the colony's railway. See Governor Nathan to Secretary of State Chamberlain, "Railway: Employment of Br. Guiana Natives," in TNA, CO 96/409, no. 34169.
17. Blyden, *West Indians in West Africa,* 110.
18. Ibid., 111.
19. On the practice of obtaining superintendents of police from British Guiana to work in the Gold Coast police, see Governor Rodger to Secretary of State Lyttelton, 2 January 1905, TNA, CO 96/427, no. 2053, enc. 1. On West Indian hires for railway, clerical, and executive posts, see Abioseh Nicol, "West Indians in West Africa," *Sierra Leone Studies* 13 (1960): 14–23. For an overview of the long West Indian presence in the Gold Coast/Ghana, see Clifford Campbell, "Full Circle: The Caribbean

Presence in the Making of Ghana, 1843-1966" (PhD diss., University of Ghana, Legon, 2012).

20. David Kimble, *A Political History of Ghana: The Rise of Gold Coast Nationalism, 1850–1928* (Oxford: Clarendon Press, 1963), 99–100.

21. A handful of Africans were, however, employed as district commissioners, doctors, and judges through the latter part of the nineteenth century. Ibid., 65–98.

22. There is a caveat to this: West Indians who came to the Gold Coast on their own and applied for positions in the administration's clerical service, which was largely staffed by Native officers, had to be willing to be hired as "natives" of the colony. The reasoning for this was laid out by Governor Maxwell in an 1897 dispatch to Secretary of State Chamberlain in which he stated, "It would be a distinct disadvantage to the Government to employ a West Indian (who comes under the special leave rules) when clerical offices can be filled by local candidates who do not require constant leave of absence in temperate climates." Maxwell to Chamberlain, 5 January 1897, PRAAD, ADM 12/3/6.

23. For instance, when the Gold Coast found itself in need of trained customs officers, it requested men from either the home customs office or the customs services of other colonies. Few applicants from the home customs service were willing to come to West Africa, which meant that the majority of posts were filled by customs officers from the West Indies, where the largest supply of trained customs officers existed. See Colonial Office minutes addressed to Mr. Antrobus and Mr. Harris, TNA, CO 96/419, no. 33739; Rodger to Lyttelton, "Native West Indians Appts. to G. Coast," PRAAD, ADM 12/1/26.

24. Rodger to Lyttelton, 2 January 1905, TNA, CO 96/427, enc. 1. For Governor Nathan's 1901 proposal, see PRAAD, ADM 12/3/8.

25. Governor Nathan to Secretary of State Chamberlain, 26 August 1903, TNA, CO 96/409, no. 34169. Also see Nathan to Chamberlain, 16 May 1903, TNA, CO 96/407, no. 21144; and Nathan to Secretary of State Lyttelton, 30 January 1904, TNA, CO 96/416, no. 6265.

26. Here I draw upon the centrality of both migration and cultural conflict to Robert Park's theorization of the marginal man to understand the way in which West Indians were being constructed as "marginal men," rather than to suggest that they were wholly "marginal" in the sense of Park's theorization, although elements of his model do seem to apply. See Park, "Human Migration and the Marginal Man," *American Journal of Sociology* 33, no. 6 (1928): 881–93.

27. Governor Rodger to Secretary of State Lyttelton, 12 September 1904, PRAAD, ADM 12/3/11 (also TNA, CO 96/419, no. 33739).

28. Ibid.

29. Colonial Office Minutes, 5 October 1904, TNA, CO 96/419, no. 33739.

30. Ibid.

31. Secretary of State Lyttelton to Governor Rodger, 26 October 1904, PRAAD, ADM 12/1/26.

32. Ibid. Rodger did not respond to this suggestion.

33. Ibid.

34. Marcus Clarke, Confidential File, PRAAD, PF 1/15/24.

35. All quoted terminology comes directly from the Comptroller of Customs report. Governor Rodger to Secretary of State Lyttelton, 5 December 1904, TNA, CO 96/421, no. 43129, Enclosed report by the Comptroller of Customs, November 30, 1904.

36. Ibid.

37. Kimble suggests that it was the chiefs and *Asafo* captains in Cape Coast that were "particularly anxious about the competition of 'foreigners of their own colour'" for government posts, as they preferred educated Africans to occupy these positions. For this and an overview of pay scale grievances, see Kimble, *Political History of Ghana*, 93, 98–109. For a contemporary reflection on colonial employment inequalities, see *Gold Coast Leader*, "An Address by J. Murray: Some of the African's Grievances and Their Remedies," 22 November 1902.

38. Governor Rodger to Secretary of State Lyttelton, 5 December 1904, TNA, CO 96/421, no. 43129, enclosed report by the Comptroller of Customs, 30 November 1904.

39. Executive Council Minutes, 25 May 1911, PRAAD, ADM 13/1/7.

40. Blyden, *West Indians in West Africa*, 122. Not surprisingly, such a response completely failed to take into consideration that prior to the advent of colonial rule, authority had always been exercised by Africans over other Africans, and this continued to be the case throughout the duration of colonial rule via the system of indirect rule, as well as in other domains of African social, religious, political, and economic life.

41. Secretary of State Lyttelton to Governor Rodger, 20 June 1905, PRAAD, ADM 12/1/27.

42. Ibid.

43. Rodger to Crewe, 19 October 1909, PRAAD, ADM 12/3/16.

44. Rodger to Elgin, 10 August 1907, TNA, CO 96/459, no. 31137, enc. 2.

45. Rodger to Elgin, 10 August 1907, TNA, CO 96/459, no. 31137. By this time Clarke had already left the Gold Coast on leave and was residing in London.

46. Heike I. Schmidt, "Colonial Intimacy: The Rechenberg Scandal and Homosexuality in German East Africa," *Journal of the History of Sexuality* 17, no. 1 (2008): 26.

47. Rodger to Elgin, 1 September 1907, TNA, CO 96/459, no. 33570, enc. 2 (emphasis added).

48. Ibid. (emphasis added).

49. John M. Sarbah, *Fanti Customary Laws: A Brief Introduction to the Principles of the Native Laws and Customs of the Fanti and Akan Sections of the Gold Coast, with a Selection of Cases Thereon Decided in the Law Courts* (London: Clowes and Sons, 1897), 45–49.

50. Rodger to Elgin, 1 September 1907, TNA, CO 96/459, no. 33570, enc. 2.

51. Penelope A. Roberts, "The State and Regulation of Marriage: Sefwi Wiawso (Ghana), 1900–1940," in *Women, State and Ideology: Studies from Africa and Asia*, ed. Haleh Afshar (Albany: State University of New York Press, 1987), 49.

52. Rodger to Elgin, 1 September 1907, TNA, CO 96/459, no. 33570, enc. 2. According to Yarn, the installment plan included an initial payment of £10/- (to buy cloth for Saraku), with the remaining payments to be made over the course of the next two months. In addition, he claimed that Clarke had agreed to pay £1 each month for "chop money."

53. Ibid.

54. Ibid.

55. Ibid. In an example of the kinds of problems encountered when working with translated and transcribed material, Saraku's testimony about her visits to Clarke was contradictory. She is reported as saying, "I do not go to defendant except he sends for me. I sometimes go on my own accord." It is unclear whether she contradicted herself,

whether the interpreter translated her testimony incorrectly, or whether the transcripts were recorded incorrectly. Fortunately, in this instance it does not adversely affect our ability to ascertain that she did not reside with Clarke on a regular basis.

56. Irina Sinitsina, "African Legal Tradition: J. M. Sarbah, J. B. Danquah, N. A. Ollennu," *Journal of African Law* 31, nos. 1–2 (1987): 52.

57. Rodger to Elgin, 1 September 1907, TNA, CO 96/459, no. 33570, enc. 2.

58. Ibid.

59. Ibid.

60. Rodger to Elgin, 10 August 1907, TNA, CO 96/459, no. 31137, enc. 2.

61. Clarke to Under Secretary of State, 29 October 1907, TNA, CO 96/464, no. 38139 (emphasis added).

62. Clarke to Under Secretary of State, 16 October 1907, TNA, CO 96/464, no. 36688.

63. Ibid.

64. Ibid.

65. In addition to West Indian government officers, sizable numbers of West Indian missionaries were present in the Gold Coast as part of the Basel Mission congregation. See Sill, *Encounters in Quest of Christian Womanhood*, 109–32.

66. Blyden, *West Indians in West Africa*, 54. Although referring to West Indians in Sierra Leone, Blyden's description of their privileged backgrounds is broadly applicable to West Indians in the Gold Coast, like Marcus Clarke, who served in administrative positions. On education in the British West Indies, see M. K. Bacchus, *Education for Economic, Social and Political Development in the British Caribbean Colonies from 1896 to 1945* (London, ON: Althouse Press, 2005).

67. Clarke to Under Secretary of State, 2 January 1998, TNA, CO 96/478, no. 175.

68. For Clarke, this conflict may have been particularly heightened because of his apparently racially ambiguous appearance: he is described in the records first as a "quadroon" and then as a "mulatto."

69. Frantz Fanon, *Black Skin, White Masks* (New York: Grove Press, 1967), 100.

70. Clarke to Under Secretary of State, 16 October 1907, TNA, CO 96/464, no. 36688.

71. Ibid.

72. Ibid.

73. Rodger to Elgin, 1 September 1907, TNA, CO 96/459, no. 33570, enc. 2.

74. For these practices during the precolonial period in Asante, see Tom McCaskie, "State and Society, Marriage and Adultery: Some Considerations Towards a Social History of Pre-Colonial Asante," *Journal of African History* 22, no. 4 (1981): 491. For Anlo, see Sandra E. Greene, *Gender, Ethnicity, and Social Change on the Upper Slave Coast: A History of the Anlo-Ewe* (Portsmouth, NH: Heinemann, 1996), 111.

75. McCaskie, "State and Society, Marriage and Adultery," 489.

76. Clarke to Under Secretary of State, 16 October 1907, TNA, CO 96/464, no. 36688

77. Clarke to Under Secretary of State, 10 November 1907, TNA, CO 96/494, no. 39707.

78. Clarke to Under Secretary of State, 27 November 1907, TNA, CO 96/494, no. 39707.

79. Ibid.

80. Rodger to Elgin, 1 September 1907, TNA, CO 96/459, no. 33570, enc. 4.

81. Ibid.
82. File minute, 25 November 1907, TNA, CO 96/494, no. 39707.
83. File minute, 27 November 1907, TNA, CO 96/494, no. 39707. Antrobus's view that the institution of customary marriage was akin to slave-dealing was not uncommon among Europeans. On this point, see Zabel, "Legislative History of the Gold Coast and Lagos Marriage Ordinance: III," 20.
84. Murray's address was serialized in the *Gold Coast Leader* between October and December 1902. For material quoted here, see the final installment, "An Address by Dr. J. Murray: The Social Position of West African Women," 13 December 1902.
85. *Gold Coast Leader*, "Lome," 17 February 1917. Also see Atu, "Scrutineer," *Gold Coast Leader*, 4–11 December 1915; and "Tarkwa," 26 March 1921.
86. Reginald Antrobus to Marcus Clarke, 3 December 1907, TNA, CO 96/491, no. 39707. Also see Clarke's Confidential File, PRAAD, PF 1/15/24.

CHAPTER 3: "A NEW WHIM OF A MOST UNPOPULAR GOVERNOR"

1. Curling to Bryan, 12 January 1909, in Rodger to Crewe, 13 March 1909, TNA, CO 96/482, no. 11081, enc. 2.
2. Bryan to Curling, 29 December 1908, in Rodger to Crewe, 13 March 1909, TNA, CO 96/482, no. 11081, enc. 1.
3. Curling to Bryan, 12 January 1909, in Rodger to Crewe, 13 March 1909, TNA, CO 96/482, no. 11081, enc. 2.
4. Ibid. Narkoyo's admission that she lied about Curling giving her an abortifacient is confirmed by Otitsu Otibo in his testimony. See Notes of the proceedings of the Committee of Enquiry, sworn testimony of Otitsu Otibo, 23 February 1909, in Rodger to Crewe, 13 March 1909, TNA, CO 96/482, no. 11081, enc. 3C.
5. Thomas Gale, "Segregation in British West Africa," *Cahiers d'Etudes Africaines* 20, no. 4 (1980): 498.
6. Ibid., 505.
7. T. C. Macnaghten, file minute, 8 November 1909, TNA, CO 96/491, no. 36719.
8. Extract from a letter from Commissioner Eastern Province (C. N. Curling), 19 August 1908, LMP 1036/134/06, in Rodger to Crewe, 13 March 1909, TNA, CO 96/482, no. 11081, enc. A.
9. Ibid.
10. Report by the acting Commissioner of Police (Mr. Collins), 26 September 1908, in Rodger to Crewe, 13 March 1909, TNA, CO 96/482, no. 11081, enc. B.
11. Ibid.
12. For a listing of the nine different charges in detail, see Bryan to Curling, 29 December 1908, in Rodger to Crewe, 13 March 1909, TNA, CO 96/482, no. 11081, enc. 1.
13. Ibid.
14. Curling to Bryan, 12 January 1909, in Rodger to Crewe, 13 March 1909, TNA, CO 96/482, no. 11081, enc. 2.
15. Curling to Bryan, 11 November 1908, in Rodger to Crewe, 13 March 1909, TNA, CO 96/482, no. 11081, enc. O.
16. Rosemary Weatherston, "When Sleeping Dictionaries Awaken: The Re/Turn of the Native Woman Informant," *Post Identity* 1, no. 1 (1997): 113–44.

17. Pamela Scully, "Malintzin, Pocahontas, and Krotoa: Indigenous Women and Myth Models of the Atlantic World," *Journal of Colonialism and Colonial History* 6, no. 3 (2005): ¶¶16–19.

18. Curling to Bryan, 11 November 1908, in Rodger to Crewe, 13 March 1909, TNA, CO 96/482, no. 11081, enc. O.

19. Ibid. Samuel Marshall, Curling's Native clerk, testified to the committee of inquiry that Narkoyo had been married by "native custom" to Berrago. Marshall had been informed of the marriage by a judicial clerk in Akuse, named Nyako, in late 1905. Sworn statement of Samuel Marshall, Proceedings from the Committee of Enquiry, 23 February 1909, in Rodger to Crewe, 13 March 1909, TNA, CO 96/482, no. 11081, sub-enc. D to enc. 3.

20. Curling to Bryan, 11 November 1908, in Rodger to Crewe, 13 March 1909, TNA, CO 96/482, no. 11081, enc. O.

21. Ibid.

22. Curling to Bryan, 12 January 1909, in Rodger to Crewe, 13 March 1909, TNA, CO 96/482, no. 11081, enc. 2.

23. Bryan to Curling, 29 December 1908, in Rodger to Crewe, 13 March 1909, TNA, CO 96/482, no. 11081, enc. 1.

24. Committee of Enquiry to Colonial Secretary Bryan, 26 February 1909, in Rodger to Crewe, 13 March 1909, TNA, CO 96/482, no. 11081, enc. 3.

25. Notes of the proceedings of the Committee of Enquiry, sworn testimony of Otitsu Otibo, 23 February 1909, in Rodger to Crewe, 13 March 1909, TNA, CO 96/482, no. 11081, enc. 3C.

26. Sworn statement of Amanquah Otibo, 9 September 1908, in Rodger to Crewe, 13 March 1909, TNA, CO 96/482, no. 11081, sub-enc. to enc. J.

27. Sworn statement of Amanquah Otibo, Proceedings from the Committee of Enquiry, 23 February 1909, in Rodger to Crewe, 13 March 1909, TNA, CO 96/482, no. 11081, sub-enc. C to enc. 3.

28. Curling to Bryan, 12 January 1909, in Rodger to Crewe, 13 March 1909, TNA, CO 96/482, no. 11081, enc. 2.

29. Sworn statement of Amanquah Otibo, Proceedings from the Committee of Enquiry, 23 February 1909, in Rodger to Crewe, 13 March 1909, TNA, CO 96/482, no. 11081, sub-enc. C to enc. 3.

30. Curling to Bryan, 12 January 1909, in Rodger to Crewe, 13 March 1909, TNA, CO 96/482, no. 11081, enc. 2.

31. Sworn statement of Otitsu Otibo, Proceedings from the Committee of Enquiry, 23 February 1909, in Rodger to Crewe, 13 March 1909, TNA, CO 96/482, no. 11081, sub-enc. C to enc. 3.

32. Jean M. Allman, "Fathering, Mothering and Making Sense of 'Ntamoba': Reflections on the Economy of Child-Rearing in Colonial Asante," *Africa* 67, no. 2 (1997): 305.

33. Curling to Bryan, 12 January 1909, in Rodger to Crewe, 13 March 1909, TNA, CO 96/482, no. 11081, enc. 2.

34. Curling to Under Secretary of State for the Colonies, 5 June 1909, TNA, CO 96/491, no. 18995.

35. Curling to Bryan, 11 November 1908, in Rodger to Crewe, 13 March 1909, TNA, CO 96/482, no. 11081, enc. O.

36. Heike I. Schmidt, "Colonial Intimacy: The Rechenberg Scandal and Homosexuality in German East Africa," *Journal of the History of Sexuality* 17, no. 1 (2008): 30.
37. Curling to Bryan, 11 November 1908, in Rodger to Crewe, 13 March 1909, TNA, CO 96/482, no. 11081, enc. O.
38. Curling to Bryan, 12 January 1909, in Rodger to Crewe, 13 March 1909, TNA, CO 96/482, no. 11081, enc. 2.
39. Ibid.
40. Curling to Bryan, 11 November 1908, in Rodger to Crewe, 13 March 1909, TNA, CO 96/482, no. 11081, enc. O.
41. H. T. Palmer to Acting Principal Medical Officer, 20 January 1909, in Rodger to Crewe, 5 February 1909, TNA, CO 96/481, no. 6925, enc. 5.
42. Ann L. Stoler, *Carnal Knowledge and Imperial Power: Race and the Intimate in Colonial Rule* (Berkeley: University of California Press, 2002), 49, 239n47.
43. Rodger to Crewe, 13 March 1909, TNA, CO 96/482, no. 11801.
44. Ibid.
45. Ibid. Here, Governor Rodger recommended a slightly stronger punishment than had Palmer's supervisor, Principal Medical Officer Dr. Garland, who had suggested that a censure alone would be sufficient.
46. Secretary of State for the Colonies, Lord Crewe, to the Officer Administering the Government of the Gold Coast, 4 May 1909, PRAAD, ADM 12/1/31.
47. Curling to Under Secretary of State for the Colonies, 5 June 1909, TNA, CO 96/491, no. 18995.
48. Ibid.
49. Committee of Enquiry to Bryan, 26 February 1909, in Rodger to Crewe, 13 March 1909, TNA, CO 96/482, no. 11081, enc. 3.
50. Curling to Under Secretary of State for the Colonies, 5 June 1909, TNA, CO 96/491, no. 18995.
51. Ibid.
52. Curling to Colonial Secretary Bryan, 12 January 1909, in Rodger to Crewe, 13 March 1909, TNA, CO 96/482, no. 11801, enc. 2.
53. File minute, 7 April 1909, TNA, CO 96/482, no. 11801.
54. T. C. Macnaghten, file minute, 4 April 1909, TNA, CO 96/482, no. 11801.
55. File minute, 18 May 1909, TNA, CO 96/492, no. 17012.
56. File minute, 19 May 1909, TNA, CO 96/492, no. 17012.
57. Alexander Fiddian, file minutes, 5 June 1909 and 11 June 1909, TNA, CO 96/491, no. 18995. Fiddian joined the Colonial Office, at the rank of a second-class clerk, in 1897. *Edinburgh Gazette*, 8 October 1897, p. 958.
58. File minutes, 16 June 1909, TNA, CO 96/491, no. 18995.
59. J. M. Robertson to Colonial Secretary Bryan, 13 November 1908, TNA, CO 96/482, no. 10220, enc. 1.
60. Ibid.
61. Chief Commissioner, Northern Territories, A. E. Watherston, to Colonial Secretary Bryan, 6 January 1909, TNA, CO 96/482, no. 10220, enc. 3.
62. J. M. Robertson to Colonial Secretary Bryan, 13 November 1908, TNA, CO 96/482, no. 10220, enc. 1.
63. Ibid.

64. Ibid.
65. Ibid.
66. Fred Shelford, "The Development of West Africa by Railways," *Journal of the Royal Colonial Institute* 25, no. 6 (1904): 353.
67. David E. Apter, "Some Economic Factors in the Political Development of the Gold Coast," *Journal of Economic History* 14, no. 4 (1954): 415.
68. Thomas C. McCaskie, "State and Society, Marriage and Adultery: Some Considerations Towards a Social History of Pre-Colonial Asante," *Journal of African History* 22, no. 4 (1981): 491.
69. Lt. Col. A. E. Watherston to Colonial Secretary Bryan, 6 January 1909, TNA, CO 96/482, no. 10220, enc. 3.
70. J. A. Robinson to F. W. Greig, 31 May 1908, TNA, CO 96/482, no. 10220, sub-enc. to enc. 3.
71. Ibid.
72. Shirley Zabel, "The Legislative History of the Gold Coast and Lagos Marriage Ordinance: III," *Journal of African Law* 23, no. 1 (1979): 20.
73. Jean M. Allman, "Adultery and the State in Asante: Reflections on Gender, Class, and Power from 1800 to 1950," in *The Cloth of Many Colored Silks: Papers on History and Society, Ghanaian and Islamic, in Honor of Ivor Wilks*, ed. John Hunwick and Nancy Lawler (Evanston, IL: Northwestern University Press, 1996), 33. Also see McCaskie, "State and Society, Marriage and Adultery."
74. Allman, "Fathering, Mothering and Making Sense of 'Ntamoba,'" 304.
75. Tom McCaskie, "The Consuming Passions of Kwame Boakye: An Essay on Agency and Identity in Asante History," *Journal of African Cultural Studies* 13, no. 1 (2000): 55.
76. Anne McClintock, *Imperial Leather: Race, Gender and Sexuality in the Colonial Conquest* (New York: Routledge, 1995), 6.
77. Lt. Col. A. E. Watherston to Colonial Secretary H. Bryan, 6 January 1909, TNA, CO 96/482, no. 10220, enc. 3.
78. Extract from Director of Public Works, Mr. Wilkinson, in Governor Rodger to Secretary of State for the Colonies, 4 March 1909, TNA, CO 96/482, no. 10220.
79. Lt. Col. A. E. Watherston to Colonial Secretary H. Bryan, 6 January 1909, TNA, CO 96/482, no. 10220, enc. 3.
80. Draft reply, Secretary of State for the Colonies to Governor Rodger, 22 April 1909, TNA, CO 96/482, no. 10220.
81. File minutes, 4 March 1909 and 24 March 1909, TNA, CO 96/482, no. 10220.

CHAPTER 4: THE CREWE CIRCULAR

1. The term *askari*, translated from both Arabic and Swahili as "soldier," is generally used to refer to the African troops who served in East Africa's colonial armies; however, the term was also applied to African men, like Mgulla, who served as policemen in these colonies. For a brief history of the police force in Kenya, and the role of the askari in it, see Hans-Martin Sommer, "The History of the Kenya Police, 1885–1960" (research report prepared for the Coast Provincial Police Headquarters, Mombasa, Kenya, November 2007), 1–16. Although focused on neighboring German East Africa, Michelle Moyd offers a groundbreaking analysis of askari identity

politics and their sociocultural world in *Violent Intermediaries: African Soldiers, Conquest, and Everyday Colonialism in German East Africa* (Athens: Ohio University Press, 2014).

2. Routledge to Sadler, 29 February 1908, in Governor Sadler to Secretary of State for the Colonies, 21 May 1908, TNA, CO 533/44, no. 21793, enc. 1.

3. Ibid.

4. For Sadler's locally issued circular, see Governor Sadler to Secretary of State for the Colonies, 21 May 1908, TNA, CO 533/44, no. 21793. For the Routledges' exposé, see R. Socresby Routledge, *Times*, 3 December 1908.

5. For press coverage, see "A Canker in Imperial Administration," *Spectator*, 12 December 1908; One Who Knows, "A Canker in Imperial Administration," *Spectator*, 19 December 1908; D. S. S., "To the Editor of the Spectator," *Spectator*, 19 December 1908. For a discursive analysis of these press reports, see Christopher Lane, "Managing 'The White Man's Burden': The Racial Imaginary of Forster's Colonial Narratives," *Discourse* 15, no. 3 (1993): 105–8.

6. Memorandum by Colonel Seely, 8 December 1908, TNA, CO 533/52, no. 45005.

7. Crewe to the Officer Administering the Government of the Gold Coast, 11 January 1909, PRAAD, ADM 12/1/31.

8. Ibid.

9. Ronald Hyam, "Concubinage and the Colonial Service: The Crewe Circular (1909)," *Journal of Imperial and Commonwealth History* 14, no. 3 (1986): 180–81.

10. Lane, "Managing 'The White Man's Burden,'" 105.

11. "Moral Sanitation," *Gold Coast Leader*, 20 December 1902; Dr. J. Murray, "Bushua: An Address by Dr. J. Murray—The Social Position of West African Women," *Gold Coast Leader*, 13 December 1902; Nigeria, "One Thing and Another," *Gold Coast Leader*, 20 April 1907.

12. Jo Anne Van Tilburg, *Among Stone Giants: The Life of Katherine Routledge and Her Remarkable Expedition to Easter Island* (New York: Scribner, 2003), 65.

13. Crewe to the Officer Administering the Government of the Gold Coast, 11 January 1909, PRAAD, ADM 12/1/31, enc. A.

14. Ibid.

15. Crewe to the Officer Administering the Government of the Gold Coast, 11 January 1909, PRAAD, ADM 12/1/31, enc. B.

16. Lord Crewe to the Officer Administering the Government of the Gold Coast, 11 January 1909, PRAAD, ADM 12/1/31.

17. T. C. Macnaghten, file minute, 16 December 1908, TNA, CO 533/52, no. 45005.

18. Illegible signature, file minute, 12 June 1909, TNA, CO 96/491, no. 18995.

19. Illegible signature, file minute, 8 December 1908, TNA, CO 96/491, no. 18995 (emphasis added).

20. Macnaghten to Antrobus, 6 January 1909, TNA, CO 533/52, no. 45005.

21. Antrobus to Macnaghten, 7 January 1909, NA, CO 533/52, no. 45005.

22. Alexander Fiddian, file minute, 13 November 1907, in Clarke to Under Secretary of State, 10 November 1907, TNA, CO 96/494, no. 39707.

23. Northeastern Rhodesia was the only Crown colony that was not scheduled to receive the circular. This was likely the case because even though it appeared on the list as a Crown colony, in practice the British South African Company controlled it. In 1911 it was amalgamated with Northwestern Rhodesia into Northern Rhodesia and after 1924 it was administered by the British government. Although the date is unclear,

at some point N. Rhodesia came under the purview of the Crewe Circular as indicated by its inclusion in discussions about the circular's fate.

24. T. C. Macnaghten to R. L. Antrobus, 6 January 1909, Memo by Col. Seely, Case of Mr. Silberrad and Mr. Haywood, December 1908, TNA, CO 533/52, no. 45005. The Colonial Office's view of the West Indies as home to racially egalitarian societies is of course at odds with scholarly treatments of race relations in the colonial Caribbean, which point to the racially stratified nature of those societies. See Ralph R. Premdas, "Racism and Anti-Racism in the Caribbean," in *Racism and Anti-Racism in World Perspective*, ed. Benjamin P. Bowser (Thousand Oaks, CA: Sage, 1995), 241–60; Michael G. Smith, *The Plural Society in the British West Indies* (Berkeley: University of California Press, 1965); David Lowenthal, "Race and Color in the West Indies," *Daedalus* 96, no. 2 (1967): 580–626; Daniel A. Segal, "'Race' and 'Colour' in Pre-Independence Trinidad and Tobago," in *Trinidad Ethnicity*, ed. Kevin Yelvington (Knoxville: University of Tennessee Press, 1993), 81–115.

25. T. C. Macnaghten to R. L. Antrobus, 7 January 1909, Memo by Col. Seely, Case of Mr. Silberrad and Mr. Haywood, December 1908, TNA, CO 533/52, no. 45005.

26. Memo by Col. Seely as to Case of Mr. Silberrad and Mr. Haywood, enclosed list of departments scheduled to receive Crewe's Circular, TNA, CO 533/52, no. 45005.

27. Draft circular, TNA, CO 533/52, no. 45005.

28. Ann L. Stoler, *Carnal Knowledge and Imperial Power: Race and the Intimate in Colonial Rule* (Berkeley: University of California Press, 2002), 8, 220.

29. Angus McLaren, *Sexual Blackmail: A Modern History* (Cambridge, MA: Harvard University Press, 2002), 3.

30. W. A. Kisseadoo to Commissioner, Western Province, 18 July 1909, sub-enc. 1 to enc. 3, in Rodger to Crewe, 13 October 1909, TNA, CO 96/485, no. 36342.

31. Ibid.

32. N. H. Dakeyne to A. J. Philbrick, 22 July 1909, sub-enc. 2 to enc. 3, in Rodger to Crewe, 13 October 1909, TNA, CO 96/485, no. 36342.

33. Ibid. (emphasis in original).

34. T. C. Macnaghten, file minute, 8 November 1909, TNA, CO 96/491, no. 36719.

35. N. H. Dakeyne to A. J. Philbrick, 22 July 1909, sub-enc. 2 to enc. 3, in Rodger to Crewe, 13 October 1909, TNA, CO 96/485, no. 36342.

36. N. H. Dakeyne to Under Secretary of State, Colonial Office, 6 November 1909, in TNA CO 96/491, no. 36719.

37. See, for example, "Bushua: An Address by Dr. J. Murray—The Social Position of West African Women," *Gold Coast Leader*, 13 December 1902; and "Immoral Sanitation," 3–10 January 1920.

38. Jacqueline Nassy Brown gives a compelling analysis of the problems and possibilities of the term "local" in relation to the women who participate/d in interracial relationships with "global" men in Liverpool. Many of her cautionary insights are applicable here. See Brown, *Dropping Anchor, Setting Sail: Geographies of Race in Black Liverpool* (Princeton, NJ: Princeton University Press, 2009).

39. N. H. Dakeyne to A. J. Philbrick, 22 July 1909, in Rodger to Crewe, 13 October 1909, TNA, CO 96/485, no. 36342, sub-enc. 2 to enc. 3.

40. T. C. Macnaghten, file minute, 8 November 1909, TNA, CO 96/491, no. 36719 (emphasis added); File minute, 9 November 1909, TNA CO 96/491, no. 36719.

41. File minute, 9 November 1909, TNA, CO 96/491, no. 36719.

42. Lewis Harcourt to Thorburn, 31 January 1911, PRAAD, ADM 12/1/33.
43. Mary Ajeley Charway to Acting Governor Herbert Bryan, 27 May 1911, PRAAD, ADM 12/3/17, enc. 4.
44. Samuel Charway to Officer in Charge of Prison, Tamale, 19 July 1911, PRAAD, ADM 12/3/17, sub-enc. B to enc. 1.
45. Ibid.
46. C. H. Armitage to Colonial Secretary, report on the circumstances of the imprisonment of Mr. Samuel Andrew Charway, 2 September 1911, PRAAD, ADM 12/3/17, sub-enc. to enc. 1.
47. Ibid.
48. Ibid.
49. Ibid.
50. File minute, 29 November 1911, TNA, CO 96/514, no. 38484.
51. Major Festing to Secretary of State for the Colonies, 13 November 1911, TNA, CO 96/514, no. 36863.
52. File minute, 7 December 1911, TNA, CO 96/514, no. 38484.
53. Major Festing to Secretary of State for the Colonies, 26 November 1911, TNA, CO 96/514, no. 36863.
54. C. H. Armitage to Colonial Secretary, report on the circumstances of the imprisonment of Mr. Samuel Andrew Charway, 2 September 1911, PRAAD, ADM 12/3/17, sub-enc. to enc. 1.
55. Thorburn to Lewis Harcourt, 27 January 1912, TNA, CO 96/515, no 5761.
56. Kortright to R. A. Irvine, Acting Chief Commissioner, Northern Territories, TNA, CO 96/515, sub-enc. 4 to enc. 1.
57. Thorburn to Acting Colonial Secretary, 8 May 1911, PRAAD, ADM 11/1/922. Also see Carina E. Ray, "Sex Trafficking, Prostitution, and the Law in Colonial British West Africa, 1911–43," in *Trafficking in Slavery's Wake: Law and the Experience of Women and Children in Africa*, ed. Benjamin N. Lawrance and Richard L. Roberts (Athens: Ohio University Press, 2012), 104.
58. Thorburn to Lewis Harcourt, 27 January 1912, TNA, CO 96/515, no. 5761.
59. File minute, 24 February 1912, TNA, CO 96/515, no. 5761.
60. Governor Guggisberg to Secretary of State for the Colonies, "George Brewer: Removal From Service: 1927," 6 April 1927, PRAAD, ADM 12/5/173.
61. W. E. Smith, General Manager, Gold Coast Government Railways, 29 September 1910, enclosed in Governor Thorburn to Secretary of State for the Colonies, ADM 12/3/17.
62. W. E. Smith, General Manager, Gold Coast Government Railways, 2 August 1910, enclosed in Governor Thorburn to Secretary of State for the Colonies, ADM 12/3/17.
63. W. E. Smith, General Manager, Gold Coast Government Railways, 21 July 1911, enclosed in Governor Thorburn to Secretary of State for the Colonies, ADM 12/3/17.
64. Ibid.
65. File minute, 27 January 1912, TNA, CO 96/515, no. 5761.
66. File minute, 28 February 1912, TNA, CO 96/515, no. 5761.
67. File minute, 23 February 1912, TNA, CO 96/515, no. 5761.
68. See, for example, Sandra E. Greene, *Gender, Ethnicity, and Social Change on the Upper Slave Coast: A History of the Anlo-Ewe* (Portsmouth, NH: Heinemann, 1996), 105–6.

69. J. F. O'Shaughnessy to Acting Postmaster General, 6 December 1917, PRAAD, ADM 12/3/28, sub-enc. to enc. J.

70. Officials in Uganda also reported that the circular had been discontinued in 1911. In 1916, the governor of Kenya reported that distribution of the circular to new officers had been discontinued for approximately fifteen months and asked for permission to drop the circular altogether, as he believed that concubinage was "no longer common." The Colonial Office refused this request on the grounds that it would be impossible to make an exception to a general rule for one colony. File minute, 5 November 1924, TNA, CO 583/127.

71. Sir Hugh Clifford to Secretary of State for the Colonies, 25 September 1924, TNA, CO 583/127.

72. File minute, 5 November 1924, TNA, CO 583/127.

73. Ibid.

74. Ibid.

75. File minute, 31 December 1924, TNA, CO 583/127.

76. File Minute, 5 December 1924, TNA, CO 583/127.

77. Ibid.

78. Gold Coast Census, 1921, PRAAD, ADM 5/2/5.

79. File Minute, 5 December 1924, TNA, CO 583/127.

80. File Minute, 31 December 1924, TNA, CO 583/127.

81. A "native" letter writer named Enno was hired to produce the affidavit, thereby illustrating the multiple channels through which these kinds of charges circulated among Gold Coasters.

82. Rex versus Hajara alias Kachina and J. K. Omar, 7 January 1927, in Governor Guggisberg to Secretary of State for the Colonies, L. S. Amery, 6 April 1927, PRAAD, ADM 12/3/47, enc. 3.

83. Ibid.

84. Ibid.

85. Ibid.

86. Gocking, "British Justice and the Native Tribunals of the Southern Gold Coast Colony," 98n30; Mathieu Deflem, "Law Enforcement in British Colonial Africa: A Comparative Analysis of Imperial Policing in Nyasaland, the Gold Coast and Kenya," *Police Studies* 17, no. 1 (1994): 45–68.

87. Rex versus Hajara alias Kachina and J. K. Omar, 7 January 1927, in Governor Guggisberg to Secretary of State for the Colonies, L. S. Amery, 6 April 1927, PRAAD, ADM 12/3/47, enc. 3.

88. The attorney general's report was included in Governor Guggisberg to Secretary of State for the Colonies, L. S. Amery, 6 April 1927, PRAAD, ADM 12/3/47, enc. 3.

89. H. M. Bamford to Colonial Secretary, 31 January 1927, PRAAD, ADM 12/3/47, enc. 2.

90. Governor Slater to Secretary of State Passfield, 21 August 1929, enclosed memorial; Drake Brockman to Secretary of State Passfield, 13 August 1929, PRAAD, ADM 12/3/50.

91. Governor Slater to Secretary of State Passfield, 21 August 1929, PRAAD, ADM 12/3/50.

92. Ibid.

93. Ibid.

94. Governor Guggisberg to Secretary of State for the Colonies, "George Brewer: Removal From Service: 1927," 6 April 1927, PRAAD, ADM 12/5/173.

95. Helen Callaway, *Gender, Culture, and Empire: European Women in Colonial Nigeria* (Urbana: University of Illinois Press, 1987), 48–50.

96. Northcote to Cunliffe-Lister, 22 September 1934, PRAAD, ADM 12/3/61, enc. 1.

97. Concubinage with Native Women, Secretary of State for the Colonies, Sir Cunliffe-Lister, to Officer Administering Fiji, Western Pacific, Nyasaland, Sierra Leone, Gambia, Gold Coast, Nigeria, Kenya, Uganda, Somaliland, Ceylon, Hong Kong, Straits Settlements, N. Rhodesia, Zanzibar, Tanganyika Territory, 8 November 1934, TNA, CO 850/47.

98. Ibid.

CHAPTER 5: "A MANIFESTATION OF MADNESS"

1. Governor Alan Burns to Gerald Creasy, Concubinage with Native Women, 29 June 1945, TNA, CO 850/218.

2. Illegible signature, Concubinage with Native Women, file minute, 17 July 1945, TNA, CO 850/218.

3. Ibid.
4. Ibid.
5. Ibid.

6. P. A. Tegetmeier, "Concubinage with Native Women," file minute, 16 July 1945, TNA, CO 850/218.

7. Sir C. Jeffries, "Concubinage with Native Women," file minute, 17 July 1945, TNA, CO 850/218.

8. Ann L. Stoler, *Carnal Knowledge and Imperial Power: Race and the Intimate in Colonial Rule* (Berkeley: University of California Press, 2002), 39.

9. For a lengthier treatment of the colonial government's resistance to strengthening its antiprostitution and antitrafficking legislation, see Carina E. Ray, "Sex Trafficking, Prostitution, and the Law in Colonial British West Africa, 1911–43," in *Trafficking in Slavery's Wake: Law and the Experience of Women and Children in Africa*, ed. Benjamin N. Lawrance and Richard L. Roberts (Athens: Ohio University Press, 2012), 101–20.

10. On the logistical and diplomatic history of what became known as the "Takoradi Route," see Deborah Wing Ray, "The Takoradi Route: Roosevelt's Prewar Venture beyond the Western Hemisphere," *Journal of American History* 62, no. 2 (1975): 340–58.

11. Nate Plageman, *Highlife Saturday Night: Popular Music and Social Change in Urban Ghana* (Bloomington: Indiana University Press, 2013), 105.

12. "Prostitutes—Control of by Police," memorandum by E. C. Nottingham to Colonial Secretary, Accra, "Traffic in Women and Children," PRAAD, CSO 15/1/222, 30 May 1941.

13. Charles M. Wiltse, *The Medical Department: Medical Service in the Mediterranean and Minor Theaters* (Washington, DC: Office of the Chief of Military History, Dept. of the Army, 1965), 67.

14. "Prostitutes—Control of by Police," memorandum by E. C. Nottingham to Colonial Secretary, Accra, "Traffic in Women and Children," PRAAD, CSO 15/1/222, 30 May 1941.

15. Acting Attorney-General Raymond Browne to Colonial Secretary, "Traffic in Women and Children," 8 September 1943, PRAAD, CSO 15/1/222. A copy of the complete set of amendments to both the Criminal Code and the Immigration Ordinance can be found in Governor Alan Burns to Bourdillon, "Traffic in Women and Children," 11 October 1943, PRAAD, CSO 15/1/222. For a fuller analysis of the war as a watershed moment in the legislative history of prostitution and sex trafficking in British West Africa, see Carina E. Ray, "World War Two and the Sex Trade in British West Africa," in *Africa and World War II*, ed. Judith Byfield, Carolyn Brown, Timothy Parsons, and Ahmad Sikainga (Cambridge: Cambridge University Press, 2015), 339–56.

16. M. Burner, Commissioner, Western Province, to Colonial Secretary, Accra, 2 May 1944, PRAAD, PF 1/38/411.

17. M. Burner, Commissioner, Western Province, to Colonial Secretary, Accra, 29 June 1944, PRAAD, PF 1/38/411.

18. Acting Colonial Secretary, file minute, 3 June 1949, PRAAD, PF 1/38/411.

19. M. Burner, Commissioner, Western Province, to Colonial Secretary, Accra, 2 May 1944, PRAAD, PF 1/38/411, enc. 1.

20. M. Burner, Commissioner, Western Province, to Colonial Secretary, Accra, 17 July 1944, PRAAD, PF 1/38/411.

21. Colonial Secretary, file minute, 31 July 1944, PRAAD, PF 1/38/411.

22. The name and the birth date of their son were obtained from Inward Passenger Lists, 1958, Liverpool, RMMV *Aureol*, TNA, BT 26/1419/26.

23. European Service Record, Donald Sidney Turner, PRAAD, PF 1/38/411.

24. For a comparative case study, see the entry for William Hugh Beeton in Anthony H. M. Kirk-Greene, *A Biographical Dictionary of the British Colonial Service, 1939–1966* (London: Zell, 1991), 27.

25. Felicia Knight, interview, Accra, August 2007.

26. Donald Sidney Turner, *England and Wales Death Index* 38 (1916–2007): 1452; "Gladys Turner: Obituary," *Manchester Evening News*, 4 September 2007.

27. Cathleen Ellis, Skype interview, 29 October 2013. Ellis is the daughter of Margaret Mary Hawe (née Barette) and granddaughter of Essie Mansah.

28. Ibid.

29. Cathleen Ellis, e-mail message to author, 19 September 2014.

30. *Supplement to the London Gazette*, no. 39863 (26 May 1953): 2974; *Fourth Supplement to the London Gazette*, no. 41730 (5 June 1959): 3743.

31. "John Holt Medalist," *Liverpool Echo*, 28 July 1965. Awarded by the Liverpool School of Tropical Medicine (LSTM), the medal is named after the English merchant and shipping magnate John Holt, who was an early benefactor of the LSTM.

32. Kwame Nkrumah to B. G. Maegraith, 20 August 1965. I wish to thank Tom Ellis, the grandson of Albert and Margaret Mary Hawe, for providing me with a copy of this letter, as well as other useful documents pertaining to his family's history.

33. Cathleen Ellis, Skype interview, 29 October 2013.

34. Dr. A. J. Hawe to Nationality Division, Home Office, 11 June 1963.

35. Director of Medical Services to Colonial Secretary, Accra, 1 June 1945, PRAAD, PF 1/32/74.

36. Charles Bowesman to Director of Medical Services, undated, PRAAD, PF 1/32/74.

37. Docia Kisseih, "Developments in Nursing in Ghana," *International Journal of Nursing Studies* 5, no. 3 (1968): 206.

38. Secretary of State for the Colonies to Governor Alan Burns, 3 May 1945, PRAAD, PF 1/32/74.

39. Given that the wedding took place in 1945, the Aggrey in question was not the famous Gold Coast educationist James Emman Kwegyi Aggrey, who died in 1927.

40. Charles Bowesman, *Being Caught in a Thorn Bush He Plucks a Rose: A Medical Anthology* (Sussex: Book Guild, 1987), 116.

41. Ibid.

42. Charles Bowesman to Director of Medical Services, PRAAD, PF 1/32/74.

43. Charles Bowesman to Director of Medical Services, excerpted in Acting Director of Medical Services to Colonial Secretary, Accra, 19 June 1946, PRAAD, PF 1/32/74.

44. Acting Colonial Secretary to Director of Medical Services, 1 June 1946, PRAAD, PF 1/32/74.

45. Illegible signature, file minute, 21 June 1946, PRAAD, PF 1/32/74.

46. Emmanuel Evans-Anfom, *To the Thirsty Land: Autobiography of a Patriot* (Achimota: Africa Christian Press, 2003), 252, 257.

47. Stephen Addae, *The Evolution of Modern Medicine in a Developing Country: Ghana 1880–1960* (Durham, NC: Durham Academic Press, 1997), 419; Reggie Bowesman, "Charles Bowesman, Obituary," *British Medical Journal* 307 (October 2, 1993): 864.

48. Charles Bowesman to the Establishment Secretary, 7 December 1956, PRAAD, PF 1/32/74.

49. Permanent Secretary, Ministry of the Interior, to Permanent Secretary, Ministry of Health, 5 November 1959, PRAAD, PF 1/32/74.

50. Bowesman, *Being Caught in a Thorn Bush He Plucks a Rose*, 174.

51. Ibid., 190.

52. Bowesman, "Charles Bowesman, Obituary," 864.

53. For the awarding of the OBE, see *The Fourth Supplement to the London Gazette*, no. 41271 (31 December 1957): 47; and Bowesman, *Being Caught in a Thorn Bush He Plucks a Rose*, 189.

54. Bowesman, *Being Caught in a Thorn Bush He Plucks a Rose*, 134.

55. Prior to 1933, courses in "Colonial Administrative Service" were known as the "Tropical African Service" at both Cambridge and Oxford, the United Kingdom's major institutions for training in colonial administration. Robert Heussler, *Yesterday's Rulers: The Making of the British Colonial Service* (Syracuse, NY: Syracuse University Press, 1963), 130. For Knight's administrative biography, including his Cambridge degree, see Kirk-Greene, *Biographical Dictionary of the British Colonial Service*, 206.

56. Felicia Knight, interview, Accra, August 2007.

57. Ibid.

58. Ibid.

59. J. C. M. Paton, Regional Officer to Secretary, Ministry of Education, Accra, 20 January 1956, "Exclusion from Social Institutions on Grounds of Race," PRAAD, SEK, WRG 24/1/140.

60. Felicia Knight, interview, Accra, August 2007.

61. Illegible signature (Secretary of the Cabinet) to Hon. Tawia Adamafio (Minister for Presidential Affairs), 2 February 1961, PRAAD, PF 1/38/242.

62. Hans Buser, *In Ghana at Independence: Stories of a Swiss Salesman* (Basel: Basler Afrika Bibliographien, 2010), 33.

63. Hans and Mercy "Kwadua" Roth, interview, Rombach, Switzerland, March 2010.

64. Hans R. Roth, *Because of Kwadua: Autobiography of Hans Rudolf Roth* (Accra: Afram, 2008), 18 (hereafter cited in text as *BK*).

65. Hans and Mercy Roth, interview, Rombach, Switzerland, March 2010.

66. Hans and Mercy Roth, e-mail message to author, 16 October 2013.

67. Hans and Mercy Roth, interview, Rombach, Switzerland, March 2010.

68. Ibid.

69. Frederick Cooper, "Reconstructing Empire in British and French Africa," *Past and Present* 210, no. 6 (2011): 199.

70. Frederick Cooper, *Africa Since 1940: The Past of the Present* (Cambridge: Cambridge University Press, 2002), 37.

CHAPTER 6: "THE WHITE WIFE PROBLEM"

1. The Register General of Shipping and Seamen forwarded her letter to the Colonial Office. Ena Parker to Register General of Shipping and Seamen, 23 October 1933, "Mr. and Mrs. John Parker—Repatriation of, from England to the Gold Coast," PRAAD, CSO 21/14/47.

2. Alex Fiddian to Ena Parker, 1 November 1933, "Mr. and Mrs. John Parker – Repatriation of," PRAAD, CSO 21/14/17.

3. G. S. Northcote, Governor's Deputy, Gold Coast, to Secretary of State, 18 January 1934, "Mr. and Mrs. John Parker – Repatriation of," PRAAD, CSO 21/14/47.

4. File minute, 19 December 1933, "Mr. and Mrs. John Parker—Repatriation of," PRAAD, CSO 21/14/47.

5. These couples included the Canns, the Robertses, the Egalis, and the Heldens. On the Canns, see "Repatriation of Natives to West Africa/Destitute Natives," 10 March 1927, TNA, CO 554/74/8. For the Robertses, see "White Wives of Natives," TNA, CO 554/105/6, 1936. On the Egalis, see "Repatriation of Destitute Natives to West Africa, M. B. Egali: Passport facilities for Mrs. Egali," TNA, CO 554/93/1, no. 1405/1. For the Heldens, see "Repatriations: Herbert Helden and Wife (An Italian) from Barcelona to the Gold Coast," PRAAD, CSO 21/14/67.

6. Throughout the time period under consideration in this chapter, the term "coloured" was widely used in Britain to refer to a broad range of people, including West Indians, West Africans, Portuguese, Indians, Cingalese, Malays, Egyptians, Somalis, and Arabs (generally from Aden). It was also not uncommon for persons to describe themselves as "coloured" during this time period when not identifying themselves in more specific ways. The term formed part of the lexicon of British racism and imperialism and has been replaced by "black" in both popular and academic usage; however, when quoting directly from source material, I retain the use of "coloured."

7. Laura Tabili, "Women 'of a Very Low Type': Crossing Racial Boundaries in Imperial Britain," in *Gender and Class in Modern Europe*, ed. Laura L. Frader and Sonya O. Rose (Ithaca, NY: Cornell University Press, 1996), 165.

8. Ibid., 166.

9. For general treatments of the riots, see Jacqueline Jenkinson, *Black 1919: Riots, Racism and Resistance in Imperial Britain* (Liverpool: Liverpool University Press, 2009); Jenkinson, "The 1919 Riots," in *Racial Violence in Britain in the Nineteenth and Twentieth Centuries*, ed. Panikos Panayi (Leicester: Leicester University Press, 1996),

93–111; Neil Evans, "Across the Universe: Racial Violence and the Post-War Crisis in Imperial Britain, 1919–25," in *Ethnic Labour and British Imperial Trade: A History of Ethnic Seafarers in the UK*, ed. Diane Frost (London: Cass, 1995), 59–88; Roy May and Robin Cohen, "The Interaction between Race and Colonialism: A Case Study of the Liverpool Race Riots of 1919," *Race and Class* 16, no. 2 (1974): 111–26.

10. Charles J. Jeffries, *The Colonial Office* (London: Allen and Unwin, 1956), 30.

11. Alexander Fiddian, Colonial Office, to British Foreign Office, 18 July 1933, "Repatriation of Destitute Natives to West Africa: M. B. Egali, Passport Facilities for Mrs. Egali," TNA, CO 554/93/1.

12. Ibid.

13. J. Pyke, British Consulate General, Hamburg, to British Foreign Office, 10 November 1933, "Repatriation of Destitute Natives to West Africa: M. B. Egali, Passport Facilities for Mrs. Egali," TNA, CO 554/93/1.

14. J. Pyke, British Consulate General, Hamburg, to British Foreign Office, 2 June 1933, "Repatriation of Destitute Natives to West Africa: M. B. Egali, Passport Facilities for Mrs. Egali," TNA, CO 554/93/1.

15. Lucy Bland, "White Women and Men of Colour: Miscegenation Fears in Britain after the Great War," *Gender and History* 17, no. 1 (2005): 52.

16. In a fascinating study of interracially married couples in the Netherlands from the late nineteenth to mid-twentieth centuries, Marga Altena find that some couples eschewed more conventional modes of protesting the racism directed at them in favoring of harnessing the power of the media and the public sphere to claim a place for themselves in the metropole. See Altena, *A True History Full of Romance: Mixed Marriages and Ethnic Identity in Dutch Art, News Media, and Popular Culture (1883–1955)* (Amsterdam: Amsterdam University Press, 2012).

17. Ann L. Stoler, *Carnal Knowledge and Imperial Power: Race and the Intimate in Colonial Rule* (Berkeley: University of California Press, 2002), 2.

18. As early as the seventeenth century West Africans had been employed onboard British ships, but their numbers surged in the mid-nineteenth century with the introduction of steamships and the new hierarchies of labor they created. As historian Diane Frost argues, West Africans "were recruited to perform . . . heavy manual work since it was believed they were better suited to the soaring temperatures that prevailed in the engine rooms," where they worked as donkeymen, greasers, and stokers. Frost, "Racism and Social Segregation: Settlement Patterns of West African Seamen in Liverpool since the Nineteenth Century," *New Community* 22, no. 1 (1996): 86. Frost develops these themes further in *Work and Community among West African Migrant Workers Since the Nineteenth Century* (Liverpool: Liverpool University Press, 1999).

19. For more on the restrictive clauses in lascar contracts that bound them to return to India, see "Lascars. Transfer of Lascars in the United Kingdom," TNA, MT 9/650.

20. Laura Tabili, "The Construction of Racial Difference in Twentieth-Century Britain: The Special Restriction (Coloured Alien Seamen) Order, 1925," *Journal of British Studies* 33, no. 1 (1994): 66.

21. Jenkinson, "1919 Race Riots," 93–90. Also see May and Cohen, "Interaction between Race and Colonialism," 118–19; and Evans, "Across the Universe," 68–70.

22. Head Constable, Liverpool, to Watch Committee, 17 June 1919, TNA, HO 45/11017/377969/28.

23. Newspaper clipping from the *Western Mail* (Cardiff), 13 June 1919, TNA, HO 45/11017/377969/11.

24. L. Everett, Asst. Head Constable, Central Police Office, to Under Secretary of State, 10 June 1919, TNA, HO 45/11017/377969/6.

25. Newspaper clipping from the *Sunday Express* (London), 15 June 1919, TNA, HO 45/11017/377969/68.

26. Newspaper clipping from the *Western Mail* (Cardiff), 13 June 1919, TNA, HO 45/11017/377969/11.

27. Newspaper clipping from the *Daily Mail* (London), 13 June 1919, TNA, HO 45/11017/377969/8.

28. Chief Constable, Cardiff City Police, to Under Secretary of State, 18 June 1919, HO 45/11017/377969/20, TNA.

29. For an account of Wootton's lynching, see Head Constable, Liverpool, Report on Racial Riots, 17 June 1919, TNA, HO 45/1107/377969/28. For a brief overview of the history of lynching in Britain, see Marika Sherwood, "Lynching in Britain," *History Today* 49, no. 3 (1999): 21–23.

30. Black men, of course, were not the only victims of lynching; so, too, were black women. For a powerful reminder of this history and an analysis of why it has been forgotten, see Elsa Barkley Brown, "Imaging Lynching: African American Women, Communities of Struggle, and Collective Memory," in *African American Women Speak out on Anita Hill–Clarence Thomas*, ed. Geneva Smitherman (Detroit, MI: Wayne State University Press, 1995), 100–124.

31. Williams to the Under Secretary of State, 13 June 1919, TNA, HO 45/1107/377969/11.

32. Ibid. For a general overview of the discriminatory nature of the police's response to the 1919 riots, which targeted blacks for punishment despite the fact that whites were primarily the aggressors, see Jenkinson, "1919 Race Riots," 98–100.

33. Head Constable, Liverpool Police, to Watch Committee, 17 June 1919, TNA, HO 45/11017/377969/28. Marika Sherwood has also used population statistics and arrest and conviction patterns to show how claims of black culpability were underpinned by police bias not only in Liverpool and Cardiff, but also in Glasgow, Barry, Newport, and Hull. Sherwood, "Lynching in Britain," 21.

34. Jenkinson, "1919 Race Riots," 111.

35. Fola Thomas to the House of Commons via the Colonial Secretaryship, 13 June 1919, TNA, CO 554/44, no. 35408.

36. Ibid.

37. For a report on the police roundup of an estimated five hundred black men, see the press clipping from the 11 June 1919 edition of the *Liverpool Post*, enclosed in TNA, HO 45/11017/377969/6.

38. War Office to Under Secretary of State, 18 June 1919, TNA, HO 45/11017/377969/19.

39. L. Everett, Asst. Head Constable, Central Police Office, to Under Secretary of State, 10 June 1919, TNA, HO 45/11017/377969/6.

40. May and Cohen, "Interaction between Race and Colonialism," 114.

41. "Memorandum on the Repatriation of Coloured Men," 23 June 1919, TNA, CO 323/814, cited in Jenkinson, "1919 Race Riots," 104–5. Enhanced incentives included the extension of resettlement packages first offered to white colonials, to black men who had served in the war; a separate gratuity was established through the Ministry of Labor to encourage men who had not participated in the war to repatriate. In order to expedite the pace of repatriation, these entitlements were offered for a period of two

months only, between 9 July and 9 September 1919. Ministry of Shipping to Home Office, 9 July 1919, TNA, HO 45/11017/377969/68; "Minutes of Meeting at Ministry of Labour," 20 July 1919, TNA, HO 45/11017/377969/98; Ministry of Labour, Employment Department, to Chief Constables of Salford, Liverpool, Cardiff, Glasgow, Hull, S. Shields, and London, 30 July 1919, TNA, HO 45/11017/377969/98.

42. Chief Constable, Cardiff City Police, to Under Secretary of State, 18 June 1919, TNA, HO 45/11017/377969/20.

43. By early July, the Home Office had been able to recruit only seventy-five West Africans to board the *Batanga*, an Elder Dempster liner that had been hired to repatriate 240 men back to West Africa. "After Loyal War Service, West Africans Returning Home," *Gold Coast Nation*, 12 July 1919.

44. Chief Constable, Cardiff City Police, to Under Secretary of State, 18 June 1919, TNA, HO 45/11017/377969/20.

45. "Repatriation of Coloured Men: Note on Conference at Colonial Office," 19 June 1919, TNA, HO 45/11017/377969/21.

46. Ministry of Labour to Chief Constables of Salford, Liverpool, Cardiff, Glasgow, Hull, S. Shields, London, in "Minutes of Meeting at Ministry of Labour," 30 July 1919, TNA, HO 45/11017/377969/98.

47. Minute by Mr. Maclennan, "Passports: Mr. Oladele Adebayo Ajose and His White Wife Beatrice," 23 March 1936, TNA, CO 554/103/3.

48. In order to be jointly repatriated with their black wives, this group of men had to wait until ships with special accommodations for women became available. The fact that there were far fewer repatriation requests from West African men married to black women was a reflection of the fact that they primarily partnered with white women in the ports. This was largely due to the demographic makeup of early twentieth-century British port cities, which were home to smaller numbers of black women than men. On Joseph Queashie's repatriation, see Colonial Office (draft letter) to the Secretary of the Repatriated British Civilians Help Committee, 11 November 1919, "Natives Awaiting Repatriation," TNA, CO 554/44.

49. "Report on the Repatriation of Negroes," TNA, HO 45/11017/377969/44.

50. Ibid.

51. On the failure of the repatriations, see May and Cohen, "Interaction between Race and Colonialism," 123; Evans, "Across the Universe," 79.

52. Mr. Francis, Local Government Board, as recorded by an unnamed author in an untitled report about the Colonial Office conference on the repatriation schemes, 19 June 1919, in "Position of Coloured Men Stranded in the UK," TNA, CO 323/814/28.

53. On this concession to West Indians, see "Case of Jamaican seaman, T. Savis," 12 August 1919, TNA, CO 137/735, no. 46926.

54. Jenkinson, "1919 Race Riots," 106.

55. T. C. Macnaghten to R. L. Antrobus, 6 January 1909, in "Memo by Col. Seely, Case of Mr. Silberrad and Mr. Haywood," TNA, CO 533/52, no. 45005.

56. See, for example, "Repatriation of D. Russell and Family," 18 June 1919, TNA, CO 137/735, no. 37977.

57. Minute by Alexander Fiddian, "Repatriation of Natives with White Wives: Minutes as to Policy to Be Adopted in Regard To," 7 August 1919, TNA, CO 137/735, no. 48782.

58. Bush, *Imperialism, Race, and Resistance: Africa and Britain, 1919–1945* (London: Routledge, 1999), 77–78.

59. File minute, "Repatriation of Natives with White Wives: Minutes as to Policy to be Adopted in Regard To," 8 August 1919, TNA, CO 137/735, no. 48782.

60. Laura Tabili, "Empire Is the Enemy of Love: Edith Noor's Progress and Other Stories," *Gender and History* 17, no. 1 (2005): 8.

61. Ibid.

62. One possible explanation for why the policy of prevention does not appear to have originally been applied to East Africa in the wake of the riots is that there were comparatively few East Africans who married white women in the British ports. Rather, it was West Indians and West Africans who were identified as having the highest rates of intermarriage with white women. Although, as Tabili's work on Edith and Ismail Noor indicates, Somalis did intermarry, their lower rate of intermarriage in Britain, according to Joel A. Rogers, was primarily a function of religion rather than race. Rogers, *Sex and Race: Negro-Caucasian Mixing in All Ages and All Lands* (New York: Rogers, 1940), 148.

63. German women were not alone in this regard. European women of other nationalities, including but not limited to British, Swiss, and French women, along with women from North and South America, were all at various times in the nineteenth and twentieth centuries at risk of losing their citizenship upon marriage to a foreign national. See, for example, Brigitte Studer, "Citizenship as Contingent National Belonging: Married Women and Foreigners in Twentieth Century Switzerland," *Gender and History* 13, no. 3 (2001): 622–54; Kif Augustine-Adams, "'She Consents Implicitly': Women's Citizenship, Marriage, and Liberal Political Theory in Late-Nineteenth and Early-Twentieth-Century Argentina," *Journal of Women's History* 13, no. 4 (2002): 8–30.

64. Suffice it to say that German men, as was the case for men in other parts of the world, did not lose their citizenship upon marriage to foreign women and were often able to confer their citizenship status on their wives and children. The caveat to this is that after 1933, German men who were Jewish lost their citizenship under numerous conditions.

65. While the majority of British colonial subjects in Europe resided in Britain, others were scattered across the Continent. This was especially the case after the war when employment opportunities in Britain became increasingly scarce. On British colonial subjects, especially those who were distressed, across mainland Europe and the British Empire, see Amy E. Robinson, "Tinker, Tailor, Vagrant, Sailor: Colonial Mobility and the British Imperial State, 1880–1914" (PhD diss., Stanford University, 2005).

66. Foreign Office, Mr. G. Lyall, British Consulate, Berlin, to the Secretary of State, 22 November 1927, TNA, CO 554/74/8.

67. Colonial Office to Foreign Office, 23 December 1927, TNA, CO 554/74/8.

68. Secretary of State, Colonial Office, to Governor Slater, 6 October 1930, "Mr. Alfred Annan, alias Alfred Larsen—Repatriation of to the Gold Coast," PRAAD, CSO 21/14/6.

69. Minute, Attorney General Abrahams, 3 January 1931, "Mr. Alfred Annan, alias Alfred Larsen—Repatriation of to the Gold Coast," PRAAD, CSO 21/14/6.

70. Ibid.

71. Tabili, "Empire Is the Enemy of Love," 13.

72. Governor Slater to Secretary of State Lord Passfield, 21 January 1931, "Mr. Alfred Annan, alias Alfred Larsen—Repatriation of to the Gold Coast," PRAAD, CSO 21/14/6.

73. Minute, Attorney General Abrahams, 15 January 1931, "Mr. Alfred Annan, alias Alfred Larsen—Repatriation of to the Gold Coast," PRAAD, CSO 21/14/6. Although both Slater and Abrahams referred to Alfred Annan as illiterate, his eldest daughter, Ellen, distinctly recalls that as a young girl in Hull her father used to read to her. Perhaps Alfred became literate during his years in Hull, but the salient point to be made here is that the phrase "illiterate African sailor" reflected the prejudices and assumptions of colonial administrators far more than it reflected Alfred's literacy or intellect.

74. Governor Slater to Secretary of State Lord Passfield, 21 January 1931 "Mr. Alfred Annan, alias Alfred Larsen—Repatriation of to the Gold Coast," Colonial Office, PRAAD, CSO 21/14/6.

75. Ibid.

76. Tabili, "Empire Is the Enemy of Love," 12.

77. Minute, 25 February 1932, Attorney General Abrahams, "Mr. Alfred Annan, alias Alfred Larsen—Repatriation of to the Gold Coast," PRAAD, CSO 21/14/6.

78. Minute, 15 March 1932, "Repatriation of Natives to West Africa/Destitute Natives/A. Annan," TNA, CO 554/89/5.

79. Alfred Annan to Colonial Office, 17 March 1932, "Repatriation of Natives to West Africa/Destitute Natives/A. Annan," TNA, CO 554/89/5.

80. Alfred Annan to Governor Hodson, 25 September 1937, "Mr. Alfred Annan, alias Alfred Larsen—Repatriation of to the Gold Coast," PRAAD, CSO 21/14/6.

81. Alfred Annan to Colonial Office, 18 December 1940, "Repatriations: Alfred Annan," TNA, CO 554/123/17.

82. File minute, 20 January 1941, TNA, CO 554/123/17.

83. Alfred Annan to Governor Hodson, 25 September 1937, PRAAD, CSO 21/14/6.

84. File minute, 20 January 1941, TNA, CO 554/123/17.

85. Ibid.

86. Known as the "Hull Blitz," the port city of Hull was the target of eighty-two wartime German air raids that resulted in approximately 1,200 fatalities and massive destruction of property, which rendered more than 150,000 people homeless. Tony Geraghty, *A North-East Coast Town, Ordeal and Triumph: The Story of Kingston upon Hull in the 1939–1945 Great War* (Hull: Kingston upon Hull, 1951); Philip Graystone, *The Blitz on Hull* (Hull: Lampada, 1991).

87. George Annan, interview, Cardiff, Wales, July 2009.

88. Ellen Robinson (née Annan), interview, Long Island, USA, April 2010.

89. Continuous Certificate of Discharge, no. R 140502, Alfred Annan, TNA, BT 382/34.

90. Information about the ON 005 Convoy obtained from: http://www.warsailors.com/convoys/onconvoys.html.

91. Ellen Robinson, interview, Long Island, USA, April 2010.

92. Continuous Certificate of Discharge, no. R 140502, Alfred Annan, TNA, BT 382/34.

93. See http://ww2eagles.blogspot.com/2011/11/battle-of-convoy-pq-15.html.

94. Continuous Certificate of Discharge, no. R 140502, Alfred Annan, TNA, BT 382/34.

95. Ellen Robinson, interview, Long Island, USA, April 2010. The couple's son George Annan also recalls his mother's complete devastation upon learning of Alfred's death. George Annan, interview, Cardiff, Wales, July 2009.

96. Ellen Robinson, interview, Long Island, USA, April 2010.

97. Sophie Gilliat-Ray, *Muslims in Britain: An Introduction* (Cambridge: Cambridge University Press, 2010), 37.

98. George and Robert Annan, interview, Cardiff, Wales, July 2009.

99. Allison J. Gough, "Messing Up Another Country's Customs: The Exportation of American Racism during World War II," *World History Connected* (October 2007), accessed 17 July 2012, http://www.historycooperative.org/journals/whc/5.1/ghough.html.

100. Robert Annan, interview, Cardiff, Wales, July 2009.

101. Ellen Robinson, interview, Long Island, USA, April 2010.

102. This phrase is borrowed from the title of France Winddance Twine's innovative ethnography of interracial intimacy and white transracial mothering in Leicester. See Twine, *A White Side of Black Britain: Interracial Intimacy and Racial Literacy* (Durham, NC: Duke University Press, 2010).

103. Memorandum by Mr. Maclennan on the position of white wives of natives desirous of entering West Africa, 1936, "White Wives of Natives," TNA, CO 554/105/6.

104. Similarly situated couples include the Ajoses and the Boardmans, who entered Nigeria in 1936 and 1939, respectively, and an unnamed Sierra Leonean man who entered Sierra Leone with his white wife in 1936. See TNA, CO 554/105/6 and CO 554/103/3.

105. On I. B. Asafu-Adjaye's prominence in the lead up to Ghanaian independence, see Jean M. Allman, "The Youngmen and the Porcupine: Class, Nationalism and Asante's Struggle for Self-Determination, 1954–57," *Journal of African History* 31, no. 2 (1990): 271, 277.

106. Janice Noble, e-mail message to author, 14 September 2014.

107. Janice Noble, e-mail message to author, 13 September 2014.

108. Ibid.

109. Ibid.

110. Ibid.

111. Ibid.

112. M. Page Baldwin, "Subject to Empire: Married Women and the British Nationality and Status of Aliens Act," *Journal of British Studies* 40, no. 4 (2001): 537–38. Also see W. E. Beckett, "The Recognition of Polygamous Marriages Under English Law," *Law Quarterly Review* 48 (1932): 341–73.

113. The Phillips case is referenced in TNA, CO 554/103/3.

114. See, for example, TNA, CO 554/105/6 and CO 554/118/2.

115. Bush, *Imperialism, Race, and Resistance*, 86.

116. "Case of Annie Muller," TNA, CO 96/712/3. So infamous was Annie Muller's case that it was cited by the governor of the Gambia as a reason why white women of "immoral character" had to be kept out of the West African colonies. "Repatriation of destitute natives to West Africa, M. B. Egali: Passport facilities for Mrs. Egali," 18 May 1933, TNA, CO 554/93/1, no. 1405/1.

117. Rogers, *Sex and Race*, 148. Also quoted in Bush, *Imperialism, Race, and Resistance*, 86.

CHAPTER 7: "WHITE PERIL"/BLACK POWER

1. Atu, "Scrutineer," *Gold Coast Leader*, 26 July 1919.

2. Ibid.

3. In their deployment of the phrase "tensions of empire," Frederick Cooper and Ann L. Stoler urge scholars to bring metropole and colony into a single analytic frame in order to better account for the full range of tensions that fractured empire, and to foreground struggle in analyses of colonialism rather than privileging questions of control. See Cooper and Stoler, "Introduction Tensions of Empire: Colonial Control and Visions of Rule," *American Ethnologist* 16, no. 4 (1989): 609–21. Also see "Between Metropole and Colony: Rethinking a Research Agenda," in Cooper and Stoler, *Tensions of Empire: Colonial Cultures in a Bourgeois World* (Berkeley: University of California Press, 1997), 1–56.

4. "Immoral Sanitation," *Gold Coast Leader*, 3–10 January 1920. The series consisted of two articles that appeared under the title "Immoral Sanitation" in the 3–10 January and 7–14 February 1920 editions of the *Leader* and a third article that appeared in the Scrutineer column in the 21–28 February 1920 edition of the *Leader*. Each commentary in the series was separately authored. Although subsequent related commentaries throughout 1920 did not directly invoke the "Immoral Sanitation" series, they were preoccupied with the same concerns. These include but are not limited to the following, which all appeared in the *Leader*: "Editorial Notes," 22–29 May 1920; Kobina Sekyi, "The English Colonials Heaviest Handicap," 5–20 June 1920; Atu, "Scrutineer," 5–20 June 1920; "Mixed Pickles," 19 June 1920; "Our Girls," 13 November 1920; Atu, "Scrutineer," 13 November 1920.

5. Atu, "Scrutineer," *Gold Coast Leader*, 21–28 February 1920.

6. See the following articles from the *Gold Coast Leader*: Dr. J. Murray, "An Address by Dr. J. Murray," 13 December 1902; "Moral Sanitation," 20 December 1902; Lux, "Literary Chat," 16 September 1905; Kwamin Koom, "The African Should Not Be Put to Scorn!" 3 October 1912; "General News: Coomasie," 11 January 1913; "The Whiteman's Prestige and the Colour Question," 10 May 1913; "Tarkwa," 13 June 1914; An Akrampah, "Self Knowledge and Patience Are True Markers of Virtue," 20 October 1915; Atu, "Scrutineer," 4–11 December 1915; A Reader, "Mixed Pickles: Moral Sanitation," 24 August 1918.

7. Linking illicit interracial sex to colonial maladministration, however, was not an altogether new phenomenon. During World War I, the *Gold Coast Leader* ran numerous stories that used allegations of German men's promiscuity and coercive sexual practices, among other abuses of power, in neighboring German Togoland to illustrate German misrule. See, for example, Agoha of Quittah, "The Atrocities of the Togo Germans," 3 May 1913; "General News," 24 May 1913; A Reader, "The Germans in Togoland," 17 June 1913; A Native of Aneho, "The Germans in Togoland," 6 September 1913, 27 September 1913, 3 January 1914, 24 January 1914, 7 March 1914, 25 April 1914, and 2 May 1914; Quashie, "Gold Coast and German Togoland," 13 June 1914; A Native of Aneho, "German Policy in Africa," 20 May 1916 and 17–24 June 1916; "Lome," 17 February 1917.

8. Although he glibly dismisses its political significance, Ronald Hyam cites Canton, Kabul, South Africa, Kenya, and Bechuanaland as places where the sexual abuse of native women provoked anticolonial resistance. See Hyam, *Empire and Sexuality: The British Experience* (Manchester: Manchester University Press, 1990), 2–3. For Indonesia, German Southwest Africa, Madagascar, Nigeria, Sierra Leone, and South Africa, respectively, see Elsbeth Locher-Scholten, "Morals, Harmony, and National Identity: 'Companionate Feminism' in Colonial Indonesia in the 1930s," *Journal of Women's History* 14, no. 4 (2003): 47, 49; Benjamin Madley, "Patterns of

Frontier Genocide, 1803–1910: The Aboriginal Tasmanians, the Yuki of California, and the Herero of Namibia," *Journal of Genocide Research* 6, no. 2 (2004): 183–85; Henrik Lundtofte, "'I Believe That the Nation as Such Must Be Annihilated . . .'—The Radicalization of the German Suppression of the Herero Rising in 1904," in *Genocide: Cases, Comparisons and Contemporary Debates*, ed. Steven L. B. Jensen (Copenhagen: Danish Center for Holocaust and Genocide Studies, 2003), 27; Jennifer Cole, *Sex and Salvation: Imagining the Future in Madagascar* (Chicago: University of Chicago Press, 2010), 102; Lisa A. Lindsay, "A Tragic Romance, a Nationalist Symbol: The Case of the Murdered White Lover in Colonial Nigeria," *Journal of Women's History* 17, no. 2 (2005): 132; Richard Phillips, *Sex, Politics and Empire: A Postcolonial Geography* (Manchester: Manchester University Press, 2006), 205–8; Solomon T. Plaatje, "The Mote and the Beam: An Epic on Sex-Relationship 'twixt White and Black in British South Africa," reprinted in *English in Africa* 3, no. 2 (1976): 85–92; Lucy V. Graham, *State of Peril: Race and Rape in South African Literature* (New York: Oxford University Press, 2012): 72–78.

9. Frances Gouda, "The Gendered Rhetoric of Colonialism and Anti-Colonialism in Twentieth-Century Indonesia," *Indonesia*, no. 55 (1993): 7.

10. "The London Aborigines Society and the Empire Resources Development Committee," *Gold Coast Leader*, 3–17 November 1917; and Lux, "Literary Chat," *Gold Coast Leader*, 16 September 1905.

11. By the early twentieth century the sexual exploitation and abuse of native women by European men in Indonesia and German Southwest Africa was already fomenting anticolonial resistance. See Locher-Scholten, "Morals, Harmony, and National Identity"; Madley, "Patterns of Frontier Genocide, 1803–1910."

12. Partha Chatterjee, "Whose Imagined Community?," *Millennium* 20, no. 3 (1991): 521. Also see Chatterjee, "Colonialism, Nationalism, and Colonialized Women: The Contest in India," *American Ethnologist* 16, no. 4 (1989): 622–33. For a fuller articulation, see Chatterjee, *The Nation and Its Fragments: Colonial and Postcolonial Histories* (Princeton, NJ: Princeton University Press, 1993).

13. The two most emblematic cases in point are those of the "female circumcision controversy" in colonial Kenya and its link to the rise of nationalism in Kenya, and the mass unveiling campaigns undertaken by French colonial authorities in Algeria and the veil's later symbolic and strategic importance to the Algerian anticolonial movement. On Kenya, see Susan Pedersen, "National Bodies, Unspeakable Acts: The Sexual Politics of Colonial Policy-Making," *Journal of Modern History* 63, no. 4 (1991): 647–80. For an alternative approach to the "female circumcision controversy" that examines its import in a wider frame than the dichotomy of colonial oppression versus anticolonial resistance allows for, see Lynn M. Thomas, *Politics of the Womb: Women, Reproduction, and the State in Kenya* (Berkeley: University of California Press, 2003). On Algeria, see "Algeria Unveiled," in Frantz Fanon, *A Dying Colonialism* (New York: Grove Press, 1965), 35–63; Neil Macmaster, *Burning the Veil: The Algerian War and the 'Emancipation' of Muslim Women, 1954–62* (Manchester: Manchester University Press, 2012); Rick Fantasia and Eric L. Hirsch, "Culture in Rebellion: The Appropriation and Transformation of the Veil in the Algerian Revolution," in *Social Movements and Culture*, ed. Hank Johnston and Bert Klandermans (Minneapolis: University of Minnesota Press, 1995), 144–59; Jeffrey Louis Decker, "Terrorism (Un)Veiled: Frantz Fanon and the Women of Algiers," *Cultural Critique*, no. 17 (1990–1991): 177–95. Although the most sustained unveiling campaigns occurred during the dubiously named "emancipation" program to liberate

Algerian women from Islamic patriarchy undertaken by the French colonial authorities during the Algerian war, the French attack on the veil, which formed part of their "civilizing mission," dates back to the early twentieth century. On this longer French colonial preoccupation with the veil, see Vivian Bradford, "The Veil and the Visible," *Western Journal of Communication* 63, no. 2 (1999): 115–39.

14. That women surface as a central concern of anticolonial nationalist rhetoric but are marginalized from its articulation in the Gold Coast would remain, with few exceptions, the norm throughout the nationalist period, despite the fact that women from all sectors of Gold Coast society, from market women to the small group of highly educated elite women, were key supporters of and participants in the mass nationalist movement. And as Jean Allman has poignantly demonstrated, even those select few elite women who were central to the articulation of Gold Coast nationalism have been marginalized in subsequent historical accounts of Ghana's nationalist movement. See Allman, "The Disappearing of Hannah Kudjoe: Nationalism, Feminism, and the Tyrannies of History," *Journal of Women's History* 21, no. 3 (2009): 13–35. On the restricted participation of women in anticolonial movements and their marginalization in the subsequent historiography of those movements in Asia, Africa, Latin America, and the Middle East, as well as an attempt to correct these omissions, see Robert J. C. Young, "Women, Gender and Anti-colonialism," in *Postcolonialism: An Historical Introduction* (Oxford: Blackwell, 2001), 360–82. Also see Joyce M. Chadya, "Mother Politics: Anti-Colonial Nationalism and the Woman Question in Africa," *Journal of Women's History* 15, no. 3 (2003): 153–57.

15. On the familiarity of Gold Coast writers with the uses and abuses of "black peril" accusations, see S. Coleridge-Taylor, "In Defence of the Negro," *Gold Coast Leader*, 29 August 1908; "Editorial Notes," *Gold Coast Leader*, 11 August 1917; and "E. D. Morel on Warpath," *Gold Coast Leader*, 21 August 1920. For a genealogy of the terms "black peril" and "white peril," and a critical analysis of their deployment, see Carina E. Ray, "Decrying White Peril: Interracial Sex and the Rise of Anticolonial Nationalism in the Gold Coast," *American Historical Review* 119, no. 1 (2014): 78–110.

16. Ann L. Stoler, *Carnal Knowledge and Imperial Power: Race and the Intimate in Colonial Rule* (Berkeley: University of California Press, 2002), 58.

17. "Immoral Sanitation," *Gold Coast Leader*, 3–10 January 1920.

18. Emily Callaci's work on racial respectability and nationalism in colonial Tanganyika offers an interesting point of comparison, albeit focused on the domain of youth dance rather than interracial sex. Callaci, "Dancehall Politics: Mobility, Sexuality, and Spectacles of Racial Respectability in Late Colonial Tanganyika, 1930s–1961," *Journal of African History* 52, no. 3 (2011): 365–84.

19. "Immoral Sanitation," *Gold Coast Leader*, 3–10 January 1920.

20. W. Asmis, "Law and Policy: Relating to the Natives of the Gold Coast and Nigeria," *Journal of the Royal African Society* 12, no. 45 (1912): 48. Asmis's observation about the paucity of intermarriage was reprinted in the *Gold Coast Leader*. See "A German Study of British West Africa," 17 May 1913. F. W. Migeod, a long-serving colonial officer in the Gold Coast (1900–1919), similarly commented on the waning practice of intermarriage in one of a serialized set of commentaries he published in the *Gold Coast Leader* under the title "Some Aspects of Thinking Black," 30 September 1916.

21. Atu, "Scrutineer," *Gold Coast Leader*, 4–11 December 1915.

22. J. M. Stuart-Young, "Miscegenacious Unions," *Gold Coast Leader*, 29 April 1922. On Stuart-Young's identity as a "literary gent," see Stephanie Newell, "Remembering

J. M. Stuart-Young of Onitsha, Colonial Nigeria: Memoirs, Obituaries and Names," *Africa* 73, no. 4 (2003): 505.

23. One focus of the vast literature on marriage practices in the Gold Coast is the introduction of the colonial Marriage Ordinance of 1884, which provided Gold Coasters with an alternative to marriage by customary law. In keeping with its Christian underpinnings, the 1884 ordinance stipulated that such marriages had to be monogamous. On the advent of the 1884 ordinance, see Shirley Zabel, "The Legislative History of the Gold Coast and Nigerian Marriage Ordinances: I," *Journal of African Law* 13, no. 2 (1969): 64–79; Zabel, "The Legislative History of the Gold Coast and Nigerian Marriage Ordinances: II," *Journal of African Law* 13, no. 3 (1969): 158–78; Zabel, "The Legislative History of the Gold Coast and Lagos Marriage Ordinance: III," *Journal of African Law* 23, no. 1 (1979): 10–36. On the implications of this dual system for women and children, see Takyiwaa Manuh, "Wives, Children, and Intestate Succession in Ghana," in *African Feminism: The Politics of Survival in Subsaharan Africa*, ed. Gwendolyn Mikell (Philadelphia: University of Pennsylvania Press, 1997), 77–95.

24. For a comprehensive yet succinct overview of the social tensions created by these two competing forms of marriage, as well as the pushback against ordinance marriage by members of the educated elite, see Stephanie Newell, *Marita: or the Folly of Love. A Novel by A. Native* (Leiden: Brill, 2002), 1–37. Also see Roger Gocking, *Facing Two Ways: Ghana's Coastal Communities under Colonial Rule* (Lanham, MD: University Press of America, 1999), 88–105. Gold Coasters were by no means alone in their varied reception of the 1884 ordinance. It also went into effect in Lagos, then still governed as part of the Gold Coast colony. The ordinance remained in effect even after Lagos became a separate colony in 1886 and thereafter amalgamated with the Southern Nigeria Protectorate into the Colony and Protectorate of Southern Nigeria in 1906. Kristen Mann has published widely on elite Lagosians' responses to the ordinance and the social changes it engendered. See, for example, Mann, "Marriage Choices among the Educated African Elite in Lagos Colony, 1880–1915," *International Journal of African Historical Studies* 14, no. 2 (1981): 201–28; Mann, "The Dangers of Dependence: Christian Marriage among Elite Women in Lagos Colony, 1880–1915," *Journal of African History* 24, no. 1 (1983): 37–56; Mann, *Marrying Well: Marriage, Status, and Social Change among the Educated Elite in Colonial Lagos* (Cambridge: Cambridge University Press, 1985).

25. "Lome," *Gold Coast Leader*, 17 February 1917. Also see Atu, "Scrutineer," *Gold Coast Leader*, 4–11 December 1915; and "Tarkwa," *Gold Coast Leader*, 26 March 1921.

26. Owen White, *Children of the French Empire*, 20.

27. Hans R. Roth, *Because of Kwadua: Autobiography of Hans Rudolf Roth* (Accra: Afram, 2008); Hans Buser, *In Ghana at Independence: Stories of a Swiss Salesman* (Basel: Basler Afrika Bibliographien, 2010).

28. "Pilot Boys in Takoradi Area," PRAAD, Sekondi, WRG 24/1/323; John Sackey, "A Tale of Takoradi Harbour: A Social History, 1928 to Present," PRAAD, Sekondi, WRG 56/24/1; K. A. Busia, *Report on a Social Survey of Sekondi-Takoradi* (London: Crown Agents for the Colonies, 1950), 108; Emmanuel Akyeampong, "Sexuality and Prostitution among the Akan of the Gold Coast c. 1650–1950," *Past and Present*, no. 156 (1997): 145–46.

29. In the context of the Gold Coast, Stephanie Newell includes "clerks, teachers, middlemen, entrepreneurs and catechists" in the group of newly educated Africans who formed the sub-elite and were "seen to have developed cultural affiliations and

economic aspirations that threatened the system of indirect rule in British West Africa." To this category of sub-elites I would add the figure of the West African maritime laborer, who was widely traveled and often possessed basic literacy skills but lacked the upper-class status and long tradition of education that characterized the educated elite. Newell, "Local Cosmopolitans in Colonial West Africa," *Journal of Commonwealth Literature* 46, no. 1 (2011): 108.

30. For Liverpool, see Chief Constable Everett to Under Secretary of State, 10 June 1919, TNA, HO 45/11017/377969/6. For Cardiff, see Williams to the Under Secretary of State, 13 June 1919, TNA, HO 45/1107/377969/11.

31. For an example of this kind of subtle invocation, see the comments of Mr. D. T. Aleifasakure Toummanah, secretary of the Ethiopian Hall, in the *Liverpool Post*, 11 June 1919, TNA, HO 45/11017/377969/6.

32. *Liverpool Post*, 11 June 1919, TNA, HO 45/11017/377969/6.

33. "The Colour Bar: Significance of Race Riots in English Ports," *Evening Express* (Liverpool), 11 June 1919 (emphasis added).

34. A. W. Neizer and Christian Wilson, "Editorial Notes," *Gold Coast Leader*, 2–9 August 1919.

35. Fola Thomas to the House of Commons via the Colonial Secretaryship, 13 June 1919, TNA, CO 554/44, no. 35408.

36. Although not focused specifically on the domain of interracial sex, a growing body of literature is examining how colonialism more generally impacted ideas about and practices of masculinity in Africa. See, for example, Lisa A. Lindsay and Stephan F. Miescher, eds., *Men and Masculinities in Modern Africa* (Portsmouth, NH: Heinemann, 2003); Stephan F. Miescher, *Making Men in Ghana* (Bloomington: Indiana University Press, 2005).

37. In her work on colonial Gabon, Rachel Jean-Baptiste makes a similar observation about the link between post–World War I political and socioeconomic crisis and increased scrutiny of interracial sexual relationships between European men and African women in public discourse. Jean-Baptiste, "'A Black Girl Should Not Be with a White Man': Sex, Race, and African Women's Social and Legal Status in Colonial Gabon, c. 1900–1946," *Journal of Women's History* 22, no. 2 (2010): 70. Jean-Baptiste takes up this issue in greater detail in *Conjugal Rights: Marriage, Sexuality, and Urban Life in Colonial Libreville, Gabon* (Athens: Ohio University Press, 2014).

38. Paul Gilroy, *The Black Atlantic: Modernity and Double Consciousness* (Cambridge, MA: Harvard University Press, 1993).

39. On this point, see Laura Chrisman, *Postcolonial Contraventions: Cultural Readings of Race, Imperialism, and Transnationalism* (Manchester: Manchester University Press, 2003), 91. For studies that emphasize the dynamic presence of West African writers and activists in the Black Atlantic world and the way in which their nationalist aspirations were nurtured within the context of its transnational spaces, see Marc Matera, *Black London: The Imperial Metropolis and Decolonization in the Twentieth Century* (Oakland: University of California Press, 2015); Jinny K. Prais, "Imperial Travelers: The Formation of West African Urban Culture, Identity, and Citizenship in London and Accra, 1925–1935" (PhD diss., University of Michigan, 2008); Jennifer A. Boittin, *Colonial Metropolis: The Urban Grounds of Anti-Imperialism and Feminism in Interwar Paris* (Lincoln: University of Nebraska Press, 2010); and for a slightly later time period, see Carol Polsgrove, *Ending British Rule in Africa: Writers in a Common Cause* (Manchester: Manchester University Press, 2009).

40. "Treatment of Blacks in England" and "Fatal Feud in Wales," *Gold Coast Nation*, 5 July 1919; "Official Bid to Stop Colour Riots," "The Colour Bar," and "After Loyal War Service," *Gold Coast Nation*, 12 July 1919; "Official Bid to Stop Colour Riots (continued)," *Gold Coast Nation*, 19–26 July 1919; "The Salford Negro Colony," *Gold Coast Leader*, 19 July 1919; "Scrutineer," *Gold Coast Leader*, 26 July 1919; "Editorial Notes" and "A Coloured Empire," *Gold Coast Leader*, 2–9 August 1919; "Justice," *Gold Coast Leader*, 30 August 1919; "A Serious Omission," *Gold Coast Leader*, 6–13 September 1919; "Colour Prejudice," *Gold Coast Leader*, 18 October–8 November 1919.

41. The colony's diverse reading public comprised several groups: highly literate long-standing coastal elites, most of whom were male, but also included a small number of women; newly literate and semiliterate readers—often young male migrants to the colony's cities and towns who had received some formal education; and illiterate men and women who received news from their literate counterparts, thereby expanding the circulation of newspaper content beyond just the literate. For an incisive overview of British West Africa's newspaper readerships, see Stephanie Newell, "Articulating Empire: Newspaper Readerships in Colonial West Africa," *New Formations* 73, no. 1 (2011): 26–42. On the transmission of newspaper content from literate to nonliterate Gold Coasters, see John Wilson, "Gold Coast Information," *African Affairs* 43, no. 172 (1944): 115; also see Stephanie Newell, *West African Literatures: Ways of Reading* (Oxford: Oxford University Press, 2006), 72–73.

42. David Kimble, *A Political History of Ghana: The Rise of Gold Coast Nationalism, 1850–1928* (Oxford: Clarendon, 1963), 98–100.

43. Ibid., 94, 100. In the early 1880s, Africans filled approximately 20 percent of the higher posts in government service, but by 1908 this number had fallen to less than 2 percent. Indeed, Africans held only five senior service appointments out of a total of 274, and four out of the five were of comparatively junior rank. Also see G. I. C. Eluwa, "Background to the Emergence of the National Congress of British West Africa," *African Studies Review* 14, no. 2 (1971): 205–6.

44. For an overview of this process of displacement, see Vivian Bickford-Smith, "The Betrayal of Creole Elites, 1880–1920," in *Black Experience and the Empire*, ed. Philip D. Morgan and Sean Hawkins (Oxford: Oxford University Press, 2004), 194–227.

45. Kwabena O. Akurang-Parry, "'Disrespect and Contempt for Our Natural Rulers': The African Intelligentsia and the Effects of British Indirect Rule on Indigenous Rulers in the Gold Coast c. 1912–1920," *International Journal of Regional and Local History* 2, no. 1 (2006): 44; K. A. B. Jones-Quartey, *A Summary History of the Ghana Press, 1822–1960* (Accra: Ghana Information Services Department, 1974), 19. Jones-Quartey makes the important observation that the "traditional rulers" also made use of the press, mainly through *Leader* rival and information organ of the Aborigines' Rights Protection Society (ARPS), the *Gold Coast Nation*. By the early 1920s both the ARPS and the *Nation* were regarded by the intelligentsia as striking a more conservative tone. Also see Stephanie Newell, "Writing out Imperialism? A Note on Nationalism and Political Identity in the African-Owned Newspapers of Colonial Ghana," in *Exit: Endings and New Beginnings in Literature and Life*, ed. Stefan Helgesson (Amsterdam: Rodopi, 2011), 84.

46. Audrey Sitsofe Gadzekpo, "Women's Engagement with Gold Coast Print Culture from 1857 to 1957" (PhD diss., University of Birmingham, 2001), 74–75.

47. Ibid. Many of these prominent Gold Coast pressmen were multiracial, including James Hutton Brew, "pioneer of West African journalism in the 1880s," who

successively founded and edited several papers (*Gold Coast Times, Western Echo, Gold Coast Echo*); F. V. Nanka Bruce (*Gold Coast Independent*); and J. E. Casely Hayford, the matrilineal descendant of the mid-eighteenth-century Irish slave trader Richard Brew and his wife, Efuah Ansah, the daughter of John Currantee, the Omanhene of Anomabu. For James Hutton Brew and F. V. Nanka Bruce, respectively, see Michel R. Doortmont, ed., *The Pen-Pictures of Modern Africans and African Celebrities by Charles Francis Hutchison: A Collective Biography of Elite Society in the Gold Coast Colony* (Leiden: Brill, 2005), 137, 48. For Casely Hayford, see Margaret A. Priestley, *West African Trade and Coast Society: A Family Study* (London: Oxford University Press, 1969); and Priestley, "Richard Brew: An Eighteenth-Century Trader at Anomabu," *Transactions of the Historical Society of Ghana* 4, no. 1 (1959): 29–46.

48. Newell, "Articulating Empire," 31. The short life span of many of the colony's newspapers is vividly illustrated in K. A. B. Jones-Quartey, "The Gold Coast Press: 1822–1930, and the Anglo-African Press: 1825–1930—The Chronologies," *Institute of African Studies* 4, no. 2 (1968): 30–46.

49. For the 1902 figure, see Gadzekpo, "Women's Engagement with Gold Coast Print Culture from 1857 to 1957," 85. For the 1912 figure, see Newell, "Writing out Imperialism?" 84.

50. Whether Casely Hayford's own multiracial genealogy, originating in the bygone era of intermarriage, played any role in the *Leader*'s criticism of illicit interracial relationships in the early twentieth century is unclear, but it is worth noting the possible link, especially since his tenure as editor began in 1919, just when the politicization of indigenous opposition to interracial sexual relations commenced.

51. Eluwa, "Background to the Emergence of the National Congress of British West Africa," 216. On the link between the *Leader* and the NCBWA, see Kimble, *Political History of Ghana*, 375.

52. Although government regulation of the press began with the Newspaper Registration Law of 1894, it was not until the 1930s that press censorship in the Gold Coast became an acute issue with the introduction of the Sedition Bill of 1934. See Gadzekpo, "Women's Engagement with Gold Coast Print Culture from 1857 to 1957," 78–80; Stanley Shaloff, "Press Controls and Sedition Proceedings in the Gold Coast, 1933–39," *African Affairs* 71, no. 284 (1972): 241–63.

53. For a representative sample of these commentaries appearing in the *Gold Coast Leader*, see A Negro, "Dwin Hwe Kan (Think and Look Ahead)," 17–24 January 1920; "Editorial Notes," 22–29 May 1920; Kobina Sekyi, "The English Colonial's Heaviest Handicap," 5–12 June 1920; "Racial Unity," 24–31 July 1920; "The Native Civil Service and The Native Salaries Committee" and "The African Civil Service," 11 September 1920; "The Police Magistrate and Colour Prejudice," 2–9 October 1920; "The Strangers Within Our Gates," 23 October 1920; "Editorial Notes," 30 October 1920; "Noblesse Oblige" and "The Prostitution of Education to Imperialistic Aims," 20 November 1920; "Recognition and Support of Our Institutions," 11 December 1920; "A Distinction Without a Difference," "A European Lady M.O.H. for Cape Coast," and "Our White Officials and Their Maintenance," 22 January 1921; "West Africa and the British West African Conference," 30 October 1920; "Recognition and Support of Our Institutions," 11 December 1920; V.H., "The West African Problem," 12 February 1921; Kobina Sekyi, "Sir Hugh Clifford and the Congress," 26 February 1921. For a brief overview of the controversy surrounding the implementation of indirect rule, see David Kimble, *Political History of Ghana*, 374–96.

54. Stephanie Newell, "An Introduction to the Writings of J. G. Mullen, an African Clerk, in the *Gold Coast Leader*, 1916–1919," *Africa* 78, no. 3 (2008): 387.

55. Newell, "Writing Out Imperialism?" 84–85.

56. Audrey Gadzekpo, "Gender Discourses and Representational Practices in Gold Coast Newspapers," *Jenda* 1, no. 2 (2001). A similar set of concerns about young girls in colonial Lagos came to occupy the attentions of both elite Lagosian women and the colonial state. See Abosede George, *Making Modern Girls: A History of Girlhood, Labor, and Social Development in Colonial Lagos* (Athens: Ohio University Press, 2014).

57. On what has become known as the period of "gender chaos" in the Gold Coast, see Jean M. Allman, "Rounding up Spinsters: Gender Chaos and Unmarried Women in Colonial Asante," *Journal of African History* 37, no. 2 (1996): 195–214; Penelope A. Roberts, "The State and Regulation of Marriage: Sefwi Wiawso (Ghana), 1900–1940," in *Women, State and Ideology: Studies from Africa and Asia*, ed. Haleh Afshar (Albany: State University of New York Press, 1987), 48–69. For an earlier moment in which young women in the Gold Coast also sought greater control over their sexual and marital lives, see Sandra E. Greene, "In the Mix: Women and Ethnicity among the Anlo-Ewe," in *Ethnicity in Ghana: The Limits of Invention*, ed. Carola Lentz and Paul Nugent (New York: Palgrave Macmillan, 2000), 40. For the wider political context of these developments, see Beverly Grier, "Pawns, Porters, and Petty Traders: Women in the Transition to Cash Crop Agriculture in Colonial Ghana," *Signs* 17, no. 2 (1992): 305.

58. Dorothy L. Hodgson and Sheryl McCurdy, "Wayward Wives, Misfit Mothers, and Disobedient Daughters: 'Wicked' Women and the Reconfiguration of Gender in Africa," *Canadian Journal of African Studies* 30, no. 1 (1996): 3. See more generally the essays in Hodgson and McCurdy, eds., *"Wicked" Women and the Reconfiguration of Gender in Africa* (Portsmouth, NH: Heinemann, 2001). Also see Jean M. Allman, "Of 'Spinsters,' 'Concubines' and 'Wicked Women': Reflections on Gender and Social Change in Colonial Asante," *Gender and History* 3, no. 2 (1991): 176–89.

59. On the history of colonial sanitation programs in the Gold Coast, see Thomas S. Gale, "The Struggle against Disease in the Gold Coast: Early Attempts at Urban Sanitary Reform," *Transactions of the Historical Society of Ghana* 16, no. 2 (1995): 185–203; Stephen Addae, *The Evolution of Modern Medicine in a Developing Country: Ghana 1880–1960* (Durham, NC: Durham Academic Press, 1997), 113–55. For an excellent case study of the resistance to colonial sanitation measures among the Anlo in southwestern Ghana, see Sandra E. Greene, *Sacred Sites and the Colonial Encounter: A History of Meaning and Memory in Ghana* (Bloomington: Indiana University Press, 2002), esp. chap. 3.

60. "Immoral Sanitation," *Gold Coast Leader*, 3–10 January 1920. The author of this commentary was not the first to suggest that Gold Coast women comported themselves in a manner designed to attract the attention of white men. The Frenchman Nicolas Villaut wrote in his mid-seventeenth-century account of the Gold Coast that women there "make it their whole business from morning to night to spruce up themselves, and make themselves acceptable, above all to whites, whom they seem to care much more about than those of their own complexion." Nearly a half century later Willem Bosman similarly noted that the women of the coast donned "a veil of silk or some other fine sort of stuff, while their arms are beautified with rings of gold, silver and ivory . . . so well-skilled in their fashions that they know how to dress themselves up sufficiently tempting to allure several Europeans." Another account, published in the mid-1740s by William Smith, plagiarized Bosman's description of Gold Coast women,

helping to perpetuate the same image. Although hundreds of years apart and written from competing although not dissimilar perspectives, it is striking how sexual licentiousness and interracial desire are so consistently signified in these accounts through descriptions of female bodily comportment that emphasize its intentionality and the display of luxury fabrics, especially silk. For Villaut's account, see Ty M. Reese, "Wives, Brokers, and Laborers: Women at Cape Coast, 1750–1807," in *Women in Port: Gendering Communities, Economies, and Social Networks in Atlantic Port Cities, 1500–1800*, ed. Douglas Catterall and Jodiy Campbell (Leiden: Brill, 2012), 302; for Willem Bosman's account, see Bosman, *A New and Accurate Description of the Coast of Guinea* (London: Knapton, 1705), 121; for William Smith's account, see Smith, *A New Voyage to Guinea* (London: Nourse, 1745), 210. Harvey Feinberg discusses Smith's plagiarism of Bosmen's account in "An Eighteenth-Century Case of Plagiarism: William Smith's *A New Voyage to Guinea*," *History in Africa* 6 (1979): 45–50. I wish to thank Emily Osborn for bringing Smith's description to my attention.

61. Anne McClintock, *Imperial Leather: Race, Gender and Sexuality in the Colonial Conquest* (New York: Routledge, 1995), 365. Therein McClintock draws on Frantz Fanon's theorization of national dress in the context of Algeria and the colonized more generally. For an analysis of how female bodily comportment and dress remain charged sites of national identity-making in postcolonial Africa in ways that are shaped by and respond to colonial discourses, see Ayo Coly, "Un/clothing African Womanhood: Colonial Statements and Postcolonial Discourses of the African Female Body," *Journal of Contemporary African Studies* 33, no.1 (2015): 12-26.

62. "Immoral Sanitation," *Gold Coast Leader*, 3–10 January 1920.

63. The author's denial of the possibility that love or other forms of affect could coexist alongside or even be forged through exchanges of material resources for sex is mirrored in the failure of scholars today, argue Lynn M. Thomas and Jennifer Cole, to "explore how sentiment also inhabited such exchanges." Cole and Thomas, *Love in Africa* (Chicago: University of Chicago Press, 2009), 8.

64. "Immoral Sanitation," *Gold Coast Leader*, 3–10 January 1920.

65. "Our Girls," *Gold Coast Leader*, 13 November 1920.

66. The image of the "gold digger" is one that increasingly saturated local depictions of women who formed relationships with European men in the Gold Coast. See Stephanie Newell, *Literary Culture in Colonial Ghana: "How to Play the Game of Life"* (Bloomington: Indiana University Press, 2002), chap. 6.

67. Emmanuel Akyeampong, "'Wo pe tam won pe ba' ('You like cloth but you don't want children'): Urbanization, Individualism and Gender Relations in Colonial Ghana, c. 1900–39," in *Africa's Urban Past*, ed. David M. Anderson and Richard Rathbone (Oxford: Currey, 1999), 224. This strategy was by no means limited to women in the Gold Coast. For similar examples in Nigeria and Kenya, see Benedict B. B. Naanen, "'Itinerant Gold Mines': Prostitution in the Cross River Basin of Nigeria, 1930–1950," *African Studies Review* 34, no. 2 (1991): 57–79; Luise White, *The Comforts of Home: Prostitution in Colonial Nairobi* (Chicago: University of Chicago Press, 1990).

68. Akyeampong, "Wo pe tam won pe ba," 226.

69. On this practice in Nigeria, see Lindsay, "A Tragic Romance, a Nationalist Symbol," 125. For Gabon, see Jeremy Rich, "'Une Babylone Noire': Interracial Unions in Colonial Libreville, c. 1860–1914," *French Colonial History* 4, no. 1 (2003): 151.

70. "Immoral Sanitation," *Gold Coast Leader*, 7–14 February 1920.

71. Ibid.

72. Atu's fiery remarks were prompted by the publication of "Memoir on the State of Education in the Gold Coast," by G. W. Morrison, the archdeacon of the Anglican Church in Kumasi, in which he claimed that Africans possessed the traits of sexual immorality, dishonesty, conceit, and selfishness. Atu, "Scrutineer," *Gold Coast Leader*, 5–12 June 1920.

73. Atu, "Scrutineer," *Gold Coast Leader*, 21–28 February 1920.

74. Joane Nagel, *Race, Ethnicity, and Sexuality: Intimate Intersections, Forbidden Frontiers* (New York: Oxford University Press, 2003), 146.

75. On the rise of Fanti nationalism, also known as the "Gone Fantee" movement, see Samuel Tenkorang, "The Founding of Mfantsipim, 1905–1908," *Transactions of the Historical Society of Ghana* 15, no. 2 (1974): 165–75. On the "local peculiarities" of early nationalism in the Gold Coast, see Kofi K. Saah and Kofi Baku, "'Do Not Rob Us of Ourselves': Language and Nationalism in Colonial Ghana," in *Identity Meets Nationality: Voices from the Humanities*, ed. Helen Lauer, Nana Aba Appiah Amfo, and Jemima Asabea Anderson (Accra: Sub-Saharan Publishers, 2011), 74–99. Stephanie Newell observes that "the word 'nation' is often used in newspaper reports to describe particular ethno-linguistic groups, especially the Fante," but the consistency with which white peril commentaries lacked any referent to particular ethnic groups suggests that they truly were reaching beyond the narrower confines of ethnicity. See Newell, "Entering the Territory of Elites: Literary Activity in Colonial Ghana," in *Africa's Hidden Histories: Everyday Literacy and Making the Self*, ed. Karin Barber (Bloomington: Indiana University Press, 2006), 233.

76. Northcote to Cunliffe-Lister, 22 September 1934, PRAAD, ADM 12/3/61, enc. 1.

77. On the reputation of the Easmon family first in Sierra Leone and later in the Gold Coast, see Adell Patton, *Physicians, Colonialism Racism, and Diaspora in West Africa* (Gainesville: University of Florida Press, 1996).

78. Harry Philip Yates, "Affidavit of Harry Philip Yates," High Court of Ghana, Western Region, Sekondi, 25 September 1979, courtesy of Reggie Yates (Jr.).

79. Frank Vardon was identified as the registrar of Sekondi's divisional court in numerous articles that appeared in the *Gold Coast Leader*, including the 6 February 1915 edition, and as a patron of the Optimism Club in "The Optimism Club of Seccondee," in the 17 August 1918 edition.

80. My knowledge of the relationship between Dorothy Lloyd and George Yates comes from a range of sources, including a sworn affidavit, newspaper reports, passenger lists, and oral histories that were conducted with members of her extended family by researchers for the BBC's genealogy program, *Who Do You Think You Are?* This information was shared with me as part of my participation in an episode of the program that traced the genealogy of Dorothy's great-grandson Reggie Yates, not to be confused with his father, also known as Reggie Yates, whose immigration battle I discuss in the conclusion.

81. Kobina Sekyi, "The English Colonial's Heaviest Handicap," *Gold Coast Leader*, 5–12 June 1920.

82. Scholars from across the disciplines have made this observation. See, for example, Robert J. C. Young, *Colonial Desire: Hybridity in Theory, Culture, and Race* (London: Routledge, 1995); bell hooks, "Eating the Other: Desire and Resistance," in *Media and Cultural Studies: Keyworks*, ed. Meenakshi G. Durham and Douglas M. Kellner (Malden, MA: Blackwell, 2000), 366–80; Winthrop D. Jordan, *White over Black: American Attitudes toward the Negro, 1550–1812* (Chapel Hill: University of

North Carolina Press, 1968). Ann Stoler has probed this connection in a number of her publications, but see especially Stoler, *Carnal Knowledge and Imperial Power*, 41–78.

83. Kobina Sekyi, "The English Colonial's Heaviest Handicap," *Gold Coast Leader*, 5–12 June 1920.

84. Kobina Sekyi, "Archdeacon Morrison's 'Moral Causes,'" *Gold Coast Leader*, 22–29 May 1920.

85. Kobina Sekyi, "Sir Hugh Clifford and the Congress," *Gold Coast Leader*, 26 February 1921.

86. For new research on the political and social consequences of World War I in Europe and the colonies, see Santanu Das, ed., *Race, Empire and First World War Writing* (Cambridge: Cambridge University Press, 2011).

87. A Reader, "Mixed Pickles: Colour Prejudice," *Gold Coast Leader*, 18 October–8 November 1919 (emphasis added). The significance of this quote is made fully appreciable in Marilyn Lake and Henry Reynolds, *Drawing the Global Colour Line: White Men's Countries and the International Challenge of Racial Equality* (Cambridge: Cambridge University Press, 2008), a global history of the strategies of exclusion enacted to preserve the racial purity of "white men's countries" in the face of the struggle for racial equality in the early twentieth century.

88. Elite women were writing letters and other forms of commentary in the Gold Coast press as early as the late nineteenth century, but the common contemporary practice of writing anonymously makes identifying them difficult. Audrey Gadzekpo captures how anonymity acted as a double-edged sword for female writers of the time: "Anonymity may have allowed women to stretch the boundaries of the possible, but it has also exacted a great historical price by concealing the identities of many noteworthy women writers and perpetuating their invisibility in the Gold Coast press." Gadzekpo, "The Hidden History of Women in Ghanaian Print Culture," in *African Gender Studies: A Reader*, ed. Oyeronke Oyewumi (New York: Palgrave Macmillan, 2005), 296. Stephanie Newell has produced a brilliant study of anonymous and pseudonymous writing practices in British West Africa's indigenous newspapers that further explores the gendered aspects of these practices. See Newell, *The Power to Name: A History of Anonymity in Colonial West Africa* (Athens: Ohio University Press, 2013), 122–169. For more on the publication of letters to the editor from elite Gold Coast women in the late nineteenth-century Gold Coast press, see Kwabena O. Akurang-Parry, "Aspects of Elite Women's Activism in the Gold Coast, 1874–1890," *International Journal of African Historical Studies* 37, no. 3 (2004): 477–78.

89. See Gadzekpo, "Gender Discourses and Representational Practices in Gold Coast Newspapers"; and Prais, "Imperial Travelers," 237–325.

90. Dove also wrote as Dama Dumas in the *African Morning Post* (1935–1940); Ebun Alakija in the Nigerian *Daily Times* (1937); and Akosuah Dzatsui in the *Accra Evening News* (1950s and 1960s). Stephanie Newell and Audrey Gadzekpo, eds., *Mabel Dove: Selected Writings of a Pioneer West African Feminist* (Nottingham: Trent Editions, 2004), xii.

91. In the context of the Gold Coast, the phrase "frock girls" or "frock women" referred to African women who donned European dress and were enamored by the cosmopolitan lifestyle and material culture of the colony's urban centers.

92. Newell, *Literary Culture in Colonial Ghana*, 126.

93. Newell and Gadzekpo, *Mabel Dove*, 92.

94. Ibid.

95. Joseph Renner Maxwell, *The Negro Question or Hints for the Physical Improvement of the Negro Race, with Special Reference to West Africa* (London: Fisher Unwin, 1891), 98.

CHAPTER 8: WASU, WHITE WOMEN, AND AFRICAN INDEPENDENCE

1. The original version of this account was given by Joe Appiah in his autobiography, but has been subsequently recounted in numerous publications. See Appiah, *Joe Appiah: The Autobiography of an African Patriot* (New York: Praeger, 1990), 164; Marika Sherwood, "Kwame Nkrumah: The London Years, 1945–47," in *Africans in Britain*, ed. David Killingray (London: Cass, 1994), 181–82; Ahmad Rahman, *The Regime Change of Kwame Nkrumah: Epic Heroism in Africa and the Diaspora* (New York: Palgrave Macmillan, 2007), 101; Marc Matera, *Black London: The Imperial Metropolis and Decolonization in the Twentieth Century* (Oakland: University of California Press, 2015), 232.

2. Appiah, *Joe Appiah*, 164; Sherwood, "Kwame Nkrumah," 182.

3. Akintola J. G. Wyse, *H. C. Bankole-Bright and Politics in Colonial Sierra Leone, 1919–1958* (Cambridge: Cambridge University Press, 1990), 3, 103–4.

4. For more on the history of WASU, see Hakim Adi, *West Africans in Britain (1900–1960): Nationalism, Pan-Africanism, and Communism* (London: Lawrence and Wishart, 1998); and Matera, *Black London*, esp. chapter 1.

5. Matera, *Black London*, 100.

6. Marc Matera, "Black Internationalism and African and Caribbean Intellectuals in London, 1919–1950" (PhD diss., Rutgers University, 2008), 166.

7. Barbara Bush, "Blacks in Britain: The 1930s," *History Today* 31, no. 9 (1981): 47. Bush points out that because it was fashionable among the avant-garde for white women to take black lovers, women whose sociopolitical commitments brought them into contact with black activists were eager to distinguish themselves and to defend the integrity of their interracial friendships. While it is beyond the scope of this chapter to discuss the French context, there are striking parallels. See Jennifer A. Boittin, "Black in France: The Language and Politics of Race in the Late Third Republic," *French Politics, Culture and Society* 27, no. 2 (2009): 23–46; Boittin, *Colonial Metropolis: The Urban Grounds of Anti-Imperialism and Feminism in Interwar Paris* (Lincoln: University of Nebraska Press, 2010). Also see Tyler Stovall, "Love, Labor, and Race: Colonial Men and White Women in France during the Great War," in *French Civilization and Its Discontents: Nationalism, Colonialism, Race*, ed. Tyler Stovall and Georges Van Den Abbeele (Lanham, MD: Lexington Books, 2003), 297–321; Stovall, "Murder in Montmartre: Race, Sex, and Crime in Jazz Age Paris," in *Minor Transnationalism*, ed. Françoise Lionnet and Shu-mei Shih (Durham, NC: Duke University Press, 2005), 135–54.

8. St. Clair Drake, as cited in Matera, *Black London*, 228.

9. Matera, *Black London*, 236. Matera provides a comprehensive and compelling study of black London during the interwar years that includes a detailed exploration of the politics surrounding interracial sexual relationships between black men, largely Afro-Caribbean and African, and white women in the chapter titled, "Black Masculinities and Interracial Sex and the Heart of Empire."

10. Susan Miller's remarks are found in her afterword to Albert Memmi's *The Colonizer and the Colonized* (Boston, MA: Beacon, 1991), 164.

11. Matera, *Black London*, 227.

12. Matera, "Black Internationalism," 254–55, 261–62.

13. Ibid., 270.

14. Appiah, *Joe Appiah*, 154–55.

15. Ibid., 155.

16. Kwame Nkrumah, *Ghana: The Autobiography of Kwame Nkrumah* (New York: Nelson, 1957), 56. Even after independence, Nkrumah continued to entrust many of his most important tasks to white women. Erica Powell served as Nkrumah's private secretary from 1955 until 1966 when he was removed from power. She became one of Nkrumah's closest friends and confidants during that time, which she recounts in her memoire *Private Secretary (Female)/Gold Coast* (London: Hurst, 1984). Likewise, Nkrumah appointed his longtime research assistant, June Milne, to serve as his literary executor, endowing her with incredible power to shape his legacy.

17. British authorities used the same strategy to paint Jomo Kenyatta as a hypocrite and to call into question his anticolonial credentials as the Mau Mau liberation struggle broke out in 1952. Indeed, just a month before the Kenyan colonial government declared a state of emergency and arrested Kenyatta, reporters from Britain's *Daily Express* coerced Edna, the English wife he had left behind in Britain, into being photographed with their son Peter for, as Edna herself put it, "a big feature on the man, now so anti-European, who enjoyed the best of England for 16 yrs. & even took to himself a white wife & had a son." Quoted in Matera, "Black Internationalism and African and Caribbean Intellectuals in London, 1919–1950," 248.

18. Philip Holden, "Imagined Individuals: National Autobiography and Postcolonial Self-Fashioning," Asia Research Institute Working Paper Series, no. 13 (Singapore: National University of Singapore, 2003), 1–22. The letter itself can be found in TNA, CO 964/24, Watson Commission—Gold Coast Commission of Enquiry, Exhibits, vol. 1, exhibit 46.

19. Sir Charles Arden-Clarke to Sir Thomas Lloyd, 2 January 1952, TNA, CO 967/175, "Possibility of Dr. Nkrumah marrying an Englishwoman."

20. Ibid.

21. George Shepperson and St. Clare Drake, "The Fifth Pan-African Conference, 1945 and the All African Peoples Congress, 1958," *Contributions in Black Studies* 8, Article 5 (1986): 39.

22. Marika Sherwood, "Kwame Nkrumah: The London Years, 1945–47," in *Africans in Britain*, ed. David Killingray (London: Cass, 1994), 164–67; Ama Biney, *The Political and Social Thought of Kwame Nkrumah* (New York: Palgrave Macmillan, 2011), 29.

23. Erna Kankam-Boadu, interview, Accra, Ghana, October 2012.

24. Jordanna Bailkin, *The Afterlife of Empire* (Berkeley: University of California Press, 2012), 80.

25. Paul B. Rich, *Race and Empire in British Politics* (Cambridge: Cambridge University Press, 1990), 178.

26. Appiah, *Joe Appiah*, 192–93.

27. Ibid., 196.

28. Ibid., 213, 221.

29. Richard Pendelbury, "The Despot and His Sunburn Mistress," *Daily Mail* (London), 20 December 1997.

30. "London Journalist Weds Jamaican," *Jet* 4, no. 17 (3 September 1953): 15; Kwame Appiah, "Kwame Anthony Appiah on Honour," The Telegraph, 15 October 2010, http://www.telegraph.co.uk/culture/books/bookreviews/8063931/Kwame-Anthony-Appiah-on-Honour.html.

31. Predictably, however, in South Africa and Rhodesia there was some outcry over the Appiahs' nuptials, with South Africa's minister of justice, Charles Swart, calling it "disgusting" and others warning that it would threaten the stability of British rule in Africa. "Peggy Appiah," http://www.telegraph.co.uk/news/uknews/1511303/Peggy-Appiah.html.

32. Erna Kankam-Boadu, interview, Accra, Ghana, October 2012. Also see Vernon D. Wickizer, *Coffee, Tea and Cocoa: An Economic and Political Analysis* (Stanford, CA: Stanford University Press, 1951), 356.

33. Erna Kankam-Boadu, interview, Accra, Ghana, October 2012. While it is difficult to quantify how many interracial couples settled in the Gold Coast in the years immediately preceding indpendence, as well as those who came in the years after it, in my conversations with Erna Kankam-Boadu she made it clear that she and Frederick were one of many that settled in Ghana during the independence era. Although her social circle came to include some of these couples, it was primarily made up of Ghanaians. For readers interested in gleaning a deeper sense of what life was like for interracial couples during and after the era of independence, see the self-published memoire by Barbara Baddoo, *To Ghana With Love: The Story of My Life*, 3rd ed. (Lulu.com, 2012). Baddoo's memoire of her life as the English wife of a Ghanaian doctor is peppered with references to other interracial couples who settled in Ghana during the mid-1950s and early 1960s.

34. Gamal Nkrumah, "Fathia Nkrumah: Farewell to All That," *Al-Ahram Weekly*, 14–20 September 2000, http://weekly.ahram.org.eg/2000/499/profile.htm.

35. Carina Ray, "The Marriage That Sent the West into a Panic," *New African* 448 (February 2006): 26–27.

36. Nkrumah, "Fathia Nkrumah."

37. "Welfare of Women in Ghana," Appendix, 1963, PRAAD, ADM 13/2/101. My thanks to Jeremy Pool for bringing this document to my attention.

38. Ibid.

CONCLUSION: SEXUALITY'S STAYING POWER

1. Stephen Cook, "'Legitimacy' Dispute Halts Deportation," *Guardian*, 7 April 1982.

2. "Patrial—But Not If You're Black," *Caribbean Times*, 1982; Duncan Campbell, "Yates and the 'Custom of the Time,'" *City Limits*, 1982.

3. "Reggie Yates and Felicia Must Stay," *Young Socialist*, 1982.

4. Harry Philip Yates, "Affidavit of Harry Philip Yates," High Court of Ghana, Western Region, Sekondi, 25 September 1979.

5. Campbell, "Yates and the 'Custom of the Time.'"

6. Ibid.

7. Stephen Cook, "'Legitimacy' Dispute Halts Deportation," *Guardian*, 7 April 1982.

8. "Reggie Yates Can Stay," *Caribbean Times*.

9. Campbell, "Yates and the 'Custom of the Time.'"

10. Jordanna Bailkin, *The Afterlife of Empire* (Berkeley: University of California Press, 2012), 1.

11. Ian R. G. Spencer, *British Immigration Policy Since 1939: The Making of Multi-Racial Britain* (London: Routledge, 1997), 22.

12. David Dixon, "Thatcher's People: The British Nationality Act 1981," *Journal of Law and Society* 10, no. 2 (1983): 163.

13. Ibid., 162–63.

14. Ibid., 162.

15. See Emmanuelle Saada, *Empire's Children: Race, Filiation, and Citizenship in the French Colonies*, trans. Arthur Goldhammer (Chicago: University of Chicago Press, 2012), 121–45.

16. Home Office, *Confirmation of British Nationality Status* (United Kingdom, June 2014), 5.

17. "Changed Patriality Rule for Immigrants," *Glasgow Herald*, 17 June 1971.

18. Ghana Constitution of 1992, chap. 3, art. VII, § 1. While the 1979 Constitution had a provision allowing Ghanaian women to confer citizenship on their non-Ghanaian husbands, it was far more restrictive than the provision for Ghanaian men, which had the net effect of reinforcing rather than ameliorating the law's gender based discrimination. See Ghana Constitution of 1979, chap. 5, art. XV.

19. Ghana Constitution of 1979, chap. 5, art. XII.

20. Ibid., chap. 3, art. VI, §2.

21. Micah Bump, "Ghana: Searching for Opportunities at Home and Abroad," Migration Policy Institute, 1 March 2006, accessed 2 June 2014, http://www.migrationpolicy.org/article/ghana-searching-opportunities-home-and-abroad.

22. Ghana Immigration Act, 2000 (Act 573), part 2, art. XVI and art. XVIII(1).

23. "Foreign Spouses of Ghanaian Nationals Want Citizenship," 29 August 2002, accessed 10 June 2013, http://mobile.ghanaweb.com/wap/article.php?ID=26903.

24. Ibid.

25. Ghana Citizenship Act, 2000 (Act 591), part 3, art. XVI(1).

26. Ibid., art. XVI(2).

27. *Free Press*, as cited in Rosemary Chinery, "The Dilemma of Rawlings Revolution," 8 December 2000, accessed 5 April 2014, http://www.nyu.edu/classes/keefer/ww1/chin.html. On the antagonistic relationship between the *Free Press* and Rawlings, see Jennifer Hasty, *The Press and Political Culture in Ghana* (Bloomington: Indiana University Press, 2005), 113.

28. Betty de Hart, "Children's Citizenship, Motherhood and the Nation State," in *Gender, Migration, and the Public Sphere, 1850–2005*, ed. Marlou Schrover and Eileen Janes Yeo (New York: Routledge, 2010), 109.

29. "How To with Immigration," accessed 3 April 2014, http://www.accraexpat.com/help/howto.php?read=11410.

30. Jenna Burrell, *Invisible Users: Youth in the Internet Cafés of Urban Ghana* (Cambridge, MA: MIT Press, 2012), 5. Jennifer Cole richly documents a similar phenomenon among Malagasy women who use the Internet to facilitate their search for European husbands in *Sex and Salvation: Imagining the Future in Madagascar* (Chicago: University of Chicago Press, 2010).

31. Mildred Loving, "Loving for All," http://www.freedomtomarry.org/page/-/files/pdfs/mildred_loving-statement.pdf.

32. Cole and Thomas, *Love in Africa*, 5.

33. Ann L. Stoler, *Carnal Knowledge and Imperial Power: Race and the Intimate in Colonial Rule* (Berkeley: University of California Press, 2002), 2.

34. Ibid., 66–68.

35. Adejoke Tugbiyele, "Sexual Identity and 'Nigerian Culture,'" thefeministwire.com, http://thefeministwire.com/2014/02/nigerian-culture/; Chika Oduah, "Gay Nigerians Targeted as 'Un-African,'" aljazeera.com, http://www.aljazeera.com/indepth/features/2014/01/gay-nigerians-targeted-as-un-african-2014125143518184415.html.

36. Alex Duval Smith, "Ghana Official Calls for Effort to 'Round Up' Suspected Gays," 22 July 2011, http://www.independent.co.uk/news/world/africa/ghana-official-calls-for-effort-to-round-up-suspected-gays-2318507.html.

37. Jean M. Allman, "Rounding Up Spinsters: Gender Chaos and Unmarried Women in Colonial Asante," *Journal of African History* 37, no. 2 (1996): 195–214.

38. Adam Nossiter, "Nigeria Tries to 'Sanitize' Itself of Gays," *New York Times*, 8 February 2014, http://www.nytimes.com/2014/02/09/world/africa/nigeria-uses-law-and-whip-to-sanitize-gays.html?_r=0.

39. Katy Steinmetz, "Kansas Bill Allowing Refusal of Service to Gay Couples Moves Forward," *Time*, 11 February 2014, time.com, http://nation.time.com/2014/02/11/kansas-bill-allowing-refusal-of-service-to-gay-couples-moves-forward/; Ray Sanchez and Miguel Marquez, "Arizona Lawmakers Pass Controversial Anti-Gay Bill," CNN.com, http://www.cnn.com/2014/02/21/us/arizona-anti-gay-bill/.

40. Marc Epprecht, "The Making of 'African Sexuality': Early Sources, Current Debates," *History Compass* 8, no. 8 (2010): 768.

41. For an insightful analysis of this kind of response among African Americans, see Michele Mitchell, *Righteous Propagation: African Americans and the Politics of Racial Destiny after Reconstruction* (Chapel Hill: University of North Carolina Press, 2004).

42. Epprecht, "Making of 'African Sexuality,'" 769, 775. Epprecht's theorization of "patriotic heterosexuality" in the African context, owes much to the work of Jacqui Alexander, who writes skillfully about allied concerns in the Caribbean. See especially, M. Jacqui Alexander, "Not Just (Any)Body Can Be a Citizen: The Politics of Law, Sexuality and Postcoloniality in Trinidad and Tobago and the Bahamas," *Feminist Review* 48, no. 1 (1994): 5–23; and Alexander, "Redrafting Morality: The Postcolonial State and the Sexual Offences Bill of Trinidad and Tobago," in *Third World Women and the Politics of Feminism*, ed. Chandra Talpade Mohanty, Ann Russo, and Lourdes Torres (Bloomington: Indian University Press, 1991), 133–52.

43. Michel Foucault, *The History of Sexuality* (New York: Vintage Books, 1990), 103.

44. Recent pathbreaking studies by Crystal Feimster and Danielle McGuire have convincingly demonstrated that the pervasive sexual abuse of black women by white men was a long-standing central concern of black political activists in the United States. Their work, along with an earlier body of innovative scholarship, has expanded our understanding of racialized sexual violence beyond its foundational role in sustaining white supremacy by documenting how these abuses influenced the range of movements, from abolition to black power, that challenged the successive systems of racial oppression that structured American society. Crystal N. Feimster, *Southern Horrors: Women and the Politics of Rape and Lynching* (Cambridge, MA: Harvard University Press, 2009); Danielle L. McGuire, *At the Dark End of the Street: Black Women, Rape, and Resistance—a New History of the Civil Rights Movement from Rosa*

Parks to the Rise of Black Power (New York: Knopf, 2010). For a sample of important works that probe the intersection between race, gender, and sexuality in shaping the lives and emancipatory strategies of black communities, especially among women, see Gail Bederman, "'Civilization,' the Decline of Middle-Class Manliness, and Ida B. Wells's Antilynching Campaign (1892–94)," *Radical History Review* 52 (1992): 5–30; Elsa Barkley Brown, "Negotiating and Transforming the Public Sphere: African American Political Life in the Transition from Slavery to Freedom," *Public Culture* 7, no. 1 (1994): 107–46; Glenda E. Gilmore, *Gender and Jim Crow: Women and the Politics of White Supremacy in North Carolina, 1896–1920* (Chapel Hill: University of North Carolina Press, 1996); Evelyn Brooks Higginbotham, *Righteous Discontent: The Women's Movement in the Black Baptist Church, 1880–1920* (Cambridge, MA: Harvard University Press, 1993); Darlene Clark Hine, *Hine Sight: Black Women and the Re-Construction of American History* (Brooklyn, NY: Carlson, 1994); Tera W. Hunter, *To 'Joy My Freedom: Southern Black Women's Lives and Labors after the Civil War* (Cambridge, MA: Harvard University Press, 1997); Mitchell, *Righteous Propagation*; Deborah G. White, *Ar'n't I a Woman?: Female Slaves in the Plantation South* (New York: Norton, 1985); White, *Too Heavy a Load: Black Women in Defense of Themselves, 1894–1994* (New York: Norton, 1999). On the role of interracial rape and the sexual exploitation of enslaved women in abolitionists' campaigns against slavery, see Harriet A. Jacobs, *Incidents in the Life of a Slave Girl: Written by Herself* (Cambridge, MA: Harvard University Press, 2009); Kristin Hoganson, "Garrisonian Abolitionists and the Rhetoric of Gender, 1850–1860," *American Quarterly* 45, no. 4 (1993): 558–95.

45. Frantz Fanon, *Black Skin, White Masks* (New York: Grove Press, 1967), 42.

Bibliography

ARCHIVES CONSULTED

Ghana:

Public Records and Archives Administration Department (PRAAD), Accra
PRAAD, Cape Coast
PRAAD, Sekondi
Balme Memorial Library, University of Ghana, Legon

United Kingdom:

The National Archives, Kew
British Library, London
Colindale Newspaper Library, London
Rhodes House Library, Oxford
Hull City Archives, Hull

NEWSPAPERS

Caribbean Times
City Limits
Daily Mail
Liverpool Echo
Liverpool Post
Sunday Express

Glasgow Herald
Gold Coast Leader
Gold Coast Nation
Guardian
Western Mail
Young Socialist

BOOKS AND ARTICLES

Addae, Stephen. *The Evolution of Modern Medicine in a Developing Country: Ghana 1880–1960.* Durham, NC: Durham Academic Press, 1997.
Adi, Hakim. *West Africans in Britain (1900–1960): Nationalism, Pan-Africanism, and Communism.* London: Lawrence and Wishart, 1998.
Akurang-Parry, Kwabena O. "Aspects of Elite Women's Activism in the Gold Coast, 1874–1890." *International Journal of African Historical Studies* 37, no. 3 (2004): 463–82.
———. "'Disrespect and Contempt for Our Natural Rulers': The African Intelligentsia and the Effects of British Indirect Rule on Indigenous Rulers in the Gold Coast c. 1912–1920." *International Journal of Regional and Local History* 2, no. 1 (2006): 43–65.
Akyeampong, Emmanuel. "Sexuality and Prostitution among the Akan of the Gold Coast c. 1650–1950." *Past and Present*, no. 156 (1997): 144–73.
———. "'Wo pe tam won pe ba' ('You like cloth but you don't want children'): Urbanization, Individualism and Gender Relations in Colonial Ghana, c. 1900–39." In *Africa's Urban Past*, edited by David M. Anderson and Richard Rathbone, 222–34. Oxford: Currey, 1999.
Akyeampong, Emmanuel, and Hippolyte Fofack. "The Contribution of African Women to Economic Growth and Development: Historical Perspectives and Policy Implications, Part I, the Pre-Colonial and Colonial Periods." World Bank. https://openknowledge.worldbank.org/handle/10986/6056.
Aldrich, Robert. *Colonialism and Homosexuality.* London: Routledge, 2003.
Alexander, M. Jacqui. "Not Just (Any)Body Can Be a Citizen: The Politics of Law, Sexuality and Postcoloniality in Trinidad and Tobago and the Bahamas." *Feminist Review* 48 (1994): 5–23.
———. "Redrafting Morality: The Postcolonial State and the Sexual Offences Bill of Trinidad and Tobago." In *Third World Women and the Politics of Feminism*, edited by Chandra Talpade Mohanty, Ann Russo, and Lourdes Torres, 133–52. Bloomington: Indian University Press, 1991.
Allman, Jean M. "Adultery and the State in Asante: Reflections on Gender, Class, and Power from 1800 to 1950." In *The Cloth of Many Colored Silks: Papers on History and Society, Ghanaian and Islamic, in Honor of Ivor Wilks*, edited by John Hunwick and Nancy Lawler, 27–65. Evanston, IL: Northwestern Univeristy Press, 1996.
———. "The Disappearing of Hannah Kudjoe: Nationalism, Feminism, and the Tyrannies of History." *Journal of Women's History* 21, no. 3 (2009): 13–35.
———. "Fathering, Mothering and Making Sense of 'Ntamoba': Reflections on the Economy of Child-Rearing in Colonial Asante." *Africa* 67, no. 2 (1997): 296–321.
———. "Of 'Spinsters,' 'Concubines' and 'Wicked Women': Reflections on Gender and Social Change in Colonial Asante." *Gender and History* 3, no. 2 (1991): 176–89.

———. "Rounding up Spinsters: Gender Chaos and Unmarried Women in Colonial Asante." *Journal of African History* 37, no. 2 (1996): 195–214.

———. "The Youngmen and the Porcupine: Class, Nationalism and Asante's Struggle for Self-Determination, 1954–57." *Journal of African History* 31, no. 2 (1990): 263–79.

Altena, Marga. *A True History Full of Romance: Mixed Marriages and Ethnic Identity in Dutch Art, News Media, and Popular Culture (1883–1955)*. Amsterdam: Amsterdam University Press, 2012.

Amnesty International. *Making Love a Crime: Criminalization of Same-Sex Conduct in Sub-Saharan Africa*. London: Amnesty International, 2013.

Appiah, Joseph. *Joe Appiah: The Autobiography of an African Patriot*. New York: Praeger, 1990.

Appiah, Kwame Anthony. "Kwame Anthony Appiah on Honour." The Telegraph, 15 October 2010. http://www.telegraph.co.uk/culture/books/bookreviews/8063931/Kwame-Anthony-Appiah-on-Honour.html.

Apter, David E. "Some Economic Factors in the Political Development of the Gold Coast." *Journal of Economic History* 14, no. 4 (1954): 409–27.

Arnfred, Signe, ed. *Re-Thinking Sexualities in Africa*. Uppsala: Nordiska Afrikainstitutet, 2004.

Arondekar, Anjali R. *For the Record: On Sexuality and the Colonial Archive in India*. Durham, NC: Duke University Press, 2009.

Asmis, W. "Law and Policy: Relating to the Natives of the Gold Coast and Nigeria." *Journal of the Royal African Society* 12, no. 45 (1912): 17–51.

Augustine-Adams, Kif. "'She Consents Implicitly': Women's Citizenship, Marriage, and Liberal Political Theory in Late-Nineteenth and Early-Twentieth-Century Argentina." *Journal of Women's History* 13, no. 4 (2002): 8–30.

Bacchus, M. K. *Education for Economic, Social and Political Development in the British Caribbean Colonies from 1896 to 1945*. London, ON: Althouse Press, 2005.

Baddoo, Barbara. *To Ghana With Love: The Story of My Life*. 3rd ed. Lulu.com, 2012.

Bailkin, Jordanna. *The Afterlife of Empire*. Berkeley: University of California Press, 2012.

Baldwin, M. Page. "Subject to Empire: Married Women and the British Nationality and Status of Aliens Act." *Journal of British Studies* 40, no. 4 (2001): 522–56.

Ballhatchet, Kenneth. *Race, Sex and Class under the Raj: Imperial Attitudes and Policies and Their Critics, 1793–1905*. New York: St. Martin's, 1980.

Ballong-Wen-Mewuda, J. Bato'ora. "Sao Jorge Da Mina (Elmina) et son contexte socio-historique pendant l'occupation portugaise (1482–1637)." PhD diss., Universite de Paris, 1984.

Barrera, Giulia. "Colonial Affairs: Italian Men, Eritrean Women, and the Construction of Racial Hierarchies in Colonial Eritrea (1885–1941)." PhD diss., Northwestern University, 2002.

———. "Dangerous Liaisons: Colonial Concubinage in Eritrea, 1890–1941." Northwestern University Program of African Studies Working Papers 1, 1996.

———. "Patrilinearity, Race, and Identity: The Upbringing of Italo-Eritreans during Italian Colonialism." In *Italian Colonialism*, edited by Ruth Ben-Ghiat and Mia Fuller, 97–108. New York: Palgrave Macmillan, 2005.

Beckett, W. E. "The Recognition of Polygamous Marriages Under English Law." *Law Quarterly Review* 48 (1932): 341–73.

Bederman, Gail. "'Civilization,' the Decline of Middle-Class Manliness, and Ida B. Wells's Antilynching Campaign (1892–94)." *Radical History Review* 52 (1992): 5–30.

Beriss, David. "If You're Gay and Irish, Your Parents Must Be English." *Identities: Global Studies in Culture and Power* 2 (1996): 189–96.

Bickford-Smith, Vivian. "The Betrayal of Creole Elites, 1880–1920." In *Black Experience and the Empire*, edited by Philip D. Morgan and Sean Hawkins, 194–227. Oxford: Oxford University Press, 2004.

Biney, Ama. *The Political and Social Thought of Kwame Nkrumah*. New York: Palgrave Macmillan, 2011.

Bland, Lucy. "White Women and Men of Colour: Miscegenation Fears in Britain after the Great War." *Gender and History* 17, no. 1 (2005): 29–61.

Blyden, Nemata A. *West Indians in West Africa, 1808–1880: The African Diaspora in Reverse*. Rochester, NY: University of Rochester Press, 2000.

Boittin, Jennifer A. "Black in France: The Language and Politics of Race in the Late Third Republic." *French Politics, Culture and Society* 27, no. 2 (2009): 23–46.

———. *Colonial Metropolis: The Urban Grounds of Anti-Imperialism and Feminism in Interwar Paris*. Lincoln: University of Nebraska Press, 2010.

Bosman, Willem. *A New and Accurate Description of the Coast of Guinea*. London: Knapton, 1705.

Bowesman, Charles. *Being Caught in a Thorn Bush He Plucks a Rose: A Medical Anthology*. Sussex: Book Guild, 1987.

Bowesman, Reggie. "Charles Bowesman, Obituary." *British Medical Journal* 307 (October 2, 1993): 864.

Boxer, C. R. *Race Relations in the Portuguese Colonial Empire, 1415–1825*. Oxford: Clarendon, 1963.

Boyle, Laura. *Diary of a Colonial Officer's Wife*. Oxford: Alden Press, 1968.

Bradford, Vivian. "The Veil and the Visible." *Western Journal of Communication* 63, no. 2 (1999): 115–39.

Bridge, Horatio. *Journal of an African Cruiser*. Edited by Nathaniel Hawthorne. London: Wiley and Putnam, 1845.

Briggs, Laura. *Reproducing Empire: Race, Sex, Science, and U.S. Imperialism in Puerto Rico*. Berkeley: University of California Press, 2002.

Brooks, George E., Jr. "Artists' Depictions of Senegalese Signares: Insights Concerning French Racist and Sexist Attitudes in the Nineteenth Century." *Geneve-Afrique* 18, no. 1 (1980): 76–89.

———. *Eurafricans in Western Africa: Commerce, Social Status, Gender, and Religious Observance from the Sixteenth to the Eighteenth Century*. Athens: Ohio University Press, 2003.

———. *Landlords and Strangers: Ecology, Society, and Trade in Western Africa, 1000–1630*. Boulder, CO: Westview Press, 1993.

———. "The Letter Book of Captain Edward Harrington." *Transactions of the Historical Society of Ghana* 6 (1962): 71–77.

———. *Luso-African Commerce and Settlement in the Gambia and Guinea-Bissau Region*. Vol. 24, Working Papers. Boston, MA: African Studies Center Boston University, 1980.

———. "A *Nhara* of the Guinea-Bissau Region: Mau Aurelia Correia." Paper presented at the African Studies Association, Philadelphia, 1980.

———. "The *Signares* of Saint-Louis and Gorée: Women Entrepreneurs in Eighteenth-Century Senegal." In *Women in Africa: Studies in Social and Economic Change*, edited by Nancy Hafkin and Edna G. Bay, 19–44. Stanford, CA: Stanford University Press, 1976.

Brown, Elsa Barkley. "Imaging Lynching: African American Women, Communities of Struggle, and Collective Memory." In *African American Women Speak out on Anita Hill–Clarence Thomas*, edited by Geneva Smitherman, 100–124. Detroit, MI: Wayne State University Press, 1995.

———. "Negotiating and Transforming the Public Sphere: African American Political Life in the Transition from Slavery to Freedom." *Public Culture* 7, no. 1 (1994): 107–46.

Brown, Jacqueline Nassy. *Dropping Anchor, Setting Sail: Geographies of Race in Black Liverpool*. Princeton, NJ: Princeton University Press, 2009.

Bujra, Janet M. "Production, Property, Prostitution: 'Sexual Politics' in Atu." *Cahiers d'Etudes Africaines* 17, no. 65 (1977): 13–39.

Bump, Micah. "Ghana: Searching for Opportunities at Home and Abroad." *Migration Information Source*, accessed June 2, 2014. http://www.migrationpolicy.org/article/ghana-searching-opportunities-home-and-abroad.

Burrell, Jenna. *Invisible Users: Youth in the Internet Cafés of Urban Ghana*. Cambridge, MA: MIT Press, 2012.

Burton, Antoinette. *At the Heart of the Empire: Indians and the Colonial Encounter in Late-Victorian Britain*. Berkeley: University of California Press, 1998.

Buser, Hans. *In Ghana at Independence: Stories of a Swiss Salesman*. Basel: Basler Afrika Bibliographien, 2010.

Bush, Barbara. "Blacks in Britain: The 1930s." *History Today* 31, no. 9 (1981): 46–47.

———. *Imperialism, Race, and Resistance: Africa and Britain, 1919–1945*. London: Routledge, 1999.

Busia, K. A. *Report on a Social Survey of Sekondi-Takoradi*. London: Crown Agents for the Colonies, 1950.

Callaci, Emily. "Dancehall Politics: Mobility, Sexuality, and Spectacles of Racial Respectability in Late Colonial Tanganyika, 1930s–1961." *Journal of African History* 52, no. 3 (2011): 365–84.

Callaway, Helen. *Gender, Culture, and Empire: European Women in Colonial Nigeria*. Urbana: University of Illinois Press, 1987.

Campbell, Clifford. "Full Circle: The Caribbean Presence in the Making of Ghana, 1843-1966." PhD diss., Univeristy of Ghana, Legon, 2012.

Candido, Mariana P. *An African Slaving Port and the Atlantic World: Benguela and Its Hinterland*. New York: Cambridge University Press, 2013.

———. "Concubinage and Slavery in Benguela, c. 1750–1850." In *Slavery in Africa and the Caribbean: A History of Enslavement and Identity Since the Eigtheenth Century*, edited by Olatunji Ojo and Nadine Hunt, 65–84. London: Tauris, 2012.

———. "Dona Aguida Gonçalves marchange à Benguela à la fin du XVIII siécle." *Brésil(s): Sciences humaines et sociales* 1 (2012): 33–54.

Casely-Hayford, Augustus L. "A Genealogical History of Cape Coast Stool Families." PhD diss., University of London, 1992.

Cell, John W. *British Colonial Administration in the Mid-Nineteenth Century: The Policy-Making Process*. New Haven, CT: Yale University Press, 1970.

Chadya, Joyce M. "Mother Politics: Anti-Colonial Nationalism and the Woman Question in Africa." *Journal of Women's History* 15, no. 3 (2003): 153–57.

Chanock, Martin. "Making Customary Law: Men, Women, and Courts in Colonial Northern Rhodesia." In *African Women and the Law: Historical Perspectives*, edited by Margaret J. Hay and Marcia Wright, 53–67. Boston, MA: Boston University African Studies Center, 1982.

———. *Law, Custom and Social Order: The Colonial Experience in Malawi and Zambia*. Portsmouth, NH: Heinemann, 1998.

Chatterjee, Partha. "Colonialism, Nationalism, and Colonialized Women: The Contest in India." *American Ethnologist* 16, no. 4 (1989): 622–33.

———. *The Nation and Its Fragments: Colonial and Postcolonial Histories*. Princeton, NJ: Princeton University Press, 1993.

———. "Whose Imagined Community?" *Millennium* 20, no. 3 (1991): 521–25.

Chrisman, Laura. *Postcolonial Contraventions: Cultural Readings of Race, Imperialism, and Transnationalism*. Manchester: Manchester University Press, 2003.

Christian, Mark. "The Fletcher Report 1930: A Historical Case Study of Contested Black Mixed Heritage Britishness." *Journal of Historical Sociology* 21, nos. 2–3 (2008): 213–41.

Clancy-Smith, Julia A., and Frances Gouda, eds. *Domesticating the Empire: Race, Gender, and Family Life in French and Dutch Colonialism*. Charlottesville: University Press of Virginia, 1998.

Cole, Jennifer. *Sex and Salvation: Imagining the Future in Madagascar*. Chicago: University of Chicago Press, 2010.

Cole, Jennifer, and Lynn M. Thomas, eds. *Love in Africa*. Chicago: University of Chicago Press, 2009.

Coly, Ayo. "Un/clothing African Womanhood: Colonial Statements and Postcolonial Discourse of the African Female Body." *Journal of Contemporary African Studies* 33, no.1 (2015): 12-26.

Conklin, Alice L. "Redefining 'Frenchness': France and West Africa." In Clancy-Smith and Gouda, *Domesticating the Empire*, 65–83.

Cooper, Frederick. *Africa since 1940: The Past of the Present*. Cambridge: Cambridge University Press, 2002.

———. "Reconstructing Empire in British and French Africa." *Past and Present* 210, no. 6 (2011): 196–210.

Cooper, Frederick, and Ann L. Stoler. "Introduction Tensions of Empire: Colonial Control and Visions of Rule." *American Ethnologist* 16, no. 4 (1989): 609–21.

———, eds. *Tensions of Empire: Colonial Cultures in a Bourgeois World*. Berkeley: University of California Press, 1997.

Cornwell, Gareth. "George Webb Hardy's *The Black Peril* and the Social Meaning of 'Black Peril' in Early Twentieth-Century South Africa." *Journal of Southern African Studies* 22, no. 3 (1996): 441–53.

Curtin, P. D. "'The White Man's Grave': Image and Reality, 1780–1850." *Journal of British Studies* 1, no. 1 (1961): 94–110.

Daaku, Kwame Y. "The European Traders and the Coastal States, 1630–1720." *Transactions of the Historical Society of Ghana* 8 (1965): 11–23.

———. *Trade and Politics on the Gold Coast, 1600–1720: A Study of the African Reaction to European Trade*. London: Clarendon, 1970.

Dakeyne, N. H. "Reconditioning of Old Hill Rubber and Hill Soil Conservation Generally," *Planter* 9 (1929): 233–36.

Das, Santanu, ed. *Race, Empire and First World War Writing*. Cambridge: Cambridge University Press, 2011.

Davidson, Joanna. "Rotten Fish: Polarization, Pluralism, and Migrant-Host Relations in Guinea-Bissau." In *States of Violence: Politics, Youth, and Memory in Contemporary Africa*, edited by Edna G. Bay and Donald L. Donham, 58–93. Charlottesville: University of Virginia Press, 2007.

Decker, Jeffrey Louis. "Terrorism (Un)Veiled: Frantz Fanon and the Women of Algiers." *Cultural Critique*, no. 17 (1990–1991): 177–95.

DeCorse, Christopher R. *An Archaeology of Elmina: Africans and Europeans on the Gold Coast, 1400–1900*. Washington, DC: Smithsonian Institution Press, 2001.

Deflem, Mathieu. "Law Enforcement in British Colonial Africa: A Comparative Analysis of Imperial Policing in Nyasaland, the Gold Coast and Kenya." *Police Studies* 17, no. 1 (1994): 45–68.

de Hart, Betty. "Children's Citizenship, Motherhood and the Nation State." In *Gender, Migration, and the Public Sphere, 1850–2005*, edited by Marlou Schrover and Eileen Janes Yeo, 97–117. New York: Routledge, 2010.

Dixon, David. "Thatcher's People: The British Nationality Act 1981." *Journal of Law and Society* 10, no. 2 (1983): 161–80.

Doortmont, Michel R. ed. *The Pen-Pictures of Modern Africans and African Celebrities by Charles Francis Hutchison: A Collective Biography of Elite Society in the Gold Coast Colony*. Leiden: Brill, 2005.

——. "Producing a Received View of Gold Coast Elite Society? C. F. Hutchison's *Pen Pictures of Modern Africans and African Celebrities*." *History in Africa* 33 (2006): 473–93.

Dorjahn, Vernon R., and Christopher Fyfe. "Landlord and Stranger: Change in Tenancy Relations in Sierra Leone." *Journal of African History* 3, no. 3 (1962): 391–97.

Douglas, Mary. *Purity and Danger: An Analysis of Concepts of Pollution and Taboo*. London: Routledge and Kegan Paul, 1966.

Du Bois, W. E. B. *The Souls of Black Folk: Essays and Sketches*. Chicago: McClurg, 1907.

Dumett, Raymond E. "African Merchants of the Gold Coast, 1860–1905: Dynamics of Indigenous Entrepreneurship." *Comparative Studies in Society and History* 25, no. 4 (1983): 661–93.

——. "Disease and Mortality among Gold Miners of Ghana: Colonial Government and Mining Company Attitudes and Policies, 1900–1938." *Social Science and Medicine* 37, no. 2 (1993): 213–32.

——. "John Sarbah, the Elder, and African Mercantile Entrepreneurship in the Gold Coast in the Late Nineteenth Century." *Journal of African History* 14, no. 4 (1973): 653–79.

Edwards, Penny. "Womanizing Indochina: Fiction, Nation, and Cohabitation in Colonial Cambodia, 1890–1930." In Clancy-Smith and Gouda, *Domesticating the Empire*, 108–30.

El Hamel, Chouki. *Black Morocco: A History of Slavery, Race, and Islam*. Cambridge: Cambridge University Press, 2013.

Eluwa, G. I. C. "Background to the Emergence of the National Congress of British West Africa." *African Studies Review* 14, no. 2 (1971): 205–18.

Epprecht, Marc. *Heterosexual Africa? The History of an Idea from the Age of Exploration to the Age of AIDS*. Athens: Ohio University Press, 2008.

———. *Hungochani: The History of a Dissident Sexuality in Southern Africa*. Montreal: McGill-Queen's University Press, 2004.

———. "The Making of 'African Sexuality': Early Sources, Current Debates." *History Compass* 8, no. 8 (2010): 768–79.

———. "Male-Male Sexuality in Lesotho: Two Conversations." *Journal of Men's Studies* 10, no. 3 (2002): 373–89.

———. "Sexuality, Africa, History." *American Historical Review* 114, no. 5 (2009): 1258–72.

———. "The 'Unsaying' of Indigenous Homosexualities in Zimbabwe: Mapping a Blindspot in an African Masculinity." *Journal of Southern African Studies* 24, no. 4 (1998): 631–51.

———. *Unspoken Facts: A History of Homosexualities in Africa*. Harare: Gays and Lesbians of Zimbabwe, 2008.

Etherington, Norman. "Natal's Black Rape Scare of the 1870s." *Journal of Southern African Studies* 15, no. 1 (1988): 36–53.

Evans, Neil. "Across the Universe: Racial Violence and the Post-War Crisis in Imperial Britain, 1919–25." In *Ethnic Labour and British Imperial Trade: A History of Ethnic Seafarers in the UK*, edited by Diane Frost, 59–88. London: Cass, 1995.

Evans-Anfom, Emmanuel. *To the Thirsty Land: Autobiography of a Patriot*. Achimota: Africa Christian Press, 2003.

Everts, Natalie. "'Brought up Well According to European Standards': Helena Van Der Burgh and Wilhelmina Van Naarssen: Two Christian Women from Elmina." In *Merchants, Missionaries and Migrants: 300 Years of Dutch-Ghanaian Relations*, edited by Ineke van Kessel, 101–9. Amsterdam: KIT Press, 2002.

———. "Cherchez la Femme: Gender-Related Issues in Eighteenth-Century Elmina." *Itinerario* 20, no. 1 (1996): 45–57.

Falola, Toyin, and Amanda Warnock, eds. *Encyclopedia of the Middle Passage*. Westport, CT: Greenwood Press, 2007.

Fanon, Frantz. *Black Skin, White Masks*. New York: Grove Press, 1967.

———. *A Dying Colonialism*. New York: Grove Press, 1965.

Fantasia, Rick, and Eric L. Hirsch. "Culture in Rebellion: The Appropriation and Transformation of the Veil in the Algerian Revolution." In *Social Movements and Culture*, edited by Hank Johnston and Bert Klandermans, 144–59. Minneapolis: University of Minnesota Press, 1995.

Feimster, Crystal N. *Southern Horrors: Women and the Politics of Rape and Lynching*. Cambridge, MA: Harvard University Press, 2009.

Feinberg, Harvey M. *Africans and Europeans in West Africa: Elminans and Dutchmen on the Gold Coast during the Eighteenth Century*. Philadelphia: American Philosophical Society, 1989.

———. "An Eighteenth-Century Case of Plagiarism: William Smith's *A New Voyage to Guinea*." *History in Africa* 6 (1979): 45–50.

Findlay, Eileen J. Suárez. *Imposing Decency: The Politics of Sexuality and Race in Puerto Rico, 1870–1920*. Durham, NC: Duke University Press, 1999.

Fletcher, Muriel E. *Report on an Investigation into the Colour Problem in Liverpool and Other Ports*. Liverpool: Association for the Welfare of Half-Caste Children, 1930.

Foucault, Michel. *The History of Sexuality*. New York: Vintage Books, 1990.

Frost, Diane. "Racism and Social Segregation: Settlement Patterns of West African Seamen in Liverpool since the Nineteenth Century." *New Community* 22, no. 1 (1996): 85–95.
———. *Work and Community among West African Migrant Workers Since the Nineteenth Century*. Liverpool: Liverpool University Press, 1999.
Gadzekpo, Audrey. "Gender Discourses and Representational Practices in Gold Coast Newspapers." *Jenda* 1, no. 2 (2001): 1–27.
———. "The Hidden History of Women in Ghanaian Print Culture." In *African Gender Studies: A Reader*, edited by Oyeronke Oyewumi, 279–96. New York: Palgrave Macmillan, 2005.
———. "Women's Engagement with Gold Coast Print Culture from 1857 to 1957." PhD diss., University of Birmingham, 2001.
Gale, Thomas S. "Segregation in British West Africa." *Cahiers d'Etudes Africaines* 20, no. 4 (1980): 495–507.
———. "The Struggle against Disease in the Gold Coast: Early Attempts at Urban Sanitary Reform." *Transactions of the Historical Society of Ghana* 16, no. 2 (1995): 185–203.
Gann, Lewis H., and Peter Duignan. *The Rulers of British Africa, 1870–1914*. Stanford, CA: Stanford University Press, 1978.
Garraway, Doris. *The Libertine Colony: Creolization in the Early French Caribbean*. Durham, NC: Duke University Press, 2005.
George, Abosede. *Making Modern Girls: A History of Girlhood, Labor, and Social Development in Colonial Lagos*. Athens: Ohio Univeristy Press, 2014.
Geraghty, Tony. *A North-East Coast Town, Ordeal and Triumph: The Story of Kingston upon Hull in the 1939–1945 Great War*. Hull: Kingston upon Hull, 1951.
Getz, Trevor. *Slavery and Reform in West Africa: Toward Emancipation in Nineteenth-Century Senegal and the Gold Coast*. Athens: Ohio University Press, 2004.
Ghosh, Durba. *Sex and the Family in Colonial India: The Making of Empire*. Cambridge: Cambridge University Press, 2006.
Gilliat-Ray, Sophie. *Muslims in Britain: An Introduction*. Cambridge: Cambridge University Press, 2010.
Gilmore, Glenda E. *Gender and Jim Crow: Women and the Politics of White Supremacy in North Carolina, 1896–1920*. Chapel Hill: University of North Carolina Press, 1996.
Gilroy, Paul. *The Black Atlantic: Modernity and Double Consciousness*. Cambridge, MA: Harvard University Press, 1993.
Gist, Noel P., and Roy D. Wright. *Marginality and Identity: Anglo-Indians as a Racially-Mixed Minority in India*. Leiden: Brill, 1973.
Glassman, Jonathon. *War of Words, War of Stones: Racial Thought and Violence in Colonial Zanzibar*. Bloomington: Indiana University Press, 2011.
Gocking, Roger. "British Justice and the Native Tribunals of the Southern Gold Coast Colony." *Journal of African History* 34, no. 1 (1993): 93–113.
———. "Creole Society and the Revival of Traditional Culture in Cape Coast during the Colonial Period." *International Journal of African Historical Studies* 17, no. 4 (1984): 601–22.
———. *Facing Two Ways: Ghana's Coastal Communities under Colonial Rule*. Lanham, MD: University Press of America, 1999.

Gold Coast Government. *The Laws of the Gold Coast Colony: Containing the Ordinances of the Gold Coast Colony and the Orders, Proclamations, Rules, Regulations and Bye-laws Made Thereunder in Force on the 31st Day of December, 1919, and the Principal Imperial Statutes, Orders in Council, Letters Patent and Royal Instructions Relating to the Gold Coast Colony.* London: Stevens and Sons, 1920.

Gouda, Frances. "The Gendered Rhetoric of Colonialism and Anti-Colonialism in Twentieth-Century Indonesia." *Indonesia*, no. 55 (1993): 1–22.

Gough, Allison J. "Messing Up Another Country's Customs: The Exportation of American Racism during World War II." *World History Connected* 5, no. 1 (October 2007). http://www.historycooperative.org/journals/whc/5.1/ghough.html.

Graham, Lucy V. *State of Peril: Race and Rape in South African Literature.* New York: Oxford University Press, 2012.

Graystone, Philip. *The Blitz on Hull, 1940–45.* Hull: Lampada, 1991.

Greene, Sandra E. "Crossing Boundaries/Changing Identities: Female Slaves, Male Strangers, and Their Descendants in Nineteenth- and Twentieth-Century Anlo." In *Gendered Encounters: Challenging Cultural Boundaries and Social Hierarchies in Africa*, edited by Maria Grosz-Ngate and Omari H. Kokole, 23–42. New York: Routledge, 1997.

———. *Gender, Ethnicity, and Social Change on the Upper Slave Coast: A History of the Anlo-Ewe.* Portsmouth, NH: Heinemann, 1996.

———. "In the Mix: Women and Ethnicity among the Anlo-Ewe." In *Ethnicity in Ghana: The Limits of Invention*, edited by Carola Lentz and Paul Nugent, 29–48. New York: Palgrave Macmillan, 2000.

———. *Sacred Sites and the Colonial Encounter: A History of Meaning and Memory in Ghana.* Bloomington: Indiana University Press, 2002.

Grier, Beverly. "Pawns, Porters, and Petty Traders: Women in the Transition to Cash Crop Agriculture in Colonial Ghana." *Signs* 17, no. 2 (1992): 304–28.

Hall, Bruce S. *A History of Race in Muslim West Africa, 1600–1960.* Cambridge: Cambridge University Press, 2011.

Hall, Lesley A. *Sex, Gender and Social Change in Britain Since 1880.* New York: St. Martin's, 2000.

Hansen, Karen Tranberg. *Distant Companions: Servants and Employers in Zambia, 1900–1985.* Ithaca, NY: Cornell University Press, 1989.

Hansen, Randall. "The Politics of Citizenship in 1940s Britain: The British Nationality Act." *Twentieth Century British History* 10, no. 1 (1999): 67–95.

Hansen, Thorkild. *Coast of Slaves.* Accra: Sub-Saharan Publishers, 2002.

Haour, Anne. *Outsiders and Strangers: An Archaeology of Liminality in West Africa.* Oxford: Oxford University Press, 2013.

Hasty, Jennifer. *The Press and Political Culture in Ghana.* Bloomington: Indiana University Press, 2005.

Heussler, Robert. *Yesterday's Rulers: The Making of the British Colonial Service.* Syracuse, NY: Syracuse University Press, 1963.

Hicks, George L. *The Comfort Women: Sex Slaves of the Japanese Imperial Forces.* Singapore: Heinemann Asia, 1995.

Higginbotham, Evelyn Brooks. *Righteous Discontent: The Women's Movement in the Black Baptist Church, 1880–1920.* Cambridge, MA: Harvard University Press, 1993.

Hine, Darlene Clark. *Hine Sight: Black Women and the Re-Construction of American History*. Brooklyn, NY: Carlson, 1994.
Hoad, Neville W. *African Intimacies: Race, Homosexuality, and Globalization*. Minneapolis: University of Minnesota Press, 2007.
Hodgson, Dorothy L., and Sheryl McCurdy. "Wayward Wives, Misfit Mothers, and Disobedient Daughters: 'Wicked' Women and the Reconfiguration of Gender in Africa." *Canadian Journal of African Studies* 30, no. 1 (1996): 1–9.
———, eds. *"Wicked" Women and the Reconfiguration of Gender in Africa*. Portsmouth, NH: Heinemann, 2001.
Hoganson, Kristin. "Garrisonian Abolitionists and the Rhetoric of Gender, 1850–1860." *American Quarterly* 45, no. 4 (1993): 558–95.
Holden, Philip. "Imagined Individuals: National Autobiography and Postcolonial Self-Fashioning." Asia Research Institute Working Paper Series, no. 13. National University of Singapore, 2003.
Holsey, Bayo. *Routes of Remembrance: Refashioning the Slave Trade in Ghana*. Chicago: University of Chicago Press, 2008.
———. "Transatlantic Dreaming: Slavery, Tourism, and Diasporic Encounters." In *Homecomings: Unsettling Paths of Return*, edited by Fran Markowitz and Anders H. Stefansson, 166–82. Lanham, MD: Lexington Books, 2004.
hooks, bell. "Eating the Other: Desire and Resistance." In *Media and Cultural Studies: Keyworks*, edited by Meenakshi G. Durham and Douglas M. Kellner, 366–80. Malden, MA: Blackwell, 2000.
Huber, Magnus. "Lingua Franca in West Africa? An Evaluation of the Sociohistorical and Metalinguistic Evidence." In *Gradual Creolization: Studies Celebrating Jacques Arends*, edited by Rachel Selbach, Hugo C. Cardoso, and Margot van den Berg, 257–78. Amsterdam: Benjamins, 2009.
Hulstaert, Gustave. "Le Problème des Mulâtres." *Africa* 15, no. 3 (1945): 129–44.
———. "Le Problème des Mulâtres." *Africa* 16, no. 1 (1946): 39–44.
Hunter, Tera W. *To 'Joy My Freedom: Southern Black Women's Lives and Labors after the Civil War*. Cambridge, MA: Harvard University Press, 1997.
Hyam, Ronald. "Concubinage and the Colonial Service: The Crewe Circular (1909)." *Journal of Imperial and Commonwealth History* 14, no. 3 (1986): 170–86.
———. *Empire and Sexuality: The British Experience*. Manchester: Manchester University Press, 1990.
Hyslop, Jonathan. "White Working-Class Women and the Invention of Apartheid: 'Purified' Afrikaner Nationalist Agitation for Legislation against 'Mixed' Marriages, 1934–9." *Journal of African History* 36, no. 1 (1995): 57–81.
Ipsen, Pernille. *Daughters of the Trade: Atlantic Slavers and Interracial Marriage on the Gold Coast*. Philadelphia: University of Pennsylvania Press, 2015.
———. "'The Christened Mulatresses': Euro-African Families in a Slave-Trading Town." *William and Mary Quarterly* 70, no. 2 (2013): 371–98.
———. "Intercultural Intimacy in Danish Guinea, 1680–1740," *Historie Netmagasinet* 16 (2005): 1–8.
Isert, Paul Erdmann, and Selena Axelrod Winsnes. *Letters on West Africa and the Slave Trade: Paul Erdmann Isert's Journey to Guinea and the Caribbean Islands in Columbia (1788)*. Oxford: Oxford University Press, 1992.
Iyob, Ruth. "Madamismo and Beyond: The Construction of Eritrean Women." *Nineteenth Century Contexts* 22, no. 2 (2000): 217–38.

Jackson, Lynette A. "'Stray Women' and 'Girls on the Move': Gender, Space, and Disease in Colonial and Post-Colonial Zimbabwe." In *Sacred Spaces and Public Quarrels: African Cultural and Economic Landscapes*, edited by Ezekiel Kalipeni and Paul T. Zeleza, 147–67. Trenton, NJ: Africa World Press, 1999.

———. "'When in the White Man's Town': Zimbabwean Women Remember Chibeura." In *Women in African Colonial Histories*, edited by Jean Allman, Susan Geiger, and Nakanyike Musisi, 191–215. Bloomington: Indiana University Press, 2002.

Jacobs, Harriet A. *Incidents in the Life of a Slave Girl, Written by Herself*. Cambridge, MA: Harvard University Press, 2009.

Jean-Baptiste, Rachel. *Conjugal Rights: Marriage, Sexuality, and Urban Life in Colonial Libreville, Gabon*. Athens: Ohio University Press, 2014.

———. "'A Black Girl Should Not Be with a White Man': Sex, Race, and African Women's Social and Legal Status in Colonial Gabon, c. 1900–1946." *Journal of Women's History* 22, no. 2 (2010): 56–82.

———. "'Miss Eurafrica': Men, Women's Sexuality, and Métis Identity in Late Colonial French Africa, 1945–1960." *Journal of the History of Sexuality* 20, no. 3 (2011): 568–93.

Jeffries, Charles J. *The Colonial Office*. London: Allen and Unwin, 1956.

Jenkinson, Jacqueline. "The 1919 Riots." In *Racial Violence in Britain in the Nineteenth and Twentieth Centuries*, edited by Panikos Panayi, 93–111. Leicester: Leicester University Press, 1996.

———. *Black 1919: Riots, Racism and Resistance in Imperial Britain*. Liverpool: Liverpool University Press, 2009.

Jones, Adam. "Female Slave-Owners on the Gold Coast: Just a Matter of Money?" In *Slave Cultures and the Cultures of Slavery*, edited by Stephan Palmié, 100–111. Knoxville: University of Tennessee Press, 1995.

Jones, Hilary. *The Métis of Senegal: Urban Life and Politics in French West Africa*. Bloomington: Indiana University Press, 2013.

———. "From *Mariage a La Mode* to Weddings at Town Hall: Marriage, Colonialism, and Mixed-Race Society in Nineteenth-Century Senegal." *International Journal of African Historical Studies* 38, no. 1 (2005): 27–48.

Jones-Quartey, K. A. B. "The Gold Coast Press: 1822–1930, and the Anglo-African Press: 1825–1930 — The Chronologies." *Institute of African Studies* 4, no. 2 (1968): 30–46.

———. *A Summary History of the Ghana Press, 1822–1960*. Accra: Ghana Information Services Department, 1974.

Jordan, Winthrop D. *White over Black: American Attitudes toward the Negro, 1550–1812*. Chapel Hill: University of North Carolina Press, 1968.

Kaplow, Susan B. "The Mudfish and the Crocodile: Underdevelopment of a West African Bourgeoisie." *Science and Society* 41, no. 3 (1977): 317–33.

Kea, Ray A. *A Cultural and Social History of Ghana from the Seventeenth to the Nineteenth Century: The Gold Coast in the Age of the Trans-Atlantic Slave Trade*. Lewiston, NY: Mellen, 2012.

———. *Settlements, Trade, and Polities in the Seventeenth-Century Gold Coast*. Baltimore, MD: Johns Hopkins University Press, 1982.

Kennedy, Dane K. *Islands of White: Settler Society and Culture in Kenya and Southern Rhodesia, 1890–1939*. Durham, NC: Duke University Press, 1987.

———. *The Magic Mountains: Hill Stations and the British Raj*. Berkeley: University of California Press, 1996.

Kim, Hyun Sook. "History and Memory: The 'Comfort Women' Controversy." In *Bodies in Contact: Rethinking Colonial Encounters in World History*, edited by Tony Ballantyne and Antoinette Burton, 363–82. Durham, NC: Duke University Press, 2005.

Kimble, David. *A Political History of Ghana: The Rise of Gold Coast Nationalism, 1850–1928*. Oxford: Clarendon, 1963.

Kirk-Greene, Anthony H. M. *A Biographical Dictionary of the British Colonial Service, 1939–1966*. London: Zell, 1991.

Kisseih, Docia. "Developments in Nursing in Ghana." *International Journal of Nursing Studies* 5, no. 3 (1968): 205–19.

Klein, Martin A. "Review of *Children of the French Empire: Miscegenation and Colonial Society in French West Africa, 1895–1960*, by Owen White." *Journal of Interdisciplinary History* 32, no. 1 (2001): 153–54.

Knörr, Jacqueline, and Wilson Trajano Filho, eds. *The Powerful Presence of the Past: Integration and Conflict along the Upper Guinea Coast*. Leiden: Brill, 2010.

Koikari, Mire. "Gender, Power, and U.S. Imperialism: The Occupation of Japan, 1945–1952." In Ballantyne and Burton, *Bodies in Contact*, 342–62.

Kuklick, Henrika. *The Imperial Bureaucrat: The Colonial Administrative Service in the Gold Coast, 1920–1939*. Stanford, CA: Hoover Institution Press, 1979.

Kwarteng, Kwasi. *Ghosts of Empire: Britain's Legacies in the Modern World*. London: Bloomsbury, 2011.

Lake, Marilyn, and Henry Reynolds. *Drawing the Global Colour Line: White Men's Countries and the International Challenge of Racial Equality*. Cambridge: Cambridge University Press, 2008.

Lane, Christopher. "Managing 'The White Man's Burden': The Racial Imaginary of Forster's Colonial Narratives." *Discourse* 15, no. 3 (1993): 93–129.

Lawrance, Benjamin N., Emily L. Osborn, and Richard L. Roberts, eds. *Intermediaries, Interpreters, and Clerks: African Employees in the Making of Colonial Africa*. Madison: University of Wisconsin Press, 2006.

Lee, Christopher J. *Unreasonable Histories: Nativism, Multiracial Lives, and the Genealogical Imagination in British Africa*. Durham, NC: Duke University Press, 2014.

———. "*Jus Soli* and *Jus Sanguinis* in the Colonies: The Interwar Politics of Race, Culture, and Multiracial Legal Status in British Africa." *Law and History Review* 29, no. 2 (2011): 497–522.

———. "The 'Native' Undefined: Colonial Categories, Anglo-African Status and the Politics of Kinship in British Central Africa, 1929–38." *Journal of African History* 46, no. 3 (2005): 455–78.

———. "'A Generous Dream, but Difficult to Realize': The Anglo-African Community of Nyasaland, 1929–1940." *Society of Malawi Journal* 61, no. 2 (2008): 19–41.

Lever, J. T. "Mulatto Influence on the Gold Coast in the Early Nineteenth Century: Jan Nieser of Elmina." *African Historical Studies* 3, no. 2 (1970): 253–61.

Lindsay, Lisa A. "A Tragic Romance, a Nationalist Symbol: The Case of the Murdered White Lover in Colonial Nigeria." *Journal of Women's History* 17, no. 2 (2005): 118–41.

Lindsay, Lisa A., and Stephan F. Miescher, eds. *Men and Masculinities in Modern Africa*. Portsmouth, NH: Heinemann, 2003.

Locher-Scholten, Elsbeth. "Morals, Harmony, and National Identity: 'Companionate Feminism' in Colonial Indonesia in the 1930s." *Journal of Women's History* 14, no. 4 (2003): 38–58.

Lowenthal, David. "Race and Color in the West Indies." *Daedalus* 96, no. 2 (1967): 580–626.
Lundtofte, Henrik. "'I Believe That the Nation as Such Must Be Annihilated . . .'— The Radicalization of the German Suppression of the Herero Rising in 1904." In *Genocide: Cases, Comparisons and Contemporary Debates*, edited by Steven L. B. Jensen, 15–53. Copenhagen: Danish Center for Holocaust and Genocide Studies, 2003.
Macmaster, Neil. *Burning the Veil: The Algerian War and the "Emancipation" of Muslim Women, 1954–62*. Manchester: Manchester University Press, 2012.
———. "The Role of European Women and the Question of Mixed Couples in the Algerian Nationalist Movement in France, circa 1918–1962." *French Historical Studies* 34, no. 2 (2011): 357–86.
———. "Sexual and Racial Boundaries: Colonialism and Franco-Algerian Intermarriage (1880–1962)." In *Population and Social Policy in France*, edited by Máire Cross and Sheila Perry, 92–108. London: Pinter, 1997.
Madley, Benjamin. "Patterns of Frontier Genocide, 1803–1910: The Aboriginal Tasmanians, the Yuki of California, and the Herero of Namibia." *Journal of Genocide Research* 6, no. 2 (2004): 167–92.
Mahoney, F. "Notes on Mulattoes of the Gambia before the Mid-Nineteenth Century." *Transactions of the Historical Society of Ghana* 8 (1965): 120–29.
Mamdani, Mahmood. *Citizen and Subject: Contemporary Africa and the Legacy of Late Colonialism*. Princeton, NJ: Princeton University Press, 1996.
Mandaza, Ibbo. *Race, Colour and Class in Southern Africa: A Study of the Coloured Question in the Context of an Analysis of the Colonial and White Settler Racial Ideology, and African Nationalism in Twentieth Century Zimbabwe, Zambia and Malawi*. Harare: SAPES Books, 1997.
———. "White Settler Ideology, African Nationalism, and the 'Coloured' Question in Southern Africa: Southern Rhodesia/Zimbabwe, Northern Rhodesia/Zambia, and Nyasaland/Malawi, 1900–1976." PhD diss., University of York, 1979.
Mann, Kristin. "The Dangers of Dependence: Christian Marriage among Elite Women in Lagos Colony, 1880–1915." *Journal of African History* 24, no. 1 (1983): 37–56.
———. "Marriage Choices among the Educated African Elite in Lagos Colony, 1880–1915." *International Journal of African Historical Studies* 14, no. 2 (1981): 201–28.
———. *Marrying Well: Marriage, Status, and Social Change among the Educated Elite in Colonial Lagos*. Cambridge: Cambridge University Press, 1985.
Manuh, Takyiwaa. "Wives, Children, and Intestate Succession in Ghana." In *African Feminism: The Politics of Survival in Sub-Saharan Africa*, edited by Gwendolyn Mikell, 77–95. Philadelphia: University of Pennsylvania Press, 1997.
Marais, Johannes S. *The Cape Coloured People, 1652–1937*. London: Longmans, 1939.
Marcson, Michael. "European-African Interaction in the Pre-Colonial Period: Saint Louis, Senegal, 1758–1854." PhD diss., Harvard University, 1975.
Marees, Pieter de, A. van Dantzig, and Adam Jones. *Description and Historical Account of the Gold Kingdom of Guinea (1602)*. Oxford: Oxford University Press, 1987.
Mark, Peter. "Constructing Identity: Sixteenth- and Seventeenth-Century Architecture in the Gambia-Geba Region and the Articulation of Luso-African Ethnicity." *History in Africa* 22 (1995): 307–27.

———. "The Evolution of 'Portuguese' Identity: Luso-Africans on the Upper Guinea Coast from the Sixteenth to the Early Nineteenth Century." *Journal of African History* 40, no. 2 (1999): 173–91.

———. "'Portuguese' Architecture and Luso-African Identity in Senegambia and Guinea, 1730–1890." *History in Africa* 23 (1996): 179–96.

———. *"Portuguese" Style and Luso-African Identity: Precolonial Senegambia, Sixteenth–Nineteenth Centuries*. Bloomington: Indiana University Press, 2002.

Matera, Marc. *Black London: The Imperial Metropolis and Decolonization in the Twentieth Century*. Oakland: University of California Press, 2015.

———. "Black Internationalism and African and Caribbean Intellectuals in London, 1919–1950." PhD diss., Rutgers University, 2008.

Maxwell, Joseph Renner. *The Negro Question or Hints for the Physical Improvement of the Negro Race, with Special Reference to West Africa*. London: Fisher Unwin, 1891.

May, Roy, and Robin Cohen. "The Interaction between Race and Colonialism: A Case Study of the Liverpool Race Riots of 1919." *Race and Class* 16, no. 2 (1974): 111–26.

Mbilinyi, Marjorie J. "Runaway Wives in Colonial Tanganyika: Forced Labour and Forced Marriage in Rungwe District, 1919–1961." *International Journal of the Sociology of Law* 16, no. 1 (1988): 1–29.

McCarthy, Mary. *Social Change and the Growth of British Power in the Gold Coast: The Fante States, 1807–1874*. Lanham, MD: University Press of America, 1983.

McCaskie, Thomas C. "The Consuming Passions of Kwame Boakye: An Essay on Agency and Identity in Asante History." *Journal of African Cultural Studies* 13, no. 1 (2000): 43–62.

———. "Cultural Encounters: Britain and Africa in the Nineteenth Century." In *The Oxford History of the British Empire: The Nineteenth Century*, edited by Andrew Porter, 665–89. Oxford: Oxford University Press, 2004.

———. "State and Society, Marriage and Adultery: Some Considerations Towards a Social History of Pre-Colonial Asante." *Journal of African History* 22, no. 4 (1981): 477–94.

McClintock, Anne. *Imperial Leather: Race, Gender and Sexuality in the Colonial Conquest*. New York: Routledge, 1995.

McCulloch, Jock. *Black Peril, White Virtue: Sexual Crime in Southern Rhodesia, 1902–1935*. Bloomington: Indiana University Press, 2000.

McGuire, Danielle L. *At the Dark End of the Street: Black Women, Rape, and Resistance—a New History of the Civil Rights Movement from Rosa Parks to the Rise of Black Power*. New York: Knopf, 2010.

McLaren, Angus. *Sexual Blackmail: A Modern History*. Cambridge, MA: Harvard University Press, 2002.

Metcalfe, George E. *Maclean of the Gold Coast: The Life and Times of George Maclean, 1801–1847*. London: Oxford University Press, 1962.

Miescher, Stephan F. *Making Men in Ghana*. Bloomington: Indiana University Press, 2005.

Miller, Susan G. Afterword to Albert Memmi, *The Colonizer and the Colonized*. Boston, MA: Beacon, 1991.

Milner-Thornton, Juliette B. *The Long Shadow of the British Empire: The Ongoing Legacies of Race and Class In Zambia*. New York: Palgrave Macmillan, 2012.

Mitchell, Michele. *Righteous Propagation: African Americans and the Politics of Racial Destiny after Reconstruction*. Chapel Hill: University of North Carolina Press, 2004.
Mohanram, Radhika. *Imperial White: Race, Diaspora, and the British Empire*. Minneapolis: University of Minnesota Press, 2007.
Moodie, T. Dunbar. *Going for Gold: Men, Mines, and Migration*. Berkeley: University of California Press, 1994.
Morgan, Jennifer L. *Laboring Women: Reproduction and Gender in New World Slavery*. Philadelphia: University of Pennsylvania Press, 2004.
Morrison, Toni. *Beloved: A Novel*. New York: Knopf, 1987.
Mouser, Bruce L. "Accommodation and Assimilation in the Landlord-Stranger Relationship." In *West African Culture Dynamics: Archaeological and Historical Perspectives*, edited by B. K. Swartz and Raymond E. Dumett, 495–514. The Hague: Mouton, 1980.
Moyd, Michelle. *Violent Intermediaries: African Soldiers, Conquest, and Everyday Colonialism in German East Africa*. Athens: Ohio University Press, 2014.
Munro, Brenna M. *South Africa and the Dream of Love to Come: Queer Sexuality and the Struggle for Freedom*. Minneapolis: University of Minnesota Press, 2012.
Murray, Stephen O., and Will Roscoe. *Boy-Wives and Female Husbands: Studies in African Homosexualities*. New York: St. Martin's, 1998.
Naanen, Benedict B. B. "'Itinerant Gold Mines': Prostitution in the Cross River Basin of Nigeria, 1930–1950." *African Studies Review* 34, no. 2 (1991): 57–79.
Nagel, Joane. *Race, Ethnicity, and Sexuality: Intimate Intersections, Forbidden Frontiers*. New York: Oxford University Press, 2003.
Newell, Stephanie. *The Power to Name: A History of Anonymity in Colonial West Africa*. Athens: Ohio Unviersity Press, 2013.
——. *The Forger's Tale: The Search for Odeziaku*. Athens: Ohio University Press, 2006.
——. *West African Literatures: Ways of Reading*. Oxford: Oxford University Press, 2006.
——. *Literary Culture in Colonial Ghana: "How to Play the Game of Life."* Bloomington: Indiana University Press, 2002.
——. *Marita or The Folly of Love: A Novel by A. Native*. Leiden: Brill, 2002.
——. "Articulating Empire: Newspaper Readerships in Colonial West Africa." *New Formations* 73, no. 1 (2011): 26–42.
——. "Entering the Territory of Elites: Literary Activity in Colonial Ghana." In *Africa's Hidden Histories: Everyday Literacy and Making the Self*, edited by Karin Barber, 211–35. Bloomington: Indiana University Press, 2006.
——. "An Introduction to the Writings of J. G. Mullen, an African Clerk, in the *Gold Coast Leader*, 1916–1919." *Africa* 78, no. 3 (2008): 384–400.
——. "Local Cosmopolitans in Colonial West Africa." *Journal of Commonwealth Literature* 46, no. 1 (2011): 103–17.
——. "Remembering J. M. Stuart-Young of Onitsha, Colonial Nigeria: Memoirs, Obituaries and Names." *Africa* 73, no. 4 (2003): 505–30.
——. "Writing out Imperialism? A Note on Nationalism and Political Identity in the African-Owned Newspapers of Colonial Ghana." In *Exit: Endings and New Beginnings in Literature and Life*, edited by Stefan Helgesson, 81–94. Amsterdam: Rodopi, 2011.
Newell, Stephanie, and Audrey Gadzekpo, eds. *Mabel Dove: Selected Writings of a Pioneer West African Feminist*. Nottingham: Trent Editions, 2004.
Newman, Simon P. *A New World of Labor: The Development of Plantation Slavery in the British Atlantic*. Philadelphia: University of Pennsylvania Press, 2013.

Nicol, Abioseh. "West Indians in West Africa." *Sierra Leone Studies* 13 (1960): 14–23.
Nkrumah, Gamal. "Fathia Nkrumah: Farewell to All That." *Al-Ahram Weekly*, September 14–20, 2000. http://weekly.ahram.org.eg/2000/499/profile.htm.
Nkrumah, Kwame. *Ghana: The Autobiography of Kwame Nkrumah*. New York: Nelson, 1957.
Norregard, Georg. *Danish Settlements in West Africa, 1658–1850*. Boston, MA: Boston University Press, 1966.
Nossiter, Adam. "Nigeria Tries to 'Sanitize' Itself of Gays." *New York Times*, 8 February 2014. http://www.nytimes.com/2014/02/09/world/africa/nigeria-uses-law-and-whip-to-sanitize-gays.html?_r=0.
Oduah, Chika. "Gay Nigerians Targeted as 'Un-African.'" aljazeera.com, 26 January 2014. http://www.aljazeera.com/indepth/features/2014/01/gay-nigerians-targeted-as-un-african-2014125143518184415.html.
Okuro, Samwel Ong'wen. "Our Women Must Return Home: Institutionalized Patriarchy in Colonial Central Nyanza District, 1945–1963." *Journal of Asian and African Studies* 45, no. 5 (2010): 522–33.
Oyeniyi, Bukola Adeyemi. "Rape and Sexual Abuse." In Falola and Warnock, *Encyclopedia of the Middle Passage*, 315–18.
Papastergiadis, Nikos. "Tracing Hybridity in Theory." In *Debating Cultural Hybridity: Multi-Cultural Identities and the Politics of Anti-Racism*, edited by Pnina Werbner and Tariq Modood, 257–81. London: Zed Books, 2000.
Pape, John. "Black and White: The 'Perils of Sex' in Colonial Zimbabwe." *Journal of Southern African Studies* 16, no. 4 (1990): 699–720.
Park, Robert E. "Human Migration and the Marginal Man." *American Journal of Sociology* 33, no. 6 (1928): 881–93.
Parker, John. *Making the Town: Ga State and Society in Early Colonial Accra*. Portsmouth, NH: Heinemann, 2000.
———. "*Mankraloi*, Merchants and Mulattos—Carl Reindorf and the Politics of 'Race' in Early Colonial Accra." In *The Recovery of the West African Past: African Pastors and African History in the Nineteenth Century*, edited by Paul Jenkins, 31–55. Basel: Basler Afrika Bibliographien, 1998.
Patton, Adell. *Physicians, Colonialism Racism, and Diaspora in West Africa*. Gainesville: University of Florida Press, 1996.
Paul, Kathleen. *Whitewashing Britain: Race and Citizenship in the Postwar Era*. Ithaca, NY: Cornell University Press, 1997.
Pedersen, Susan. "National Bodies, Unspeakable Acts: The Sexual Politics of Colonial Policy-Making." *Journal of Modern History* 63, no. 4 (1991): 647–80.
Phillips, Oliver. "The 'Perils' of Sex and the Panics of Race: The Dangers of Interracial Sex in Colonial Southern Rhodesia." In *African Sexualities: A Reader*, edited by Sylvia Tamale, 101–15. Oxford: Pambazuka Press, 2011.
Phillips, Richard. *Sex, Politics and Empire: A Postcolonial Geography*. Manchester: Manchester University Press, 2006.
Pierre, Jemima. *The Predicament of Blackness: Postcolonial Ghana and the Politics of Race*. Chicago: University of Chicago Press, 2012.
Plaatje, Solomon T. "The Mote and the Beam: An Epic on Sex-Relationship 'twixt White and Black in British South Africa." Reprinted in *English in Africa* 3, no. 2 (1976): 85–92.
Plageman, Nate. *Highlife Saturday Night: Popular Music and Social Change in Urban Ghana*. Bloomington: Indiana University Press, 2013.

Polsgrove, Carol. *Ending British Rule in Africa: Writers in a Common Cause.* Manchester: Manchester University Press, 2009.

Ponzanesi, Sandra. "The Color of Love: *Madamismo* and Interracial Relationships in the Italian Colonies." *Research in African Literatures* 43, no. 2 (2012): 155–72.

Porter, R. "The Cape Coast Conflict of 1803: A Crisis in Relations Between the African and European Communites." *Transactions of the Historical Society of Ghana* 11 (1970): 27–82.

———. "The Crispe Family and the African Trade in the Seventeenth Century." *Journal of African History* 9, no. 1 (1968): 57–77.

Powell, Erica. *Private Secretary (Female)/Gold Coast.* London: Hurst, 1984.

Powell, Eve M. Troutt. *A Different Shade of Colonialism: Egypt, Great Britain, and the Mastery of the Sudan.* Berkeley: University of California Press, 2003.

Prais, Jinny K. "Imperial Travelers: The Formation of West African Urban Culture, Identity, and Citizenship in London and Accra, 1925–1935." PhD diss., University of Michigan, 2008.

Premdas, Ralph R. "Racism and Anti-Racism in the Caribbean." In *Racism and Anti-Racism in World Perspective*, edited by Benjamin P. Bowser, 241–60. Thousand Oaks, CA: Sage, 1995.

Priestley, Margaret A. "The Emergence of an Elite: A Case Study of a West Coast Family." In *The New Elites of Tropical Africa*, edited by Peter C. Lloyd, 87–99. London: Oxford University Press, 1966.

———. "Richard Brew: An Eighteenth-Century Trader at Anomabu." *Transactions of the Historical Society of Ghana* 4, no. 1 (1959): 29–46.

———. *West African Trade and Coast Society: A Family Study.* London: Oxford University Press, 1969.

Quayson, Ato. *Oxford Street, Accra: City Life and the Itineraries of Transnationalism.* Durham, NC: Duke University Press, 2014.

Rahman, Ahmad. *The Regime Change of Kwame Nkrumah: Epic Heroism in Africa and the Diaspora.* New York: Palgrave Macmillan, 2007.

Ray, Carina E. "Decrying White Peril: Interracial Sex and the Rise of Anticolonial Nationalism in the Gold Coast." *American Historical Review* 119, no. 1 (2014): 78–110.

———. "The Marriage That Sent the West into a Panic." *New African* 448 (February 2006): 26–27.

———. "Sex Trafficking, Prostitution, and the Law in Colonial British West Africa, 1911–43." In *Trafficking in Slavery's Wake: Law and the Experience of Women and Children in Africa*, edited by Benjamin N. Lawrance and Richard L. Roberts, 101–20. Athens: Ohio University Press, 2012.

———. "World War Two and the Sex Trade in British West Africa." In *Africa and World War II*, edited by Judith Byfield, Carolyn Brown, Timothy Parsons, and Ahmad Sikainga, 339–56. Cambridge: Cambridge University Press, 2015.

Ray, Deborah Wing. "The Takoradi Route: Roosevelt's Prewar Venture beyond the Western Hemisphere." *Journal of American History* 62, no. 2 (1975): 340–58.

Rediker, Marcus. *The Slave Ship: A Human History.* New York: Viking, 2007.

Reese, Ty M. "Controlling the Company: The Structures of Fante-British Relations on the Gold Coast, 1750–1821." *Journal of Imperial and Commonwealth History* 41, no. 1 (2013): 104–19.

———. "Wives, Brokers, and Laborers: Women at Cape Coast, 1750–1807." In *Women in Port: Gendering Communities, Economies, and Social Networks in Atlantic Port Cities, 1500–1800*, edited by Douglas Catterall and Jodi Campbell, 291–314. Leiden: Brill, 2012.

Reynolds, Edward. "The Rise and Fall of an African Merchant Class on the Gold Coast, 1830–1874." *Cahiers d'Etudes Africaines* 14, no. 2 (1984): 253–64.

———. *Trade and Economic Change on the Gold Coast, 1807–1874*. London: Longman, 1974.

Rich, Jeremy. "Gabonese Men for French Decency: The Rise and Fall of the Gabonese Chapter of the Ligue Des Droits De l'Homme, 1916–1939." *French Colonial History* 13, no. 1 (2012): 23–53.

———. "'Une Babylone Noire': Interracial Unions in Colonial Libreville, c. 1860–1914." *French Colonial History* 4, no. 1 (2003): 145–69.

Rich, Paul B. "Philanthropic Racism in Britain: The Liverpool University Settlement, the Anti-Slavery Society and the Issue of 'Half-Caste' Children, 1919–51." *Immigrants and Minorities* 3, no. 1 (1984): 69–88.

———. *Race and Empire in British Politics*. Cambridge: Cambridge University Press, 1990.

Richards, Sandra L. "What Is to Be Remembered? Tourism to Ghana's Slave Castle-Dungeons." *Theatre Journal* 57, no. 4 (2005): 617–37.

Roberts, Penelope A. "The State and Regulation of Marriage: Sefwi Wiawso (Ghana), 1900–1940." In *Women, State and Ideology: Studies from Africa and Asia*, edited by Haleh Afshar, 48–69. Albany: State University of New York Press, 1987.

Robinson, Amy E. "Tinker, Tailor, Vagrant, Sailor: Colonial Mobility and the British Imperial State, 1880–1914." PhD diss., Stanford University, 2005.

Rocco, Fiammetta. *The Miraculous Fever-Tree: Malaria and the Quest for a Cure That Changed the World*. New York: HarperCollins, 2003.

Rodney, Walter. *A History of the Upper Guinea Coast, 1545–1800*. Oxford: Clarendon, 1970.

Rogers, Joel A. *Sex and Race: Negro-Caucasian Mixing in All Ages and All Lands*. New York: Rogers, 1940.

Romer, Ludvig Ferdinand. *A Reliable Account of the Coast of Guinea (1760)*. Translated and edited by Selena Axelrod Winsnes. Oxford: Oxford University Press, 2000.

Rose, Sonya O. "Sex, Citizenship, and the Nation in World War II Britain." *American Historical Review* 103, no. 4 (1998): 1147–76.

Ross, Robert. "Oppression, Sexuality and Slavery at the Cape of Good Hope." *Historical Reflections* 6, no. 2 (1979): 421–33.

Roth, Hans R. *Because of Kwadua: Autobiography of Hans Rudolf Roth*. Accra: Afram, 2008.

Rubin, Gayle. "The Traffic in Women: Notes on the 'Political Economy' of Sex." In *Toward an Anthropology of Women*, edited by Rayna R. Reiter, 157–210. New York: Monthly Review Press, 1975.

Saada, Emmanuelle. *Empire's Children: Race, Filiation, and Citizenship in the French Colonies*. Translated by Arthur Goldhammer. Chicago: University of Chicago Press, 2012.

Saah, Kofi K., and Kofi Baku. "'Do Not Rob Us of Ourselves': Language and Nationalism in Colonial Ghana." In *Identity Meets Nationality: Voices from the*

Humanities, edited by Helen Lauer, Nana Aba Appiah Amfo, and Jemima Asabea Anderson, 74–99. Accra: Sub-Saharan Publishers, 2011.

Sackur, Amanda. "The French Revolution and Race Relations in Senegal, 1780–1810." In *Peoples and Empires in African History: Essays in Memory of Michael Crowder*, edited by J. F. Ade Ajayi and J. D. Y. Peel, 69–87. New York: Longman, 1992.

Sanchez, Ray, and Miguel Marquez. "Arizona Lawmakers Pass Controversial Anti-Gay Bill." CNN.com. http://www.cnn.com/2014/02/21/us/arizona-anti-gay-bill/.

Sarbah, John M. *Fanti Customary Laws: A Brief Introduction to the Principles of the Native Laws and Customs of the Fanti and Akan Sections of the Gold Coast, with a Selection of Cases Thereon Decided in the Law Courts*. London: Clowes and Sons, 1897.

Schmidt, Elizabeth. "Patriarchy, Capitalism, and the Colonial State in Zimbabwe." *Signs* 16, no. 4 (1991): 732–56.

———. "Race, Sex, and Domestic Labor: The Question of African Female Servants in Southern Rhodesia, 1900–1939." In *African Encounters with Domesticity*, edited by Karen Tranberg Hansen, 221–41. New Brunswick, NJ: Rutgers University Press, 1992.

Schmidt, Heike I. "Colonial Intimacy: The Rechenberg Scandal and Homosexuality in German East Africa." *Journal of the History of Sexuality* 17, no. 1 (2008): 25–59.

Schweizer, Peter A. *Survivors on the Gold Coast: The Basel Missionaries in Colonial Ghana*. Accra: Smartline, 2000.

Scully, Pamela. "Malintzin, Pocahontas, and Krotoa: Indigenous Women and Myth Models of the Atlantic World." *Journal of Colonialism and Colonial History* 6, no. 3 (2005).

———. "Rape, Race, and Colonial Culture: The Sexual Politics of Identity in the Nineteenth-Century Cape Colony, South Africa." *American Historical Review* 100, no. 2 (1995): 335–59.

Searing, James F. *West African Slavery and Atlantic Commerce: The Senegal River Valley, 1700–1860*. Cambridge: Cambridge University Press, 1993.

Segal, Daniel A. "'Race' and 'Colour' in Pre-Independence Trinidad and Tobago." In *Trinidad Ethnicity*, edited by Kevin Yelvington, 81–115. Knoxville: University of Tennessee Press, 1993.

Shaloff, Stanley. "Press Controls and Sedition Proceedings in the Gold Coast, 1933–39." *African Affairs* 71, no. 284 (1972): 241–63.

Shelford, Fred. "The Development of West Africa by Railways." *Journal of the Royal Colonial Institute* 25, no. 6 (1904): 349–71.

Shepperson, George, and St. Clare Drake. "The Fifth Pan-African Conference, 1945 and the All African Peoples Congress, 1958," *Contributions in Black Studies* 8, Article 5 (1986): 35–66.

Sherwood, Marika. "Kwame Nkrumah: The London Years, 1945–47." In *Africans in Britain*, edited by David Killingray, 164–94. London: Cass, 1994.

———. "Lynching in Britain." *History Today* 49, no. 3 (1999): 21–23.

Shumway, Rebecca. "Castle Slaves of the Eighteenth-Century Gold Coast (Ghana)." *Slavery and Abolition* 35, no. 1 (2013): 84–98.

———. *The Fante and the Transatlantic Slave Trade*. Rochester, NY: University of Rochester Press, 2011.

Sill, Ulrike. *Encounters in Quest of Christian Womanhood: The Basel Mission in Pre- and Early Colonial Ghana*. Leiden: Brill, 2010.

Sinitsina, Irina. "African Legal Tradition: J. M. Sarbah, J. B. Danquah, N. A. Ollennu." *Journal of African Law* 31, nos. 1–2 (1987): 44–57.

Skinner, Elliott P. "Strangers in West African Societies." *Africa* 33 no. 4 (1963): 307–20.

Smith, Alex D. "Ghana Official Calls for Effort to 'Round Up' Suspected Gays." *Independent,* 22 July 2011. http://www.independent.co.uk/news/world/africa/ghana-official-calls-for-effort-to-round-up-suspected-gays-2318507.html.

Smith, Michael G. *The Plural Society in the British West Indies.* Berkeley: University of California Press, 1965.

Smith, William. *A New Voyage to Guinea.* London: Nourse, 1745.

Sommer, Hans-Martin. "The History of the Kenya Police, 1885–1960." Research report prepared for the Coast Provincial Police Headquarters, Mombasa, Kenya, November 2007.

Sparks, Randy J. *Where the Negroes Are Masters: An African Port in the Era of the Slave Trade.* Cambridge, MA: Harvard University Press, 2014.

Spencer, Ian R. G. *British Immigration Policy Since 1939: The Making of Multi-Racial Britain.* London: Routledge, 1997.

Spitzer, Leo. *The Creoles of Sierra Leone: Responses to Colonialism, 1870–1945.* Madison: University of Wisconsin Press, 1974.

St. Clair, William. *The Door of No Return: The History of Cape Coast Castle and the Atlantic Slave Trade.* New York: BlueBridge, 2007.

Steinmetz, Katy. "Kansas Bill Allowing Refusal of Service to Gay Couples Moves Forward." *Time,* 11 February 2014. http://nation.time.com/2014/02/11/kansas-bill-allowing-refusal-of-service-to-gay-couples-moves-forward/.

Stoler, Ann L. *Along the Archival Grain: Epistemic Anxieties and Colonial Common Sense.* Princeton, NJ: Princeton University Press, 2010.

———. *Carnal Knowledge and Imperial Power: Race and the Intimate in Colonial Rule.* Berkeley: University of California Press, 2002.

———. "Carnal Knowledge and Imperial Power: Gender, Race, and Morality in Colonial Asia." In *Gender at the Crossroads of Knowledge: Feminist Anthropology in the Postmodern Era,* edited by Micaela di Leonardo, 51–101. Berkeley: University of California Press, 1991.

———. "Making Empire Respectable: The Politics of Race and Sexual Morality in Twentieth-Century Colonial Cultures." *American Ethnologist* 16, no. 4 (1989): 634–60.

———. "Rethinking Colonial Categories: European Communities and the Boundaries of Rule." *Comparative Studies in Society and History* 31, no. 1 (1989): 134–61.

———. "Sexual Affronts and Racial Frontiers: European Identities and the Cultural Politics of Exclusion in Colonial Southeast Asia." In Cooper and Stoler, *Tensions of Empire,* 198–237.

Stovall, Tyler. "Love, Labor, and Race: Colonial Men and White Women in France during the Great War." In *French Civilization and Its Discontents: Nationalism, Colonialism, Race,* edited by Tyler Stovall and Georges Van Den Abbeele, 297–321. Lanham, MD: Lexington Books, 2003.

———. "Murder in Montmartre: Race, Sex, and Crime in Jazz Age Paris." In *Minor Transnationalism,* edited by Françoise Lionnet and Shu-mei Shih, 135–54. Durham, NC: Duke University Press, 2005.

Studer, Brigitte. "Citizenship as Contingent National Belonging: Married Women and Foreigners in Twentieth-Century Switzerland." *Gender and History* 13, no. 3 (2001): 622–54.

Swanzy, Henry. "A Trading Family in the Nineteenth Century Gold Coast." *Transactions of the Gold Coast and Togoland Historical Society* 2, no. 2 (1956): 87–120.

Tabili, Laura. "The Construction of Racial Difference in Twentieth-Century Britain: The Special Restriction (Coloured Alien Seamen) Order, 1925." *Journal of British Studies* 33, no. 1 (1994): 54–98.

———. "Empire Is the Enemy of Love: Edith Noor's Progress and Other Stories." *Gender and History* 17, no. 1 (2005): 5–28.

———. "Women 'of a Very Low Type': Crossing Racial Boundaries in Imperial Britain." In *Gender and Class in Modern Europe*, edited by Laura L. Frader and Sonya O. Rose, 165–90. Ithaca, NY: Cornell University Press, 1996.

Tanaka, Yuki. *Japan's Comfort Women: Sexual Slavery and Prostitution during World War II and the US Occupation*. London: Routledge, 2002.

Teixeira da Mota, Avelino, and Paul E. H. Hair. *East of Mina: Afro-European Relations on the Gold Coast in the 1550s and 1560s*. Madison: University of Wisconsin, 1988.

Tenkorang, Samuel. "The Founding of Mfantsipim, 1905–1908." *Transactions of the Historical Society of Ghana* 15, no. 2 (1974): 165–75.

Thomas, Lynn M. *Politics of the Womb: Women, Reproduction, and the State in Kenya*. Berkeley: University of California Press, 2003.

Tillet, Salamishah. *Sites of Slavery: Citizenship and Racial Democracy in the Post–Civil Rights Imagination*. Durham, NC: Duke University Press, 2012.

Trento, Giovanna. "Lomi and Totò: An Ethiopian-Italian Colonial or Postcolonial 'Love Story'?" *Conserveries mémorielles: Revue transdisciplinaire de jeunes chercheurs*, no. 2 (2007).

Tugbiyele, Adejoke. "Sexual Identity and 'Nigerian Culture.'" *Feminist Wire*, 13 February 2014. http://thefeministwire.com/2014/02/nigerian-culture/.

Twine, France Winddance. *A White Side of Black Britain: Interracial Intimacy and Racial Literacy*. Durham, NC: Duke University Press, 2010.

Van Dantzig, Albert. *Forts and Castles of Ghana*. Accra: Sedco, 1980.

Van Onselen, Charles. *New Babylon, New Nineveh: Everyday Life on the Witwatersrand, 1886–1914*. Johannesburg: Jonathan Ball, 2001.

———. *Studies in the Social and Economic History of the Witwatersrand, 1886–1914*. Johannesburg: Ravan Press, 1982.

Van Tilburg, Jo Anne. *Among Stone Giants: The Life of Katherine Routledge and Her Remarkable Expedition to Easter Island*. New York: Scribner, 2003.

Vogt, John. *Portuguese Rule on the Gold Coast, 1469–1682*. Athens: University of Georgia Press, 1979.

Walz, Terence, and Kenneth M. Cuno, eds. *Race and Slavery in the Middle East: Histories of Trans-Saharan Africans in Nineteenth-Century Egypt, Sudan, and the Ottoman Mediterranean*. Cairo: American University in Cairo Press, 2011.

Weatherston, Rosemary. "When Sleeping Dictionaries Awaken: The Re/Turn of the Native Woman Informant." *Post Identity* 1, no. 1 (1997): 113–44.

White, Deborah G. *Ar'n't I a Woman?: Female Slaves in the Plantation South*. New York: Norton, 1985.

———. *Too Heavy a Load: Black Women in Defense of Themselves, 1894–1994*. New York: Norton, 1999.

White, Luise. *The Comforts of Home: Prostitution in Colonial Nairobi*. Chicago: University of Chicago Press, 1990.

White, Owen. *Children of the French Empire: Miscegenation and Colonial Society in French West Africa, 1895–1960*. New York: Oxford University Press, 1999.
——. "The Decivilizing Mission: Auguste Dupuis-Yakouba and French Timbuktu." *French Historical Studies* 27, no. 3 (2004): 541–68.
Wickizer, Vernon D. *Coffee, Tea and Cocoa: An Economic and Political Analysis*. Stanford, CA: Stanford University Press, 1951.
Wildenthal, Lora. "Race, Gender, and Citizenship in the German Colonial Empire." In Cooper and Stoler, *Tensions of Empire*, 263–83.
Wilson, John. "Gold Coast Information." *African Affairs* 43, no. 172 (1944): 111–15.
Wilson-Fall, Wendy. "Women Merchants and Slave Depots: Saint-Louis, Senegal and St. Mary's, Madagascar." In *Paths of the Atlantic Slave Trade: Interactions, Identities, and Images*, edited by Ana Lucia Araujo, 273–303. Amherst, NY: Cambria 2011.
Wiltse, Charles M. *The Medical Department: Medical Service in the Mediterranean and Minor Theaters*. Washington, DC: Office of the Chief of Military History, Dept. of the Army, 1965.
Wyse, Akintola J. G. H. C. *Bankole-Bright and Politics in Colonial Sierra Leone, 1919–1958*. Cambridge: Cambridge University Press, 1990.
Yarak, Larry W. "West African Coastal Slavery in the Nineteenth Century: The Case of the Afro-European Slaveowners of Elmina." *Ethnohistory* 36, no. 1 (1989): 44–60.
——. "A West African Cosmopolis: Elmina (Ghana) in the Nineteenth Century." Paper presented at the Seascapes, Littoral Cultures, and Trans-Oceanic Exchanges, Library of Congress, Washington, DC, 2003.
Yoshimi, Yoshiaki. *Comfort Women: Sexual Slavery in the Japanese Military during World War II*. Translated by Suzanne O'Brien. New York: Columbia University Press, 2000.
Young, Robert J. C. *Colonial Desire: Hybridity in Theory, Culture and Race*. London: Routledge, 1995.
——. *Postcolonialism: An Historical Introduction*. Oxford: Blackwell, 2001.
Zabel, Shirley. "The Legislative History of the Gold Coast and Lagos Marriage Ordinance: III." *Journal of African Law* 23, no. 1 (1979): 10–36.
——. "The Legislative History of the Gold Coast and Nigerian Marriage Ordinances: I." *Journal of African Law* 13, no. 2 (1969): 64–79.
——. "The Legislative History of the Gold Coast and Nigerian Marriage Ordinances: II." *Journal of African Law* 13, no. 3 (1969): 158–78.
Zeiger, Susan. *Entangling Alliances: Foreign War Brides and American Soldiers in the Twentieth Century*. New York: New York University Press, 2010.

Index

Page numbers in italic refer to figures.

Aborigines' Rights Protection Society (ARPS), 286n45
Abrahams, Peter, 217
Abrahams, Sidney, 176–77
Abura Dunkwa, 46
Accra, 35–36, 143, 146, 255n59; "Accra Club," 140; population, 43; prostitution during WWII, 136–37
Accra Evening News, 292n90
Ada, 36, 77, 84, 255n59
Adangbe, 91
Addais, Akoshua, 96, 98, 99
administered colonies, 10, 163, 234
adultery compensation (*ayefare sika*), 73–74, 98–99
affective ties. *See* emotions; love and affection
African Americans, 237, 296n44; as soldiers in WWII, 183
African Crown colonies, 108
African Intimacies (Hoad), 14
Africanization of civil service, 1, 139, 147, 231
African Morning Post, 292n90
African National Congress, 9
Africans: and authority, 60, 65, 261n40; as domestic workers, 73, 80, 88; grievances, 167–68, 197, 199; racist stereotypes about sexuality of, 215, 237–38, 290n72; self-rule, readiness for, 154, 194, 199, 215. *See also* African women; black men; Gold Coast elites; Native officers
African women: agency of, 12, 33–34, 112–13, 121, 195, 200–204; bodily comportment, 200–201, 289nn60–61, 292n91; capital accumulation by, 201–4; elites, 209–11, 283n14; in Europe, 213–14; married to black men, 277n48; in medical service, 141; nurses, 141–43; portrayed as "gold diggers," 201–2, 289n66; services and skills of, 33–34, 38–39; stereotypes about, 112, 191, 193–94, 202–4; subordinate status of, 99, 111–12; unmarried, 236; voices of, 21. *See also* concubinage; marriage; sexual exploitation
Aidoo, Paul Evans, 236
Akerele, Mr., 184
Ako-Adjei, Ebenezer, 217
Akpata, Bankole, 218
Akyeampong, Emmanuel, 203, 252n24
Alexander, Jacqui, 296n42
Algeria, 282n13
Allen, A. C., 121–22
Allman, Jean, 283n14
Altena, Marga, 275n16
Amanokrom, 145, 147–48

323

Amedika Customs Station, 79
Anglo-Asante wars, 42
Angola, 222
Anlaby Road Institution, 179
Anlo region, 31
Annan, Alfred, 174–82
Annan, Cudjoe, 67–68, 78
Annan, Ellen, 181–82
Annan, Frieda (neé Meyer), 174–84
Annan, George, 183
Annan, Robert, 183
Annan family, 24, 162, 173–84, 188
Ansah, Effua, 37, 287n47
anticolonial nationalism, 3, 16, 18, 189, 238, 282n13, 283n14, 286n45; agitation and unrest, 196, 212–13; and interracial sexual relations, 24–25, 155, 191–93, 204–11, 215–17, 224–25; marginalization of women in, 193; rhetoric, 12, 155, 190, 197, 238; and sexual possession of British women, 214–15
anticoncubinage circulars, 2, 17–18, 81, 101, 103–5, 163, 195; consequences of, 18, 120, 130–31; distribution of, 171, 270n70; Gold Coasters' awareness of, 81. *See also* Crewe Circular; interracial concubinage; "Undesirable Relations" circular
antimiscegenation laws, 163
antiprostitution laws, 118, 136
anti-Semitism, 180, 218–19
Anti-Slavery and Aborigines' Protection Society, 196
Antrobus, Reginald, 75–76, 108–9
Anum, John W., 115–16
apartheid, 222, 238, 246n93
Appiah, Enid Margaret (Peggy, neé Cripps), 220–22, 221
Appiah, Joe, 212, 215, 217, *218*, 235; marriage, 220–23, 221
Arden-Clarke, Charles, 216–17
Armitage, C. H., 117–18
Arondekar, Anjali, 20–21
arranged marriages, 31–32
asafo: captains, 261n37; companies, 52
Asafu-Adjaye, Dorothy and Isaac Boaten, 184–85, 187
Asante people, 38–39, 73, 149, 205; elite, 184, 220; military defeat of, 16, 42
Asante region, 42, 95, 97, 125, 143; European population of, 43; nationality status of inhabitants, 51
askari (policeman), 102, 266n1
Asmis, Rudolf, 194
Atlantic Charter, 154
Attoh Ahuma, Samuel Richard Brew, 198
Attrill, George, 62, 64–66

Atu (*Gold Coast Leader* columnist), 4, 190–91, 194, 197, 204–5
Avebury, Lord, 227
Ayambah (Fulani woman), 115–16, 118, 120
Azikwe, Nnamdi, 222

Baddoo, Barbara, 294n33
Bailkin, Jordanna, 227
Banda, Hastings, 222
Bankole-Bright, Herbert, 213
Bannerman, James, 42
Barnes, Charles, 47, 256n77
Bartholomew, John George, 40
Basel Mission, 36, 84, 149, 210, 262n65; intermarriages, 44–45
Bassey, Grace and Dame Shirley, 182
Berney, Mr., 95, 99
Berrago, Arabara, 84
Bertschi, Koni, 149
Beverly Road Institution, 179
Birth of a Nation, The, 238
Black Atlantic, 25, 71, 196–98
Black Atlantic, The (Gilroy), 197–98
blackmail, 21, 73–74, 98, 110–14, 117, 122–23, 131
black men: proposed internment of, 168; racial violence against, 24, 165, 167–68; relationships and marriages with white women, 11–12, 22, 24, 155, 159–61, 163, 169–88, 211–25. *See also* Africans; Gold Coast elites; marriage; race riots
"black peril," 10–11, 165, 167, 178, 193, 197, 236
Black Skin, White Masks (Fanon), 72, 239
black women: sexual abuse of, 296n44. *See also* African women
Bond of 1844, 39
Bosman, Willem, 289n60
Botsio, Kojo, 217
Botswana, 222
Bowesman, Charles, 141–44, 146–48, 235
Bowesman, Martha Gladys (neé Owusu), 141–44, 146
Boye, Frants, 36
Brabo, Salome, 128
Brew, Elizabeth, and relationship with Lyall, 46–47
Brew, James (Prince Brew of Dunquah), 46
Brew, James Hutton, 198
Brew, Richard, 37, 287n47
Brew, Samuel Collins, 46
Brewer, George, 119, 128–29
Brew family, 3, 37
Bridge, Horatio, 29, 39
Britain: immigration policy, 226–30; Parliament, 93, 103; port cities, 164–65,

166, 169, 213, 277n48 (*see also* race riots); Special Restriction (Coloured Alien Seamen) Order (1925), 51; West African students in, 212–20
British colonial rule: administrative efficiency, 2, 58, 88, 96, 106, 130–31, 134–35; challenges to moral legitimacy of, 15, 24, 131, 155, 189, 191–93, 207; formalized, 4, 6, 39, 54, 130; growth of civil service, 42; local colonial authorities, 64, 77, 91, 103–5, 171, 173, 198; racial and sexual politics of, 4, 10, 13, 17, 19, 30, 42, 48–50, 54–55, 57–58, 76–78, 92; racial classifications, 58–66, 72–73, 77; reputation of colonial service, 18, 48, 58, 74–75, 83, 88–89, 93, 117, 119–21, 134, 154; stability of, 130–31, 172, 176, 178, 294n31; transition from company rule, 39, 54; welfare and development programs, 131. *See also* Colonial Office (Whitehall); European government officers; Native officers
British Commonwealth, 228
British East Africa, 172
British Empire, 105, 108–9, 130–31, 144, 147, 162–64, 168, 208, 211, 213; administered colonies, 10, 163, 234; alien political rule, 4, 14, 130; end of, 18, 192, 196, 199, 223, 229; imperial loyalty, 53, 72, 115, 199; tension between metropole and colonies, 171–72, 190. *See also* anticolonial nationalism; British colonial rule; Gold Coast colony; settler colonialism
British Guiana, 60, 70–71
British nationality law, 50–51, 162, 174, 226–31; Nationality Act (1948), 51, 228, 230; Nationality Act (1958), 141; Nationality Act (1981), 227–28; Nationality and Status of Aliens Act (1914), 50–51; patriality, 226–27, 230–31
British Parliament, 103
British protected persons, 51, 161–62
British subjects, 51, 161, 168, 174, 197, 228
Brockman, Drake, 128–29
Brooks, George, 30
Brown, Jacqueline Nassy, 268n38
Bryan, Herbert, 85, 115
Burma, 247n48
Burns, Sir Alan, 2, 133, 135, 137
Burton, Antoinette, 24
Bush, Barbara, 188, 214

calisare, 35
Callaci, Emily, 283n18
Cape Coast, 5, 52, 112, 139–40, 261n37
Cape Coast Castle, 53
Cardiff, Wales, 164–65, 167–69, 181–84, 278n62

Casely-Hayford, Augustus, 50
Casely Hayford, J. E., 198–99, 206–7
Castellain, Louis, 116
census figures, Gold Coast colony: 1891 census, 42–43, 49, 52; 1901 census, 42–43, 49; 1911 census, 42–43, 54–55; 1921 census, 256n89; 1931 census, 256n89
Charway, Mary Ajeley, 115, 117
Charway, Samuel Adams, 115–18, 120
chastity, 46
Chatterjee, Partha, 192
child marriages, 97
Christiansborg, 36, 90, 174
Citizen of the United Kingdom and the Colonies (CUKC), 51, 228, 230
citizenship, 50–51, 141, 161, 178, 226–33; dual, 231–33; gendered laws, 162; and marriage to foreign nationals, 174, 227, 231, 278nn63–64
"civilizing mission" rhetoric, 18, 208
Clancy-Smith, Julia, 8
Clarke, Marcus: charged with sexual misconduct, 56–59, 66–67; customary marriage, 67–70; defense against charges, 70–74; disciplinary action against, 74–76; job performance, 64–65; racial identity, 58–59, 65, 67, 71–77, 108, 262n68
class status: of multiracial Gold Coasters, 52–53; of West African men with white wives, 163, 176–78, 184–88
Clifford, Hugh, 122, 125
cohabitiation, 35, 46–47, 91, 102, 107, 135, 150–51, 164
Cole, Jennifer, 12, 234, 289n63
Collins, E. V., 82–83, 88–89
colonial courts, 21, 23; European defendants, 67; native law courts, 18
Colonial Office (Whitehall): and concubinage, 2, 16–19, 46, 103–5 (*see also* anticoncubinage circulars; concubinage cases); official correspondence, 23; professionalization of administration, 54–55; purview of, 44. *See also* British colonial rule; colonial courts; "policy of prevention"; public scandals
colonized and colonizer, distinction between, 18, 58, 76–77, 178
color line, 2–3, 9–11, 18, 81, 239. *See also* race and sexual politics
"coloureds," 53, 64; use of term, 274n6
Commonwealth citizen, 51
companionate marriage, 7, 194, 200, 201, 209
company rule, 30–32, 38, 39, 54; Committee of Merchants, 39; Company of Merchants Trading to Africa, 32

Index ~ 325

concubinage cases, 19–23; Allen case, 121–22; Brockman case, 128–29; charges as tool of coercion, 18, 58, 81, 98–101, 131; Clarke case, 56–59, 64–77, 108, 262n68; Curling case, 79–87, 89–90, 107, 195; disciplinary action on, 74–76, 89–94, 100, 103, 108, 117, 120–25, 128–29; exculpatory strategies, 21, 70–77, 93–94, 111–15, 118; false charges, 123, 125–27; Festing case, 116–17, 121; Greig case, 95–100, 123; grievances addressed through charges, 19–20, 81, 95–101, 125–29, 131, 191, 197; Kortright case, 115–20; Palmer case, 79–80, 82, 89–90, 93, 123, 195. See also anticoncubinage circulars; interracial concubinage
Connal, Andrew, 114
consent/coercion binary, 5–6, 113, 193
Cooper, Frederick, 8, 281n3
Creasy, Gerald, 133
"Creole" identity, 260n30
Crewe, Lord, 17, 18, 90
Crewe Circular (1909), 17–18; Circular A, 106–7, 109, 114, 122; Circular B, 106–7, 109, 114, 120, 122; Colonial Office policy discussions on, 122–25, 129–31; discontinuation of, 125, 129–30; distribution of, 103, 108–9, 122; effects of, 120, 195; formulating, 105–10; inappropriate uses of, 123, 125, 129; language used in, 107, 118; revival of, 133–34; violation of, 128. See also anticoncubinage circulars; concubinage cases; interracial concubinage; "Undesirable Relations" circular
Cripps, Stafford, 220
cross-racial intimacy, 17–18, 73, 78, 80, 87, 88, 100–101, 145
Crown colonies, African, 39, 108
CUKC. See Citizen of the United Kingdom and the Colonies
Cunliffe-Lister, Philip, 129–30, 206
Curling, Clarence Napier: allegations of colleagues' sexual misconduct, 89–90, 107; charges against, 80, 82–83, 86–87, 195; disciplinary actions against, 89–90; relationships with African women, 79–87
Currantee, John, 37, 287n47
customary law, 3–4, 6–7, 18, 29, 49–50; adultery compensation (*ayefare sika*), 73–74, 98–99; and forfeiture (*sarwie*), 33
customary law marriage ("native marriage"): between African women and European men, 3–4, 6–8, 29, 56, 67–70, 82–85, 145, 151–52, 229; Clarke court case, 56–58, 67–70; European perspectives on, 69, 75–76; legitimacy of, 76, 195; payments, 3, 68, 85–86, 126; profit from, 3, 68, 85–86, 126
Customs Department, 70–71, 260n23

Dagarti, 96
Daily Mail, 167
Daily Times (Nigeria), 292n90
Dakeyne, N. H., 110–14, 120, 123, 195
Dalton, P. N., 227–29
Danes, 32, 35–37, 252n32
Danquah, J. B., 209
Davidson, Joanna, 250n4
Davies, Jenny (neé Lewis), 185, 186
decolonization, 1–2, 152, 189, 228
de Marees, Pieter, 29, 35
desegregation, 9
developmental colonialism, 154
divorce, 125–26
Dixon, David, 228
Doortmont, Michel, 258n102
Doumer, Governor-General, 14
Dove, Mabel, 209–11, 292n90; writing as Akosuah Dzatsui, 292n90; writing as Dama Dumas, 292n90; writing as Ebun Alakija, 210, 292n90; writing as Marjorie Mensah, 209
dowry, 56, 68–70, 78
dual citizenship, 162, 231–33
Du Bois, W. E. B., 9, 17, 217
Dutch: citizenship, 232–33; interracial relationship policies, 4, 32, 35, 36
Dutch East India Company, 4
Dutch Gold Coast (Elmina), 35, 39
Dutch West India Company (WIC), 35

Earl of Elgin, 66–67
Easmon, Charles Odamtten, 143
Easmon, Kate, 129, 205–7
East Africa, 278n62
East African Protectorate (Kenya), 102
Effie, Ambah, 68–69
Egalie, Michael and Elisabeth, 162
Elder Dempster ships, 162, 277n43
El Hamel, Chouki, 9
Ellis, Tom, 272n32
Elmina, 5, 30, 34–35, 52, 251n16
emotions, 12–13, 34, 87, 99, 180, 206, 211, 215–16. See also love and affection
Epprecht, Marc, 237
equality, calls for, 50, 64, 208
European government officers, 42, 44; abuse of official position, 58, 74, 77, 83, 96, 100, 113; credibility and authority of, 7, 53–54, 110–13, 134–35; disciplinary action against, 46, 74–76, 134–35; embedded in African

326 ⏐ Index

communities, 17–18, 80–81, 83–84, 87–88, 100–101, 109; European wives of, 54–55, 124, 138, 164, 251n16; intraracial rivalries between, 19, 100, 127–29; moral misconduct, 46–47; procuring African women, 87–88; racial identities of, 108; shortages of, 114; use of term, 242n9. *See also* concubinage cases; interracial concubinage; marriage

European prestige, 24, 53, 104–5, 160, 172, 178, 187

Europeans in Gold Coast: demographics, 42–43, 164; dependence on Africans, 32, 54, 73, 78, 100–101; health and mortality rates, 42, 59–61, 80–81, 143, 198; privately employed, 20, 42–44, 94, 148–52, 206. *See also* racial segregation

Evans, William Timothy, 210
Evening Express (Liverpool), 196
Ewe, 73, 232; Anlo region, 31

Fanon, Frantz, 72, 239, 289n61
Fante, 32, 33, 37, 38, 52, 55, 73, 139; customary marriage, 68; nationalism, 205
Feimster, Crystal, 296n44
Feinberg, Harvey M., 251n16
female circumcision, 282n13
Ferguson, J. Halcro, 222
Festing, Arthur, 116–17, 121
Fiddian, Alexander, 75, 94, 171
Fifth Pan-African Congress (1945), 217
First, Ruth, 9
Flagstaff House, 1–2, 140, 147
Fletcher Report (1930), 15
forfeiture (*sarwie*), 33
Forger's Tale, The (Newell), 14
Fort Fredericksborg (Cape Coast), 252n31
Fort Kongensten (Ada), 36
Fort Prinzensten (Keta), 36
Foucault, Michel, 25, 238
Free Press (Ghana), 232
French, Merene, 222
French Empire, 229–30, 247n45, 247n47, 282n13
French West Africa, 14–15, 53, 97
"frock girls," 209
Frost, Diane, 275n18
Fulani, 115

Ga, 31, 33, 36, 52, 55; multiracial people in politics, 232
Ga-Danish marriages, 36–37
Gadzekpo, Audrey, 198, 291n88
Garland, Dr., 265n45
Garraway, Doris, 247n47
Garvey, Marcus, 17, 211

gender-based discrimination, 227–28, 231, 295n18
gender chaos, 12, 200
gender hierarchies, 99, 111
German East Africa, 67, 249n67
Germanophobia, 180
German Southwest Africa, 282n11
Germany, 162; and Annan family, 173–79, 183
Ghana: 1979 Constitution, 231; 1992 Constitution, 230–31; Africanization of civil service, 1, 139, 147, 231; Citizenship Act 2000 (Act 591), 231–32; independence, 1–2, 139, 151; Nationality and Citizenship Act (1957), 141, 230; nationality and immigration laws, 230–33; nation building, 217–24. *See also* Gold Coast colony; Gold Coast elites
Ghosh, Durba, 8, 13
Gibbs, John (St. Clair Drake), 214
Gilroy, Paul, 197–98
Glasgow, 169
Glassman, Jonathon, 9
Gold Coast colony: 1891 census, 42–43, 49, 52; 1901 census, 42–43, 49; 1911 census, 42–43, 54–55; citizenship status of inhabitants, 50–51; consolidation of, 39, 42; maps of, 40–41; race relations, 19–25; reading public, 286n41. *See also* British colonial rule; Ghana
Gold Coast elites, 51–52, 184–88, 191, 194–98, 205–7, 211; Black Atlanticism and nationalism, 197–98; in Britain, 51, 212–23; on interracial sexual relationships, 2–5, 22–25, 55, 103–5, 131; nation-building, 217–24; sub-elites, 196–97; on white men's relationships with African women, 21, 155, 190, 191–93, 197, 199, 204–5, 207–11, 224–25, 238; women as, 209–11, 283n14
Gold Coast Independent, 126
Gold Coast Leader, 4, 55, 76, 104, 198–211; on 1919 race riots, 189–90, 198; on "Dutch times," 194; "Immoral Sanitation" commentaries, 104, 190–91, 198–205, 224
Gold Coast Nation, 286n45
"gold diggers," 201–2, 289n66
Gouda, Frances, 8, 192
Great Depression, 175
Greene, Sandra E., 252n32
Greig, F. W., 95–100, 123, 195
grievances: addressed through sexual misconduct charges, 19–20, 81, 95–101, 125–29, 131, 191, 197; of black men, 167–68, 197; against colonial state, 199. *See also* anticolonial nationalism
Grunshi, Imoru (Omar), 125–27

Index ⁓ 327

Guardian (British newspaper), 226
Guggisberg, Gordon, 126–28, 131
Guinea-Bissau, 5
Guppy, Mr., 47

"half-castes," 53
Hall, Bruce, 9
Hausa, 126
Hawe, Albert Joseph, 139–41, 143, 147–48, 230; John Holt Medal, 140
Hawe, Margaret Mary (neé Barette), 139–41, 230
Heincks, Captain, 91, 93
Helden, Sarah, 57, 74, 77
Hill, Stephen, 60
Hintermann, Werner, 150–52
Hitler, Adolf, 175
HIV/AIDS epidemic, 237
Hoad, Neville, 14
Hodson, Arnold, 179
Home Office, 165, 167, 179, 226, 230, 277n43; Nationality Division, 141
homophobia, 14, 236–37
homosexuality, 13–14, 47–48, 233–38, 249n67; same-sex marriage, 233–34, 236; situational, 235
honor, 5, 194. *See also* respectability
Houghton, M. J., 119–20
Hull, England, 169, 179–81
Hutchinson, Charles Francis, 258n102
Hutton-Mills, Thomas, 198
Hyam, Ronald, 103, 281n8
hypersexuality, 215, 237

Idun, Asimaku, 149
illegitimacy, 227–30, 247n47
Immigration Act of 1971 (Britain), 226
Immigration Act of 2000 (Ghana), 231–32
Immigration Restriction Ordinance, 163, 176–77, 188
"immoral whites," 24, 131, 189, 191–93, 199, 204–5, 208–11, 222, 224–25
Imperial Customs, 70–71
indirect rule, 51, 198, 199, 261n40, 275n99, 285n29
Indochina, 14, 53
Indonesia, 4, 282n11
intelligentsia, 191, 197–98, 211. *See also* Gold Coast elites
International Spouses Association of Ghana (ISAG), 231
interracial concubinage: changes in attitudes toward, 3–8, 13–19, 30, 54–55, 235; as distinct from occasional illicit acts, 93–94, 114–21; as marriage alternative, 35; persistence of, 54, 195; purported effects of, 106–7; and racial respectability, 48–49; tacit acceptance of, 135; as threat to colonial administrative efficiency, 2, 58, 88, 96, 106, 130–31, 134–35. *See also* anticoncubinage circulars; concubinage cases; Crewe Circular; "Undesirable Relations" circular
interracial relationships: African perspectives on, 30, 31–34, 55, 190–211; changes in Gold Coast sexual economies, 3–9; children of, 150–52 (*see also* multiracial people); colonial anxieties about, 2–3, 15, 160–64, 173; in postcolonial period, 226–33; in precolonial era, 3–6, 30–34; prevalence of, 38, 87–91; procurement of African women, 87–88; secrecy and discretion about, 8, 15, 18, 45, 129, 148, 195; as shaped by the colonized, 19; situational, 235; visibility of, 29. *See also* emotions; interracial concubinage; love and affection; marriage; prostitution; public scandals
Ipsen, Pernille, 37
Ivory Coast, 195

Jean-Baptiste, Rachel, 12–13, 285n37
Jenkinson, Jacqueline, 170, 277n53
Jet, 221
Jews, 175, 177, 180–81, 184, 219, 278n64
João II, king of Portugal, 34
João III, king of Portugal, 252n24
job competition, racialized, 162, 165, 167, 196
johns, 136. *See also* prostitution
Johnson, Alfred, 129, 205–6
Jones-Quartey, K. A. B., 286n45

Kachina (Gold Coast woman), 125–27
Kanjarga, Mala, 125–27
Kankam-Boadu, Akua, 219–20
Kankam-Boadu, Erna "Miki" (neé Cohn), 218–19, 218–20, 222–24
Kankam-Boadu, Frederick, 217–20, 218–19, 222–24, 235
Kato, David, 234
Kenya, 93, 130, 222, 270n70, 282n13
Kenyatta, Jomo, 217–18, 222, 293n17
Keta, 36
Khama, Ruth (neé Williams), 9, 220, 222–23
Khama, Seretse, 9, 220, 222–23
Kimble, David, 50, 261n37
Kisseadoo, W. A., 110–13
Knight, Brendan, 1–2, 8, 133, 144–48, 231, 235
Knight, Felicia Agnes, 1–2, 22, 139, 144–48; enstooled as Nana Tetkyi Ampong I, 148
Knight, W. L. C., 144
Komfo Anokye Teaching Hospital, 143

Korle Bu Hospital, 143
Kortright, H. A., 115–21
Krooboys, 47, 256n79
Kumasi, 54, 143, 145, 149–51, 184
Kumasi Central Hospital, 143
Kwabena, 144–45
Kyeremateng, Alex, 152
Kyikyiwere, 143

labor hierarchies, 97. *See also* job competition
Lagos, 284n24, 288n56
landlord-stranger reciprocities, 30, 31–34
Larsen, Robert, 174
lascars, 164
laws: antimiscegenation, 163; antiprostitution, 118, 136; Ghanaian nationality and immigration laws, 230–33. *See also* British nationality law; customary law
Lee, Christopher, 50
legitimacy: challenges to moral legitimacy of British colonial rule, 15, 24, 131, 155, 189, 191–93, 207; of imperial power, 14; of interracial marriages, 6, 23, 76, 135, 145, 152, 195, 227–30
Lembembe, Eric Ohena, 234
Leonard, H. Selfe, 47–48
Lever, J. T., 52
LGBT Africans, 234–38
Liberia, 256n79
libertinage, 119–20; female, 194, 200–201, 289n60
Liverpool, England, 164–65, 168–70
Liverpool Echo, 140
Liverpool Post, 196
Liverpool School of Tropical Medicine, 140
Lloyd, Dorothy, 205, 226, 229
Lloyd, Thomas, 216
load carriers, 23, 79, 82–84, 86, 88
London, 164, 169, 212–13, 222. *See also* West African Students Union
London Immigration Action Group, 227
love and affection, 12–13, 127, 135, 149, 185, 201, 215–16, 239, 289n63. *See also* emotions
Love in Africa (Cole and Thomas), 234
Loving, Mildred, 233–34
Loving v. Virginia, 233, 238
lynching, 163, 167, 276n30
Lyttelton, Alfred, 63–65, 77
Lytton, Edward, 60, 65

Maclean, George, 39
Maclean, Letty, 253n53
Macmillan, Harold, 223
Macnaghten, Terence, 93, 108–9, 113
Maegraith, B. G., 140
malaria, 42

Mampong District, 143
Manley, Florence, 212, 215–17
Mansah, Essie, 139
marriage: arranged, 31–32; *calisare*, 35; child marriages, 97; Christian, 194; cloth for intended bride, 68; companionate, 7, 194, 200, 201, 209; country marriages, 29; Ga-Danish, 36–37; monogamous, 7, 234, 284n23; same-sex, 233–34, 236; situational, 235. *See also* customary law marriage; emotions; interracial concubinage; interracial relationships; love and affection
marriage between African women and European men: advantages for men, 33–34, 38–39; advantages for women, 5–6, 32, 34, 37; changes in attitudes toward, 2–9, 13, 154–55, 194; community support, 148; couples' experiences of, 22, 138–54; disapproval of, 144, 146–47, 150–51, 154; as "epidemic," 133–34, 137, 155; familial support for, 146–47; and officers' professional advancement, 133–34, 137, 144, 146; pathologized as "madness," 134, 235; in precolonial era, 30–34; public legitimation, 6, 23, 76, 135, 145, 152, 195, 227–30
marriage between European women and African men: among African nationalists in Europe, 211–25; community support, 220; presence of white wives in colonies, 10–12, 22, 24, 155, 159–61, 163–64, 169–88, 211
Marriage Ordinance (1884), 6–7, 47, 194–95, 199, 263n83
Marshall, Samuel, 264n19
Matera, Marc, 214–15
matrilineages, 52
Mauritius, 109
Maxwell, Joseph Renner, 55, 211
Maxwell, William, 47, 48, 260n22
McCarthy, Mary, 38, 251n16
McCaskie, Thomas, 30
McClintock, Anne, 99, 200
McGuire, Danielle, 296n44
Mead, Tom, 142
Mends (clerk), 116–17, 127
métis "problem," 15, 49, 229
métissage, 15, 49, 211
metropole, 11, 164, 171; movement between colony and, 190, 213
Mgulla (African policeman), 102, 104
Michelin, W. P., 56, 70
Miller, Susan, 214
Milne, June, 293n16
mining/miners, 42–43, 45, 104, 148, 206

Index ⌔ 329

missionaries, 43, 44, 53. *See also* Basel Mission
Mohamed, Dusé, 17
Mondlane, Eduardo, 222
monogamy, 7, 234, 284n23
morality, 225; moral decay, 12, 104, 195; "moral sanitization," 104, 236; regulation of, 46, 57. *See also* sexual morality
Morrison, G. W., 290n72
Mould, Jacob, 38
Mozambique, 222
Mugabe, Robert, 234, 236
"mulattoes," 49–50, 52, 64, 108, 253n35; administrative racial classification of, 59; "Mulatto treasury," 36. *See also* multiracial people
Mullens (clerk), 116–17, 127
Muller, Annie, 188
multiracial people, 15–16, 35–36, 42, 49–53, 90, 211, 229–33; colonial racial categories for, 49–50; and criticism of interracial marriage, 287n50; "quadroons," 49, 75, 262n68. *See also* "mulattoes"; West Indian officers
Murray, J., 76
Museveni, Yoweri, 234, 236

Nagel, Joane, 205
Namoo, Elizabeth, 110–13
Nanka-Bruce, F. V., 198
Nasser, Gamal Abdel, 224
Nathan, Matthew, 60, 62
National Congress of British West Africa (NCBWA), 199, 207
nationalism: and sexuality, 235–38. *See also* anticolonial nationalism; political nationalism
National Party (South Africa), 222
nation-building, 217–24
"native": as colonial category, 49–50; use of term, 246n38
Native Customs Ordinance (1892), 199
Native Jurisdiction Ordinance (1883), 49, 50, 59
"native" law. *See* customary law
"native" marriage. *See* customary law marriage
Native officers, 48, 58, 60, 62, 71, 260n21, 286n43; campaigns for equality, 64; charges against European officers, 95–100; discrimination against, 50
Native West Indians, 62–66, 77
"native wife" / "native wives," 110–14, 118; prevalence of, 195; use of term, 7, 29, 154–55. *See also* customary law marriage; interracial concubinage; marriage
Nazi Party, 175
Netherlands, 275n16. *See also* Dutch

Neto, Agostinho, 222
Newell, Stephanie, 14, 199, 209, 285n29, 290n75, 291n88
Newspaper Registration Law (1894), 287n52
nharas, 5
Nigeria, 55, 122, 129, 136, 162, 171, 184, 236, 284n24
Nkrumah, Fathia (neé Rizk), 140, 224
Nkrumah, Gamal, 224
Nkrumah, Kwame, 1, 140–41, 147, 211–12, 217–18; marriage, 224; relationships with white women, 215–17
Noble, Janice (neé Davies), 185, 186
Nogwaza, Noxolo, 234
Noor, Ismail and Edith, 172–73, 176
Northern Territories, 96, 97; "protected persons," 42, 51
Nottingham, E. C., 136–37
Nyasaland, 53

Obisanya, Opeolu, 215
Obuasi, 54
"occasional illicit acts," 93–94, 107, 114–15, 118. *See also* prostitution
Odebiyi, Afolabi, 218
Ogbe, Moses, 79, 82
Okutu, Agnes, 128
Opanwa, Amba, 46
Order of the British Empire (OBE), 140, 144
ordinance marriage (Marriage Ordinance of 1884), 6–7, 47, 194–95, 199, 263n83; Christian marriage, 194; companionate marriage, 7, 194, 200, 201; monogamous marriage, 7, 234, 284n23
Orphan Fund, 35
Osu, Accra, 36, 90, 147, 148
Otibo, Amanquah, 82, 85–86
Otibo, Matte, 84
Otibo, Narkoyo, 79–80, 82–87, 93
Otibo, Otitso, 86, 263n4
Otibo, Tettey, 84
Otibo, T. K. (Theophilus Kwabla), 82, 85
Otibo, Tsutsu, 82, 85
Owusi (cousin of Narkoyo Otibo), 80, 82–83, 85–87, 92

Palmer, Harold T., 79–80, 82, 89–90, 93, 123, 195
Pan-Africanism, 199, 217–18, 224
Park, Robert, 260n26
Parker, Ena and John Akok, 159–61, 173
Parker, John, 52
Passfield, Lord, 175
paternalism, 83–84, 192, 210
patriality, 226–27, 230–31
patriarchal power, 33–34, 99, 200

patrilineages, 52
Penno, E. F. L., 125–27
Pensions Ordinance, 138, 142
Philbrick, Arthur, 111
Phillips, M. O., 187
"pilot boys," 136, 195
Plageman, Nate, 136
police brutality, 82
"policy of prevention," 16–17, 169–73, 175, 184, 187–88
political nationalism, 12, 192
polyandry, 201, 204
polygamy, 37–38, 47, 185, 187, 204
polygyny, 6, 35
Portuguese, 32, 34, 252n24
Powell, Erica, 293n16
Powell, Eve Troutt, 9
premarital sex, 46
Prempeh, Asantahene Otumfo Nana Osei Tutu Ageyman, II, 143
press: African-owned, in Gold Coast colony, 22, 24, 126, 131, 190, 198–211, 220; regulation of, 287n52. *See also specific newspapers and magazines*
Priestley, Margaret, 3, 37
prostitution: customary marriage perceived as, 69; interracial, 5, 8, 13, 34–35, 235; investigation of cases involving, 114–21, 129; and Portuguese officers, 252n24; during World War II, 23, 135–36. *See also* interracial concubinage; "occasional illicit acts"
public health, 136. *See also* venereal diseases
public scandals on interracial relationships, 88, 92–94, 104, 188; and disciplinary proceedings, 119–20, 128–29; and homosexuality, 47; and "mulattos," 108; and "native marriage" cases, 56, 74–75; and officers' dismissal, 123; and prostitution, 136; and violence, 83

"quadroons," 49, 75, 262n68
Quayson, Ato, 4
Queashie, Joseph, 169
quinine, 42

race and sexual politics, 4, 10, 13, 17, 19, 30, 42, 48–50, 54–55, 57–58, 76–78, 92
race riots in British ports (1919), 11–12, 24, 155, 161, 165–69, 189, 196, 199, 276n33
racial classification, administrative, 58–66, 72–73, 77, 108
racial discrimination, 10, 50, 70–74, 227–28; skin color and job performance, 63–65
racial hierarchies, 42, 58, 77, 109, 155, 163, 191, 198, 224

racial integration, 220
racial respectability, 207, 237; African, 105, 194–95; of European officers, 48–49, 53
racial segregation, 20, 25, 48–49, 109, 139–40, 163; in European social clubs, 10, 48, 146; residential, 80–81, 171, 178, 200; transgression of, 178. *See also* apartheid
Racial Unity, 214, 220
racism, 50, 51, 238; British lexicon of, 274n6; colonial, 20, 149, 154; and interracial sexual desire, 207; metropolitan (in Britain), 162, 198; in Nazi Germany, 218; scientific, 42, 60; against West Indians, 58
rape, 192, 193, 238; of female slaves, 5–6
Rawlings, J. J., 232
Reese, Ty, 32
Reindorf, Carl Christian, 55, 76
Renner, Peter, 69, 74
repatriation to colonies, 168–88; of African men married to white women, 11–12, 22, 24, 155, 159–61, 169–88, 211; financial requirements, 188; incentives, 276n41; passage fees, 169–70, 175; "policy of prevention," 16–17, 169–73, 175, 184, 187–88
respectability, 3, 5, 8, 69, 152. *See also* racial respectability
Rhodesias, 53, 268n23, 294n31
Riby Williams, Charles, 91
Roberts, Penelope, 68
Robertson, J. M., and Ambah, 95–100
Rodger, John, 15, 17, 18, 57, 101, 103–4; investigations of concubinage charges, 66–67, 85, 89–90, 97, 100, 113–14; on racial identity of West Indian officers, 62–63, 65, 77; on racial segregation, 81. *See also* "Undesirable Relations" circular
Rogers, Joel A., 188, 278n62
Roth, Hans Rudolf, 24, 138, 148–54, 153
Roth, Mercy "Kwadua" (neé Kwafo), 22, 24, 138, 148–54, 153
Rottmann, Hermann Ludwig, 44, 45
Rottmann-Hesse, Regina, 44, 45
Routledge, Katherine, 102
Rubin, Gayle, 34
Russia, 237

Saada, Emanuelle, 8, 15
Sadler, J. Hayes, 103–4
Salford, 169
same-sex marriage, 233–34, 236. *See also* homosexuality
Samuels, Mr. (Gold Coaster), 175–78
São Jorge da Mina, 34
Saraku, Abba, 56, 67–70, 75–78
Sarbah, John M., 33

sarwie (forfeiture), 33
Scandinavians, 165
Scheitlin, Erwin, 149, 151–52
Schmidt, Heike, 67, 88, 249n67
scientific racism, 42, 60
Scoresby, William, 102
Scovell, Captain, 93, 94
seamen: Special Restriction (Coloured Alien Seamen) Order (1925), 51; West Africans married to white women, 11, 161, 164, 196, 223; West Indian, 161, 164–65, 169, 170–71, 277n53
Sedition Bill (1934), 287n52
Sekondi, 43, 56, 67, 80, 111–12, 143, 202–3, 206; "Accra Town," 119; social life, 191, 201–4
Sekyi, Kobina, 207–8, 211, 251n11
self-governing colonies, 108–9
self-rule, 154, 194, 199, 215. *See also* anticolonial nationalism
Senegal, 222
Senghor, Leopold, 222
settler colonialism, 163, 222; race relations and racism, 9–10; racial politics of, 53
sexual abstinence, 89
sexual exploitation of African women, 8, 10, 24, 99, 104, 189–94, 197–205, 209–11, 224–25, 282n11; anticolonial rhetoric about, 12, 155, 190, 197, 238
sexual misconduct cases: Barnes case, 47, 256n77; Brew case, 46–47; Leonard case, 47–48; Penno case, 128; Wingrove case, 128
sexual morality, 46–54, 208, 237; "immoral whites," 24, 131, 189, 191–93, 199, 204–5, 208–11, 222, 224–25. *See also* libertinage
sexual regulation, 22–25, 30, 34–39, 44–45, 234–38; adultery compensation, 73–74, 98–99; landlord-stranger reciprocities, 30, 31–34; as legitimizing colonial regimes, 14. *See also* anticoncubinage circulars; concubinage cases
sex workers. *See* prostitution
Seychelles, 109
Shepard, Matthew, 236
Sherwood, Marika, 276n33
Shumway, Rebecca, 33
Sierra Leone, 123, 169, 184, 256n79; West Indian officers in, 59–60, 65–66
signares, 5
Silberrad, Hubert, 102–5; and relationship with Nyakayne, 102
Slater, Alexander, 128, 177–78
slavery, 96; customary marriage perceived as, 76
slaves, female, 251n12, 252n24; as domestic labor, 34–35; marriages to Europeans, 31–33; rape of, 5–6
slave trade, 5–6, 30, 37; women's role in, 5, 37
"sleeping dictionary," use of term, 83–84
Slovo, Joe, 9
Smith, A., 56, 66–67, 70–71, 74
Smith, Fannie, 38
Smith, John Hope, 38
Smith, W. E., 119–20
Smith, William, 289n60
social clubs, European, 10, 48, 146
social stigma, 145, 207
Solanke, Ladipo, 213, 215
Somaliland Protectorate, 108, 164–65, 172–73
Somalis, 278n62
South Africa, 163, 222, 234–36, 294n31; Communist Party, 9
Southern Rhodesia, 163, 222
South Shields, 169
Spectator (Britain), 93
SS *Cape Corso*, 182
St. Clair Drake (John Gibbs), 214
St. Mary's Convent School, 140
Stoler, Ann L., 8, 135, 249n70, 281n3
Stuart-Young, John Moray, 194
Summers, Gerald, 172–73
Sunday Express, 165
Sunyani, 145
Surgery and Clinical Pathology in the Tropics (Bowesman), 143
Swart, Charles, 294n31
Swiss African Trading Company Limited (SAT), 45, 148–51
Switzerland, 148. *See also* Basel Mission
Syrians, 50

Tabili, Laura, 161, 172, 178
Takoradi, 136–37, 195, 202
Tamale, 115–16
Tarkwa, 43
Taylor, Williams, 91
Tegetmeier, P. A., 134
Thatcher, Margaret, 227
Therson, Elias, 57
Thomas, Fola, 168, 197
Thomas, Lynn M., 12, 234, 289n63
Thomas, Shenton, 160
Thompson, Joyce Dorthea, 222
Thorburn, James, 118–19
Times (Britain), 93
Togoland, 194, 281n7
Torrane, George, 38
Touré, Samori, 96–97
trade, 30–33; British and European traders, 3, 32, 37–39, 64–65, 90, 139, 148; illicit, 34–35; protection of, 34

tropical illnesses, 59, 80–81, 143; improvements in medicine, 42, 60, 198
Turner, Donald Sidney, 137–39
Turner, Gladys Adzo (neé Chapman), 137–39
Turner, Ian Leslie Obeng, 139
Twine, France Winddance, 280n102

Uganda, 234, 236, 270n70
"undesirable immigrants," 176–77, 187
"Undesirable Relations" circular (Rodger, 1907), 15, 17, 30, 48, 76, 80, 83, 103–4; disciplinary cases, 80–81, 107; disciplinary provisions of, 57–58; distribution of, 81, 100; effects of, 195; limitations of, 93–94; as prescriptive, 54; reception of, 87, 91–92, 100, 111. *See also* anticoncubinage circulars; concubinage cases; Crewe Circular; interracial concubinage
Union Trading Company (UTC), 45
United States: African Americans, 183, 237; anti-gay violence, 236–37; military personnel, 136, 183; prohibition on interracial marriage, 234; racial violence and lynching in, 167; same-sex marriage, 233–34; sexual abuse of black women by white men, 296n44
Upper Slave Coast (southeastern Ghana), 31
urbanization, colonial, 202–4

van den Bronk, André, 142
Vardon, Frank, 206
venereal diseases, 45, 48, 136, 236
Victorian era: sexual mores of, 46–47
Villaut, Nicolas, 289n60
violence, 83, 85, 95, 163. *See also* race riots; rape
Vogt, John, 251n16

Watherston, A. E., 97–100
Watson Commission, 212, 216
West African Students Union (WASU), 212–20, 218
West Africa Times, 209
Western culture, 200–202, 203
Western Mail, 167
West Indian officers: administrative racial classification of, 58–66, 76–77, 108; Native West Indians, 62–66, 77; in Sierra Leone, 59–60, 65–66

West Indies, 60–61, 72, 77, 108–9, 161, 164–65, 170–71, 260n23, 262n66, 268n24
White, Owen, 8
Whitehall. *See* Colonial Office
White Man's Grave, The, 17
white men: increasing numbers in Gold Coast colony, 42–43; multiracial children of, 15–16, 197, 205–7, 210. *See also* European government officers; interracial concubinage; marriage; "white peril"
whiteness: definitions of, 260n30
"white peril," 104, 190–96, 198–205, 209, 224; use of term, 192–93
white wives: of African men, 11–12, 22, 24, 155, 159–61, 163–64, 169–88, 211, 212–25; and class status of African husbands, 163, 176–78, 184–88, 223; of European government officers, 54–55, 124, 138, 164, 251n16
white women: black men as sexual threat to, 10–11, 165, 167, 197; in colonies, numbers of, 54, 124, 133, 135, 229, 235; of "immoral character," 280n116; role in African independence movements, 215–16. *See also* marriage; white wives
Widows and Orphans Pension Scheme, 142
Wingrove, Captain, 119, 128
Woman in Jade, A (Dove), 209
Wootton, Charles, 167
World War I, 159–60, 164, 281n7
World War II, 23, 133–37, 154, 179–80
World Wars: demands of colonized subjects, 208; interwar period, 131–32, 161–62, 164
Worm, Christen, 36

Yarn, Quasie, 56–57, 67–70, 78
Yates, Albert Edward, 67–68
Yates, George William, 206, 226, 229
Yates, Harry Phillip, 206, 229
Yates, Joseph, 125–26
Yates, Reggie, 226–30
Yates, Reggie, Jr., 290n78
yellow fever, 80–81
Young Socialist, 226

zany malattas, 5
Zimbabwe, 234, 236
Zimmerman, Johannes and Catherine, 44

www.ingramcontent.com/pod-product-compliance
Lightning Source LLC
Chambersburg PA
CBHW020638300426
44112CB00007B/161